The Women Outside

The Women Outside

Meanings and Myths of Homelessness

WITHDRAWN

Stephanie Golden

UNIVERSITY OF CALIFORNIA PRESS
Berkeley · *Los Angeles* · *Oxford*

University of California Press
Berkeley and Los Angeles, California

University of California Press, Ltd.
Oxford, England

© 1992 by
Stephanie Golden

Library of Congress Cataloging-in-Publication Data

Golden, Stephanie.
    The women outside: meanings and myths of homelessness / Stephanie Golden.
    p. cm.
    Includes bibliographical references and index.
    ISBN 0-520-07158-1 (alk. paper)
    1. Homeless women—United States. 2. Homelessness—Psychological aspects. I. Title.
HV4505.G65 1992
362.83'086942—dc20   91-32936
                                                               CIP

Printed in the United States of America
9 8 7 6 5 4 3 2 1

The paper used in this publication meets the minimum requirements of American National Standard for Information Sciences—Permanence of Paper for Printed Library Materials, ANSI Z39.48–1984. ♾

Contents

362.83
G618w

Now I must write for myself   for this blind
woman scratching the pavement   with her wand of thought
this slippered crone   inching on icy streets
reaching into wire trashbaskets   pulling out
what was thrown away   and infinitely precious
                    —*Adrienne Rich, "Upper Broadway"*

Acknowledgments

Riding the subway after a day at the shelter for homeless women where I was a volunteer, I used to try to figure out, logically, how it was that I could be going home while the women I had just left had no home. The issue was not understanding the causes of homelessness but rather actually conceptualizing the coexistence of two such contradictory realities. But my mind would just blank out, and I was left with the feeling that maybe I should be like the nuns who ran the shelter and give over my life to the homeless. Yet I also knew I couldn't do that.

What I did do was write about them. However, since writing about other people means in a sense living off them, I could not accept the fact that this book owes its existence to homeless women if I did not feel that it might multiply the effects of one person's advocacy.

Since the late 1970s more and more people in this country, in the course of their daily routine, have had the experience of encountering homeless humans living in largely unimaginable but clearly inhuman conditions. For many of us it is so painful to confront such destitution amid the surrounding affluence, and to feel so helpless to affect it, that we shut down our feelings and either look away or get angry at those homeless who are too intrusive to ignore. My intention here is to offer a different mode of looking, in which homeless people—not only women but men too—no longer seem so frightening, so degenerate, so alien.

Everything in this book originates from my experience at that shelter, the Dwelling Place. My first acknowledgment is to the homeless women

I knew there, and to others I've known since—less as a thank-you than as recognition of their heroic will and ability to survive, as well as of the strength of the spirit that woke in them, then expanded to touch others, once they were drawn back into community.

Next I acknowledge, in the same way, the Dwelling Place staff and volunteers—especially the five founders, Sisters Anne Regina Cassanto, Nancy Chiarello, Sally Cox, Rita Foegen, and Bernadette Mullen—whose vision created what I still believe is the most truly human and effective way to bring homeless people back into society. What I learned there remains the core of what I know about homelessness and about community.

Sections of this book were previously published, in different form, in *Conditions: Four* (Winter 1979); in *For Crying Out Loud: Women and Poverty in the United States*, edited by Rochelle Lefkowitz and Ann Withorn (New York: Pilgrim Press, 1986); in *City Limits* (January 1988); and in *Frontiers: A Journal of Women Studies* 9 (2–3), 1990.

Several friends read part or all of the manuscript and offered valuable comments and invaluable moral support. I thank most especially Bonnie S. Anderson and Phyllis Deutsch, as well as Alice Kessler-Harris, Beverly Lieberman, Harriet Serenkin, Alix Kates Shulman, and Judith P. Zinsser.

Thanks also to Barbara Black Koltuv, whose subtle wisdom informs much of this book; to my agent, Diane Cleaver, whose belief in it has always been a form of sustenance; and, in different ways, to Paul Howard, Rita Kingkade, Meeta L'huillier, Felicia Sobel, Barbara Winslow, and Kate Wittenberg. Naomi Schneider of the University of California Press has been exactly the editor I needed. I'm grateful also to Valeurie Friedman and to the copy editor, Pamela Fischer.

Finally, I want to acknowledge the late Mina P. Shaughnessy, associate dean of the City University of New York. Bending to pick up a tote bag full of books and papers, she remarked, "I look as though I must live in the subway." Nobody ever looked less like she lived in the subway. In that incongruity this book was conceived.

S. G.
Brooklyn, N.Y.
September 1991

Introduction

i could see myself making a wrong turn & falling downdowndown
    off the margin
being without income too long
losing my apartment
getting worn out by redtape changes
savings exhausted
goodwill dried up
get up & go on the road
i could see myself ending up between a rock & a hard place
    at the intersection of reduced resources &
    reverberating rage
    living on the street
          —*Hattie Gossett, "between a rock & a hard place ..."*

Driving out to the Brooklyn Women's Shelter in East New York, one afternoon in May 1989, was eerily like going to the country. Under a hot sun and blue sky lay fields of brilliant green—the vacant lots, long overgrown with weeds, that outnumbered the buildings in this neighborhood in the far reaches of Brooklyn. It was also unnaturally quiet; although this was part of New York City, there were no shops, little traffic, and few people.

"That's where the dogs hang out, in those lots," said the homeless woman riding next to me in the van. "The only time I was at BWS, I came overnight. The next morning I took one look around me and I left, I didn't even wait for coffee. It was very early and there was nothing on the way to the subway but the dogs barking. But by the time you got there, you could be dead."

Living now at another, safer shelter, she was coming to a demonstration organized to demand the immediate closing of BWS. Shelter residents and advocates for the homeless had described conditions there that could be compared only to the worst of the nineteenth-century poorhouses. Residents reported rapes, beatings, and drug trafficking by some staff. Although gangs of men attracted by crack houses and the shelter's presence made the neighborhood dangerous, women had been arbitrarily evicted at night or refused admittance if they returned even a few minutes after the 10 P.M. curfew. Guards then stood by watching as they were harassed.

Residents were also victimized by treatment seemingly calculated to strip them of basic human dignity. Sick women were not permitted to lie down in the sleeping area during the day even if they had a doctor's note. Some residents managed to hold jobs, but if they worked late shifts, they could not sleep late. No food was provided for those whose work hours made them miss regular mealtimes; and if they bought food with their own money, they had to eat it out in the street, like a dog that can't bring its bone into the house.

"This is not a *shelter*," exclaimed one advocate to the demonstrators. "It's a DOGHOUSE!" yelled back BWS residents in the crowd. A former resident named Jacqueline took the microphone. "One worker almost lost his job trying to get me out of here," she said. "He's the *only one!*" came cries from the audience. "Some of these workers don't respect you as a person," she went on. "They think we're animals." And in fact, staff had been known to send women who got into fights out into the street, telling them to "fight like dogs."

No attempt was made to assist these women. One resident said she was homeless because of a fire in which her three-year-old son died. She was happy to be at BWS only because it was near the cemetery and she could go there every day. This woman was mourning but had gotten no counseling or other support. Some women were trying to find jobs but were not given the means to obtain presentable clothing. Thus they often wound up postponing job interviews because they felt they could not dress properly.[1]

Clearly BWS had nothing to do with helping people. Its abusiveness made sense only on the assumption that its purpose—as with the old poorhouses—was punishment. Perhaps this was why the city subsequently made it the intake center for all women entering the single-adult shelter system, requiring them to be "assessed" there before they could be placed in another, more appropriate facility.[2] Homeless women I spoke to shook their heads at the thought that BWS would be the first experience of unseasoned women new to the system.

Although BWS was possibly the worst of the single-women's facilities, it was no aberration; similar conditions existed in the other municipal shelters. Yet the revelations at the demonstration, as well as in a report put out by the Homeless Women's Rights Network, a coalition of advocacy groups, got little media coverage and inspired no public response. Such indifference—let alone the existence of so extraordinary a level of abuse in the first place—was made possible, I believe, by a particular set of dehumanizing perceptions that are central to the issues of female homelessness this book explores.

These perceptions were even more clearly in evidence at the Kingsbridge Armory shelter for single women in the north Bronx, like BWS a long, long subway ride from Manhattan. A number of the male guards there, who had worked in prisons or been in the military, saw the shelter residents as frightening, violent women and treated them as inmates, not clients. These guards were upset when Widney Brown, a female martial artist, came to teach the women self-defense in response to a questionnaire on which they had listed being physically hurt as their greatest concern. While homeless men might also be potentially violent, the guards seemed to feel, it was all right for them to know how to defend themselves; that was what being a man was all about. But they saw women as dirty street fighters—cats—and their attitude was "Don't teach them this or you'll just have more catfights."

Though to the guards these shelter residents were powerful and threatening, to others they were easy victims. The Armory was a huge, windowless building covering about two city blocks. It had one entrance on the side, at a distance from the well-lighted intersection where residents got off the elevated subway. To reach the entrance they had to walk under the el for almost two blocks, dark because of ineffective street lighting. Local men occasionally stood on the subway platform and urinated down on the women's heads as they came and went.[3]

What could these men have seen when they looked at those women to feel free to commit an act so breathtakingly vicious? "Being homeless is like being a nonentity—you don't exist," said a homeless woman who spoke at the BWS demonstration—that is, you haven't even the minimal right to be a person, not an object. This book proposes to explain how, in a society that has always professed to respect women, often limiting their actions in the name of protecting them, women who become home-less—having perpetrated no criminal act that might justify punish-ment—can be hidden away at the margins of the city and treated like stray dogs.

I focus here entirely on women—not to minimize the injustices faced by homeless men but because the issues are different for women and need to be examined separately. Although much research has been done and many books written about homeless men, few works treat homeless women as a group in themselves; they have generally been assimilated into the study of men and subsumed into generalizations based on that study. Yet I found that female homelessness means something different to society than does male homelessness: whereas a homeless man can be assigned comfortably to a variety of categories (hobo, tramp, bum, va-grant) and be relatively easily dismissed, a homeless woman creates dis-comfort because she cannot be categorized. Women are so entirely de-fined in terms of whom they belong to that no category exists for a woman without family or home. A whole complex of attitudes about women in general also comes into play, for to the mystery of the outsider (always greater in a woman than in a man) the homeless woman adds the subtle aura of unsavory sexuality and secret power that attaches to a woman who exists apart from a defined social context. For women of color, who constituted the overwhelming majority of homeless women by the end of the 1980s, these attitudes are compounded by racism, es-pecially by degrading assumptions about their sexuality.

The book discusses mostly single homeless women, although—espe-cially today—it is difficult to draw a line between them and those with children. Homeless women who have their children with them generally receive better treatment or at least more services than those who are "sin-gle"; but even for them the virtue of being a mother is often canceled by the social irregularity of single parenthood. As we will see, homeless mothers as well as single women fulfill the function of all marginal women: being scapegoats for certain "sins" that society hesitates to condemn in the powerful or well off. Homeless women can serve this function because their separation from society distances them psychologically and turns them into blank shapes on which we can project various images stored up in our cultural warehouse. As someone remarked to me, "They become not human but objects in other people's minds."

When I first began thinking about homeless women, in the late seventies, hardly any information was available about them. To people who saw them on the streets but had no contact with them, they were a deep and powerful mystery that evoked intense feelings, while even to those who "serviced" them at hospital emergency rooms or city shelters, they remained enigmatic. In the absence of information, people seized on scraps of fact—such as the details of occasional ghoulish news stories—that suited their own notions of what such women must be like, or simply made up ideas based on their inner convictions.

I began this project with the intention of writing an article about people's ideas about "shopping-bag ladies"—not about the women themselves. I did a number of interviews and discovered that although each person was absolutely convinced that her or his ideas about the women represented the truth about them, all their ideas contradicted each other and so couldn't possibly be true. Some, for example, were certain that the women were homeless because their children had abandoned them, while others were positive that they had lost touch with their children because no child would allow a parent to live on the street.

I was also astonished by the intensity of these totally opposite reactions. One young man said that when such women had regressed to the point where you see them on the street, he didn't make distinctions between male and female. They lived in the open "like animals in a cage," performing their bodily functions in public; in their "primitive kind of jungle life" they were "predators on society's leftovers." But a woman asserted, "This is the wholly liberated female. She says, 'You've given me no resources but there's one thing I can do which is to create the life I lead.' She lives by her wits, which women have never been allowed to do. The bag ladies represent human dignity in extremity—they are a transcendent group." And another woman described to me a bag woman she saw every morning as she passed through Grand Central Station in Manhattan on her way to work. She developed the feeling that the woman was not human but like a seer; as long as she was still standing there, things were all right. "I gave her powers," she said. These three reactions share only the feature that they have equally little to do with fact. Each person is seeing in the homeless women only what corresponds to his or her own feelings, and the result is a set of images that range clear across the evolutionary continuum.

Contradictions were particularly revealing when they coexisted within the same person. A woman named Valerie, for example, described to me with great admiration a homeless woman she saw every day outside her office building, whom she considered "special." The woman sat on a metal milk crate next to the building entrance, wearing a wig, a black cape, and no underwear. In a singsong voice she would say, "Give me a quarter for a cup of coffee," though most of the time she seemed oblivious to the people passing. When someone came too close or did something to offend her, however, she screamed and made terrible faces; once she jumped up and whacked an astounded male passerby on the back. Occasionally she urinated or defecated on the sidewalk. This woman, Valerie felt, had "class"; she identified with her, though not with any other shopping-bag woman. Valerie had seen her reading paperback books and doing the *Times* crossword puzzle, and was intrigued because she was so "independent" and "imaginative in terms of survival. I have to think she's really smart." The black cape was new, she said, and just like one she had seen in the department store across the street for $100; "I have to imagine she spent $100 there on it." Certainly the woman always had money for coffee and danish from a nearby candy store. Valerie had heard that men coming to work in the morning gave her "pockets of change"; she remembered an article by a *New York Post* reporter who had tried panhandling and calculated that he would have made more money in a year from begging than Valerie herself made working; so she figured the woman was "pretty well off."

She had no positive feelings about any other bag women, however. They were "just wastes—they take crap from garbage—rotten orange peels, ten-week-old papers. This woman is on vacation, but the others are wasting time doing nothing." She was happy, the others were not; Valerie could tell because "appearance is a key to happiness. Happy people don't go through garbage." And she had never seen the other women do anything "for themselves"—like sunbathing, as this one did, sitting on her crate leaning her head back against the wall. She thought this woman "would make a fantastic worker—she's there every morning at 8:15 on the dot. She's awake—she has a mind and uses it."

Nevertheless, Valerie did not want the woman to pick her out as a person who was interested in her; she was not a woman Valerie could deal with, especially in public. If people at the office saw her in conversation with the woman, they would associate her in their minds with someone not acceptable to society, and some would then think less of her. Furthermore, Valerie was afraid of lice. She had heard that they jump, and she did not know how far, so she always crossed the street at a diagonal to avoid the woman or, if she forgot to cross in time, stayed on the outside of the sidewalk.

Now this is a rather large superstructure to build on a few superficial observations. In particular Valerie's arbitrary separation of this woman from all other bag women, her conviction that she was "using her mind" (another woman from the same office assured me that though the bag woman had a book and seemed to be intently reading, her eyes did not move and she just stared at the page, although how she could tell this I don't know), and the idea that she would have been a good worker because of her regularity are complete fantasies that Valerie could maintain only by ignoring the woman's homelessness and destitution.

But beyond the fantasy, notice the self-contradiction. At the same time that she was repulsed by the possibility that she might "catch" the woman's lice (her dirt, her behavior, her social disease), Valerie admired the strength that enabled the woman to cut herself off totally from people and from the norms of society. "When she pees on Madison Avenue, she's saying 'Fuck you,'" Valerie said. "I couldn't do anything so far out even if it made me happy. There's a reason that I'm so conventional-looking." Like the people quoted above, Valerie hardly saw the homeless woman at all but rather a series of images that sprang out of her own ambivalence about the restrictiveness versus the security of remaining inside conventions.

While I was interviewing, I encountered a group of nuns about to open a private shelter called the Dwelling Place and decided to become a volunteer there to find out why women really became homeless. In the next four years I learned the "truth" about homeless women, all right; but I also discovered the reality of the myths about them. The myths have reality, that is, because they determine how the women are treated. What was more, when I came to do research on the history of homeless women, I discovered that the myths have a history as much as the women do. This book, then, is a history and analysis as much of images and perceptions as of the socioeconomic context and psychology of homeless women.

Homeless women have a long history. It was a big surprise to me to discover that "bag ladies," who seemed so quintessentially modern and urban, were only a continuation of a phenomenon so common in the past that it easily escaped comment. That is one reason people today are so unaware of this aspect of history that the large-scale appearance of homeless people on city streets seems to us shocking and untoward. Two generations of welfare and unemployment insurance had allowed me, like most adults in the United States today, to grow up without encountering large numbers of street beggars as an everyday, familiar part of life. (I remember being taken on vacation as a child to pre-Castro Cuba and being completely bewildered by the sight of beggars in Havana. My mother explained that in our country we did not allow such things.) Their appearance at this particular time, moreover, is no anomaly but simply a repetition of what happened in previous historical periods when widespread economic difficulties were not offset by adequate programs of relief (welfare).

However, because the images surrounding homeless women were so powerful, historical research alone seemed insufficient. I was drawn also to explore the intense feelings female homelessness evokes and, further, the myths inspired by all marginal women. It would, however, require delicate and precise surgery to separate the real homeless women from the myths about them. What is more, all the material I gathered, past and present—through research and my own experience—came to me in fragments. In such a case, where the material is so scattered and inchoate, an effective method of analysis is to use an image. A powerfully magnetic image can draw all the bits and pieces away from the women and out of the texts, and make them cohere like iron filings into a recognizable shape. Or, to put it another way, by creating a shape, an image constrains and focuses thoughts while still allowing great freedom in moving around within it; you can come at your material from many different directions without losing coherence because the analysis acquires its form from the structure of the image. Besides, many of the homeless women conducted their conversations on this principle, and what I learned from them only loses in translation.

Using an image has another advantage. Although numerous experts have demonstrated, eloquently and convincingly, that homelessness is due primarily not to mental illness or other personal problems but to large-scale social and economic inequalities, many people still resist acknowledging such a cause—much as, years ago, people mystified by shopping-bag ladies did not believe my prosaic explanations of why these women were on the street. They wanted the mystery, which fed some deep, unconscious emotional needs. But where logical explanation and argument do not reach, an image may; it works nonlinearly, appealing more to the emotions than to the intellect.

I found my image in the figure of the witch: an ancient, well-enshrined tradition that has evoked over the centuries responses that differ more in mode of expression than in content and thus has remained constant over the entire long history of homeless women. Witch figures in Western culture range from Lilith, the night hag of the ancient Near East, to the *strix*, a destructive bird creature imagined by the Romans, to the familiar old woman of fairy tales who casts evil spells and is herself a fictional version of the medieval witches burned by the Inquisition. In whatever form she appears, the witch is connected to two themes: power and sex. Inhabiting a domain of female power and sexuality that has to remain outside society, she incarnates marginality in woman and like all marginal people fulfills a definite function for society just by not being in it.

The "bag lady," I suggest, is the modern old witch, possessing magical powers and a certain animal quality, as my interviewees perceived; the young homeless woman is a contemporary form of the young witch, who attacks men with her seductive sexuality, which also has an uncontrolled animal quality. Thus the guards who told homeless women to "fight like dogs" or complained of their "catfights" were responding within this old tradition. Similarly, staff assaults on the Brooklyn shelter residents and the implicitly sexual attempt to degrade the Bronx women by peeing on them expressed ancient assumptions about the sexuality of homeless women, whose marginality consists in large measure of their not belonging to any man. These women could not have been so treated if they had been perceived as regular, "real" women. But those who exist at the margins are never perceived as "real people."

For me, the most frightening of the many gruesome aspects of homelessness at the beginning of the 1990s was the way "the homeless" were turning into "they," a population of resident aliens, the Other. Going out to East New York was indeed almost like making a trip to a foreign country—a Third World nation within the borders of the United States. People who were homeless felt a corresponding alienation, with some expressing the conviction that homelessness was a well-executed plan that "they" (here, those in power) had designed to keep people oppressed.[4] As more and more homeless people appeared in public spaces, and people with homes grew less tolerant of seeing them, the gap seemed to be widening.[5]

I hope here to create an alternate sense of connection between homeless women and people in society, to lessen the sense of their separateness and nourish the impulse to truly accept them inside, as was done, indeed, at the Dwelling Place. This book therefore begins, in Part 1, by describing my experience at this shelter, to show who these women actually were: why they became homeless, what they were like, how they lived, what images they themselves created of their condition, and—most important—how they managed to come into community given the right conditions.

Part 2, shifting to the level of myth, lays a foundation for the analysis of our images of homeless women by interpreting a Grimm's fairy tale in which a witch/bag lady appears. It presents the fairy-tale kingdom's relation to this witch figure as a model of our society's relation to homeless women, showing how the story's central images of the female outcast's burden and treasure are still present when we look at homeless women today.

Part 3 returns to objective reality by describing the long history of homeless women in Western culture. It demonstrates how ideology about women's proper "place" and about their sexuality has always conditioned their financial survival, both by preventing them from getting jobs that men could get and by enabling them to earn money as prostitutes. The last section of this part describes how this ideology continued to affect the lives of homeless women in the 1980s.

Part 4 examines the relation of ideology about women to the issue of homeless women's "mental illness," often assumed to be the cause of their homelessness. A brief historical survey demonstrates the relativity of the concept of insanity by describing how different eras have defined the same "mad" behaviors differently. Part 4 then describes how assumptions about female roles have influenced diagnoses of mental illness in women and finally suggests that our view of madness as a stigmatized medical condition has helped separate homeless women from society by making institutionalization or other forms of permanent dependency seem an appropriate solution for most of them.

Part 5 discusses the general meaning of marginality and gives examples of the marginalizing images we create today of homeless women. A history of the witch figure is followed by an analysis of popular and literary images of witches to show that feelings about forbidden female power and sexuality that have remained constant for centuries are now associated with homeless women. Finally, I suggest possibilities for integration.

Because the presence of homeless women raises issues that go right to the heart of the concept and structure of our society, reactions to them are powerful and deeply ingrained, shaping policy decisions about services for homeless women as well as the manner in which assistance is provided. It is therefore essential to develop a conscious awareness of the sources of these reactions, so that services can be designed to meet homeless women's real needs. If, for example, we understand why women are judged more stringently than men by their appearance and we want them to find jobs, we will provide them with clothing suitable for an interview. And if we realize that almost any man will make certain assumptions about their sexuality, we will build in ongoing education for security guards or hire female guards, as well as prosecute men who abuse homeless women.

Beyond this, however, the treatment of homeless women—as of all homeless people—depends on how society at large sees them. And in fact it is difficult to look at homeless women clearly because, I think, their condition reveals so nakedly our long-standing ambivalence toward women outside society; we turn away in order to preserve a reassuring distinction between them and us.

The sense of separation created by such a distinction is what enables institutions that warehouse and abuse women to exist in the first place. Recognizing the culturally determined component in our reaction to homeless women is one step toward creating, instead, a sense of community between "us" and "them." On such a feeling effective advocacy, and true service, both depend. But, further, acknowledging the human reality of the outcast simultaneously enlarges our sense of ourselves—just as my own encounter with the women of the Dwelling Place, remote as they originally seemed from anything in my experience, revealed to me entirely new realms within myself.

PART I

Real Life Outside

The accumulation of experiences had reached a point when it was difficult to bear any more. The knowledge that I was but one of many hundreds of broken women, and that this hall held but a remnant of the legion of the dispossessed, frightened me. It was something in life that I had not guessed at; and the knowledge made me afraid.

—*Ada E. Chesterton,* In Darkest London

The Dwelling Place

A scene, reconstructed:

The living room of the Dwelling Place, a shelter for homeless women in New York City, on a November afternoon in 1977. Eight or ten homeless women sitting on chairs and couches, and me, the volunteer, on a low hassock in the center of the room. In one corner Ella, rolling a cigarette with a roller she got in Chinatown, rambles on about how much everything costs: In midtown a Coke costs fifty cents and so does a hot dog from a vendor even though he doesn't pay the overhead that they do in Penn Station, so that these girls who buy their lunch spend a whole dollar for it.

PATRICIA: (flipping rapidly through the *Daily News*, not really reading but picking out phrases at random) Now there's an adulterous situation for you! (Reads, gaily, part of an item about labor negotiations)
DORA: (in snuffling voice) Nothing is like it used to be.
ANNIS: (to me) What kind of work do you do?

(I explain that I edit manuscripts of books. Ella's monologue switches to how she used to work in a printing plant, putting the covers on the books.)

PATRICIA: (turning on her suddenly, icily) Well, if you're going to discuss me, I'll thank you not to continue!
ANNIS: (to me) What kind of books are those?

(I tell her they're mostly about literature; Annis, who has been a schoolteacher, informs me that modern writers get away with murder—they don't have complete sentences. She cites Faulkner. I assure her none of my authors gets away with that.)

PATRICIA: (jumping up and flouncing out) I can see very well that nothing is as it is!

PAMELA: (to me) Do you have a cigarette?

ME: No.

EMMA: (to me) Do you have a permanent?

ME: No, this is how my hair is.

EMMA: Well I think you have a permanent.

ME: No, I really don't.

EMMA: Well, I *know* you have a permanent because your face is red, your skin is red the way it gets from the permanent chemicals. (I look at her helplessly—how to argue? Emma's hair is completely hidden under a scarf, and she has a skin condition that causes large red patches and pimples.) Oh, never mind.

(We talk about Chicago, where Pamela is from; we talk about sewing, knitting, and crocheting.)

ELLA: I used to do that; I would walk over to Forty-second Street and get some, but the patterns cost too much.

PAMELA: I used to make my own patterns.

ME: I can knit, but I can't crochet.

JUNE: Well, I can crochet but I can't knit!

(Pamela, who has been getting more and more worked up by talking, by my attention, my admiration that she can make patterns, screws up her face in an incredible grimace and bursts into a diatribe about a psychiatrist who was supposed to do an evaluation of her but just stuck his head in the door and said hello and waved and went out again. Underneath her hysteria, rage.)

PATRICIA: (who has returned) Well, people shouldn't pretend to be what they aren't, and Dr. Steven MacKenzie, my *very good friend*, is a psychiatrist.

ANNIS: (to me) And do you précis them?

A pale version of the actuality. Particularly dizzying was the way all these conversational darts shot past the others, each into its own void: no contact being made, no meanings shared.

The Dwelling Place was created by five Franciscan Sisters of Allegany who had asked themselves, "Who are the people Francis would be with if he were alive today?" Their answer was the bag women whom they saw poking through the garbage outside the apartment they shared on West Forty-seventh Street. From the beginning their intention was to live with the homeless, not apart from them as "service providers." The realities of ministering to deeply wounded, disoriented, and disturbed people meant that this ideal could never be entirely lived up to, but it remained a guiding principle. It also influenced the large number of volunteers—Catholic and non-Catholic—who did much of the work, from mopping floors and cooking to answering the phone, "being with" the "ladies" (as the nuns chose to call the homeless women, not liking the impersonal "client"), taking them to doctor's appointments and welfare offices, and visiting them in the hospital. As one of these volunteers for over four years, I encountered a variety of women who were homeless in the city and learned much about who became homeless and why.

Occupying a five-story brownstone near the Port Authority bus terminal in midtown Manhattan, the Dwelling Place was set up as a temporary shelter where women living on the street could sleep a few nights and obtain food, clothing, showers, and delousing. If they chose, we helped them get public assistance—usually either state welfare or Supplemental Security Income (SSI), a federal program for those with disabilities—or find a place to live. Quite a number were eventually placed in some form of permanent housing—sometimes nursing or adult homes, but more often single-room-occupancy, or SRO, hotels in Manhattan.

As the staff learned, however, about the needs of the women who came, the services were repeatedly modified. It became clear that the primary need was not for handouts—though many peanut butter sandwiches, aspirins, coats, hats, cigarettes, and other necessities were dispensed—but for emotional support and the feeling that someone cared about them. Women kept returning to the Dwelling Place, not only because it was just about the only place they could get needed supplies but also because it provided what was for them the rare experience of being treated with respect and appreciated for who they were, for the sisters saw first in each woman not her symptomatology but her humanity.

It was not easy. "We are learning about our own wounds—[out of] which we sometimes [respond] when we face the ungrateful and angry and disturbed guest," said an early newsletter. It is just as human to dislike someone for herself as to love her for herself, and we had to learn to do that too—as well as to get angry. In its practical applications, too, the ideal imposed difficult choices. Respecting privacy meant not demanding information from someone who declined to give it, even though we were then unable to get her a pension. Respecting dignity meant not putting undue pressure on someone who refused all help beyond a bowl of soup and insisted on returning to the street with her leg sores raw and oozing. As it turned out, the coming together of the nuns and the women of the street involved a common working out of problems; the interaction was not one-sided. From it we also learned that to identify with the homeless so totally as to become like them means that one cannot help them. Distinctions had to remain. I am convinced, however, that it was the sisters' rigorous insistence on seeing the homeless as people to relate to, not clients to care for, that made so many inveterate street dwellers willing to come inside. They were accepted without question, and in time they came to trust—far more than anyone might have expected.

Before long a larger, more permanent community started to form and took on some of the qualities of a family. Women who had been placed in SRO hotels in the neighborhood still dropped in for meals, for help with problems, for company. Others who refused to live in hotels did accept help getting SSI, using the Dwelling Place as their address while continuing to live on the street; they came to eat and shower. Thus the number of women the shelter served was always far greater than the number staying there, which was usually twenty or fewer. The staff also worked out an arrangement with the management of the nearby Times Square Motor Hotel, a large SRO with many types of residents, that enabled the sisters to place women there and to act as intermediaries when problems arose. A fairly stable group formed in the hotel, most of whom remained oriented toward the shelter. They ate meals there, came to the staff with problems, and participated in birthday parties, holiday celebrations, excursions, and religious services. Within the hotel itself, however, they remained isolated from one another. One of the sisters therefore set up a series of separate activities at the hotel to bring them together there. The program, held in meeting rooms the management made available, included bingo, arts and crafts, an exercise class, and a coffee or social hour. After a while I took charge of this coffee hour, whose development over two years showed me a way of coping with a second phase of the solution to homelessness: after bringing people inside, keeping them there.

That, however, came later. At the beginning the ragged creatures who rang the Dwelling Place doorbell were an unknown quantity whom we came to understand only through much (often painful) experience. One of my jobs as a volunteer was to interview new arrivals and ascertain their needs. This was not always easy. Many women's experiences had made them suspicious and mistrustful, unwilling to give information about themselves. Others had become resourceful and manipulative, and they tried to pull the same number on us that they had on everyone else. Still others believed their own delusions about who they were or what had been their past, making it impossible to separate fact from fiction. Thus, for example, a woman whose check was going to an old address and being stolen (by the people there, who were cashing it) might refuse to reveal the address; why should she trust us more than she trusted them? Some would not even give their real first names but called themselves Mary, which in this culture seems to be the archetypal name for woman.[1]

Over time, though, we could usually learn something. After a while most women began to trust us and revealed selected fragments of their lives; or they might agree to apply for welfare or SSI, and we then discovered that they had a history of institutionalization. Even when a woman told us almost nothing, we often recognized in her behavior a familiar pattern and could infer much. Thus, although we never got detailed histories from most women, we were able to form fairly clear ideas of the lives of many, or at least of the significant factors that had led them to the street.

Why They Were Outside

For the sake of convenience, I have grouped the factors contributing to homelessness loosely in three categories. The first two, loss of relationships and loss of a job or housing, involved a relatively passive reaction on the part of the woman, who was more or less forced out onto the street; the third represented a more active choice.

LOSS OF RELATIONSHIPS

The most important factor was the loss of family and other relationships. In the years before an accelerating loss of low-cost housing in New York City made cheap hotel rooms virtually impossible to find, this was perhaps the most frequent reason for homelessness that the Dwelling Place staff heard. The issue was not necessarily that the women were unable to maintain relationships but rather that they were unable to carry on when these were lost. The great majority had lived within society, to some extent at least, and became homeless only when their network of support was destroyed. Because most were products of a generation that socialized women to be dependent and not to work, the determining factor that broke up their lives and plunged them into homelessness was usually not economic but relational.[1]

For many of the women I knew, problems arose when a pattern of dependency was broken, usually through loss of a husband, parent, or other relative. About half of the homeless people in the city at that time seemed to us at the Dwelling Place, and to staff at other private shelters, to have been inmates of psychiatric institutions; this observation made it tempting to assume that their difficulties were psychological.[2] However, quite a few women who showed signs of psychological disturbance when we saw them seemed to have led normal lives before the death of a mother or sister, for example, brought on an emotional crisis. To me, "mental illness" came to seem not a clear-cut phenomenon, but something that depended on context. Even when women had delusions or heard voices, the better I knew them, the more such symptoms seemed a response to circumstances rather than an indication of illness within the person. Thus, the context of a woman's life was as important to understand as her psychology—especially in cases where a "normal" woman became "abnormal" when her circumstances changed.

Mary, the youngest of several children, lived with her mother until her mother died when Mary was thirty-five. Fifteen years later she still thought about her mother's death constantly, as well as about the bad feelings among the members of her family that had led, among other things, to her father's leaving home. It was after her mother's death that Mary began having to go into mental hospitals; she had been in four in the New York area. She could not restrain her emotions, she told me; people told her she had to take care of herself, but she couldn't stop thinking about her family's problems. Yet Mary settled in permanently at the Times Square, participating in all the Dwelling Place activities. Nothing about her suggested mental illness. She was quite passive and needed reminders about keeping doctor's appointments, and she tended to get sulky and irrational when she was frustrated, but these traits hardly distinguish her from a great many other people whom no one ever thinks of sending to a hospital. Mary's dependency became an "illness" only when there was no one to take care of her.

We found, too, that a surprising number of women whose thinking and emotions appeared quite disorganized to us had spent many years as wives. When Evelyn's husband died, her life fell apart. A brother supported her; when he became ill, another brother looked after her until she had to enter the hospital—the veterans' hospital since she had been a WAC in World War II. She went in for a fairly simple medical procedure, but her behavior apparently led to her transfer to the psychiatric ward. On her release she could not return to her brother (I inferred that he wouldn't take her) and refused to go to her in-laws. If her own family wouldn't take her in, she said, her in-laws would think something was wrong with her. Besides, she added, "I hate to beg." She showed me pictures of herself, young and pretty in her WAC uniform, and, later, with her husband.

She filled the huge emptiness his death had left in her life with an obsessive, consuming involvement in the legal details of her "case" with Veterans Assistance and with a series of physical ailments. These illnesses could never be cured because until her case was settled, she had no money or Medicaid to get treatment, and her case would never be settled because she had gone the rounds already from one agency to another and knew it was impossible. She maintained this belief with unshakable conviction, just as she clung to her illness with unalterable determination: it was her treasure, her pearl, her identity. Ultimately she enforced her assertion that we could not help her by running away. Yet this woman had, at least by her own account, been happily married for years.

Millie lived with her aunt in the country but tended to wander off. On one of these flights she wound up in a hospital that referred her to the Dwelling Place. I got in touch with her aunt, who informed me, "She has been adjudged schizophrenic." This condition was the result of a broken marriage. "Before then," the aunt said, "this woman was a top secretary in the housing department, quite a position for a black person to hold in the forties." Millie's "illness" consisted basically of a hyperemotionality that led her to burst into violent floods of tears when she thought about her difficulties. "I have this trouble that I get emotional," she told me, "which is why I can't hold a job."

She wanted to live in a foster home where she could do things for herself but get support when she needed it. "I'm *forty-nine* years of age," she said, meaning that she couldn't live with her aunt (who worked all day) and just sit alone and do nothing out in the country; she was an adult who needed her own place in the world. She felt strongly that having some kind of meaningful activity would save her. But although I started the process of investigating foster homes, she wound up going back to her aunt the next day after a burst of emotion while talking to her on the phone. "The thing is, she isn't really crazy," I said later to one of the nuns. "Honey," she responded, "that's what we wind up saying about almost every one of them!"

Although Lydia's marriage was not broken like Millie's, it was intermittent; her husband periodically left her. She had been without him for a couple of months when she came to the Dwelling Place, and was comfortably settled in the hotel until one day she experienced a violent, mysterious affliction that resembled a stroke. She became incontinent and incoherent and did not recognize people or know where she was. Bellevue, the municipal hospital, would not take her, though, because she wasn't sick enough. Dwelling Place volunteers went to the hotel daily and cleaned up after her. In a few days she improved, and when another volunteer and I brought some food to her tiny room, she was sitting alone, neatly dressed, smoking. She had gone downstairs earlier to buy cigarettes, though we had trouble getting her to eat. She spoke softly and indistinctly and had difficulty hearing us as we persuaded her to take a few sips of orange juice. In fact I began to suspect that Lydia wasn't quite as helpless as she let on, that she was playing a little game, enjoying being waited on and cajoled. This suspicion was confirmed a few days later when one of the staff spoke to her brother in Alabama, who said that this same seeming breakdown had happened the last time Lydia's husband had left her. She was an alcoholic, a condition that also contributed to her behavior. Shortly thereafter Lydia's husband was discovered living in a hotel nearby; joyfully, they moved in together—until, presumably, the next time he left.[3]

The Dwelling Place policy of not requiring any information that a woman did not choose to give meant that most of the stories we heard were incomplete, fragmentary, and one-sided. There was no way to discover, for example, what Mary and Evelyn were like before the deaths that changed their lives. It did seem clear that, whatever their psychological state might have been, they and the others I have described were able to function for years in lives that included family, husband, and sometimes work. The question then arises of whether the traumatic event changed something in them or whether personalities that had been viable in the past were simply unequipped to deal with new conditions. In this case, to speak of "illness," with its implication that something was inherently wrong with their mental and emotional makeups, seems to me unfair since they had been perfectly acceptable before.

An acute version of this question arose when a woman's behavior within her family was considered objectionable by someone who then had her hospitalized.[4] Here I found myself asking how much the context—for example a husband's (and two psychiatrists' and a judge's) expectations of how a wife should behave—had to do with her being considered ill. The woman I saw, who often did seem "ill" to me, was the product of a series of experiences that included being defined as ill and hospitalized; I did not know her as she had been. Nor did I get the husband's point of view. Even without it, however, what I learned invites speculation.

Take, for example, Norma. Though she was furious with her husband,

Norma was at the same time proud of him and convinced of his superiority over other men. She had a pervading sense of her own sinfulness, which seemed related to her sexual feelings for him. By her account he was a domineering man with a hot temper, violent (he raped her twice), highly critical, jealous, and suspicious (though he was unfaithful himself). Norma had a strong tie to her father; she often ran away from her husband to her father and then went back. Her problem started, she said, when her father died; if he hadn't, she never would have been in a mental hospital. Her husband finally left her for another woman, abandoning her with two children and no money. He said she was crazy and had her put in the hospital. She showed me the scars on her wrists from being tied and straitjacketed, and told how they forced her to submit to electroshock. All the other patients were doped up with medicine that destroyed their minds, but she fought and escaped by climbing over the wall.

It was quite clear to Norma that what her husband and the hospital authorities wanted was for her to be obedient and agreeable. She refused to behave and was proud of her resistance, yet at the same time felt she was a bad ("sinful") person. She kept saying she was "stupid" but also knew that her trouble wasn't "here" (pointing to her head) but "here" (pointing to her heart), for she had been tested. Certainly she was quite intelligent and had as well a sharp moral sense unclouded by sentiment. Yet although she could express anger at her husband and the hospital authorities, she never condemned them, only herself, and continued to judge herself by their standards, making constant efforts to fit herself back into regular life. She experimented with various therapies, hoping to get better, and kept trying to find a job; she went once to the state employment office but was sent to a clinic where a doctor told her she was a "very sick girl" and couldn't hold down a job. This comment enraged her. "I got so mad the next thing I knew I found myself in the hospital," she said. Eight months later she did get a job, which she held for two months until it became "too taxing" and she ended up once more in Bellevue.

I interpreted "taxing" to mean that the contradictory tangle of feelings in her made success even harder to handle than failure. Within Norma there was continual tension between her conscious judgment of herself in the conventional terms she associated with her husband and a natural unconscious resistance to this judgment. When the stress became too much, she blew and wound up in the "booby hatch," as she put it. In such a state she was completely out of her mind and was dangerous, for she was a strong woman; on one occasion, she told me rather proudly, it took three policemen to hold her. After a couple of weeks on Thorazine, she came out and returned to her previous hotel or found a new one, and the cycle began again.

I became attached to Norma, and it was extremely painful to see her struggling against her own strength, for evidently what was strong in her had been so devalued by the people around her that she did not value it herself. In a different context—married perhaps to a less authoritarian and controlling man—her natural personality might have been acceptable; she would not have needed to repress it and would never have been driven to whatever extreme behavior had been used to justify her commitment (probably the same sort of outbursts that we saw). Yet even as she was when I knew her—fluctuating between violent ups and downs—Norma's intelligence and powerful motivation would have given her a good chance to acquire some control over her feelings and her life if she had had continuous emotional support in a stress-free environment. But she was a homeless woman, with nothing in the world but her SSI check, and the resources of the Dwelling Place were insufficient to give her this support.

Norma's turmoil was caused in large measure by the power of her personality; at the same time that she set her husband, or what he represented, over her as judge, she would not let go of an autonomous sense of herself. Some women, though, have no such sense but are totally slaves of the man—any man. When he says "Come," they go, not just blindly but unconsciously. Asking for help, Sylvia called the shelter one afternoon saying she had been robbed and had no clothes but those she was wearing. She had been at Mary House, a shelter for women run by the Catholic Worker organization on Manhattan's Lower East Side, but had stayed out an entire night, breaking their curfew, and so had lost her place. I said she could come and get clothes, though we had no room for her to stay.

When she arrived, Sylvia, who turned out to be a small woman in her forties, told me she had been given a week's rent by welfare to tide her over in a hotel because her check hadn't come. She had met a man who offered her a drink and figured she wouldn't go anywhere with him but just have a drink and a pleasant chat. After several drinks she fell asleep. "That never happened to me before," she commented (I didn't believe her). When the bartender woke her, she found that her purse, containing her money, identification, and the key to the locker that held all her things, was gone. When she went to the locker, it was empty. It was clear from the way Sylvia talked about him that this man had had a hypnotic effect on her; even though it might have been the liquor that put her to sleep, the fact that she had allowed herself to drift off that way instead of staying alert signaled a tendency to lapse into unconsciousness the moment an authority figure—that is, any man with a will—appeared to whom she could hand herself over.

When Sylvia had showered and changed, at her request I called the city Women's Shelter (also located on the Lower East Side and at that time the only public shelter for women) to see whether they had a bed. Hearing her name, the social worker sighed deeply. "Miss Prior *again?*" she said. "Where did she spend the night?" I repeated what Sylvia had told me, that she spent the nights on the trains. "All right," the social worker said, "send her over and I'll interview her." Sylvia seemed not too happy about this development—she would have preferred Mary House—but she accepted a token for the subway and left, saying she might go over that evening. A year and a half later she reappeared, obviously leading exactly the same life.

The women so far described all had originally, or had developed, elements in their personalities that contributed largely to (though did not entirely determine) their being homeless. June's case, however, is less clear-cut. June was not passive or dependent or obsessed or anything else that would lead one to infer psychological problems; but she was full of anger. The anger was justified, from what I could gather, but, in much the manner of a psychiatric symptom, it sometimes got in the way of her functioning. She had periodic outbursts of fury, which she handled by going off alone until she calmed down. This rage seemed to spring from not having been treated as a real person, first by her father, then her husband. One day she informed me that her husband had "lost" himself. "He got lost," she said, "so I did too, and I've been lost ever since." She meant that he had a habit of leaving and staying away for a while without, she said indignantly, any sense that he shouldn't do that to her, that she had a right to know where he was. When he did it once too often, she walked out herself.

Anger like that is a luxury, however, that only women with an adequate job or someone to go to can afford; and for this reason I would give circumstances more weight than her own character in making June homeless. Such anger is not unusual in "normal" society; there, however, a supporting social framework of family or job compensates for or cushions its destructive effects. But June, lacking such support once she left her husband (in itself an act of strength that perhaps saved her from severe emotional problems like Norma's), was started on a career that ultimately led to homelessness. Without marketable skills and being black, she could get only low-paying and insecure work; one day she just didn't go back to her job. When I asked why, she couldn't (or wouldn't) tell me. "I just didn't go," she repeated. I finally concluded that her anger had operated here too. People with options are not necessarily penalized for leaving jobs they dislike, but June's only option was the street. She took it.

Many SRO tenants, too, had long ago lost whatever human connections they might have had, and amid the brutal life of the hotel their mental and emotional condition deteriorated through sheer fear and isolation. These hotels were dirty, cold, depressing, and dangerous. The way landlords made a profit from the low rents charged was by not maintaining the buildings. Toilets and faucets did not work; heat was often nonexistent; locks were insecure; and the shared bathrooms in the hallways were particularly dangerous because men tried to break in while women were in the shower. A few larger hotels provided meals, recreational activities, and assistance from social workers. But such assistance had to be sought out, and SRO tenants were often unwilling to approach a caseworker for any reason (having once been ground through the welfare mill) or simply too disoriented.

Many, in fact, were former patients discharged from state mental hospitals during a wave of deinstitutionalization beginning in the late 1960s (see "Since World War II" in Part 3 for the history of SROs and deinstitutionalization in relation to homelessness). Whatever their original condition, long-term hospital inmates had been rendered incapable of coping in the outside world simply by the nature of life in the institution. Lacking any emotional or practical support, unable to handle even the normal business of living, let alone the stresses of SRO life, they deteriorated still further. They stopped going to appointments with their caseworkers and ceased taking the drugs that calmed them, silenced the voices they heard, and repressed their more antisocial behavior. As their behavior worsened, even casual contacts with others became more and more abrasive, until the hotel threw them out or they left on their own. After a time on the street they would most likely be picked up by the police—usually after some incident in which they disturbed others in a public place—and taken to the hospital, which treated them briefly with drugs and discharged them again as soon as possible, with a new caseworker and a new prescription.

The history of one such long-term inmate was shockingly revealed one day in the mid 1970s to Raye, a middle-aged grandmother who had known her when they were both children in the Bronx forty years before. Deborah, the little girl who was to become the homeless woman, lived in the house next to Raye's, in a close-knit Jewish neighborhood. Deborah's father committed suicide when she was small by throwing himself off a roof. Her mother was the caretaker for the synagogue. As a child Deborah had been "a little slow," as Raye put it, though not retarded; she went to school but had no friends her own age. Though Raye was a little younger, Deborah followed her and her friends around, holding the jump rope for them, for example. They, understanding that she "wasn't like the rest of us," watched out for her. When Deborah was about sixteen, her mother committed suicide too. Raye never knew what became of her after that. Then one rainy day, forty years later, Raye went into a five-and-ten on Twenty-third Street in Manhattan during her lunch hour. As she shopped, she passed someone whose dirty clothes and shopping bags marked her as a bag woman. As Raye stood in line waiting to pay, the bag woman came up and said Raye's first name and maiden name. "It gave me a chill," Raye recalled. "Then I looked into her eyes and I saw the little girl—the eyes don't change—the smile and the eyes." Deborah's voice too was the same little girl's voice. Her name came back to Raye "like something out of a dream," and she was able to say, "You're Deborah, yes, I remember you."

As they went out into the street, Raye asked Deborah to have coffee, but Deborah refused, so they stood in the pouring rain under Raye's umbrella. In answer to Raye's questions, Deborah said she had been in Creedmoor, a state mental hospital in Queens. She had in fact been in institutions all her life (until, I assume, being discharged to an SRO) and was deeply embittered. Don't trust those places, she said to Raye, don't believe everything you hear; they're horrible places. "They lie," she said, "they do terrible things." Later Raye found out that Deborah had been married and had a child who was taken from her by the father's parents. Speaking to Raye that afternoon, however, she was perfectly rational. She said she slept in subway cars, but since that was dangerous she sometimes used the library. She would not say where she got money but only, in response to Raye's offer, that she had no need of it: "Oh, no, Raye, I won't take any money from *you*." "For weeks afterward it haunted me, and I tried to find her," Raye said, but she couldn't. Nor, I think, if she had succeeded, could she have prevailed on Deborah to accept help.

Deborah's story illustrates the complex factors that create an individual's homelessness. If Deborah had not been "slow," or had not lost both parents so early in so devastating a way, or had had other family mem-

bers to take her in and enable her to avoid the years of institutionalization that created such distrust and bitterness, perhaps she would not have
become so attached to the life of the bag woman, whose extreme solitude
and independence she clearly needed. Though she wanted the connection
involved in recognizing Raye and talking to her, she drew a line at a place
that to her represented the margin of safety. Many homeless women drew
such lines, although for each one familiarity turned to danger at a different point. But like Deborah's, each boundary could be mapped with reference to specific bruisings in the past.

LOSS OF JOBS AND HOUSING

With jobs and housing, the next two factors responsible for homelessness, circumstances definitely weighed more heavily. The homeless
women I knew, most of whom were over forty, had worked—if they
worked at all—largely in marginal jobs that offered no security in the
present and often no Social Security in the future. When I knew them,
most were in any case no longer able to work by reason of physical or
mental disability or both. But even for those who could have worked—
both skilled and unskilled—there were no jobs. They did not have even
the opportunity older homeless men had to work as dishwashers or seasonal farm laborers, or as casual laborers unloading trucks. Recruitment
systems existed for such labor, and references and appearance were un-
important, but women were not part of this labor pool.[5] The only comparable unskilled work available to them was domestic service, but a
woman off the street had little chance of being hired for that. Thus, while
men could pick up occasional work that enabled them to get by without
public assistance or to supplement their checks, women had to choose
between dependence on the government as absolute as their previous dependence on father or husband, or nothing at all.

Wilhelmine, a heavy, reddish-blonde-haired woman of fifty-four, said
when I interviewed her that she wanted a job. She spoke in a mumble,
not incoherently but too fast, so she was hard to hear. At the moment she
was living with a man in his room in a boarding house, but since it was
supposed to be a single, he had to sneak her in; she needed a place of her
own. She had been married for over thirty years to a longshoreman who
had died; her widow's pension was only $100 a month, not enough to
live on. Her checks went to her brother's house in Queens, but she
couldn't live with him because he was violent. She had applied for welfare
but was refused because she was, they said, able to work. In fact they

could have given her a supplemental income until she found a job, but getting that required an assertiveness that Wilhelmine clearly was not capable of, even had she known she was entitled to the money. She wanted to do housekeeping or baby-sitting. She had been a waitress off and on, substituting for a friend, but the owner sold the restaurant and didn't give her a recommendation to the new owner, and she wasn't hired because she was too old. I called a housekeeping agency, which said she should come over. But she didn't have her Social Security number; her brother had it and would bring it with her pension check. Wilhelmine always had to wait for her brother to bring the check to Manhattan because by the end of the month she never had the fare (at that time fifty cents) to travel to Queens to get it.

I don't think Wilhelmine was unusually passive, at least not originally—certainly no more so than many other women whose husbands support them for thirty years—but she had been trapped by circumstances she had no experience coping with. Living too long with uncertainty and helplessness can wear down even strong people until they lose any capacity they might have had to act. I thought Wilhelmine could probably have held a job; there seemed nothing wrong with her except that she could not present herself effectively. But would anyone hire her when so many younger, more prepossessing women were available?

While the lack of jobs affected relatively few of the homeless women I met, the lack of housing affected them all. By the early eighties, the problem that the SROs were impossible to live in had been superseded by the problem that they were ceasing to exist, as more and more were converted into middle-class and luxury housing. Not only did the old tenants (who included many types of people, not just former mental patients) lose their housing, but less housing of any kind was available for the people newly discharged from hospitals; we heard reports of patients being "discharged" into the street.[6]

The tenants of an SRO about to be converted were frequently evicted brutally. Commonly the landlord hired a management company that locked the tenants out, throwing them onto the street with their belongings, and hired thugs who threatened to beat them up if they tried to get back in. Often this trauma prevented them from expending the effort required to find a new place to live. In April 1980 the Dwelling Place staff opened the door to three former residents of one Upper West Side hotel whose management had given the tenants $200 apiece and told them to leave in two weeks—a somewhat gentler proceeding than being thrown out without warning, but the effects were not much different. One of the three was a woman in her late seventies. Sometimes we could get such women into adult or nursing homes, but finding one that was decent and had space available was difficult. Other women were evicted for similar reasons from apartments.

Loss of housing was complicated by another difficulty in the eviction of Caroline, who was about seventy, thin and tiny, somewhat bent, and senile. She couldn't remember anything for more than five or ten minutes, and when I arrived at the shelter one Monday in April, she was moaning and wailing loudly about her apartment, furniture, and cats. She had been brought in the previous Friday night by a policeman from Brooklyn, with a note saying that a man from the Department of Protective Services would come to pick her up that Monday morning. No one had, however, so I called the office and spoke to a supervisor.

Caroline was evicted for not paying rent for three months. She had been in court, she had had legal representation, the judge had given her several extensions, but she still hadn't paid. Having over a thousand dollars in the bank, she was not eligible for emergency relief. But she refused to spend her money. The department had found an adult home for her in Far Rockaway (a section of Queens far from Manhattan), but she wouldn't go there. She was examined at a hospital and given a clean bill of health both medically and psychologically, so was not admitted. I objected that she seemed senile (and the policeman's note had called her "senile and destitute"), but the supervisor shrugged it off. Either he didn't want to hear this objection, or he wouldn't credit anything I said against the hospital psychiatrist's evaluation. The department had gotten her into the Women's Shelter's Brooklyn annex, but after she made a racket all night, the staff there apparently gave up and had her brought to the Dwelling Place.

I next called the city marshal, who said that her furniture was in a city warehouse and that her cats had probably run away. Caroline did not remember anything about the court proceedings and, when I mentioned the home in Far Rockaway, said, "I don't even know where Far Rockaway is." But when a staff member (with much difficulty) took her there, she entered it. Whether she woke up the next morning and began wailing about her furniture and cats, and how the people there handled her, we never knew; but given the possibilities, simply getting her into the place constituted success.

Alone and quite incapable of any action on her own behalf, Caroline became simply an object to be processed through the legal and welfare systems, which by their nature were unable to match their procedures to her condition. Only when the Women's Shelter evaded its legal responsibility to secure appropriate placement for her by fobbing her off on the Dwelling Place did she get the kind of attention that gave her some chance of being helped. But Caroline's complete inability to understand—let alone deal with—the need to pay rent was only an extreme version of a common pattern resulting from the standard way in which women are socialized. The eviction of Elise affords a typical example.

Elise, who was in her fifties, had lived for years with her mother. The mother had remarried, so her name was different from Elise's, and when she died Elise was thrown out of their apartment because her name wasn't on the lease. I thought it possible that the apartment was rent-controlled, and the landlord wanted her out so he could raise the rent; however, Elise would not say whether she had continued to pay rent after her mother's death, and the rest of her story suggested that this could have been the problem. She was in bed with her six cats one morning around eight or nine when there came a terrific pounding on the door. Five men were there—two lawyers and three policemen—who showed her a piece of paper and said she had twenty minutes to pack and get out. She claimed she had had no prior notice, but I knew from experience that she might not have paid attention to it. For women unused to dealing with "business" such as rent and taxes, official-looking letters either had no reality at all or were confusing and frightening, and the women tended to disregard them. One of the policemen was "considerate" and took Elise to the Women's Shelter, which placed her in a hotel where she lived for two years until they raised the rent and she had to leave. She said she couldn't pay for "three squares" a day, although she was on welfare, which was supposed to provide an increase to cover such expenses.

Elise carried around a great deal of anger beneath a suave exterior, and her story was not entirely consistent; still, whatever happened after her mother's death, she seemed to have led a perfectly normal life previously. She told me she had worked since she was a teenager as a stenographer/typist. Becoming interested in clothes, she left the patent office, where she had worked at first, for a large export-import company that paid more, so that she could buy herself furs. In this sheltered niche she had lived quietly; only when the niche was destroyed did she become a "social problem."

The poverty of these Dwelling Place women, who could not understand why they had to pay the rent or who were evicted because they would not take their money out of the bank, tends to obscure their similarity to those middle-class elderly mothers whose children suddenly realized, as they listened to me describe the Dwelling Place women during the many conversations I had about homelessness while writing this book, that if it were not for the children's surveillance of the mothers' finances and superintendence of "business," those mothers too would be on the street that very minute. Social class and income level do not create this type of woman; she exists everywhere. Whether she is on the street is determined by whether there is money and someone taking care of it and her.

At issue here is women's relation to money and legal matters. Elise's refusal even to discuss the topic of paying rent was typical. The feeling I had in trying to talk to many women about these matters was that such things existed on a plane quite removed from their own. One said this to me in so many words. Agnes was an educated, refined woman who did not look her sixty-seven years and was quite clear-minded until I asked about money; then she became agitated. She said yes, she got it but didn't know what money it was or where it came from. It was all in the hands of lawyers and bankers, she said, and she and I couldn't understand those things. I said I *could* understand, but this she refused to credit: she knew more than I because she was older, and since she didn't know, I couldn't. It was like asking for the secrets of the gods—not allowed. Agnes had lived with her sister in a hotel where this mysterious money paid the rent. We found out later that it was some kind of trust fund. When the checks were suddenly no good, the hotel evicted Agnes. At the time, her sister, who handled business for both of them, was in the hospital. When the sister came out, she took over again and got them both into another hotel—fortunately for Agnes, who without her sister would doubtless have ended up on the street.

I met many women who, like Agnes, had a vague spot in their minds when it came to money. They had trouble managing their funds—not only with paying rent and making the rest of their check stretch over a month, but with being able to feel a sense of actual ownership of money in the first place. This difficulty might be aggravated by psychological disability but certainly did not depend on it. I came to believe that more was involved in the tendency many women had to spend their whole check right away than being unable to budget or to resist impulse. Simply possessing it seemed to make them uncomfortable. Thus, some would give away money they should have spent on legitimate needs of their own. This desire to avoid owning one's money was exemplified by Jessie, who lived for years with a man she was not married to and had her SSI checks come in his name. When he finally left her, she had no money. In the face of the three-month wait required to start getting checks in her own name—not to mention the prospect of having to explain to the caseworker why she had lied in the first place—she simply went to live in Penn Station.

This attitude toward money is only one aspect of a more general female passivity, which as I have suggested tended to be hidden when a woman lived within a social framework but was thrown into sharp relief when she became homeless. Jessie's willingness to allow a man who had no legal obligations to her to receive her funds is another version of the willingness to follow a total stranger; and both these reactions are only the attempts of women in irregular situations to create the regularized passivity of the traditional marriage they were raised to believe in. When catastrophe struck, women who had no man or anyone else to act for them often did not try to figure out what they could do or search for someone to advise them; instantly overwhelmed, they went to Penn Station.

There, for example, a Dwelling Place outreach team found Barbara, a middle-aged, sweet-natured, frightened woman whose welfare check had not come that month. She had been too inert, too intimidated, to call the welfare office and ask about it; her solution was the station. So I called on her behalf. The caseworker I spoke to was a nice young man who was at first quite upset that she had waited so long without doing anything (it was two weeks after the check had been due). I tried to explain Barbara's incapacity but he didn't really hear me; bureaucratic procedures are deeply ingrained in bureaucrats, who have trouble understanding that there are people to whom they don't come naturally. He did say he would stop payment on the check and that next week Barbara had to come in and explain how she had supported herself in the interim. I said she had been in Penn Station. He sighed but said nothing, as though he preferred to avoid thinking about that.

I explained to Barbara that she had to call sooner next time. She heard me, but I was sure she'd never do it. Women like her seemed to have no sense of owning themselves, even in the minimal sense that would lead one to protect a valuable piece of property. This is one reason why they so often left themselves open to being robbed or assaulted. To themselves, as to the welfare bureaucracy, they were not only objects but worthless ones as well.

CHOOSING TO GO OUT

Not all homeless women were passive victims; some acted to shape their situations. Nevertheless the exercise of will by someone in a dependent position usually involves considerable sacrifice. The women willing to make it were the ones who came closest to the myth of the bag lady who "chooses" the street. Once I learned, however, how damaging to the personality this choice could be, I ceased to feel even the theoretical enthusiasm being expressed at the time by some feminists who saw the bag women as independent souls rejecting the domination of the patriarchy.

Some women did make straightforward, rational decisions to go on the street, not as a permanent choice but as a response to a specific situation. Cynthia, seventy-eight but looking ten years younger, walked out of a nursing home on the Upper West Side one November. The residents of such places turned their checks over to the management, which was legally required to give them $28.50 back as spending money; but Cynthia said her home took it all, so she left. Though she was diabetic, as we found out later, she had survived on her own for three months and was quite vigorous, calm, and cheerful—only stubbornly resistant when it came to giving a straight answer as to whether she would turn over her check if we got her into another home. I spent an afternoon on the phone trying to find one, and finally reached a social worker at an adult home who explained that sometimes a check is short, so the management keeps the spending money to make up the difference. Cynthia, and many like her, refused even to understand this reasoning—not surprisingly since no one with a spark of self-respect (and Cynthia had plenty) could imagine that her rights should be sacrificed for someone else's profit.

The social worker called the former home, which assured her that Cynthia was very nice. With so many clients to choose from, the homes could pick out the ones who didn't give trouble, leaving the independent spirits out in the cold. However, people sometimes came to a home, stayed a month, then refused to turn over their checks and left, which meant the home was out $300. Thus the management tried to protect itself. Most of the old people, however, couldn't protect themselves; an unscrupulous management could say anything about the check since the poor and infirm (and now homeless) old person was hardly going to take the home to court. Cynthia was accepted by the new home, but within a few months she left it too and went back on the street. Shortly after, she died in a hospital.

The dangers of SROs impelled quite a few women to leave them simply because they felt safer on the street. Sarah, a somewhat incoherent
and deluded Jewish woman of about sixty, was raped at her hotel and
went wandering off; she lived on the street and eventually found her way
to the Dwelling Place. Danger also drove Kathleen from her SRO. She
was a handsomely coiffed, white-haired woman who, in answer to the
question "What age would you like to be?" (part of a game we played
once at the coffee hour), said, "Ninety-one, because then it would all be
over." When asked her real age she said, "Seventy-five and proud of it."
She had lived in an Upper West Side hotel that was so terrible she was
afraid to stay there; people banged on her door in the middle of the night,
for instance, trying to break in. She went on the street but still paid rent
because her belongings remained in the room. She also continued going
to church and described her situation to the priest, who got angry and
fought to get her into a senior citizens' project. It took two years, but
finally, she said, she had a home. She told me how much she loved her
bathroom, after having had no bathroom of her own for five years in the
hotel. She sometimes went into it just to sit and read; twice she fell asleep
in there, she felt so good. Now in the evenings she bought copies of the
Daily News from a vendor for twenty-five cents and sold them on the
street for thirty-five cents. By this means she made twenty or thirty cents
a night, which at the end of the week provided her with two dollars for
the collection at her church. That was her only reason for selling the papers—two dollars being, apparently, the amount her self-respect required
her to give. Her son lived on Long Island, and she had grandchildren, but
her daughter-in-law was "bossy," so she preferred being on her own. The
project where Kathleen lived stood on a spot previously occupied by an
apartment building in which she had had a six-room apartment. When it
was torn down, she had had to leave.

Kathleen's and Cynthia's rather matter-of-fact choice to go on the
street illustrates an attitude I was surprised to discover was common.
People far removed from such a necessity tend to think of being on the
street as a catastrophe that shakes people loose from the category of humanity—a concept closely connected to the idea of shelter. Animals sleep
outside (though, being domesticated, dogs get doghouses). Nevertheless
a remarkable number of women considered the street a reasonable option, at least as an interim measure. Although the Women's Shelter was
always full and turned away many more women than it accepted, the
Dwelling Place staff saw many who refused to go there because of the
demeaning restrictions and regulations imposed on its residents (includ-

ing a compulsory gynecological examination and a prohibition against lying down on their beds in the middle of the day).[7] Their feelings about it may be summed up by the somewhat enigmatic comment of one who told a Dwelling Place staff member that she would rather be on the street because if she went into the Women's Shelter, she "would lose my life." Perhaps this woman was just deluded, but I prefer to interpret her remark as an expression of the feeling shared by many that the rules there deprived them of their personhood.[8]

One day before the high point of SRO conversion, I was compiling a list of cheap hotels while Susan, looking over my shoulder, made comments; she knew them all. One, she complained, was very dirty: "I'd rather sleep on the street than put up with that." Another charged forty-nine dollars a week—at that time rather high in this category—and made you pay for two weeks in advance, which used up all your money. Susan was one of the women who drifted from one such hotel to another. If by accident or choice all their money was spent, they hit the street until the next check came. Some deliberately chose to live in a nicer, more expensive hotel for only half the month and on the street for the rest. Their highest value was maintaining their self-respect; and while this attitude led them to walk out of degrading living conditions, it also made them happy to accept better ones.

The danger in holding to this value for someone in such circumstances was that one moment of justified anger could precipitate a sudden change that turned out to be irreversible. The social frameworks of many Dwelling Place women were much less stable than other people's, and the ties attaching them to the social fabric were fragile. When their one thread broke, they fell away. I was once sitting on a bench outside a store on Third Avenue when a woman next to me started talking. She was terribly agitated, having just come from the office where she had to sign for her check. The caseworker had scolded her for having received money from her family. She was distressed that they could know so much about her, but mostly she felt she had lost so much self-respect that the money wasn't worth it. She kept repeating that she should have refused to sign and just walked out, but the place "hypnotized" her and she couldn't.

This woman had a place to live, probably one of the hotels. But I could see that her encounter with the bureaucracy was so deeply wounding that to preserve her sense of who she was she would one day refuse to sign and walk out. She would then be terminated (as they say), be unable to pay rent, and soon be on the street. Once there, she would sink further into her rage and isolation. Unless her family intervened (and they probably could not find her if she chose not to contact them, which out of pride she might well do), she could easily become a permanent street dweller. It was unlikely that she would encounter the kind of support that kept Mary, at the Times Square, from succumbing to a similar moment of rage.

At the coffee hour one day Mary was very angry. She had already withdrawn all her spending money from the hotel cashier, so that there was nothing left but her rent money for the rest of the month (it was the fourteenth). Emotionally, she insisted she would take that too and go on the street; how could she get along with no money? Mary was diabetic and had heart trouble; on the street she would die. But she was too angry and too fixated on her lack of money for this fate to be real to her. Without persuasion from one of the sisters, and the promise of help in working out a budget, she would certainly have done it.

Women like Mary and the one on the bench were not by nature street people, although having once gone out in a state of rage and despair they risked becoming street people the longer they stayed out. So, I think, did the hotel drifters, as they grew older. Some such development, in which increasing anger combines with increasing alienation, may account at least in part for the women whom the Dwelling Place staff came to call "real bag ladies," people who stayed on the street because they needed to remain outside. Some were not bag women but what we called locker people. Instead of spending ten to twelve dollars a day on a hotel room, they spent about two dollars to support three to six lockers in a railroad or subway station. Although in some cases this life-style resulted from a pragmatic decision that it was more important to eat than to have a roof over one's head (especially after 1980, when hotel rates rose drastically), in my experience it was more often a necessary psychological compromise between being inside and being totally outside.

Marsha, a fat, pretty woman in her forties, was usually jolly and talkative but also had a terrible temper; her uncontrollable rages made her unable to fit into the structure of everyday life or to hold a job. She spent nights in Penn Station and had accepted the fact that she couldn't sleep more than two or three hours at a time. "You have to keep moving," she said. She would sometimes start out at Grand Central, then shift to Penn Station when Grand Central closed at 1:00 A.M. She kept herself neat and clean so that she looked like a traveler, and loved to sit and chat with the real travelers all night. Marsha needed this distance; her anger prevented her from wanting to live in normal proximity to other people.

One winter she developed pneumonia and went into the hospital. On

her release she came to the Dwelling Place and told me she had been on a
diet there and lost eighteen pounds. She said she felt good, but after she
had rushed up and down the stairs to say hello to everyone, she could
scarcely breathe and could speak only in a whisper. Two sisters sat her
down and told her flatly that if she didn't get on welfare so she could live
someplace, she would die. "This is the end of the street for you!" one
exclaimed, but Marsha only smiled; obviously she had her own ideas. To
me, watching, the whole business was absurd and disgusting. What was
the point of curing her and then throwing her back into her old situation?
Not that there was anything else constructive that the hospital social
worker could have done.

Joan, too, could not be near people. She lived in a vacant lot and for a
long time had refused to come to the shelter, although she accepted food
brought by staff members. At first she was violent and hostile but gradually began to trust the sisters. On the day I met her, in early March, she
had come to the Dwelling Place for soup at lunchtime. She wore a pon-
cho over a synthetic leather coat over one or two shirts; on her feet were
black rubber boots tied with cord above the ankles and folded over. She
explained that she was going to apply for SSI, using the shelter as her
address. I asked whether she didn't want to get a place to live when she
had money, and she said no, the hotels were terrible and had sick people
in them, good people mixed in with sick people; as she was, she was free
to come and go. This dislike of hotels and sick people was repeated over
and over; her speech, which had been so rational and clear that I had had
trouble believing she was really a street person, became too fast and took
on a compulsive, obsessive quality. She talked about "circumstances"
and how they made it better that she stay in her lot. I asked whether she
wasn't cold. She said that when she was, she came to the Dwelling Place
for a couple of hours to warm up, for supper, and so on, as she had today.

This, however, was a lucid phase of Joan's. The following winter I saw
her again, sitting on the sidewalk half a block from the shelter door, en-
veloped in a huge mass of blankets, muttering under her breath with
deadly fury. She had been staying at the Dwelling Place but had become
so hostile that the staff felt it was unsafe to let her stay unless she went to
the hospital and got medication. This she refused to do, and left.

Joan was middle-aged. Cathy, however, was in her twenties. When she
first started coming to the shelter, she never talked and always looked
sour and unhappy. The first time I saw her, she was standing by a wall,
stock still and wrapped in a blanket like a cigar-store Indian, head
slightly to one side. Next to her was her shopping cart filled with miscel-

laneous gatherings. She was so utterly disconnected that she seemed almost autistic, except that her presence itself constituted a message: she was asking for something yet refusing all contact. Although she was staying at the shelter, she had consistently refused a bed, kept away from everyone, and would not even go into the dining room to get food but had someone bring it to her. Gradually she came to move around and talk more, and get food for herself. The staff could do no more for her, however, and eventually she left. The next time I saw her, six months later, she was much more open and communicative. She had come for delousing, which she did about once a month. She still had to maintain a certain distance, however, which she achieved by refusing to eat sitting at a table with others and declining part of what was offered; she let me give her lunch, for example, except for the iced tea.

Cathy once told a staff member that she couldn't help the way she was living, that she went around in circles and lived like an animal. Although Cathy was intelligent and educated, some kind of block prevented her from doing anything except lead this shiftless, shifting existence. Eventually the staff managed to get her SSI for mental disability. With the money she lived for a while at the Times Square, though she disliked it because the men who hung around there made it dangerous for young, attractive women.

While Cathy and even Joan had some insight into themselves, other women located the source of their need to stay outside entirely in the external world. Thus there was a group who claimed that they couldn't come in because of certain enemies (especially the FBI or CIA) who eternally pursued them, destroying their chances to promulgate the message that it was their mission to reveal to the world. The women I met who had such delusions were originally middle-class and well educated, and their ideas were fantastically elaborated. Fran informed me that she had been "blacklisted from the human right to work" by the "entourage" of "intelligence" that followed her everywhere. With the assistance of library research, she had tied her own persecution by the CIA into the Kennedy and King assassinations so brilliantly that I couldn't draw the line where her delusion took over from the more respectable conspiracy theories. Another, who had been a high school speech teacher, said her child had been taken from her by the Mafia and police agents. They were after ten million dollars that belonged to her husband, who had a healing mission from God (now passed on to her). Women like these must stay outside because their secret persecutors poison every contact they make with other people.

Despite suspicions that the FBI and the Mafia had penetrated the Dwelling Place, these two women were willing to stay, probably because nobody challenged their beliefs. Wilma, however, would not even cross the threshold; she spent the entire day outside the door, eating meals that staff members brought her, asking occasionally for new clothes or some other small need. Once I tried to use her request for a new pair of pants to entice her in, but to no avail. The saint had told her she must stay outside for the sake of humility, she told me. To others she said she would be killed if she went in. At times she complained that she was cold, but her voices told her not to go in. Wilma was sweet and friendly, not at all suspicious; her beliefs referred only to herself. My sense was that she had a strong feeling of sinfulness, much like Norma's, for which the angels (as she also called her voices) were requiring her to do penance. After several years, one of the nuns noticed that Wilma wasn't looking well and tried to talk her into going to a hospital, but she wouldn't, and she died.

All these women claimed they wanted to be on the street or had to be. Others said they didn't and asked—often insistently—for help. But to every real possibility of help they said no, sometimes subtly, but consistently. The Dwelling Place carried on a truly epic struggle to overcome this eternal No over two years of dealing with Lenore, a small, theatrical, sharply dressed woman who came in off the street saying she wanted a job; she had been a waitress in a coffee shop and had been "nervous" ever since she stopped working, when the hotel her restaurant was in had closed. She had been offered a job in another hotel coffee shop but refused it because, she said, the prices there were so high that she wouldn't make any tips. I thought she might be able to get some other waitressing job, but she created so many conditions—it had to be the right shift in the right neighborhood—that I began to see that finding Lenore a job would not be so simple. She had been to the state employment office but didn't like what they offered. She was separated from her husband, who did not support her; to get support she needed a lawyer, but she would not go to Legal Services because—she was convinced—Legal Services would only help single people. Although she lived at the Dwelling Place, she would not take a bed but slept across three chairs or on the floor. Yet she was always complaining about how she was treated. If you reminded her about the bed, she denied it—it wasn't there, or they forgot about it, or nobody told her.

At length she was made to leave and was provided with a few days' rent at the Times Square until she could get emergency welfare or a job. But she objected to her room; she didn't like the institutional faucets, which wouldn't stay on. They gave her another room, which she also re-jected. So she went on the street and settled into living at Penn Station, where she got to know all the homeless women and developed a routine of making the rounds every night. She continued to dress very well and wear elaborate makeup, which she applied using the free display samples in nearby department stores.

A year later Lenore was once again taken into the Dwelling Place. Through the staff's efforts she got new glasses, which she had needed for a long time, but she wouldn't wear them. I noticed that she tended to abuse the nuns and the shelter to the extent that she was being helped and that, further, she insisted not only on refusing to be grateful but on de-manding more. When the nuns had to say no, she had fresh justification for abuse. It was clear that she overwhelmingly, desperately needed love—more love than anyone can ever give, and certainly more than an overworked staff of eight could give one of over a hundred women who all needed a great deal. So ultimately Lenore was told to leave again, and this time she did not return.

Life on the Street

Though women might decide to live on the street for a positive reason—financial or psychological self-preservation—the effects of that life were so negative that while I could admire the strength of character that often lay behind the decision and understand the reasons for it, I always wanted to get people inside again if possible. With long-timers, this could be difficult once they had adapted to life outside.

ADAPTATION TO STREET LIFE

Whether they had been forced into or had chosen street life (and sometimes, as we will see, the one turned into the other), once there women had to develop techniques to keep themselves alive. These varied considerably, but what struck me particularly was that by and large they reflected much less a rejection of conventional values than an attempt to affirm them in the midst of living outside. This attempt, however, was conditioned by the amount of distance each woman needed to maintain from other people. Living patterns ranged from that of passive women like Barbara, who on their own could not mobilize the energy to get shelter but gratefully accepted assistance and settled happily into life inside, to that of women like Lenore, who operated in cycles of making connections and then withdrawing, to that of the real isolates (relatively rare), who created lives almost totally outside.

The homeless women I knew used all the techniques of street survival that grew familiar later as homeless people became ubiquitous. They slept in phone booths, in subways (both in stations and on the trains), in store entrances, by vents that blew hot air onto sidewalks in winter, on park benches in summer. (One told me she lived in Central Park.) Some built constructions of cardboard cartons that they lined with newspaper. Sleeping outside at night was particularly dangerous for women, however, so quite a few kept moving or sat up in the stations by night and slept during the day. They used the ladies' rooms in Grand Central or Penn Station or other public restrooms to wash bodies, hair, and clothing; some stripped completely to wash. Others went to private shelters to shower. One woman gave me a graphic description of the difficulties of getting her period on the street when she had no money for sanitary napkins and no access to a bathroom. Women found clothes by going through trash or got them from churches and private shelters. Those who received checks bought secondhand clothes at thrift shops. Because of the difficulty of getting clothes washed, they always needed new ones.

That this much energy was expended on getting clean may seem surprising. The dirtiness of bag women became part of their mystique, probably because, like sleeping without shelter, dirt is a primary concept distinguishing the nonhuman from the human. One of the earliest studies of homeless women reported that some "shopping-bag ladies" claimed to use "filth and odor . . . as a conscious and articulated defense against" male attackers.[1] But to me this assertion runs counter to human nature—or at least female nature as socialized in our culture. If a woman had given me such an excuse, I would have seen it as another type of defense—an attempt to avoid admitting what bad shape she was really in or a rationalization that was necessary just because being dirty so contradicted her sense of who she was.

In my experience even women who were not otherwise concerned to keep up a respectable appearance did want to be clean; the most inveterate street dwellers came regularly to use the Dwelling Place showers. Without exception, lice and body odor accompanied a disintegration (sometimes temporary) in a woman's sense of herself. Among both street and hotel dwellers, relapses into infestation were always accompanied by mental and emotional deterioration and a falling away from habitual relationships with others.[2] Nevertheless the idea that the women chose to be dirty took hold because, I think, they had a magical quality that led people to believe they could dispense with elemental needs like keeping clean.

Bags were essential to street life. Unless a woman used lockers, she had no other place to keep things. Even women who lived in hotels often carried bags because the rooms were so unsafe that they had to keep their valuables with them. Women varied in their use of bags. At one extreme was Sylvia, who asked me for only one new outfit to replace the dirty clothes she was wearing, explaining that she didn't carry things with her because they would only get stolen. At the other was a well-known, much-photographed woman who used to live on Fourteenth Street in Manhattan, pushing around a large postal cart piled so high with her possessions that it severely restricted her mobility.[3] For her, as well as for other women who clearly had an intense relationship with their bags, carrying things around had a psychological component in addition to the practical one.

A small, thin woman named Allie spent the first several weeks of her stay at the Dwelling Place sitting near the front door with her possessions, a motley assortment of bags, bundles, and cases. During her first few days she was occupied with taking things out, rearranging them, and putting them back in; this repacking seemed to soothe her. Soon she took on the job of answering the door, though after a while she no longer needed to keep so close to the exit and was willing to come upstairs. Within two months she was living in a hotel and carried only two bags around.

Gertrude, a middle-aged woman (whom I so name because she looked exactly like Gertrude Stein, even to the crew-cut hair), also once made an inventory demonstrating the relationship of a collector to the things she collected. Sitting on a couch in the Dwelling Place living room, she took everything out of the two plastic shopping bags she always kept with her, went through it, recrumpled it up, and put it all back in, except for one empty potato-chip bag and a small Dr. Scholl's box. Among the things she put back in were old manila envelopes and various items of clothing, particularly one rather remarkable silver and pink knit T-shirt, far too small for her. She took each piece of clothing out, unfolded it, held it up and inspected it, refolded it, crammed it back into the bag, stuffed in crumpled papers, then stuck that whole bag into another. During the entire operation she remained obsessively intent on the contents, almost tranced, oblivious to the rapt attention she was getting from nearly everyone else in the room and unresponsive to several admiring remarks about the T-shirt. The woman sitting on the chair next to the couch leaned so far forward she seemed about to fall into the bags, and her eyes bugged out. Gradually all conversation in the room ceased; the women (myself included) were absorbed in Gertrude's movements, responding not so much to the things themselves (even the T-shirt) as to the quality of her relationship to them.

Gertrude seemed to me (perhaps partly because I was still new to the shelter) unearthly strange, almost a moon woman. She dressed in a peculiar assortment of clothing, as though she had been outside so long she had forgotten the function of each item. But within a few weeks she had begun to pull herself together, a process signaled by her changing style of dress. She used the Dwelling Place clothing room to experiment, creating outfits that became increasingly well matched; her previous oddness remained as a flair for distinctive combinations. I concluded that inventories like hers and Allie's were correlatives of a psychological sorting-out that was occurring as a result of the change in their living conditions. As a corollary, homeless women's different styles of dress—from those in Penn Station who looked like middle-class travelers to the classic bag women who looked like collections of rags—would also then reflect the state of their minds and feelings.

Another necessity for survival on the street was almost always money. Some women got checks, which were sent to general delivery or a post office box. Sometimes checks continued to go to a hotel where a woman no longer lived, and she went there to pick them up, an arrangement that could create problems if her relationship with the manager was not good or if he was unscrupulous. Although, conceivably, some women managed without any money at all, most had worked out some way to get it, usually by panhandling. Most women did not like to beg and did it only when they felt forced to. Fortunately quite a number of passersby gave homeless people—especially women—food or change without being asked. Several women told Dwelling Place staff members that women panhandlers did not have to ask for money the way men did; businessmen passing through the stations gave the women money if they just stood there.

Some women carried on more conventional enterprises. One sold flowers. After she bought her stock she came to the Dwelling Place to borrow several large white plastic pails to arrange them in. Another sang on the street for money. But the most conventional entrepreneurs, in a sense, were the prostitutes. We saw few of these at the shelter, partly because regular prostitutes had enough money to avoid homelessness and partly because many of them were younger than our minimum age of twenty-one. (Another program specifically for teenagers existed nearby.) Some of the younger women we saw did engage in casual prostitution when they wanted money. One of these combined prostitution with severe mental disability. When she first came to the Dwelling Place, she told a volunteer that she felt "disoriented" and didn't know what to do or where she was, and that this disturbed her. Nevertheless she declined to talk about her history and rejected offers of help. She seemed to be taking good care of herself, however, and I wondered how until, months later, I overheard her tell someone that she "saw guys." Soon after that she stopped coming but reappeared a year later, very much deteriorated. She had stopped keeping herself clean; there was a distant, blank look in her eyes; and her formerly soft voice had become monotonal and too loud, as though there was a wall between her and the world and she was shouting over it without being able to see what was on the other side. The last time I saw her, walking down Forty-second Street in a daze, even the shouting was gone; she seemed to have retrenched entirely into madness.

Fortunately, money was not always necessary to obtain food. Free food programs distributed sandwiches and coffee or soup, or served meals. Managers of small, inexpensive restaurants (I never heard of fancy ones doing this) gave homeless people handouts, often on a regular basis. At one coffee hour the women traded information on which local doughnut shops gave away day-old doughnuts; more even than most people, they were hooked on sugar, so this type of handout was important to them. However, because none of these sources could adequately feed all the homeless in the city, many people went through garbage to find edible bits, particularly damaged produce thrown out by supermarkets and vegetable stands and waste food from restaurants. Those with nerve and skill did more. A man eating in a coffee shop with a U-shaped counter once saw an old woman dash in, run around the counter eating all the leftover food and drinks at each place, then dash out. It happened so fast that most of the people there were unaware of what she was doing. This tactic backfired, however, for a woman who was found dead in the Automat sometime in the early 1970s. She had seen a man across the room slump over on his table and had rushed to retrieve the leftovers on his plate. She soon collapsed herself. It turned out that the man had poisoned himself because of debt. (Investigators going through the woman's bags found bankbooks showing a sum so large that the interest on it would have paid his debts.)[4]

Resourcefulness can occasionally be carried to heights that have to be admired, although such an achievement in such a context inevitably is constructed of negative elements, making the admiration somewhat equivocal. Johnnie, a seemingly sweet and childlike young woman, came to the Dwelling Place and explained that though she was living in New

York, the SSI office had said that it would send her next check to Alabama, where she was from originally. She wanted the check to come to New York, she said—how could she get to Alabama? I asked what she wanted to do when she left the shelter. Well, she had a husband in Rochester, and she wanted to go to him. Would he want her back? Yes, he said she could come any time. She had left him because he drank, and then he got mean. Well, I said, he'd still drink. Are you willing to put up with that? Yes, she said, I couldn't handle it before but I can now. Besides he always kept me in a house, with food and shoes. We talked about how she could locate him since she didn't have his address. She was passive and soft-spoken but quite clear about what she had to do. Then I called the SSI office to find out why her check was being sent to Alabama. This is what the man said:

We know Johnnie Carey. She's famous here. We've known her three years, and this is what she does: every month she travels to Birmingham, to New York, and then to Rochester. She's in Birmingham the first of every month. If she's in New York now, she probably wants to go to Rochester, right? Yes, I said, rather staggered. It seemed that for a year Johnnie had told SSI each month that her check was lost, had been issued a duplicate, and had cashed both. Therefore, they refused now to mail her checks; she had to come into an office and sign for them. Further, they were withholding seventy-five dollars a month until the overpayment was made up (which would take three or four years); and because she had changed her address so often, they chose the Alabama office to issue the checks at the Alabama rate, which was much lower than the New York rate. Johnnie was left with $92.80 a month, not enough to live in one place, so the result was to perpetuate her circuit.

The combination of institutional self-righteousness, viciousness, and justified indignation had fixed her good, except I had the feeling she had it all well under control. When I got off the phone and told her the man had said that she did go to Alabama all the time, her whole attitude changed; she stopped listening and more or less brushed me off. Having realized the game was up, she simply stopped playing. In a sense I had been used, but it was hard to get angry at Johnnie or pass judgment on her for not wanting to live the kind of life that is imposed by dependence on an SSI check. A year and a half later, she reappeared, just up from Birmingham.

While Johnnie manipulated the system, another woman, one of the isolates, rejected it entirely and built an existence so totally outside that even normal objects from our world became transformed in hers. We called this woman by her last name, Richards, because when asked her first name, she responded with one of many religious titles she claimed to possess (from several religions), and the staff chose not to go along with this. Generally she accepted being so addressed, but once when I called her Richards she rebuked me. "Really," she said, "I have a thousand Ph.D.'s and ten religious dignities, and at the very least that's worth a Reverend or a Doctor. Call me Doctor, or I won't answer." "I was only asking if you wanted iced tea," I said. "Well, you could be polite," she retorted.

The skill and creativity of the techniques Richards had developed for living on the street were awesome. She transformed whatever she could get to serve her purposes. She made a dress into a sack, for example, to carry her things; and one rainy day she came in all pinned up in a plastic shower curtain arranged so that she was bone dry underneath. On the night of her arrival she wore a headpiece that held white curtains in front of her face like a veil, with a strange hat on top. She had been at the Dwelling Place for only a short time when it had to close its overnight program to make repairs. After she left, she created several living spaces—we called them campsites but they were more than that—in various vacant lots nearby and continued to come almost daily for lunch and a shower. The campsite I saw, which was set against a building wall and surrounded on the other sides by bushes, was fixed up with an old mattress from the shelter, a chair, and boxes that served as bed table, dresser, and cabinets. The bed was covered with a plastic spread (serving as protection from rain as well as decor), the floor was a layer of newspapers, canned goods stood in the boxes (though there was no way to cook). A broom leaned against the wall, and she swept the place out every day. It had a well-kept homeyness.

After a while I began to see that Richards was a brilliant woman, as I imagine she knew in claiming all those Ph.D.'s and insisting on appropriate deference. One day she came into the kitchen talking about people who had black "mocks" and pointing at Kathy, a black woman who was washing dishes. At first I thought it was some kind of racist accusation (Richards was white); but the next week I was sitting at lunch with her (she used three chopsticks, very old and dirty, which she manipulated adroitly) when a white woman with platinum bleached hair passed by, and Richards began abusing her. "You look like an idiot with that hair," she said. "Don't you know it's against the law to bleach your hair?" Fortunately the other woman was in a vague, abstracted state of mind and, after being puzzled a moment, drifted on. But Richards continued talking about the blond hair being a mask and people going around behind masks. I realized then that it wasn't the blackness or whiteness that was on her mind but the idea that everybody is in disguise.

At the same time she was deluded and self-destructive. She took off her shoe once to try on a new pair I had brought her; in it I saw a nickel and pointed it out. "That's for the electronic waves," she informed me. She had a bad wound running from the instep about seven inches up one leg that she refused to let anyone touch, although once she asked for a knife to lance it with (the sisters said no). The feelings behind her choice of the street (she adamantly refused to apply for SSI) became clearer as her association with the Dwelling Place extended to four months and then five. Everyone adored her (in response, I suspect, not only to the power and inventiveness of her personality but to her absolute I-don't-give-a-shit attitude), and she manipulated us effectively to get special treatment and extra attention. But she occasionally disappeared for several days at a time. After one of these absences two sisters went to speak to her at her campsite, and she told them—amid much deluded monologuing—that she loved them, or something nearly as explicit. At the same time she said that she stayed away because they were poisoning her and that they had to give her time before she came back.

Ultimately her fear of closeness won out. She allowed the shelter to pay for her to live for two weeks at the Times Square, until the swelling in her leg went down; after that she vanished. Three weeks later one of the women said she had seen Richards in the Port Authority, screaming at police, who tied her up and took her off to Bellevue. But she got out, for after that the same woman saw her coming out of a Chinese restaurant, tapping on the window at intervals with her chopsticks as she passed, while the people eating looked at her through it and a man ran out shouting at her to pay. We never saw her again, but at least, I thought, she was still taking care of herself.

EFFECTS OF STREET LIFE

Despite her moments of feeling close to the Dwelling Place staff, Richards lived so wholly closed off inside her private world that she was essentially unreachable. The very effectiveness of her technological adaptation (so to speak) to street life, by making her so self-sufficient, enhanced a psychological process by which people became so comfortable in that life that they began to prefer it. The longer a woman remained outside, the more radical this change became.

Thus two women in Penn Station, asked by a nun to come to the Dwelling Place, said they could not leave. "I have something to do first," said one; the other said she was "hooked." Certainly Margaret, whom the staff met doing outreach at Grand Central, described the life there as though it was rather pleasant. She had had an SRO room uptown but left because she felt unsafe and went to Grand Central. She walked around all day and looked at the people; she liked being where there were so many. Some gave her money to buy candy and cigarettes. A rich woman wearing beautiful clothes going home on a commuter train once gave her a dollar. Margaret did not understand why, but thought the woman wanted to give it so she might as well accept it. She did not leave Grand Central easily; only after several invitations were extended to her there did she appear at the Dwelling Place door. For a while she accepted only soup, then departed, until one day she asked to come in. Then it was hard to get her to leave.

After some months—including a stint back on the street when she refused to stop wearing her old clothes, which were bug-infested, and a long stretch in the hospital for care of her legs, which were badly inflamed—Margaret moved into the Times Square, but her stay there was short. She roamed around the lobby, carrying her bags, and refused to go up to her room to sleep. We thought that her long experience sleeping sitting up in public made the solitude and closed-in quality of the room frightening to her; indeed she tried to sleep in a chair in the lobby.[5] The management was not pleased, and soon she had to leave.

Several months later I saw her once again in Grand Central, as completely lost to the world around her as if she had never sat on a couch in the Dwelling Place living room chatting amiably and rationally about her perfectly normal-sounding life. After a childhood in Eastern Europe, she worked in an upstate textile mill in the twenties, as a live-in housekeeper for a series of well-to-do families during the depression, and in some kind of war work in the forties. She had been a maid again in the fifties and at some point after that spent four years in a state mental hospital. I never found out what sent her there, but it was probably significant that Margaret had lost her parents early and since the 1930s had lived with a series of relatives. I would guess that losing one by one the people she was connected to affected her emotionally; certainly living as an outsider in someone else's home is an alienating experience.

It seemed to me that circumstances had slowly detached Margaret from human relationship, initiating an inner transformation that, by the time I knew her, had rendered her unable to endure normal living conditions. I must add, though, that she was willing to live at the shelter, being waited on and pampered. Possibly a long period there, with gradual, gentle pressure to function in the regular world, could have restored her to some form of life inside, perhaps not. In any case the Dwelling Place's limited resources made trying impossible.

Because we saw people only after they had spent varying amounts of time on the street, it was usually not possible to know how much of whatever psychological disorganization they manifested was the result of this experience, as opposed to the cause of their being on the street in the first place. In many cases street life appeared to have exacerbated an emotional weakness that already existed, but often it seemed to me that perfectly normal women had become so ground down by it that they quite lost themselves. Some of these, whom we rescued before they became so lost inside the experience that they had no perspective on it, were able to describe to me the actual process by which this deterioration occurred.

The first effect of being on the street is a demoralization so profound as to be paralyzing. Sonia was a Russian-French woman who had come to this country from France about three months before I saw her. She had been working as a secretary for a temporary employment agency, but they ran out of work for her, and she did not know that she could go to another agency. Unable to pay rent, she had to leave her hotel. Though she had been only a few nights on the street, she was in shock, not just from physical exhaustion but from the sense of degradation the experience produced in her. "It's debilitating," she said. Watching her struggle to maintain the bearing that expressed the cultured person she normally was, I began to see that a woman can degenerate through sheer misfortune. The worse she feels about herself, the worse she registers on others, and their reactions make her feel still worse until, finding herself so removed from the person she has always felt herself to be, she can no longer respond with that person's responses.

This plight was aptly described by Lily Smith, a homeless woman, in testimony submitted for a congressional hearing in 1984:

> Life on the streets is a ritual that forces the mind to go against the teaching that you have learned as a child. . . .
> You fall into a character that is not you, and you get scared to death, standing in the middle of the street with no destination. . . .
> . . . You find yourself two people: One will break down and one will survive. . . . You become paranoid and frightened to death. Some break down and end up in mental hospitals and others just go on and not caring. . . .
> . . . I am still trying till I fall apart.[6]

Demoralization is exacerbated by another effect of street life, produced by being outdoors all the time without a structure to one's life: a disorientation both physical and mental. One woman who had spent four days on the street—sleeping on a bench, riding the subway, and walking the streets all night—told me she felt a "restlessness," a compulsion to keep moving. At the same time she lost her sense of time and continuity. You know it's night because it's dark, she told me, and you know it's day because the sun shines or dawn because it's rising, but you no longer know which day it is. Another, who had been on the street much longer, said she had had a sudden perception that walking around so much had the effect of making her not pay attention to what was going on behind her; she only stared straight ahead. This bothered her because she realized it was dangerous.

A precise description of this experience is provided by Ada Chesterton, an English journalist who spent some time homeless in London in the 1920s to see what it was like:

> At first when you have walked about for two or three hours you get very tired. Your head aches and your limbs are like lead; the fact that you have no fixed objective is like a pall on your spirits—you urge yourself forward on mere will. But if you keep on for another hour, or two, or three, your pains vanish— in some strange way you forget cold, hunger and thirst. Your brain is light, your feet move on air. The noises of the street form a monotonous accompaniment which gradually merges into silence; you see little, hear less, feel not at all. Trouble and regret fall from you—it is as though you were doped. You have no sense of distance or of time, and gradually you adopt the slouch of the tramp; you feel yourself one with the streets; you have lost your entity.[7]

This last phrase is the key; physical and spatial disorientation initially loosened a woman's connection to herself. Then, under the physical privations of street life—exposure, inadequate food and sleep—her mental condition deteriorated further. In experimental subjects sleep deprivation alone has produced symptoms not that different from some exhibited by street people. Certainly women who entered the Dwelling Place quite spacy and hallucinated often woke up after three days' sleep surprisingly lucid.[8]

As a woman remained longer outside, she was affected further by solitude. Even though she mixed with others at a lunch program or bread line, she did not experience the kind of reciprocal relations that constitute true human contact. One writer described the effects of such a life on the French tramp, or *clochard*:

Everywhere, it is silence that greets and surrounds him; each man lives on his own, eats on his own, sleeps on his own, without taking any account of his neighbor. . . . The lack of money severs one's contact with other men, and one grows accustomed to this lack of human contacts. One ends by no longer knowing what day it is, and also by no longer caring, in the absence of human connections.[9]

An extended period of living like this leads to a "degradation of . . . needs," as the *clochard* abandons more and more the attempt to take action to satisfy even the most elementary ones, such as hunger; and habitual undernourishment, although no longer felt as such, "tends to render more and more fatiguing each effort necessary to a concerted action." Ultimately, "the privations that are prolonged, then accepted, are at the origin of a mutilation of the personality."[10]

The end result is a kind of numbing, which for someone like Chesterton—a strong personality who knew she could always go home—is only temporary. But for a fragile character, especially if she has no structure to return to and winds up spending a long stretch outside, it offers an escape. This is how street life could, for some, become easier than life inside. Because physical sensation and emotion are closely connected, the loss of physical feeling involved an emotional numbing as well. And since it is through feelings that one knows oneself, when the feelings go, so does the self. Given the likelihood of an unhappy recent past, plus the probable unpleasantness of any attempt made now to get help, any emotion the woman outside might feel was far more likely to be painful than otherwise. Numbness, therefore, came as a relief; and more, the prospect of feeling anything again became more and more terrifying the longer she remained outside. This is why she resisted attempts to bring her in.

Numbness also explains how women were able to endure life on the street. They often, for example, did not feel the cold (or the heat, in the case of those who wore heavy coats on hot summer days). Some of the Dwelling Place women went out in inadequate clothing in the winter, and if you asked them whether it was cold outside, they didn't know. This lack of awareness was no protection, however; they might not feel the cold, but they still could die of it. Ellen, who spent three years in a box on Ninth Avenue, lost several fingers from frostbite without realizing what was happening.

Women who for whatever reason remained sufficiently connected to their feelings to be miserable on the street were more likely to want to come inside. Mamie, who was not a street person but who through mismanaging money once had to spend about ten days on the street before getting into the Women's Shelter, told me that ten years living like that would make anyone crazy; she herself nearly went crazy after ten days. She met people at the Women's Shelter who said that after a while they couldn't take it physically; when they got up in the morning after a night in a doorway, or wherever, they ached all over. You could only live like that in your twenties or thirties, they said; in your forties, forget it.

Still, this does not necessarily mean that the women who chose to apply to the Women's Shelter were in better shape psychologically than those who didn't; I could as easily maintain that people who were willing to put up with the way the Women's Shelter treated them tended to be more compliant and have less sense of self than those who refused to go there. I discovered, in fact, that it was impossible to generalize about who would decide to come in and who wouldn't because so many variables went into such a decision. Strong, intelligent women who seemed capable of facing their feelings would refuse close human contact and sink gradually into isolation, while weaker ones could come to accept it and settle into a real community life. Other strong women did come in and became leaders. At most I would say that it depended on how permanent was whatever wounding each had suffered in the past. Moreover, rescue (like everything else about street life) did not depend entirely on personality; here again circumstances played a large part. A major factor seemed to be chance—for instance, that a person doing outreach from the Dwelling Place happened to encounter a particular woman on a particular day when she happened to be capable of responding to an overture.

The transformation produced by life outside on a woman who had spent all her life inside—and, in fact, seemed to have no psychological disability beyond some fairly common neuroses—was witnessed by Ann Marie Rousseau, a photographer and writer researching a book on shopping-bag ladies. Rousseau met this woman in Penn Station after the woman had been living on the street for two months.[11] She had an upper-middle-class background and a college education, had been married, and had supported herself for years. Rousseau was able to corroborate the details of her story with someone who had known her when her troubles were just beginning and who, further, had not perceived her as a person with psychological problems.

This woman had had a great deal of trouble with welfare—not through her own fault—that had led her to leave the hotel where they had placed her without telling them while continuing to collect her checks. She slept outside in boxes, with other people nearby, but kept herself well dressed and clean by using the Penn Station ladies' room. She talked about wanting to find a job and a place to live, so Rousseau tried to get her into other, better hotels, but she either missed appointments or found fault, deciding without trying, for example, that she couldn't get the shopping cart containing her possessions (which she took everywhere with her for fear of losing it) up the stairs. "But isn't this better than the boxes?" Rousseau asked. "I don't mind the boxes," she responded, even though she had been attacked there by men with knives. Similarly, she could not find a job. At first she answered ads but had trouble at the interviews because she had the cart with her and, later, after it was stolen, because she had no clean dress.

Over the months Rousseau saw a change in her. At first she maintained herself well; but after her cart was stolen, though she got new clothes, she became somewhat disheveled and each time Rousseau saw her, she looked a little worse. Along with this went a change in her psychology; the energy she put into hunting for a job and a place to live diminished as she adjusted to living outside. Ultimately she refused to continue the search, though she did not admit that to herself but went on saying, "If only I had a job or a place I could get back on my feet" (a pattern I saw often myself). Rousseau realized that the longer this life continued, the more difficult it would be to get her back inside. She was becoming more comfortable outside, complaining less about the difficulties; the boxes had become familiar, and in her perception less threatening (despite the men) than the adjustment she would have to make to a new hotel. With her intellect and self-awareness (she had been psychoanalyzed) one might have expected her to be easier to bring back inside than most; but she had evidently reached a point where her inner resources were so weakened that the radical simplicity of her new life was a greater temptation than the struggle for something better.

The Effects of the Relief System

The choice Rousseau's acquaintance made to stay on the street was essentially the result of an interaction between her psychology and the conditions of that life. But the trigger that sent her out there originally was pulled by the welfare bureaucracy. To understand how this could have happened and, even more, why so many homeless people refused to apply for assistance requires some idea of the daily realities of welfare: what you have to go through and what you get for it.

Except for a few veterans for whom the Veterans Administration was responsible, the Dwelling Place women, being single, depended on one of two relief (or, more loosely, welfare) programs.[1] SSI was a federal program that provided a monthly pension for physically or mentally disabled people of any age and also supplemented the income of persons over sixty-five receiving Social Security when it fell below a specified minimum. Those ineligible for SSI could get public assistance (welfare in the strict sense, known in New York State as home relief) from the state. The federal government also provided food stamps.

A perpetual tension existed between the state and federal agencies, with the state always trying to get welfare recipients off the state rolls and onto SSI, and the Social Security Administration rejecting as many applicants as possible. This tension, as well as the complexities, inconsistencies, and inefficiencies that are inevitable when huge bureaucracies try to administer programs toward which society's attitude is at best equivocal, made getting assistance daunting.

My own experience with various agencies demonstrated that the amount of effort required to accomplish even the simplest task under the best of circumstances goes way beyond imagining if one is operating under conventional assumptions about the act to be performed. I once had to call the Immigration and Naturalization Service to find out how to obtain a passport for a woman who was a naturalized citizen but had lost her papers. Her son in Italy had invited her to come home, and she needed the passport to go. I spent the first ten minutes dialing continuously, always getting a busy signal. At last I got a ring—about twenty rings—then a recording telling me to wait, then a silent ten-minute wait. Ten minutes is a long time to hang on to a telephone with nothing but dead silence at the other end. If I had been a homeless person I would probably have had to use a pay phone. How long would I have been willing to feed dimes into nothing—assuming I had enough dimes?

Similarly, the first time I helped someone fill out a welfare application I was overcome by a sense of exhaustion just from looking at the form. I also had trouble understanding it. It was ten pages long; there were four pages of mimeoed instructions and an extra folder explaining the documentation needed to prove one's eligibility. This included birth certificate or other proof of identity; proof of citizenship or legal-alien status; marriage license and divorce or separation papers or spouse's death certificate; plus evidence of previous employment or proof of how a woman had been supported if unemployed. The form asked for her life history, including the case number for each time she had been on public assistance in the past, with the dates of when checks came and stopped coming, and so on. These are things that people occupied with day-to-day survival, and continuously vulnerable to theft, have difficulty keeping track of. After someone had gone through this once, however, she learned to keep official-looking papers, which was one reason why homeless women's bags and handbags were stuffed with packets of frayed papers with all the numbers written down—somewhere.

The agencies themselves did provide help in filling out the forms, and many people got assistance that way. But a homeless woman who was fearful and disoriented might be unwilling to give such personal information (often connected with painful memories) to a total stranger who was, frequently, not very sympathetic. Or she might simply lack the moral energy to take the stress involved, especially if she had had a bad experience with welfare in the past. The endless waiting was particularly demoralizing. A Dwelling Place volunteer who arrived at a welfare office at two o'clock one afternoon with one of the women found people waiting who had come at eight o'clock that morning and had not yet been seen. For the hundreds of people seeking help, there were only seven case-workers, of whom four were talking to each other. This basic level of stress is more or less unavoidable; but there are also more subtly intimi-dating practices that compound it. For example, at the welfare office de-scribed above, applicants got a number and then waited to be called. When the caseworkers called clients in, they said the names and numbers in such low voices that people didn't hear them and missed their turns. After hours spent waiting, this could have been the final blow that made someone give up.

The complexity of the rules and procedures meant, further, that the caseworkers often made mistakes. Although you were supposed to have all the documentation mentioned above to get welfare, there was also a rule that if you didn't have all the papers, you had only to show evi-dence that you were trying to get them (a carbon of a letter to the town clerk in the place where you were born, requesting a copy of your birth certificate, for example); or sometimes another form of identification was acceptable. At one interview a caseworker told a Dwelling Place woman that she would be terminated because she didn't have a birth certificate. But the volunteer accompanying the woman objected that she needed only a welfare identification card, which she did have. The caseworker did not believe this, and the volunteer had to argue force-fully until the caseworker discovered the volunteer was right. If the volunteer had not been there, the woman would have been turned down. Again, an individual was required to have an address in order to receive assistance; but in fact one welfare center had been designated to pro-vide benefits to people without one. However, the caseworkers at the other centers did not so inform the homeless whose applications they rejected.

What it came down to, the same volunteer told me, was that there was no single system one could rely on to function consistently. Not only were the rules vastly complex, but each caseworker had great leeway to do what she or he wanted to. Thus the same woman coming at different times might get widely different benefits, depending on who handled her case: restaurant allowance or not, food stamps or not, and so on. Bene-fits were sometimes refused quite irrationally. Jeannie, who had been brought in by the outreach team after a long period in Penn Station, re-ported that when the doctor who examined her (part of the routine of getting SSI) saw her frostbitten toes he said, "Woman, you deserve a pen-sion!" This was in March 1979. By the following December she had been denied SSI three times, the third time because she had supposedly failed to submit a certain form. But she had submitted it—had gone to the office with one of the nuns and spent all day there doing it. The work program for welfare recipients was also extremely inconsistent. Some did not have to work at all (usually the ones welfare was trying to transfer to SSI). Some had to work several days a week; others three days every two weeks; and so on. (They did clerical work in city offices.)

Although the advantage of welfare was that it could be tailored to someone's individual needs—rent allowance based on actual rent, restaurant allowance provided if she had no cooking facilities—whereas SSI was a flat, invariable amount, the psychic stress of welfare was much greater. The checks came twice a month, so that recipients had to endure twice as often the usual anxiety before they were due (foul-ups were so frequent that the women never felt confident that they would arrive); and welfare also required a periodic interview, called a face-to-face, in which the caseworker decided whether the recipient was still entitled to assistance. The arbitrary nature of the system meant that one could not rely on consistency, so many women suffered considerable additional anxiety every time an interview was in prospect.

Sheer bureaucratic inefficiency could take a tremendous toll even though the mistake was quite small. Arriving one day at the Times Square, I found a woman I knew waiting in the lobby, very nervous and angry. Her welfare check was late, and she was waiting for the hotel's social worker, who had promised to call and find out why but then had gone to lunch and was already an hour late in returning. The woman was in imminent danger of being thrown out for not paying rent. Later she came down to the coffee hour, and though the problem had been straightened out, her hands still shook so badly that I had to sugar and cream her coffee for her. The check had gone to her old hotel, even though she had filed the address change over a month before. She had not been getting mail from there, so if welfare had terminated her she would never have received the warning letter, and as she put it, "I would have had to start that shit all over again."

Like the woman I met on Third Avenue, the Dwelling Place women complained about the caseworkers' nastiness. I experienced it myself once when I called an agency for someone and the man to whom I spoke was shockingly snide. He treated me like an idiot for asking a perfectly reasonable question. When I snapped back that he had no business talking to me like that, he was startled, for he had assumed that I was the client and had responded in his habitual mode. He then apologized a little, enough at any rate to demonstrate that he was not always overbearing and offensive. Indeed, I dealt with many concerned caseworkers trying to help and even some who saw their clients as persons like them-selves. But their job was brutalizing; those who lasted in it often had to become insensitive to some extent just to survive. The enormity of the suffering they saw and the awareness of how limited even their best ef-forts were in alleviating it, plus the frustration of repeatedly failing to counteract people's self-destructive behavior, demoralized them too.

In fact they, like their clients, were trapped by the traditional Ameri-can "loathing of 'reliefers.'" The caseworkers' official mandate to dis-pense relief contradicted a basic belief of American society: that success "is a matter of individual merit," that people who fail do so because there is something wrong with them. Even before the Reagan administration began to attack the relief system, the agencies were always under fire for giving too much to people who were undeserving. Relief officials were in a sense forced to degrade their clients because "the general public re-quire[d] it." The endless waiting, the abusive behavior of caseworkers, as well as humiliations like having to pay in supermarkets with food stamps, constituted "rituals of degradation" of the same order as the pauper's badge that relief recipients had to wear in the eighteenth cen-tury.[2]

The ambivalence behind the provision of relief also helps explain the seeming irrationality of some denials of benefits, for an unofficial, un-stated mandate of relief agencies is not to confer benefits but to refuse them as much as possible. One way this is accomplished is by a set of administrative mechanisms that constitute a largely unwritten, unac-knowledged policy.[3] An informal example is that of calling numbers in too low a voice. A more "official" policy was discovered by a Dwelling Place volunteer when she was in court with one of the women contesting a denial of SSI benefits. As it turned out, the judge was furious that the woman had been denied and ruled that she was eligible; but in the mean-time his secretary took the volunteer aside and told her not to worry be-cause anyone who went that far through the appeals process always got benefits. It seemed that all who applied for SSI were rejected and got a letter stating that they were not eligible. On the back of the letter, how-ever, was a note saying that one could appeal. Those who did so got what was called a fair hearing, where they were again rejected. The next step was to go to court; and then they were ruled eligible. This procedure was confirmed to me later by a woman who had been on welfare but devel-oped a physical ailment that made her eligible for SSI. Welfare thus began the process of shifting her over, which, the welfare worker told her, would require three applications before she was accepted.

An archetypal tale of life on public assistance was told at one coffee hour by June, who had gone that morning to the Bellevue outpatient clinic because her thumb was swollen and painful. You had to get there at 8:30 A.M., register, and wait for a doctor. If one showed up, then you could see him or her. June said the doctor didn't even look at her thumb but stood there turning over the papers in her file. Finally he told her, "It's an old fracture." She wanted to know what was happening to her thumb now, but he wouldn't look at it. Then she got angry, and he said he didn't like her attitude. She responded that she didn't like his attitude. That surprised him. Yes, she said, she had to go to welfare and to all these places where they treated her like he did, and she didn't like it. There was a poster on the wall of the two robots from *Star Wars* (at least I think so; June, having no money to go to movies, did not know what *Star Wars* was), above which was tacked a sign that said something condescending about Earthlings. Pointing to the poster, June asked the doctors (there were two there by then), "Is that you? Why don't you go back where you came from?" and walked out. She was so worked up that she forgot to stop at the desk and get the sixty cents carfare given to welfare patients. She decided not to go back because she felt she was too angry and would just get into an argument. Fortunately she had sixty cents on her.

When June finished telling this story everyone applauded, for all the women understood the bind she had been in. People on relief always have to pay for refusing to relinquish their self-respect. June's anger made it difficult for her to submit to bureaucratic requirements; what kept her on welfare was the emotional support she got from the shelter staff each time her reevaluation came up.

Not only specific required procedures but many incidents of daily life make absolute dependence on a government pittance a kind of continuous, low-grade punishment whose small daily degradations throw additional light on the reasons why some refuse to deal with the relief system. One day I had a long conversation with Gloria about a pair of pantyhose she had bought in Woolworth's; they didn't fit right and kept slipping down. She had gotten the same size as always, but this particular pair was defective. They had cost $1.80. She was thinking of trying to exchange them, but this was her only pair, and she said it was too chilly to walk back to the store with bare legs. I suddenly realized that this was not what it first seemed, a case of unnecessary preoccupation with a trivial item; for Gloria it was a real problem. She had so little money (being on SSI) that having to spend another two dollars on another pair of pantyhose that same month was an actual hardship. This was only one of many incidents that brought home to me what it means to live on SSI. Repeatedly women had strong reactions to the loss or breakage or defectiveness of some small item that to me would mean little. But for them replacing it meant sacrificing something else—cigarettes, coffee, food.

Indeed after the coffee hour had been going some time I began to realize that one reason the atmosphere was frequently not particularly convivial, especially toward the end of the month, was that the women were hungry. They had too little money to buy enough food, especially since they were unable to cook. Thus the little food we provided at the coffee hour became the focus of a need that got in the way of socializing. The Dwelling Place received some government surplus food, particularly large cans of peanut butter and five-pound blocks of cheese. When these were available, we brought them to the coffee hour, along with crackers, and everyone could eat as much as she needed. When these supplies did not come, however, we had to make do with less. Not knowing the mechanism by which such food was provided, I used to wonder whether those who sent it had any idea of the difference it made in these individual lives.

Since buying new clothing also required sacrifice, most women wore secondhand things, even shoes (not very comfortable). If children who have to wear hand-me-downs resent it, how much more do adults who don't have the prospect of one day becoming independent? The Dwelling Place had a clothing room full of donated items, and I used to take women who needed clothes downstairs to it and let them choose from whatever was there. Most women loved doing this, and though I often felt uncomfortable in the role of dispenser, they did not usually appear to resent it.

Once, however, I brought a young woman there under pressure—the kind of pressure that a suggestion from someone who is your benefactor can create. Terry had not asked for clothes, but her own were dirty, and the staff member on duty thought she should have new ones. She came, but when I started going through a pile of jeans, she rejected them all and finally said she would rather buy new ones when her check came. I said she should take something to wear in the meantime. She responded irritably that she hated thrift-shop clothes and never wore them but threw them out when she got them, and so would I. For a split second I saw rage in her eyes; then instantly she put the lid on it and turned toward the door, saying, "Let's go upstairs, it's too cold down here." Such intense fury, even though momentary, may seem inappropriate to the occasion, but it was less a response to the situation itself than evoked by it—that is, by what was probably one more experience of being systematically deprived of selfhood. Like June's, Terry's anger was a stream that ran throughout her life—an underground hot spring, rather, that boiled up whenever a fissure opened in the crust of her defenses.

Incidents like this illuminated much for me about the antagonisms surrounding welfare. Commonly welfare recipients are thought to be getting something for nothing, and there is "general outrage when recipients show evidence of ingratitude or impenitence."[4] But, as should be clear, relief does not come free; it has its price. And since this price is one's dignity, some people not unreasonably feel it is too high. Therefore, said George Orwell, "A man receiving charity practically always hates his benefactor—it is a fixed characteristic of human nature."[5]

We can now understand the solitary bag woman on the street who suddenly begins shrieking unaccountably at a startled, innocent passerby. While Terry fought to keep her rage bottled up because she was still trying to live among people, the woman on the street has given up; she is all cracks and fissures, and her anger pours out continuously. Having never been able to express it in the appropriate place, she now expresses it everywhere; and what makes such behavior possible is her isolation. The more cut off she is from human contact, the less effect will the release of her feelings have on others. She has made herself safe.

Ten Years Later

By 1990 most of the women I knew either had settled into some form of housing or—if still on the street—had rendered themselves unnoticeable by taking off their layers and behaving less flamboyantly. The Dwelling Place still sheltered a few women who were homeless because they lost a job, were evicted from an apartment that went co-op, or had to leave a doubling-up situation. And the proportion who appeared mentally ill remained similar: between 35 and 40 percent. However, the women were younger, averaging about forty (the shelter's minimum age was now thirty); and, starting around 1985, a new group had begun to appear: homeless drug users.[1]

Women whose only problems were financial were not eligible for most city-owned renovated apartments and so had great difficulty finding housing because so little was affordable. Those who had lost a job couldn't find another that paid enough to support a private apartment. Besides, as Sister Nancy Chiarello, the Dwelling Place director, said to me, "When you're homeless, how do you go to job interviews?" One employer refused to hire a woman who gave the Dwelling Place as an address because he knew it was a shelter. Such women therefore wound up on welfare, whose mandatory work requirement (for example, cleaning welfare offices at night, handing out towels at public pools) had the effect of tying them firmly to the system by leaving them too little time to look for paying work.

Young mentally ill women, having come of age after deinstitutionalization, had never been in state hospitals.[2] Most, it seemed, had either
been kicked out by their families or had walked out themselves. Some,
after being picked up because of violent behavior or for crimes like stealing, might get into the hospital and be put on medication. While hospitals, more than in the past, helped them find a placement, young women
without a long history of mental illness were likely to tell the social
worker that they had a family or someplace else to go but then return to
the street, where they were introduced to alcohol or drugs. Once they
became what was known as dual diagnostic—mentally ill substance
abusers—it was nearly impossible to get treatment since detoxification
programs would not take people who were mentally ill, and mental
health programs would not take people actively using drugs. Yet these
women were not addicts: if they did get off drugs or alcohol and onto
medication for their psychological problems, they did not crave drugs.
Once stabilized, they could be placed in halfway houses or residential
programs.

The least support, however, was available for those who needed it
most: the large proportion of Dwelling Place women who were non–
mentally ill drug users. Some were heroin addicts on methadone maintenance, but most were on crack. Typically they had been thrown out by
families unable to tolerate their behavior. They found a community on
the streets, where they supported each other's habits, as well as sharing
food, blankets, needles, and crack vials. Afraid of contracting AIDS
through needle-sharing, many intravenous drug users had switched to
crack but then became infected with the AIDS virus through prostitution, which they were driven to by their need for frequent vials.

Yet unless they manifested severe medical symptoms, there was no
help for them; they had to remain homeless. After two- or three-day
binges, they crashed at the Dwelling Place (where they could sleep for a
few hours as long as they weren't violent or actively high), in abandoned
buildings, or in cardboard boxes on the streets when it was warm. Some
died in street violence or after being hit by cars. Others might get into the
hospital or be sent to prison for drug possession or dealing; but from
these places they were "discharged to nowhere," as Sister Nancy put it,
and wound up back on the street with the "same old crowd."

Was there any hope for them? "There's always hope as long as the issue
presents itself as a problem," said Sister Nancy. But most crack users
were "not even conscious of themselves—it's day to day, minute to minute, for them. Sometimes when they're coming down from a high, they

get depressed and realize they have to change. They feel sorry they've hurt other people and themselves. But nothing breaks the cycle, so they repeat it. There are people out there who really want a chance, but there's no place that gives them one, so they wind up in the city shelters, which are drug havens in themselves. When you work with a system that doesn't care, what's to motivate you?"

Community

Against such odds, can women who have gone outside come in again? My own experience—supported by some later examples—says that, given the right conditions, most can; only a few cannot. The crucial motivating factor, it seems to me, is community—connections among people. And creating community depends on seeing homeless women as people, not clients who are needy and defective. I once commented to a Dwelling Place staff member that while many of the women had been diagnosed as schizophrenic, it didn't seem particularly meaningful for our dealing with them in the house. "Yes," she said, laughing, "after you know they're schizophrenic you still have to live with them."

It was because of this perspective, I think, that the Dwelling Place staff was able to entice women into the shelter and then keep them off the street, including many whom social service professionals considered "hard to reach." Some were too violent or otherwise disruptive to remain in a group living situation. But within this limit a remarkably wide range of behavior could be tolerated. If the social context does not define as bad or otherwise unacceptable a habit such as hearing voices, it simply becomes one part of someone's personality, and others are free to react to it individually as they would, say, to cigarette smoking. Thus I could say, "Listen, Louise, I can't follow you when you talk about the poisonous chemicals sprayed on your bed, especially since I haven't seen anyone with a spray gun around here. Besides, we need help with dinner. Can you come into the kitchen?" Someone who believes she has a mission from God or that she is a reincarnation of Saint Barbara can still make zucchini bread or do laundry or even answer the phone. What is more, as she creates real connections with other people, Saint Barbara—or the chemicals or the FBI—recedes into a small corner of her life because the part of her experience that it is connected with is no longer so important. The FBI may never go away, but it does not poison the new friendships. This may not be a cure in the conventional sense, and it certainly does not enable Saint Barbara to go out and get a job; but it does permit her to remain inside, as part of a community whose other members are important to her, as she is to them.[1]

Even drug users can be brought into a permanent residential community, although for it to work they must be off drugs or at least working at getting clean. The Heights, a residence for homeless single adults (male and female) in the Washington Heights neighborhood of Manhattan, which opened in 1986, successfully integrated people of different ages, races, and physical and mental abilities not only as residents but also in planning and daily administration. The connections that developed among the tenants provided support that enabled them to overcome many personal problems and also to band together to tackle an initial serious drug problem in the building.[2]

In creating their community the Heights residents got a boost from the design of their building. Conrad Levenson, the architect who renovated it, focused on creating an attractive environment that would enhance residents' dignity and security, balancing privacy with community in the context of a feeling of home. "Design itself can't cure psychological problems," Levenson told me, "but it can facilitate overcoming them by allowing the creation of human community." When the residents of the Federal City Shelter in Washington, D.C., home of the Community for Creative Nonviolence, moved back in after Levenson's conversion of the building in 1986, "their behavior was totally different. A lot of tension and acting out was suddenly gone. Unbelievably, it still looks exactly as it did when it was new."[3]

The best example I can give of the kind of change that is possible is the development of the coffee hour and the community of women in the Times Square Motor Hotel. When I started the coffee hour with one of the sisters, nobody wanted to come; sitting around as a group conversing was not a meaningful experience to the women there. We had to bribe them with coffee and doughnuts, luxuries to them. We had seven or ten women sitting around a table but not together; each was off in her own world, talking to herself or demanding our exclusive attention.

Over some months, however, more came; they settled down somewhat and became used to being in a room together (most, of course, had been accustomed to the isolation of street life). Gradually we noticed that they were coming for the companionship as much as the food (which, as the result of a speech I made one day about nutrition, had been changed by consensus to cheese and crackers). At this point we introduced a discussion topic to get everyone talking about the same thing. The women agreed to this change, and the first topic was clothes: favorite colors, dresses versus pants, and so on. The second was celebrities; they discussed the Pope (then visiting New York), then several movie stars, establishing by pooling their memories a catalogue of Elizabeth Taylor's husbands.[4] After only a month or so, however, I found that a topic was no longer necessary. As a result of this and the other activities in the hotel, the women had formed friendships and naturally began chatting among themselves; they were together. They still needed at least one volunteer there, me, but I was no longer the arbiter of all discussion, the only one who could fulfill needs; I didn't even have to serve or clean up any more.

The women now gave each other emotional support; they remembered each other's birthdays, took each other to the doctor, visited each other in the hospital. What was more, the group accommodated members who had chronic psychological problems. When they got angry, they might accuse each other of being crazy, but they all understood. If someone had an emotional crisis and had to go into the hospital, the others sent cards and visited; and when she came out, she was part of the group again.

One more story will give an idea of how tying people into such a community can keep them inside. Ellen had lived on the street in a nest of cardboard cartons for three years (it was she who lost her fingers from frostbite). She was with difficulty persuaded to come into the Dwelling Place and was eventually established at the hotel. When she first came in off the street, she was like a wild woman—she was not violent, but I had the feeling she had simply forgotten how to be human. Her speech was so incoherent that it had to be interpreted like the symbols in a dream. But two and a half years later, the mere fact of living in a social setting had made an amazing change in her. Her former angular, isolated quality had given way to a new softness, which showed in the expression on her face and in her eyes, the cadences of her speech, and her movements. She became able to ask directly for things she wanted and even to answer the phone and take messages. She retained a certain otherworldliness—and had still to be helped each month to pay her rent—but looking into her eyes now, one felt, as not before, that someone was there.[5]

I think that such a rescue is made possible by the experience of community, which in itself is healing. Studies of former mental patients "indicate that the most significant factors in successful reintegration of such people have to do with the quality of one's surroundings and the nature of social ties to others."[6] My experience—especially in the Times Square, which was certainly a surrounding of low quality—indicates that social ties are even more important than physical environment. The women I knew could not make demands to satisfy—often could not even experience—their own needs; but they could be held by the knowledge that someone else needed them. What they could not do for themselves they could do for each other; being able to give something, anything—help with cleaning or cooking, information, sympathy, physical assistance— to another woman or to the group was a powerful bond. If Ann Marie Rousseau's friend in Penn Station had been brought into a community like this one, could she not have received enough of the energy that flows through such human channels to get the strength to try again? For "what makes the *clochard* is the fact of having no one to love."[7]

Here then is another scene:

A Monday afternoon, two years after the scene that opened this part; the basement of the Times Square: a shabby, depressing, fluorescent-lit room full of rickety long tables and plastic chairs. Around two tables pushed together and covered by old stained sheets are gathered about twenty women and me, the volunteer. June is here; so are Gloria, Norma, and a number of the others I have described. As the coffee water heats and the women distribute crackers and cheese among themselves, Gloria starts the conversation by asking if I've heard the latest about the possible release of the American hostages in Teheran. Norma wants to know what the student militants want with the shah—he's gone, why not just leave him alone? I compare their anger to how she feels about her husband (who put her in the hospital), explaining that the shah had had people tortured and murdered. This she understands and asks why Henry Kissinger and David Rockefeller want to help him if he's so awful; they must be bad too. They are, I assure her.

Gloria describes her trips every other Friday night to do outreach ("reach out" she calls it) at Penn Station with two Dwelling Place volunteers: they approach the homeless women there and try to persuade them to come to the shelter. The women are frightened, she says, so she assures them that at the Dwelling Place there *is* someone who cares. She then recites a list of her blessings—that she has food and a place to sleep and lives in America, where we have freedom of expression (she's thinking of the shah). This is not the first time that the shah has come up at the coffee hour, and it now dawns on me that the reason the women are so interested in him is that he also is a homeless person, whose people don't want him.

Nobody else is particularly feeling their blessings today, however, because it's the Christmas season and they are jittery, depressed, tense. All have had families or still have them (Norma's wish for 1980 is to see her children, whom she hasn't seen in seven years), and this horrible season brings painful memories and thoughts to the surface. All talk at once and get into squabbles over nothing. Maria starts everyone singing Christmas carols, but June and Phyllis keep arguing while the rest are singing and the noise is unbearable. One of the carols makes Kathy cry, which upsets Maria.

I have been sitting feeling helpless (not being in a particularly cheerful mood either), but I pull myself together and manage to yell them all into submission. I remind them that everyone is unhappy, and there's nothing to do but simply calm down. Surprisingly, quiet settles over the table. I add that we must just let Kathy cry and all accept each other's being upset. Then, although it's not quite time yet, I figure it's best to cut a bad business short, and I go to spill out the leftover coffee water. When I return, I find them all sitting there singing together, as cozy as peas in a pod. Norma and Maria sing a couple of songs in Spanish, which though badly sung are immensely charming and soothing. The mood is now so close and warm that we sit together a few minutes longer. It is the first time in my experience that the women have managed to come together over bad feelings instead of being split apart by them; in the future I will see more. Although the scar tissue that has grown over these women's wounds still pulls and distorts the faces they present to the world, at least the wounds have closed over and are no longer too sore to be touched.

PART 2

Mythmaking

The root principle of reform is to remove the distance between yourself and those whose life you want to understand.

—*Mary Higgs,* Down and Out

Week after week at the Dwelling Place, as I listened to women telling me their problems, I noted the social, economic, and psychological reasons they were homeless, but my head also buzzed with the images they used to frame their delusions. I found these intensely seductive. Richards's perception that we all wear "mocks" to disguise our true selves or the paper another woman wore pinned to her shoulder that read "I am a lifetime Jew" seemed marvelously perceptive (even if unconscious) capsulations of the truths that underlay their lives. But I soon learned that encouraging the women to produce these images by listening to them so raptly only reinforced their separation from reality and increased their already high anxiety level. Once I began trying to lead them away from their delusions, my own fantasies died away, and I was also able to see that other people's notions about homeless women were often fantasies too.

There were a lot of these. In fact, the extent to which "shopping-bag ladies" were present in people's minds (particularly women's)—at least in New York, where there were so many—floored me. Because homeless women lived in such an extreme situation, people tended to perceive them as symbols more than fellow humans: "the thing itself, unaccommodated woman," as one person paraphrased *King Lear* to me. So although people asked me for the "real truth" about who the women were, they were likely to provide their own answers before I could speak (weren't they all rich eccentrics? orphans? old people whose children had thrown them out?). Often someone would recount an encounter with a homeless woman that held such profound personal meaning that the person was convinced the woman was special or unique. When, responding to entreaties to clear up the mystery surrounding her, I said she fit into a pattern I knew well, my interlocutor often stopped listening, not wanting to hear that there was no mystery.

The most telling bag-woman story I heard, however, was one in which no bag woman appeared. A suburban housewife, hearing what I was writing about, seized my arm and pulled me into a corner, insisting that I must hear about this incident. She had gone into a Fanny Farmer store to buy some candy to satisfy a nervous hunger. Her empty white candy bag fell to the floor and coasted some distance away. She saw a man look down at it, but instead of picking it up he walked off. She went to get it herself, but when she touched it, she discovered he had spat on it and her hand was full of green slime. For days she felt like Lady Macbeth; but her immediate thought was, "This must happen to bag ladies"—they see some gorgeous thing in the garbage, go to pick it up, and find blood or slime on it.

Evidently this experience touched deep feelings in this woman that instantly called up the bag-woman image; the image was so powerful and present for her that no real woman was needed to evoke it, just a situation. The spot that Lady Macbeth could not remove was created by the guilty consciousness of her own evil deed; but the stain here was acquired from another. By touching that man's spittle, this woman felt she had been contaminated by his sliminess, as a bag woman would acquire the rot, the stench, the slime of even a good-looking piece of garbage. A mechanism is operating here by which the bag woman (and her non-homeless counterpart) is taking on the negative qualities of someone or something else: psychological projection.

THE OLD WISE WOMAN AND THE GOOSE-GIRL

Indeed homeless women—old and young—carry around (along with everything else) a huge load that consists of everybody's fantasies about them. Solitary women have always carried this load, and it has always consisted of much the same batch of fantasies. In my research I found them cropping up across the centuries. One particularly good example is a Grimm's fairy tale called "The Goose-Girl at the Well," where they appear in full flower.

Fairy tales are expressions of the collective psyche that can be interpreted to diagnose a society's imbalances much as a dream is interpreted for an individual.[1] This particular tale both shows which fantasies attach to young and which to old women and provides the two fundamental images that symbolize the marginal woman's mythological function: her burden and her treasure. As a framework for my analysis of the historical and contemporary psychological dynamic between homeless women and society, I will summarize and interpret "The Goose-Girl" here.

An old woman who lives in a remote clearing in the forest is out gathering wild apples and pears and grass for her flock of geese when she meets a young count. Although fathers in that country commonly warn their sons to keep away from her since she is a witch "with claws beneath her gloves," the young man agrees to carry her enormous load, which seems much too heavy for her. He finds it as heavy as cobblestones, but the old woman will not let him stop to rest and laughs maliciously as the burden sticks fast to his back, so he cannot throw it off.

Just as he feels he must collapse, they arrive at her house, where she is met by her geese and an ugly old goose-girl, whom she tells to go into the house, lest the young man fall in love with her. After laughing to himself at this idea, the count falls asleep. When he wakes the old woman quite kindly gives him a box made from an emerald and sends him away. After wandering in the forest for three days, he reaches a large town and presents the box to the Queen. Inside she discovers a pearl that has fallen from the eyes of her youngest daughter, who has the gift of weeping pearls and jewels instead of tears.

This daughter, however, is lost. Three years before, when she was fifteen, her father asked his three daughters how much they loved him in order to decide how to divide up his kingdom. One sister professed to love him like sugar, the second "as dearly as my prettiest dress," but the youngest said she loved her father like salt. Flying into a rage, he banished her into the forest with a sack of salt bound on her back. Now, however, he has repented, and he and the Queen leave with the count to seek out the old woman.

She, meanwhile, sits spinning at her wheel, and at the cry of an owl sends the goose-girl out into the forest at night to do her "work." The girl goes to a well, where in the bright moonlight she removes a skin that has covered her face and washes it and herself in the well water. Without the skin she appears as a beautiful young girl with golden hair, who sits and weeps for a long time. All this is witnessed by the count, perched in a tree. He makes a noise and the girl runs home, where she finds the old woman cleaning and sweeping the house.

When the count arrives with the King and Queen, the old woman is expecting them. She brings out the girl, who without the skin is revealed to be their daughter. After embracing her parents, she perceives the young man and turns red. The King wants to know what he can give her now, since he has divided his realm between her sisters, and the old woman replies: "She needs nothing. I give her the tears that she has wept on your account; they are precious pearls, . . . worth more than your whole kingdom, and I give her my little house as payment for her services." She disappears, and the house turns into a "splendid palace." "Whether the snow-white geese . . . were verily young maidens . . . whom the old woman had taken under her protection, and whether they now received their human form again, . . . I do not exactly know," speculates the storyteller in conclusion, "but I suspect it. This much is certain, that the old woman was no witch, as people thought, but a wise woman, who meant well. Very likely it was she who, at the princess's birth, gave her the gift of weeping pearls instead of tears."[2]

The endless forests in which an old woman might live alone, feared and suspected by the inhabitants of the surrounding countryside, have disappeared, as has the cultural and social setting reflected in this fairy tale; but there still exist isolated women who live on the fringe of society, feared and despised by its respectable citizens. In accord with changing times, however, these women have become urbanites, inhabitants of the contemporary wilderness—homeless women, who go foraging for garbage, the only harvest the city provides. We are no longer a culture of storytellers, and we have no comparable modern legends to explain our marginal women; but the basic issues have not changed, and the fairy tale provides a good starting point for analyzing them. The story is concerned with an incomplete, unbalanced, and therefore destructive attitude toward the feminine side of experience, expressed both in the father's relationship to his daughter and in the society's feeling about the old wise woman.

This woman shares a number of characteristics with "shopping-bag ladies." She is old, lives alone, and her principal activity involves collecting and carrying. It is not made clear just what leads the people of the countryside to mistrust her. It could be discomfort associated with the mystery created by her isolation—of who she is and how she manages to survive. Or perhaps it is the fact that she seems able to carry a burden anyone would have thought much too heavy for her, which hints that she may have powers beyond what old women should have, for one expects an old woman to be weak. In any case, though she has apparently done nothing evil, these characteristics are enough to create a general assumption that she is a witch. (But note that it is the fathers who warn their sons against her, not the mothers their daughters.) Still, while this woman resembles modern marginal women in some ways, she has a whole other side of purposeful action and control, not to mention supernatural power. She applies this power to resolve the problem created by the King's anger at his daughter for loving him like salt and his driving her out into the forest.

Why was the King angry? The princess who refuses to make a conventional sentimental assertion of her love for her father and gets punished for it is common in European folklore; this motif is the basis of *King Lear*, with its contrast between Goneril's and Regan's honeyed words and the plain savor of Cordelia's honesty. The motif also occurs in a traditional tale of India, where six older princesses love their father "like the sweetest sugar," but the youngest loves him like salt, and in a rage he orders her to be taken off to a dense jungle.[3]

In all these cases the daughter recognizes that something about the question is wrong and does not want to speak; it is only after the King insists that she comes out with her uningratiating answer, and then he instantly falls into an unthinking rage. To understand why the idea of salt should so enrage him and why it should be the response of this daughter who is obviously the only sincere one, we must consider what salt is and what it means.

The King's preference for his other daughters' answers recalls a child's craving for sweets; it takes growing up a little to recognize that constant sweetness becomes cloying and sickening, whereas food tastes flat without salt. Certainly salt has been recognized from ancient times as an important seasoning and dietary necessity, a preservative, and an essential element in religious offerings.[4] From this literal, material value of salt has grown a considerable set of figurative meanings. One derives from its importance as "an ingredient or element that gives savor, piquancy, or zest" (*Webster's Third New International Dictionary*), as in the phrase "the salt of honesty." But the word is also used "with reference to the bitter saline taste of tears" ("the salt of most unrighteous tears," *Hamlet*). There is also a slang meaning of "costly, dear" (*Oxford English Dictionary*).

Another figurative meaning appears in the Bible, where the Lord tells Moses that the Israelites' offerings must be seasoned with salt, not honey, which, being associated with fermentation, is rejected as not being lasting; conceivably the preservative quality of salt made it an apt emblem for the faithfulness involved in keeping a covenant.[5]

Salt is thereby linked to personal integrity, an association that is taken a step further in the New Testament, where it symbolizes the superior, enlightened quality of those who have accepted Christ: Jesus calls the disciples "the salt of the earth" (Matthew 5:13). Salt may therefore be said to symbolize the wisdom of the "elect" personality that has discovered its own absolute inner integrity and wholeness, having managed to accept and integrate the often conflicting elements that constitute the individual psyche.[6]

This idea of a wholeness that includes opposing elements leads to yet another meaning. Salt is found in body fluids—tears, blood, perspiration, semen, and vaginal fluid. It is therefore related to the physical reality of the body and by extension (since emotion is so closely connected to physical sensation) to the feelings manifested by the salty tears of joy or sorrow or the sweat of fear, and also to sexuality. Another meaning of salt is "common sense, earthiness" (*Webster's Third*), and in fact to insist on salt, as the princess does, is to insist on recognizing a down-to-earth aspect of oneself. This earthiness is implicit in the phrase "salt of the earth," which I take to recognize a second kind of enlightenment. It does not descend from above but arises from the experience recorded in the body and is not necessarily pleasant, just as body fluids are not always so easy to deal with. Still, such experience is hard to avoid because the body sends its messages whether we like it or not. And the wisdom of the elect is simply the knowledge of the salty aspect of experience. Paradoxically, this aspect is a great treasure, which is why the princess's tears fall as pearls and jewels, and why salt and not sugar is the attribute of those who belong to the kingdom of heaven. The princess is rich to the extent of her ability to weep.

The salt in this story has a specific reference. The King asks his question when his youngest daughter is fifteen, the age of puberty.[7] The beginning of her mature sexuality provokes a crisis in his mind that he attempts to avoid by asking her symbolically to deny this aspect of herself. Her refusal to do so provokes his rage. Implicitly she insists that he recognize the full range of her womanhood, meaning not only the simple fact that she has become a sexual being but also the new element this introduces into her relationship with her father. As soon as she does this she acquires a burden—the salt that symbolizes her integrity, her true inner self.

On one level, then, the fairy tale is a paradigm of the psychology of the father who cannot deal with his daughter's emerging sexuality and either turns upon her and castigates her for it or (as here) simply refuses to see it and continues to pretend that the daughter is still a sweet little girl. In trying to get his daughter to deny her sexuality, the King is also asking her to deny part of her feelings, since if she does, he will not have to deal with his own; but this princess—no doubt because she is endowed with an especially close connection to her inner truth, as symbolized by her tears being pearls—refuses to go along.

Being a king, however, this father may be taken as representative of his entire society, which means that his refusal to acknowledge this sexual aspect of womanhood afflicts the society in general. But since, as I said, the body sends its messages anyway, remaining blind to certain feelings means repressing them; and repression has negative effects that in the story emerge as the collective suspicion and dislike of the old woman. Those aspects of femininity that were denied the princess get projected onto the old woman and colored by fear. There is further a destructive effect on women's own attitude toward themselves in an environment where a considerable part of their psychological and physical reality is devalued and denied. As a result, the part of reality represented by the feminine vanishes from the general awareness, and the entire society is psychologically maimed.

The general fear and suspicion of the old wise woman in the story are explained by this negative projection. The old woman herself does not possess overt sexuality, but powerful sexual associations are contained in the attribute *witch* and in her connection with animals. These associations are implicit in the warning the fathers give their sons, for in this unbalanced world the sexuality not allowed the princess gets transferred to the old woman and is perceived as ravening bestiality, though no one, apparently, has seen the claws hidden under her gloves with which she catches (and presumably devours) young men. Because of all these projections, no one can see what the old woman is actually like, particularly that she has special powers that she uses for good. Eventually, however, we discover that although she does indeed have a connection with the animal world, it is different from the fathers' image of it.

The story traces the reeducation of the masculine side of society, which is carried out by means of the young count. When he picks up the old woman's burden—the load of negative projection she has had to carry around—it becomes his burden, for until he acknowledges these projections as his own, his (and the society's) relationship to the feminine cannot be righted. And indeed, once he has suffered through the trial of bearing it, everything takes on a new aspect. The old woman is now kindly and gives him the emerald box. He then wanders in the wilderness, an apt image for the experience of letting go of old concepts that have become a hindrance and simply trusting to one's instincts to tell one where to go next. The count winds up finding the Queen, who recognizes his pearl.

Meanwhile we learn that the ugly goose-girl is really the beautiful princess in disguise and that the old woman has taken her in and been very good to her. Who then is this old woman? First, she has a maternal quality. The count, when he first sees her, addresses her as "good little mother." The goose-girl too calls her "mother." She also "stroked and fondled her geese as if they were children." This extension of her maternal quality beyond the human realm suggests a supernatural connection with the animal world that is confirmed by the appearance of the owl later on to signal the hour for the daughter's "work."

Second, the old woman is a spinner. Considering the fact that emerges at the end—that she has caused and controlled all the events leading to the resolution—this activity expresses her active "spinning" of the tale, in the manner of the Greek Fates, who spin the destiny of humans. Indeed she is a goddess: a manifestation of that ancient original female divinity referred to as the Great Goddess or Great Mother, who took many forms all over the world (Isis, Ishtar, Demeter, Cybele) and was still extant in Europe as late as the nineteenth century, when the Grimm brothers did their collecting, in various forms clearly recognizable under the Christian overlay.

This figure represented the full range of the feminine and contained all the opposites that such a range implies. The Fates, for example, are associated with death as well as with life: they both spin the thread of destiny and cut it off; the two are inseparable. Similarly the Egyptian Isis was represented as a fertility goddess with genital area exposed at the same time that she was associated with spiritual-transformation mysteries.[8] A society that worshipped such a figure would not require that young girls deny their sexuality. The society that produced the Grimm tale, however, was Christian; and looking at the Christian female divine being, we see that such a split has indeed occurred: the Virgin has to do only with purity, spiritual transcendence into eternal life, and a form of love absolutely detached from the body.[9] The side of female experience that involves physical death and sexuality, as well as the feelings and needs connected with them, is left entirely without official cultural recognition and so must express itself through a magical old woman who, as the natural complement to the Virgin, appears entirely negative. The fairy tale's function is to counteract this one-sidedness by revealing what she is really like.

The symbols associated with her represent specific aspects of the feminine that her society has rejected. First are the wild apples and pears and the grass she collects. In her character of fertility goddess, the Great Mother is associated with all vegetative processes, including agriculture; but since the story emphasizes that the fruits are wild—nondomesticated—it seems that here she represents a connection with nature that lies outside the civilized human domain. Apples also recall the apple from the tree of knowledge in Eden; and it is indeed an aspect of the Edenic knowledge that the old woman has come to impart.

She gathers pears too, however. Apples are masculine; like the Edenic apple, they represent a principle of transformation that has to do with mind and spirit rather than body and feeling. But pears, with their womblike shape and soft milky flesh, are feminine.[10] Their presence along with the apples suggests the specifically female, physical aspect of knowledge that was not included in the legacy of Eden, which left Eve forever subordinate to Adam.

The grass the old woman carries is for her geese. The suggestion made by the greeting they give her and her affectionate response—that these are no ordinary geese—is confirmed by the storyteller's remark at the end that they were probably young maidens taken under her protection. What they needed protection from is suggested by the princess's experience; why they had to be geese has to do with the need to educate them into that side of their own femininity of which they, like she, had been deprived. The goose is another attribute of the Great Mother.[11] Further, in Greek religion it represented the goddess Nemesis, "a principle of natural justice by which everyone gets what they deserve."[12] This is a specifically nonrational, nonlegal form of "justice" that is not based on a concept but rather is inherent in what people mean when they say that someone "made a goose of himself"; that is, some quality in the person's own character produced the result. As such the goose represents the working of nature in a blind, "stupid" (because nonintellectual) way; and geese certainly are known for being stupid, although here stupidity involves not a lack of wisdom but a lack of thinking, a functioning on an instinctual level.[13]

Thus the maidens have been regressed into a primitive state of instinctual femininity, while the princess has been made to assume the low state of goose-girl; to balance out her father's one-sided view of her, she is required to live out the side he will not recognize. The society's clinging to a limited, unreal view of women has driven these young women to the opposite extreme, where they experience, and act out, the disallowed part of themselves in a primitive, nonhuman way—which is to say that in rigidly rational, authoritarian environments, women often seem to act like silly geese.

Finally there is the owl whose cry announces the hour for the goose-girl's "work." The owl is a night spirit, associated with death and with witches; but it is also the bird of Athena and symbolizes wisdom.[14] Here it represents a kind of night wisdom—the knowledge of death, sexuality, and the processes of nature that this society has shut away from the daylight.

All these themes come together in the scene where the princess washes her face by the well. On the one hand, in her father's house she is like the sun: the Queen says that her hair is "radiant as sunbeams," and when she comes in for the King's question, "it was just as if the sun were rising."

The goose-girl, on the other hand, seems to the count "ugly as night." Why, one might ask, should night be thought of as ugly? Only when darkness is fearsome because you are using it to hide something from yourself. The goose-girl, however, has been undergoing a transformation that will ultimately enable day and night to meet.

By the time she reaches the well, the moon has risen, shedding a light not as brilliant as that of the sun but still bright enough to permit very fine perception: "It was so light that one could have found a needle." The moon is a powerful feminine symbol. Aside from the correspondence between the lunar and the menstrual cycles, the moon represents a feminine principle of illumination that appears quite opposite to the hard, clear light of rationality associated, for instance, with the sun god Apollo. The soft dimness of moonlight permits the slow, organic unfolding of an element of personality governed by instinct or intuition rather than intellect, a process that is not amenable to rational analysis and would in fact be damaged by it. Moonlight symbolizes a kind of spiritual understanding—that is, connection to one's true inner self—in which spirituality is not divorced from the realm of the physical. Thus the princess undergoes her self-transformation by moonlight.

For three years she has been coming each night to the well, to remove her mask and wash her face, cleansing herself of the false versions of herself. Note that she washes the mask as well as her face. Both are false; they represent the two extremes to which women can be driven when a society cannot accept them as whole persons. The water she uses, arising from the depths of the earth, is an essence of female earthiness. She then sits and weeps, for she has to experience the opposite of her previous purely sunny disposition, until she hears the count and runs away.

But he has seen enough; having encountered her day-self, he now perceives its connection to her night-self. This balanced picture of interaction among the components of a whole personality contrasts to his immediate reaction when he first saw the goose-girl, that she could never touch his heart. He was seeing her then as one-sidedly as had her father, although from the opposite side.

The old woman, who knows the meaning of these events, responds by cleaning her house, making a clean sweep so that the princess and count can have a new beginning together. At the end the princess is reconciled to her father, but her old relationship to him is over. Her turning red when she sees the count indicates her readiness to experience the masculine element in her world and in herself in a new, mature way. This maturity is expressed by the pearls and by the transformation of the old woman's hut into a palace. The princess "needs nothing" from the King because her tears have made her rich. Like the "pearl of great value" in Matthew 13:45, her treasure consists not of literal riches but of a spiritual or psychological awareness worth more than worldly wealth could be. With this knowledge of self the princess has built her own "house," for the transformation of the hovel into a palace expresses not only the new external circumstances of her life but her discovery of splendor within. She thus provides a model, particularly for those whose intense identification with the homeless state reflects an inner feeling of also being "unaccommodated."

BURDEN AND TREASURE

Our own myths of homeless women are woven out of the same stuff as the fairy tale. Later on I will show how these myths grow out of fears of young women's active sexuality (expressed as accusations of promiscuity) and of old women's occult, implicitly sexual powers (expressed as accusations of witchcraft). Here, however, I will analyze the images of the burden and the treasure.

Like the old woman in the story, bag women collect and carry. These activities touched a chord in many people I interviewed; in particular the bags themselves held many associations for women, who related them to their own and other women's habit of collecting shopping bags or their feelings of needing to carry bags with them. "The bags are their security and identity. Anything that identifies them is in those bags—the bags are their home," said one.[15] Another said: "The bag ladies carry their selves around with them—they're transportable." Another: "Shopping bags are so important to them that they carry their whole lives in them."

Like the fairy tale's old woman, "there's something maternal about shopping-bag ladies—they carry so much," as one woman put it. "Bags are a particularly female image. Women had to be the ones to take care of everyone so they had to be prepared for all different situations," remarked a twenty-year-old who said she loved bag women because she felt they knew how to survive and carried around in their bags a kind of arrogance that came from choosing to be strong. But to another young woman the idea of living out of bags was "horrible." Why? "When you're little and your mother has shopping bags, it's a symbol of security. She brings bags from the A&P—they're associated with food, cooking. The shopping bag is *food*. So the shopping-bag lady is a travesty of the shopping bag," she said with violent revulsion. For her it was the idea of mother that had to be sugar-coated.

Along with the bags themselves, the impulse to collect, and also to hoard what is collected, constituted for many people the essence of the bag woman. In *The Rag Bag Clan*, a mystery-detective novel by Richard Barth, bag women are central characters, only they aren't homeless; they are defined entirely by their habit of picking through all the garbage cans in the neighborhood.[16] In fact the collectors' own involvement in collecting and intense connection to the objects gathered were matched by a fascination on the part of those who watched them, which arose from identification with—if not actual participation in—this activity. I heard many stories of compulsive hoarders, people whose rooms or apartments (in one case, house) were piled with all sorts of objects that they could not let go of, whose uselessness matched that of Gertrude's pink T-shirt or the "broken radios, . . . toasters, electric clocks" that bag people carried around "even though they have no access to electricity."[17]

Another reason for the fascination with collecting is that it occurs by accretion—that is, in layers. The bag woman's habit of dressing in many layers of clothes was briefly mirrored in the late seventies by the fashionable "layered look," whose resemblance to the dress of homeless women was noted frequently by fashion writers. But the actual connection went much deeper. "Women are co-natured with their clothes—that is, one partakes of the other," said the woman quoted in the introduction who considered homeless women feminist heroines. Their layers of rags, she said, were "a fragmented symbol of what they're rejecting—of their Barbie Doll sisters! But women seem to layer themselves in many ways. Fatness is a protection from a lack of ability to express themselves physically, that is sexually. Or you could layer yourself with words—talking a lot when you can't express something directly. Or you can wrap yourself in silence. Madwomen weave gossamer around themselves that nobody can get through."

More than oneself could be layered. "There's something very attractive in the idea of having all your possessions able to fit into a finite object like a shopping bag," another woman told me. "You own your possessions rather than the other way round. And you can have shopping bags within shopping bags. When your outer one gets worn and frayed you just put a new one over it."

"Why not just throw the old one out?" I asked.

"Because you're carrying your past with you. There's something comforting in looking back on the colors and sizes of the old ones. One bag lady I knew—a middle-class Jewish girl I went to Europe with—had five at a time."

This particular fantasy corresponded, as it happens, with the homeless women's actual need to carry around all the papers that documented their lives. Gradually the accumulation of an entire lifetime—which included not only official papers but letters, photographs, articles, and pamphlets with personal significance—acquired a magical quality: someone's identity became lodged in a slip of paper that bore a number, tucked inside a plastic bag wrapped in an old coat lying inside the inmost of several shopping bags. One day I realized why so many women were reluctant to bring these papers out when asked for them: it was like revealing their secret selves, the selves hidden under their layers of clothing, of incoherent speech, or of silence, wrapped in folds of dark velvet like the family jewels.

Certainly there seemed to be general agreement that homeless women carried around something precious, for another motif that dominated fantasies about them was the notion that what they had in those bags was valuable. A persistent assumption was that they possessed secret hoards of money. The *New York Post* once reported and refuted "the rumor that shopping bag ladies are rich eccentrics carrying wads of money in their paper sacks"; a magazine article referred to "muggers who believe the myth that many of the women are carrying around huge sums of cash concealed in their shopping bags."[18] This image of the destitute woman carrying a treasure was reinforced by the fact that occasionally a homeless woman who did possess a large amount of money got written up in the newspapers.

One example is the woman in the Automat described in Part 1. In another gruesome incident, a homeless woman sleeping on a bench in the New York subway was set on fire by four youths who threw lit matches on her. Two Transit Authority employees beat out the flames and took her to a hospital. When police went through her bags looking for identification, they found bankbooks showing twenty thousand dollars in deposits. The shock value of the burning and this amount of money got the event considerable news coverage.

One article, written by a female reporter who went to the hospital and saw the homeless woman, concentrated on the woman herself, how she felt about what had happened and why she lived on the streets when her son lived in a middle-class suburb in New Jersey. The article was titled "A Bag Lady Fights for Her Life," and the fact of the bags containing "several locker keys, some inexpensive jewelry, $27.55 in cash and two

bank books showing a total balance of about $20,000" was mentioned
only in passing about a third of the way through. A second story, head-
lined "Boys Set Fire to Bag Lady in IRT with 20G," was written by a man
who spoke only to Transit Authority and hospital officials. It began: "A
71-year-old shopping-bag lady—who had bankbooks showing $20,000
in savings and piles of jewelry stashed among her rags—was severely
burned early yesterday when a group of young boys tossed lit matches on
her as she slept in the Herald Square subway station, police said." At the
end appears this detail: "She also had $27 in cash and jewelry 'so filthy
that we haven't been able to determine the value yet,' a hospital spokesman said."[19] Clearly the reporter was playing on the treasure idea when
he transformed some jewelry of indeterminate value into "piles."

This motif was so compelling that secret treasure in the bags was a
standard item in imagined portraits of bag women. In September 1981,
for example, the comic strip *Dondi* featured a bag woman who had been
duped by smugglers into transporting their stash of diamonds hidden inside a chicken in an extra bag. Upon discovering them, she exclaimed,
"I'm like a walking jewel box stuffed with diamonds!" I came across
many other examples of fictional bag women who were secretly rich.[20]

But the notion of treasure was not just a fantasy projected on the
homeless women by observers; the women themselves collaborated in it.
For example, a Dwelling Place staff member described a homeless
woman who was brought into a hospital emergency room, greatly debilitated. In her bra were pinned five-, ten-, and twenty-dollar bills,
wrapped in cloth bags. Someone asked why she lived on the street when
she had so much money. "I couldn't let anyone know I had it," she replied, "or I'd get mugged." At the level of common sense, this answer is
absurd; but at the level of symbol, it is highly suggestive. Why stay out on
the street when you have the financial means to obtain shelter? Because
the most important thing is to protect your treasure; if anyone knew you
had it, as they would if you spent it, they would attack you. The fact that
they attack you anyway—as they did the woman set on fire—only rein-
forces your conviction that the danger is real. The fact that you would be,
at the least, less vulnerable indoors does not enter into consideration because the basic question is not physical safety but the preservation of the
treasure, which is just as endangered by being inside as by remaining on
the street—for the treasure has acquired a psychological importance that
goes beyond its literal value; its symbolic and its real values interpene-
trate. This explains the general fascination with what the women carry

in their bags: if the value of real money can go beyond money, anything else in the bags can also acquire such value.

Richards, so conversant with symbolic forms of meaning, provides an example. Her campsite described in Part 1 was eventually discovered by the police, who made her leave. A team of reluctant sanitation men, under prodding, moved hesitantly into her clearing to clean out her possessions, officially denominated "garbage." One of them picked up a white plastic bag that held an orange bucket. "You give that back to me," Richards snapped; "that's my jewels." He handed it back. Later I looked into it; it was half full of water. She refused to talk about what had happened, so I never found out what the bucket meant to her. But it doesn't matter whether it had some specific meaning or was precious to her just because it was hers and she had so little. In either case the bucket had no value in itself but was endowed with a value that—as with the papers stowed away in the bags or Gertrude's T-shirt—was connected with the personality, or the self, or the being of its owner. What is more, people inside society seem to "catch" this sense of value from the women, although since it isn't clear exactly what the value attaches to, the feeling gets expressed through the fantasy that all bag women are rich.

So we have a paradox: the worthless garbage is also priceless jewels; the outcasts of society—who in reality carry around what the *New York Post* once termed "cartsful of nothingness"—possess treasure.[21] This paradox accounts for the ambivalence of people like Valerie, described in the introduction, who was reacting to both sides of it: admiration for the specialness of the woman outside her office building coexisted with repulsion and a need to keep her distance.

The paradox further points to the nature of the connection that exists between homeless women and people inside, which all the examples above have demonstrated. Talking to Valerie I began to get the feeling that all her made-up ideas about what the woman was like were so many additional weights being loaded into the woman's bags. "Women always have to have so much with them," Valerie said at one point. "I don't know why." "There's something about being a carrier," said the twenty-year-old. "It's a symbol of all the psychological shit we have to carry around with us—being laden with something." The bag women are indeed carriers, and their load is both real and metaphorical. "They're filling a role that's expected of them," suggested another woman. "It almost becomes a responsibility."

Indeed it is one—to carry all the projections I have been describing—

and it turns on the fact of the women's being outside. The function they thereby serve can be analyzed with reference to the fairy tale. There, the significance of the treasure is that it has been created by the princess's suffering because she refused to give up the part of herself that the King rejected. This suffering is the price of her integrity; thus her integrity becomes her burden. She is driven out into the forest because as long as she keeps it, she cannot remain in society. We, in projecting the idea of treasure on the bag women, are giving them as burden our own rejected part, which we have been unable to live with and so have cast out; it constitutes our integrity and would be our treasure (as the princess's pearls—her own integrity—are hers) if we could repossess it. Our unconscious awareness of this truth is responsible for the treasure projection in the first place. But since we are not aware of it consciously, what we see in the homeless women is frightening, and we have all sorts of uncomfortable feelings about them, just as the people in the story suspected the old woman for her ability to bear so much.

That old woman is able to bear all these projections easily; she is not damaged by the one-sided way in which her contemporaries see her and indeed acts to restore the lost aspect of the feminine to active functioning. Our own marginal women, however, often are damaged; they become the projection and self-destructively act it out. Nevertheless their strange behavior is, like the goose-girl's mask, essentially a protective measure for preserving a true inner core. The difference is that while the princess is protecting a delicate process from interference until her transformation is accomplished, most of the homeless women I knew were simply traumatized into rigid defense of a tiny and desperately vulnerable core of self—which is still their treasure.

The sudden appearance of the palace at the end of the story—that is, the fact that the change in the princess's inner self creates the transformation in her outer habitation—suggests another meaning of homelessness: that at least on one level of experience, home has to be inside oneself before it can be anyplace else. In that sense, physical shelter does not automatically provide a home, for homelessness may also involve not feeling at home in oneself or not having a clear sense of self seated inside one. The refusal of women described in Part 1 to come under a roof can then be seen as an expression of their inner sense of having no home, and no self.

While the homeless women have lost a positive aspect of themselves, those inside society have lost a negative one. Negative or not, it is still of great value, and for us as well as them repossession is necessary, for by bringing them in we restore not just their "homes" but our own whole-ness. I am not speaking metaphorically: one consequence of working at the Dwelling Place, for me and for other volunteers and staff members, was a profound encounter with unacknowledged aspects of our own na-tures.[22]

THE WOMAN OUTSIDE AS WITCH

One way of repossessing the self is to know its past, for a sense of history can give both definition and depth to experience. The very existence of the fairy tale indicates that the dynamic in which certain women serve a function by being outside is not new; and indeed it has a long history.

In the fairy tale the accusation prompted by fear and suspicion of the old woman was that she was a witch. In that cultural context this in-volved a belief that she had magical powers which she used to harm oth-ers. Although literal belief in witchcraft is rare in Western society today, something rather similar does still operate. This is why Valerie felt im-pelled to cross the street to avoid the woman outside her building, as though the woman's lice had supernatural powers of jumping. The cur-rent witch image involves not working black magic in the old-fashioned sense but possessing a certain psychological potency that makes the women seem to have "powers," as one woman I quoted put it.

If you translate accusations of casting spells and so on into psycholog-ical terms, the old witch stories take on a startlingly modern application. For example, the witch myth has insinuated itself into the second article about the woman burned in the subway. In this article the woman begins to lose her humanness and turn into a bare set of symbols: she is de-scribed as "wearing ragged clothing and clutching two bags filled with rags"—a figure that is far from the "frail withered woman" lying in a hospital bed who looked up, as an attendant brought in the first reporter, with "hopeful disbelief." Some similarly reduced image of the woman is what the four youths must have seen, especially considering what they chose to do.

The act of burning calls up powerful associations to the traditional fate of witches that connect this modern homeless woman directly to the old woman in the fairy tale. A similar incident occurred a few years later when police in Brooklyn chose to deal with a homeless woman who had lost her apartment and begun living in a corner of Prospect Park by burning her possessions (not, fortunately, her person). Officers re-sponding to complaints about her presence in the park allegedly threw the bags containing all her belongings into a trash can and set fire to it. The precinct commander explained "that throwing the woman's property into a garbage can was the best way to 'clear the situation up.'" Although he asserted that what they threw into the can was "'junk—not clothing,'" which "'somehow ignited'" all by itself, witnesses insisted that they saw one of the officers light a match. In either case, it was an unnecessarily vicious way of getting rid of someone whose only offense was impinging on "'the quality of life in this community.'" I think the policemen were impelled toward this act in particular because the homeless woman (young, this time) was contaminated with associations attaching to women who have for centuries been conceived of as enemies of society.[23]

Another way to analyze the relationship between society and women outside, then, is to investigate the history of the witch image. A useful version of this history was provided by the nineteenth-century French historian Jules Michelet, whose account of the making of a medieval witch traces (in a somewhat fantastical way) the changes in a single fictional Sorceress (as he calls her) as they parallel changes in medieval and early modern society. He interprets the development of satanism, the alleged religion of the accused witches, as a compensation for the antinature, antilife repressiveness of the medieval church, whose emphasis on purity and devaluation of sexuality left the entire natural world as the devil's domain and the witches as his supposed priestesses.[24]

Michelet's story starts in the twelfth century, when the Sorceress is a little peasant wife still worshiping, in a half-acknowledged way, the old pagan gods now reduced by the imposition of Christianity to the level of outlawed spirits. The peasants suffer great hardship, but they do not become desperate until the fourteenth century, when the king and nobility, needing gold to fight the Crusades and buy luxury goods from the East, demand payment of feudal obligations in coin instead of in kind. The peasant wife has already turned to her own little familiar pagan spirit and pledged herself to him in return for his promise of assistance; thus when the need for gold arises, she is ready. Since Satan, in Michelet's metaphorical terms, is the spirit of Nature that the church had set itself to repress, this pact represents woman's rejection of the teachings of Christianity in favor of her own instinctual relation to life and the natural world.

With this source of power working for her, she has unexpected success at selling grain in the market; her husband is made bailiff of the manor; they prosper, and she holds her head high, "proud as Lucifer." The villagers hate her for the harsh measures she uses to extract their payments but are also proud of her. However, after the outraged chatelaine has her beaten, they turn against her with an accusation of what they suspected all along: " 'For sure the Devil must be in the Dame!' " Fleeing the village to avoid a charge of witchcraft—it being assumed that any woman so resplendently successful must be possessed by evil—she finds refuge in a cave in wild hilly country, the hermitage of Satan.[25]

Michelet makes it clear that resentment of the Sorceress is due largely to her ability to rise to a level of well-being that puts her above her station, thus upsetting the medieval "rank and order" and threatening not only the secular hierarchy but also the power of the church against the still-lively paganism of the people, as well as the theologically enforced dominance of man over woman.[26] The mere nature of woman released from patriarchal constraints is a force so strong that it threatens every established power. It therefore becomes defined as evil and must lead a shadowy, semicriminal existence.

This indeed is the fate of the Sorceress, who settles in the west-central hills of France, "between the land of Merlin and the land of the Faery Queen," and undergoes a transformation as Satan "lays in her hand the precious fruit of Science and of Nature"—teaching her nature's language, putting her in touch with the life force of sexuality, bestowing on her the ability to see into the realm of the dead. The people of the area, though fearful of "the implacable Proserpine," visit her for aid they cannot get from the Church; she can call back the spirits of the departed, succor the sorrow of widows, mix love potions. In time the embittered outlaw woman becomes a healer, especially of other women, whom, as representatives of the flesh, the Middle Ages consider "radically impure. . . . Medieval medicine concerns itself exclusively with the superior, the pure being (to wit, man)."[27]

But with the awakening of secular culture at the end of the fourteenth century, Michelet says, the reign of Satan is over. Later centuries will redefine him into a common, grotesque devil who has lost his old dignity as Prince of Nature, and the witch will degenerate accordingly into a "mere trafficker" claiming "ridiculous powers" over unsavory matters.[28]

Despite its romanticized form, Michelet's fable is not entirely fanciful. Recent research supports his assertion that the presence in medieval society of women said to be witches derived from the social and economic conditions of feudalism. The many European folk tales featuring old women who live in cottages outside villages and cultivated lands reflect the actual position of peasant widows unable to meet the obligations owed the lord for the lands they inherited from their husbands.[29] Aside from specific expenses entailed by the husband's death, these obligations involved working on the lord's land and on their own. A widow without sons might be unable to fulfill them and could be forced off her land. If she was an expert midwife or herbal healer, she would naturally turn to the type of "sorceress" practice Michelet describes to make a living.

Such could well have been the background of stories like "The Goose-Girl," in which " 'the old woman in the forest' " possessed a "white magic of rescues and transformations" as well as "the potions and curses of black magic," both believed to be the special province of women, related to "the gift of their reproductive ability."[30] By being made into a fable, however, the old woman lost her historical reality and has come down to us as a magical figure with no specific social context.

Michelet's fable also illustrates how this power over the domain of sexuality functions as a link between the society and the woman outside. The Sorceress gets cut off from society but in a paradoxical way remains connected by being separated, for needs are still being met on both sides: the Sorceress earns her living by dealing in matters that no one inside the society can touch. Or, to put it another way, she owns an entire area of life that belongs outside with her; it is her working capital. In one way or another, such a separation between society and certain women has always existed in Western culture; and to explore it we now return to objective history.

PART 3

Homeless Women Have Always Existed

Many a woman may be deterred from entering a suitable Home by fear of cross-questioning. Poor thing! The only thing that belongs to her is her past.

—*Mary Higgs,* Glimpses into the Abyss

The Ancient World through the Eighteenth Century

A homeless woman's personal past may belong to her, but her historical one does not. The assimilation of women into Mankind that characterizes historical studies in general has operated even more thoroughly in the case of those who were homeless than for the rest; their history often has to be combed out of sources that are about something else. When this history is detached from other contexts and assembled, however, even bag women no longer appear so anomalous, so unheard-of as before.

Nor is the story of homeless women the same as that of homeless men. While men have been outcasts, and more often than women, not only have they had more options but, just as today, the male outsider has been defined in terms of work and the female in terms of sexuality. If a woman did not belong to a family or live within some other restrictive social context (such as a convent), her sexuality was seen as anarchic and threatening. At the same time (as for Michelet's Sorceress) sexuality was often the instrument of her economic survival—sometimes as a wise woman or midwife but most often as a prostitute.

Thus, although the history of homeless women is intertwined with that of two other venerable, non–sex-related social phenomena—begging and vagabondage—it is also closely related to one activity men generally do not share: prostitution. This was an option almost always open to a destitute woman; Henry Mayhew, the chronicler of the poor of Victorian London, describes sick and disfigured prostitutes over sixty who did business in the parks at night, wearing veils so their customers could not see them. Although beggars, vagabonds, and prostitutes all evoke in the members of settled society a similar mixture of fear, envy, loathing, attraction, and moral disapproval, the element of sexuality and the mystery associated with it have entered into the public perception of homeless women and made them seem special in a way that has not been true for men. Despite the fact that for women prostitution was essentially a reasonable economic choice, given their other alternatives, reformers have always discussed it in terms of morality, and specifically of the flaws in women's characters—or, rather, in Woman's Nature. The rhetoric presents an inflated vision of the prostitute's evil powers that is based on a deep fear of what is perceived as unbridled sexuality. Such fear is aroused by any woman who is not "bridled" by living within social restraints; and it can be traced through centuries, from the frightful hags in Roman literature who gather noxious herbs in cemeteries by night, to the medieval witches accused of blasting crops and causing impotence or sterility, to the Victorian prostitute, "the terrible avenger of her sex," whose "potent influence" is seen "in the downward tendency of all that is pure and holy in life!"—down to the contemporary bag woman likened to a "toad" or "gargoyle."[1]

Historically, a separation between certain women and society occurred in two ways. First, the women who made their living by sex were set explicitly apart—with their status generally signaled either by clothing regulations that prescribed specific items of apparel (as in classical Greece and Rome) or by a self-chosen, easily recognizable style of dress (as today). Second, receiving assistance that would make prostitution unnecessary also involved outcast status. Giving alms has been likened to primitive hospitality to strangers, which is based on fear of the stranger's unknown, mysterious quality; the giving is a way of appeasing the stranger to protect oneself from whatever bad magic she or he may have. Thus people who give to a beggar may well be doing it for their own sake, not the beggar's.[2] Institutionalized charity too is based on the principle of giving hospitality to strangers, which "means that the 'poor person' has become a stranger to the society."[3] Giving gives outcast status, especially since people receiving assistance generally lose most of their rights as citizens. This enforced outside-ness, compounded by the issue of sex, makes the homeless woman the ultimate outcast.

THE ANCIENT WORLD

Women were always among the enormous number of poor and homeless people who existed from early times until the institution of massive social welfare programs in the twentieth century. These people are now largely invisible, for they left few records of their own and those who documented the society generally did not dwell on them. But in fact, until relatively recently, the existence of huge numbers of starving poor was largely taken for granted as an eternal fact of life.[4]

Part of the history of homeless women, therefore, involves the measures taken by societies to deal with poor and homeless people in general. Yet since women, having fewer rights than men, were more vulnerable, there also had to be special provisions for them. In the ancient Near East, for example, a woman's connection with society was through the men of her family; lacking these, she became an outsider.[5] The Code of Hammurabi provided a woman with gifts from her father and husband and the right to stay in her husband's house if she was widowed or if another wife was brought in. In the Old Testament the widow (defined as "a once-married woman who has no means of financial support"—that is, no new husband, adult son, or father-in-law) is always classed with the orphan and "sojourner," or resident alien.[6] One might think that a woman born and bred in the society would have a different relation to it than an alien, but in fact the same legal dispositions applied to both; they received public charity, in the form of gleaner's rights and a share in the tithe of produce given to the priesthood. The need to promulgate such codes and the frequent exhortations in the Old Testament to the Israelites to remember their duty to the poor indicate that the indigent were not always properly provided for. Many women had, therefore, to fend for themselves; and in such a case prostitution was one of their few alternatives.[7]

A woman who became a prostitute in the ancient world passed to a more explicit outsider status. In societies where marriage was essentially a property transaction, prostitution satisfied male sexual needs while preserving the safety of family women, whose chastity was necessary to the secure inheritance of property through the male line.[8] For this reason alone the prostitute had to be outside the social structure so that her children could have no claims on the inheritance; but as we shall see, fear of the mystery of sex operated as well.

Prostitutes often came initially from outcast groups, who were frequently too poor to maintain the large extended-family households that sheltered the unmarried sisters and widowed daughters of more well-to-do families.[9] These homeless poor appear in the literature of classical Greece and Rome, warming themselves near public baths or forges and gathering "the leftovers after great festivals."[10] Although some high-class prostitutes, such as the Greek hetairai, did quite well, at least while they were young, the great masses of them led miserable existences; the poorest prostitutes of Rome, for example, "did not even have the security of a brothel but practiced their trade out-of-doors under archways."[11] And unless she was shrewd enough to provide for her future, even the most successful hetaira faced destitution in old age. Several sources describe the desperation of the old Greek streetwalkers, who used makeup to hide their age and served their customers in darkened rooms.[12]

These old women evoked violent horror and disgust in the classical writers, who described them, and especially their sexuality, with a revulsion approaching nausea.[13] In light of the sexual fears implied by this hatred, it is significant that most prostitutes of ancient Greece and Rome not only were outside the social structure but also were slaves; their status permitted a distancing and control of this potentially anarchic area of life of which women are the locus. The equivocal relation between society and its female outcasts implied by such an arrangement has persisted, in somewhat different forms, for centuries.

THE MIDDLE AGES

The homeless of the medieval period included "criminals, socially disgraced persons, maladjusted individuals, and even some insane persons," as well as people who for some other reason had gotten detached from their native areas.[14] Contributing to the homeless population were attempts by medieval cities to eliminate prostitution by summarily banishing prostitutes and to get rid of insane inhabitants by expelling them or turning them over to sailors: "Madmen then led an easy wandering existence. The towns drove them outside their limits; they were allowed to wander in the open countryside, when not entrusted to a group of merchants and pilgrims."[15]

Although the rigidity of feudalism excluded many from the system, it did protect those inside it. The medieval manor had a "built-in system of poor relief" that provided for many widows and aged persons. The widow's right to inherit all or part of her husband's holding and have it worked by a relative who agreed in return to support her saved many old women from the fate (common in Europe as earlier in Mesopotamia) of being turned out of the house by their children. The poor had other "customary privileges," including the right to glean for three days before the harvested fields were turned over for pasture and "permission to sleep in the church if they had no other accommodation."[16] In addition, alms were regularly given by individuals to their local poor, who depended on

handouts of food and clothing to survive. This tissue of custom and priv-
ilege kept many aged and infirm women from becoming homeless.

Those who were homeless got assistance both from private almsgivers
and from the church, whose institutions—monasteries, refuges, and asylums—cared directly for the incapacitated and destitute.[17] In addition,
the church collected tithes that, along with private donations, were administered by local priests to relieve the destitute in their parishes. Because they knew everyone personally, there was no question about who
deserved help. This assistance was based on two principles: first, that
"poverty was not a disgrace," and, second, that the purpose of almsgiving
was primarily to save the souls of those who gave, not to relieve the destitute.[18]

Over time, however, this system became inadequate. Fundamental social and economic changes broke down the manorial system, destroying
the security it provided, and the state gradually assumed more and more
responsibility for relief, which, however, it administered primarily for
purposes of its own, rather than simply to assist the poor. Although similar difficulties and attempted solutions existed throughout Europe, the
following discussion focuses largely on Britain since the public welfare
system developed there directly influenced that of the United States. Despite changing conditions, the relation between government and homeless people in general has consistently been conditioned by politics, economics, or both, while for women in particular it has been based on the
need to control their sexuality in the interest of property relations.[19] At
the same time, these components of the relationship have been obscured
by the images created in the public mind by its psychological component.

Three events broke down the system of church relief and ultimately
changed the ideological basis of giving aid. The first was the outbreak in
the fourteenth century of the plague, which by depopulating the country
created a labor shortage. Peasants left their land and wandered, looking
for the best market in which to sell their labor. The government thereupon enacted the Statute of Laborers of 1349, which required people to
work for anyone who asked them to at prepestilence wages and prohibited giving alms to "able-bodied" beggars (those who could work).
Those who really could not work—the "impotent" poor—could get alms
only "at their present residence, in a neighboring town, or at their place
of birth"; they were thus prevented from moving around.[20] In this early
attempt to use relief to enforce labor lies the foundation of government's
future relation to the homeless.

The second event was the enclosure of agricultural land for pasture on a wide scale in the fifteenth century, which drove more people off the land, creating many vagabonds and upsetting the system of local assistance to the indigent. The third was Henry VIII's seizure of church lands in 1536, which dissolved the monasteries that had cared for the poor. As a result this responsibility fell entirely on the individual parish, whose voluntary relief system, in the face of the great civil disorder that existed, provided insufficient funds. Slowly, therefore, the national government took over. During the sixteenth century it passed the Elizabethan Poor Laws, which required local officials to register and license the legitimate poor of each parish; outlawed almsgiving to unlicensed beggars; empowered local officials to levy taxes, called poor rates, specifically for relief; and finally, in 1601, created a system that became the basis of relief in England until the mid-twentieth century and of the system developed in the United States as well. The law of 1601 created in each parish an "overseer of the poor," empowered to raise money by taxing and to set up a workhouse for the able-bodied. It established the principle of "local responsibility for the poor" but provided at the same time that "towns were liable only for and to their own residents." As a result, each parish became concerned to avoid spending money on strangers, which meant it had an interest in refusing relief rather than giving it. (This attitude continues in full force today, as the Dwelling Place women, caught between welfare trying to get them onto SSI and SSI trying to reject them, could testify.)[21]

The nature of the conditions this legislation was designed to alleviate emerges from contemporary descriptions of beggars. After the plague, the country swarmed with the "begging poor," including poor scholars and wandering friars, real and fake; robbers and other criminals disguised as beggars and cripples; and mad people. In *Piers Plowman* (1362), William Langland pities those beggars who "want their understanding, . . . lunatic vagrants, and wanderers about, who are more or less mad according to the phases of the moon."[22] Two centuries later little had changed. Sixteenth-century vagrants included "fulloks"—"wanton girls" who lived in summer "in ditches and under bushes, loitering and wandering by by-ways from place to place without working, living upon haws and blackberries, and indulging in hedge-breaking"; in winter they went to town and wandered around. An act of 1562 provided measures to return female servant runaways to their "Maistresses or Dames."[23]

Among the horde of vagrants were great numbers of "common women" and "strumpets." Prostitution had flourished throughout Europe since the Dark Ages, even though the tolerance shown it by the ancient world had ended with Christianity's emphasis on celibacy. The early church fathers nevertheless felt it necessary to "tolerate prostitution" as "the price of social purity"; Thomas Aquinas compared prostitution "to a sewer in the palace; if the sewer was removed the palace would be filled with pollution."[24] The ambivalence between acknowledging the need and trying to repress it was reflected in a centuries-long debate over whether to tolerate prostitution and control it through regulation or to suppress it altogether. Throughout, however, the debaters remained faithful to the image of woman as a conduit for draining off men's filth. Even when it was acknowledged that women had been forced into prostitution by destitution, they were degraded, ostracized, and sometimes severely punished.

Attempts to suppress the trade, often by exiling prostitutes, invariably failed, so that by the end of the Middle Ages prostitution was well established in most cities of Europe, though confined to specified areas, as if it were a disease. In fact, the city of Bristol "classed prostitutes with lepers and would allow neither group within the city walls."[25] As in the ancient world, prostitutes were required to wear specific clothing or badges, or even to dye their hair a certain color. In Strasbourg "an edict of 1420 forbade prostitutes to enter the cabarets; another of 1558 prohibited tavern-keepers from entertaining them. . . . Prostitutes were only allowed . . . to stand without and drink what was handed to them from within."[26] The more successful these efforts to cut the women off from society, the less able they were to find some other way to survive. Thus, when, in the sixteenth century, Martin Luther closed the brothels in the Reformed cities of Germany, the Strasbourg prostitutes "drew up a petition stating that they had pursued their profession not from liking it but only to earn bread; they asked for honest work if they were to quit it."[27]

Who were these women? Many had been sold into prostitution as young girls by their parents or by kidnappers; probably their families were too poor to support them. By the twelfth century slave markets existed; although these were closed down in the sixteenth century, the practice continued into the nineteenth century, using more discreet means. Other prostitutes were servants who had been seduced and dismissed or women in any trade who were out of work. Thousands of women were camp followers during the many wars of these centuries.[28] Laws of the Italian duchy of Asola prevented a father from disinheriting his daughter if she became a prostitute after he had opposed her marrying beyond the age of twenty-five—a direct acknowledgment of economic necessity.[29]

Despite the overwhelmingly economic nature of the motive that led any unattached woman into prostitution, another possible cause should be recognized. "In many cases," remark two historians of prostitution, "economic pressures are all important; but it also seems clear that in societies where women are socially acceptable only as wives and mothers, many women rebel against the legal bondage which marriage entails. . . . Often [prostitution] was the only way in which a woman could advance" to "influence and affluence."[30] Affluence, let alone influence, is hardly relevant to homeless women; but the desire for independence is, and it definitely was a factor in a number of cases of vagrancy as well as prostitution, past and present.

THE SEVENTEENTH AND EIGHTEENTH CENTURIES

Luther's closing of the brothels in the cities under Protestant influence signaled a cultural shift that, in the seventeenth century, was to change the situations not only of prostitutes but of vagrants and poor people in general; they came to be redefined in terms of new cultural norms that were developing in accordance with new social and economic conditions. The harsh English laws against vagabonds reflected the point of view of those who made them: the political leaders, with a stake in power, and the landowners, with a stake in wealth. The common people, especially before the seventeenth century, were sympathetic toward vagrants; later their attitude seems to have varied according to how much they were influenced by the developing individualism associated with capitalism and private property. "Among the vices of that rude age," says one historian of the fifteenth century, "parsimony was rarely one, the exercise of charity being in fact regarded as a religious duty. Universal begging implies universal giving."[31]

In fact, making vagabondage a crime, as the statute of 1349 did, was a new idea. Previously, legal dispositions of vagrants had not involved punishment for vagrancy as such. A vagrant might be enslaved (in Rome any free man could enslave a poor one who owed him money, a beggar, or a vagabond); punished as a fugitive (many vagrants were escaped slaves); or simply banished, as under Germanic law. Christianity had then introduced the attitude that "poverty is a superior state and that the beggar has more merit than the rich man." However this idea coexisted with the opposite doctrine that "the sufferings imposed on the poor person constitute an expiation of his sins."[32] During the seventeenth century, this second attitude, reinforced by the developing work ethic, became dominant, changing both the definition of the poor and homeless and the way they were treated.

The effect of this transition on the relationship between the poor and society is well illustrated by Keith Thomas's analysis of the social status of English witches. Most of the witches brought to trial in England during the sixteenth and seventeenth centuries were poor. "They are usually such as are destitute of friends, bowed down with years, laden with infirmities," according to a contemporary. In fact "their names appear among the witchcraft indictments just as they do among the recipients of parochial relief." Many were women "in the habit of going 'from house to house, and from door to door for a pot full of milk, yeast, drink, pottage, or some such relief, without which they could hardly live.'" This was the medieval almsgiving tradition in action; in the sixteenth century it was still "in many places essential for the routine maintenance of the elderly and infirm. . . . [It was] probably as important a means of poor relief as the public levies." Thomas notes that "the overwhelming majority of fully documented witch cases" arose after the supposed witch had been denied the relief to which traditionally she was entitled. This almsgiving norm had begun to conflict with "a growing sense of private property" and "the increasingly individualistic forms of behaviour which accompanied the economic changes of the sixteenth and seventeenth centuries." It was also being weakened by the Poor Law injunction against giving alms indiscriminately. Thus the witchcraft accusations reflected social tensions that "arose from the position of the poor and dependent members of the community." People "hated [the poor] as a burden to the community and a threat to public order. . . . They also recognised that it was their Christian duty to give them charity when no public relief was forthcoming. The conflict between resentment and a sense of obligation produced the ambivalence which made it possible for men to turn begging women brusquely from the door, and yet suffer torments of conscience after having done so." This guilty conscience led them instantly to accuse the begging woman the minute something in the household went wrong. Thus "class hatred constituted a major stimulus to [the witch's] prosecution."[33]

Of course not all witch prosecutions necessarily had such a cause; but Thomas's analysis allows us to see how, through a simple projection mechanism, homeless and other outcast people could come to be suspected, if not of specific crimes, then at least of generalized evil, in a way that neatly avoided awareness of the class or economic inequity they suffered. Poverty could thereby become "a sign that a person had displeased

God, and dependency . . . an indication of moral failure. . . . The poor were sinners in need of reform or punishment."[34]

In 1662 the Law of Settlement and Removal provided that persons not in their own parish who could not prove that they would not become a public charge "could be sent back to [their] original place of 'settlement'—to [their] legal residence." That place was required to give them relief.[35] Thus began a veritable circus of shipping poor people around the country as each parish tried to get rid of them; it lasted nearly two centuries.

A 1670 pamphlet advocating the establishment of a workhouse in each county gives a typical picture:

> As for instance, *a poor idle Person*, that will not Work, or that no Body will employ in the Country, comes up to *London, to set up the Trade of Begging*, such a person probably may *Begg* up and down the Streets seven Years, it may be seven and twenty, before anybody asketh why she doth so, and if at length she hath the ill hap in some Parish, to meet with a more vigilant *Beadle* than one of twenty of them are, all he does is but to lead her the length of five or six Houses into another Parish, and then concludes, as his *Masters* the *Parishioners* do, that he hath done the part of a most diligent officer: But suppose he should yet go farther. . . . Suppose he should carry this poor wretch to a *Justice* of the Peace, and he should order the *Delinquent* to be *Whipt* and sent from *Parish* to *Parish,* to the place of her *Birth* or last abode, which not one *Justice* of twenty (through Pity or other Cause) will do; even this is a great charge upon the Country, and yet the business of the nation is it self wholly undone: For no sooner doth the *Delinquent* arrive at the place assign'd, but for Shame or Idleness she presently deserts it, and wanders directly back, or some other way, hoping for better Fortune, while the *Parish* to which she is sent, knowing her a Lazy, and perhaps a worse qualified person, is as willing to be rid of her, as she is to be gone from thence.[36]

This was the seventeenth-century revolving door. Then, as now, poor people tended not to have documentation of their birthplaces or identities, so that many remained in perpetual motion.

The institution of the workhouse at the end of the seventeenth century was designed to attack this problem on several levels. The workhouse was part of a system of confinement on a large scale that appeared all over Europe during this century; the poor, unemployed, criminals, and the insane were all locked up together—often in the same buildings that centuries before had housed the lepers—and made to work. By thus contributing to their upkeep, they were supposed to keep the poor rates down, while confining so many people had the further purpose of repressing social disorder during the economic crises that accompanied large-scale changes in agriculture and manufacturing. When the crises subsided and workers were again needed, the horrendous conditions in the workhouses ensured "that no one with any conceivable alternatives would seek public aid."[37] In accordance with this principle, the poorhouses, even though they were intended for the aged and other "deserving poor" who could not work, were equally terrifying.

But further, confinement relieved a certain psychological discomfort on the part of society: it was an ethical affirmation of the value of labor, apart from its economic value. The one characteristic common to the diverse categories of people who were shut up in this period was "idleness," which was for the seventeenth century *"the fault par excellence,"* in Michel Foucault's phrase. Those who labored, following the norm, "acquired an ethical power of segregation, which permitted [them] to eject, as into another world, all forms of social uselessness." This demarcation "between labor and idleness . . . replaced the [earlier] exclusion of leprosy." The "idle" were thus not only shut out of society but strictly segregated from it, relegated to the same precinct that the leper had occupied in the Middle Ages—and to which, in the future, the mad person would be assigned. Foucault refers to "the social importance of that insistent and fearful figure [the leper] which was not driven off without first being inscribed within a sacred circle." As we saw, the same magical demarcation operated with respect to prostitutes—for of course, though Foucault does not mention them, they too belonged to this category, as the city of Bristol clearly recognized when it classed them with the lepers.[38]

Like the prostitutes, too, the poor were marked. An English law of 1603 provided for branding vagrants on the left shoulder with a letter R for "rogue"; another of 1696 required everyone on relief to wear on the right shoulder "a badge or mark with a large Roman P, and the first letter of the name of the parish."[39] Although this had the practical purpose of ensuring that only the certified impotent got aid, its symbolic effect as a "ritual of degradation" is suggested by an order in the vestry book of Burton-on-Trent for June 6, 1703: "That Elizabeth Salisbury, Mary Budworth, Hannah Scott, and Ann Hinckley be taken out of constant pay for their stubborn refusal to wear the badge publickly."[40] This feature of relief was transported to the New World; paupers in eighteenth-century Pennsylvania, New York City, and Rhode Island, for example, had to wear a P on the right shoulder.[41]

In the 1690s it was estimated that half the population of England could not support themselves and "were dependent, or, at best, semi-dependent, on some help beyond what they could earn," and that of a total of 5,500,520 people, 30,000 were vagrants.⁴² The changes in agriculture during the eighteenth century—when much land was enclosed and the rural poor lost the use of common and waste lands that had enabled them to survive—along with the movement of industry to the towns, which deprived the poor of local employment, induced many to migrate to the towns.⁴³ Once they left their home parishes, however, they lost their legal settlement and thus their right to relief.

The "general uncertainty of life and trade" in the eighteenth century meant that even "labouring people" might at any moment find themselves paupers needing relief. Business fluctuations periodically threw large numbers out of work, so that in London, for example, there existed a "floating population," estimated at twenty thousand, who lived in common lodging houses or slept in garrets or cellars rented by the night, in the streets, in the brickyards that surrounded the city, or in stalls—small structures used by tradespeople such as shoemakers.⁴⁴

Beyond this, "the hardships of the age bore with especial weight upon" women. "Social conditions tended to produce a high proportion of widows, deserted wives, and unmarried mothers, while women's occupations were over-stocked, ill-paid and irregular." There were too few positions available for the country girls who came to London to be domestic servants, so that many became prostitutes. In 1763 six women were discovered in an empty house, three dead of starvation and two others nearly so. "Two of the dead women had sheltered there for some months at least; they were both basket-women who carried loads in Fleet Market, and were both known only as 'Bet.' "⁴⁵

Many homeless women had been homeless girls. Great numbers of children were "either entirely abandoned to the streets as vagrants" or turned over to the parish, either as foundlings who had been left exposed on the street or as illegitimate babies handed over with a sum of money to free the father from future responsibility. The parish placed them with wet nurses and apprenticed them when older, or sent them to the workhouse if one existed. Girls were generally apprenticed as domestics in what amounted to legal slavery: once the master or mistress had paid a fee, the child was completely under his or her power. Apprentices of both sexes commonly suffered horrendous abuses, and many "ran away to become beggars and vagrants." "Deserted children and vagrants whose settlements were often unknown . . . were virtual outlaws, outside the pale of the parochial organisation of society."⁴⁶

Exactly such an existence as an outsider amid uncertain social conditions forms the substance of an autobiographical pamphlet by Mary Saxby, an English vagrant of the late eighteenth century. But Saxby's account, which reveals a fiercely energetic, assertive character, also lets us see vagrancy as the outcome of the interaction with social conditions of the desire for independence and self-determination. Mary Saxby was able to move from a life within society to one outside and then work her way in again by means of an adroit shift of mode that created an acceptable expression for her formidable personality.

Memoirs of Mary Saxby, published around 1801 by the Religious Tract Society of London, purports to describe Saxby's conversion from the "proud perverse spirit" and "wicked and impetuous temper" of her youth to Christian principles.[47] She was born in 1738; her mother died when she was young, and her father went into the army, so that she spent her early childhood being moved from one relative to another. None would keep her long because of her "perverse temper." Her father returned and treated her well; but when she was ten he remarried. "The very name of step-mother gave me such disgust, that I could not endure it," and she several times ran away. Finally her father sent her to buy something, giving her a shilling and a plate to put the purchase on, but she lost the shilling and broke the plate and, being afraid to go home, ran away once more.

She hid in the town, sleeping under the shop stalls and eating "rotten apples or cabbage-stalks" found in markets, until she met another girl who agreed to "go into the country" with her; "and though neither of us knew where we were going, we set out, and travelled several days, without any other food than what the hedges afforded. My companion not being so hardy, and perhaps not so wicked as I, soon returned, and I was left alone."

She wandered from town to town by herself, enduring snow, cold, hunger, and dirt, until she met "a poor travelling woman" with three daughters who took her in. "In this poor state, I might have been very happy, as she was a tender, motherly woman, and would have taught me to get my bread honestly, had I been ruled by her. But here again, my proud imperious temper began to shew itself incapable of any restraint." Making friends with the woman's youngest daughter, Mary, who had a good voice, persuaded her to leave her mother so that they could "go about together singing ballads."

So "we ran into all sorts of company, singing in alehouses, and at feasts and fairs, for a few pence and a little drink" (like the New York homeless today who sing on the subways). Eventually they fell in with a band of gypsies, whom they joined; before long Saxby began living with one of the men. After a while, however, she found that he liked another woman better; and, refusing to submit to the "humiliation" of being "secondary wife, or servant to the other woman," she escaped. "I travelled as far as Dover; . . . [I stopped], at times, to ask for a bit of bread, to keep me from starving. When I reached the coast, I met with a woman who sang ballads, and she took me into partnership, till we had some words and separated. As I was not disposed to be extravagant, I had collected a little money, and now set up for myself." Shortly afterward, she joined another woman who sold hardware.

After another brush with the gypsies, Saxby got a job "weeding corn." But her arm "swelled and turned black, having . . . received poison. As I had no friends . . . I . . . was forced to bow my stubborn spirit, and go to my father, who kindly received and clothed me, and got me into an hospital." She was cured but did not return to her father.

> I went to Kent, to pick hops; and from thence into Essex; where they would not suffer any one to travel without a licence, except they could give a very good account of themselves. I, not knowing the rules of the county, sung ballads in Epping-market. In the course of the day, I became acquainted with a middle-aged woman, who looked like a traveller [tramp]; and we went to sleep together at an ale-house. . . . [But] she proved to be a common woman [prostitute]. . . . Being in her company and having been seen with her in the market, the constable came in the night, obliged us to leave our bed, and secured us till morning: when we were taken before a justice who committed us both to bridewell [a house of correction], and ordered us to be repeatedly whipped.

The "keeper," however, realizing she had been tricked, only pretended to whip her.

After another period with her original gypsy lover, "a man, whom I had met with in Kent, finding out my situation, came and took me away." They were married in 1771 and, after spending some more time as migrant agricultural workers, settled down.

After the birth of Saxby's second pair of twins, she became quite sick and had a conversion experience involving a vision of Jesus on the cross—although "not only my neighbors, but my own family, reported, that I was actually mad." This opinion does not seem to have shaken her own sense of the experience, however, for after she recovered she "walked from town to town" with the Bible, talking to "serious christians."

Some time later her husband's death left her with five children to support. "I then applied to the parish for assistance," which came to three shillings a week. After a while, "with the assistance of some kind friends, [I] went into a little business." But as the result of a fall she was laid up, and in the meantime the business failed.

Saxby does not say how she supported herself after that; her text ends with the death of a son. However, an afterword by someone else provides an account of her death in 1801, as well as some comments on her personality that round out the picture of a woman whose "faults" of character seem rather to have been the source of her success in life. Describing the physical ailments that led to her death, the commentator remarks: "Her complicated diseases, indeed, frequently deprived her of the command of her thoughts; and the natural impatience of her disposition then prevailed." Nevertheless, "the esteem with which she was universally regarded, precluded her want of any earthly support or comfort that she could enjoy during her tedious and painful confinement. . . . Her example and conversation were useful far beyond the precincts of her immediate neighborhood."

Saxby's insistent repudiation of her earlier self sounds a false note, partly because her descriptions of her tramping life convey a distinct sense that she enjoyed herself immensely and partly because her strong, self-willed nature, far from being a liability, clearly enabled her to take excellent care of herself. She seems to have been so closely identified with the dictates of her own nature that the dictates of convention never even made her hesitate; but beyond that she managed to adapt convention to her own requirements. She calls herself "a daring rebel" and "an awful instance of the depravity of our nature, and the desperate wickedness of the human heart, till changed by sovereign grace!" But it seems that she did not change so much as redefine herself; all her force of character was simply rechanneled into a Christian mode wherein the same activities that had been objectionable in a tramp now won praise. For example, the commentator tells us that in her "latter years" she took religious tracts along "while performing her usual journeys." That is, her restlessness and "natural impatience"—the desire to move that many vagrants feel—had at last found an acceptable outlet, through a kind of sleight-of-hand that bespeaks a character whose strength lies in flexibility. In Saxby's case the denial of her own strengths was a useful subterfuge that let her take on a conventional role without betraying her needs. Other women have been more rigid, or more trapped, and their denials of themselves accordingly more destructive.

The Nineteenth Century in Britain and the United States

The poor rates rose rapidly in the first years of the nineteenth century, and the desire to curb this expense led in 1834 to a Poor Law reform that established two principles of relief that lasted into the twentieth century.[1] The first, the "workhouse test," abolished what was known as outdoor relief (that given in people's homes), forcing those who wanted relief to go into the workhouse (indoor relief) as a "test" of real necessity—since no one would go into it otherwise. The second was the idea of "less eligibility," set forth by a royal commission in these words: "The condition of the person on poor relief 'shall not be made really or apparently so eligible as the situation of the independent labourer of the lowest class.'" Since many wages were below subsistence already, this meant that relief *on principle* "was to provide below-subsistence living."[2]

In the mid–nineteenth century the increasing number of vagrants who began using the workhouses "as hotels" led to the introduction of the casual ward, a separate part of the workhouse reserved for transients ("casuals"—purportedly laborers looking for work), who spent at most a few nights there.[3] These institutions were designed to be as unpleasant as possible—even more uncomfortable than the workhouse—in order to discourage people from using them, and as a consequence most of those on the road went there only as a last resort. Because no one could return to any one casual ward before thirty days had passed, the tramps who used them had to keep moving. Their floating life, broken by occasional periods of agricultural labor, changed little over time; Mary Saxby's description of its continual movement and convergence on certain areas for the hay and hop harvests is virtually identical to that given by George Orwell in *Down and Out in Paris and London*, over 150 years later.

AMERICAN RELIEF POLICY AND THE FAMILY ETHIC

American poor relief took its departure from the British system but developed a distinct character of its own. While importing "all of the English features that stigmatized the stranger as criminal or dangerous," the colonies made their own settlement and vagrancy laws even harsher, using them to exclude unacceptable people from obtaining settlement and the right to public assistance that went with it. Until 1969, when residency requirements for relief were declared unconstitutional, many homeless Americans had no settlement rights, existing "in a kind of geopolitical limbo where no jurisdiction was responsible for their care."[4]

At the same time, the prevailing ideology that women's proper place was exclusively within the home meant that homeless women, who by definition violated this norm, were judged for not being part of a conventional family. The use of welfare policy in the United States to support and stabilize the family as the linchpin of the social order has only underscored the deviance of the single homeless woman. Since the seventeenth century, in fact, conformity to this "family ethic" has been the major criterion for determining which women deserve relief and which do not; its pernicious effect persists today.[5]

Attempts to deny relief to transient strangers—as opposed to the local, resident poor—go back to the earliest days of the American colonies. In seventeenth-century Massachusetts, each town was responsible for supporting its own poor. As a result strict rules were established to regulate who could settle in or even enter a town; anyone town officials thought likely to need public assistance could be ordered ("warned") out. These controls were directed specifically at immigrants, who often arrived ill and needed to be supported. Local poor people received outdoor relief in their own homes or were boarded with families at the town's expense.[6]

The eighteenth century brought a great increase in the number of transient poor. These were probably mostly young and single, perhaps former indentured servants whose terms were up.[7] In some towns a third to a half of the paupers were women: young unmarried mothers, divorced or abandoned wives, and older widows. Except for widows, women without husbands "had a more difficult time proving their self-sufficiency and convincing town officials of their moral character" and thus were less able than other transients to satisfy the rules of settlement. Not only was their ability to earn a living and hold property limited; but also, because they did not comply with the colonial prescription that a woman should be a wife and mother, they were considered undeserving, not "real" women, and were denied settlement.[8]

Widows too were often denied settlement and sent "traveling from town to town."[9] Even in these Puritan communities, old people could not count on their children for support. "Even families did not always care for their own relatives who were in need. Wenham and Beverly had to negotiate a contract in order to force a nonresident son to care for his widowed mother. Also, the overseers of the poor of Marblehead petitioned the court of general sessions of the peace in 1752 to force the relatives of two 'aged' women to care for them." On the other hand, the law was not always inhumanly adhered to. When nonresident widow Mercy Fiske "entered Wenham without permission of the Selectmen in 1694, they nevertheless paid for a doctor and nurse to care for her."[10]

From the practice of paying town residents with public funds to take in the indigent, a "farming-out" system developed in the eighteenth century whereby the poor person's services were auctioned off to the resident who offered to charge the town least for room and board. The bid depended on how much work the pauper seemed able to do and how little she or he could be fed.[11] In the late eighteenth century, "the notion that those dependent on public aid ought to work for it was institutionalized in the workhouse and the poor farm."[12]

The evolution of relief policy in the nineteenth century was shaped by a distinctively American individualism, which defined poverty "as a moral condition," the result of "individual weakness and inferiority." Whereas in other nations "some residue remained of earlier Christian teachings that poverty was a blessing that should inspire charity in the rich and meekness in the poor, poverty in the United States came to be regarded as 'the obvious consequence of sloth and sinfulness.' "[13]

The prevailing attitude was expressed by a mid-century editorial in a Newburyport, Massachusetts, paper: "We declare it a vice and a sin for a man to be poor, if he can help it." The cause of poverty was "not a want of means, but a want of will—of real manliness and self-control."[14] As a fault not of the social system but of the individual, poverty was thought to be closely connected to criminality, insanity, and other types of defects, so that all deviant members of society were lumped conceptually into a single undifferentiated group whose features defined what one 1880 commentator referred to as "the morphology of evil."[15]

The practical consequence of this ideology was that the workhouses and poor farms (where the paupers were supposed to contribute to their support by working the land) "became places of punishment for the 'idle,' the 'vagrant,' and the drunkard as well as for the thief. . . . In a few large towns, the unemployables were put in almshouses, the able-bodied were sent to workhouses, and the criminals were kept in jails or houses of correction. Elsewhere, they were thrown in with widows, children, the aged, the sick and the insane."[16]

Not surprisingly, it was assumed that simply giving relief to poor people encouraged idleness and destroyed character, and that welfare officials must distinguish between the "worthy," or truly needy, poor and the able-bodied poor, who could work but tried to avoid it.[17] Reformers sought to make assistance contingent on entering an almshouse or poorhouse, where the able-bodied could be made to work. Private charities focused on the distinction between "worthy" and "unworthy" poor women, often refusing help to unmarried mothers, abandoned wives, and even widows who were judged intemperate or promiscuous, or who lived "in a disreputable neighborhood."[18]

After the turn of the century some states passed laws providing for monthly payments to help support the children of "worthy" women. The only other poor people considered deserving of relief were the aged and blind, and by 1934 only twenty-eight states provided assistance to these. "The refuge of most of the aged poor—and of the blind—remained the poorhouse."[19]

What assistance was given by government and private charities went almost exclusively to whites and often only to Anglo-Saxons. Black women were largely excluded from relief; both before and after the Civil War, African-Americans cared for each other, through churches, taking needy people into families, and forming charitable societies. Poor free black women in antebellum New York City, for example, got help from the Mother Society of New York, an organization founded by black women.[20]

Although transients got no relief, local jails or police stations in larger cities provided temporary lodgings for them. The nature of these facilities varied from place to place. New York City's police lodging rooms, before they were closed in 1896, were "vile dens, in which the homeless of our great city were herded, without pretence of bed, of bath, of food, on rude planks."[21] Subsequently the city set up municipal lodging houses to serve the homeless. Other large cities had similar shelters, although not all provided them for women.

Despite the growth of terrible slums in nineteenth-century American cities, and the centuries-long existence of equally terrible slums in England, in both countries substantial sections of the poor population remained unknown and mysterious to the middle class. Homeless women, moreover, were perceived through the screen of the nineteenth-century version of the family ethic, which established the home as a separate feminine sphere where women both functioned as moral guardians of society and were themselves protected from the dangers that existed in the world outside. This "cult of domesticity," as it has also been called, identified "womanhood" so closely with "home" that by implication women who were not in homes were not "true women."[22] This ideology forms the context of nineteenth-century writing about homeless women and particularly illumines the ease with which they were identified with prostitutes.

Underlying the comments of middle-class observers of the working- and lower-class milieus of the homeless is a sense of the dangers posed by the city to women who were not sheltered in a home but ventured alone into city streets. In nineteenth-century New York, for example, a respectable-looking workingwoman who simply went out alone could be taken for a prostitute or at least assumed to be "issuing a sexual invitation."[23] Other women figure as innocents ensnared by scheming men into sexual immorality. Once "fallen," such a woman became a menace to society, "synonymous with the degradation of morals and public health," a source of infection of the middle class.[24] The existence of a population of promiscuous women would lead, as one British reformer put it, straight to the "decay of manhood and the family."[25]

Grounded in fear of uncontrolled female sexuality, the family ethic shapes even sympathetic accounts of homeless women. One such is Henry Mayhew's four-volume account of the London poor at mid-century, based on his personal investigations. It documents "a large body of persons, of whom the public had less knowledge than of the most distant tribes of the earth—the government population returns not even numbering them among the inhabitants of the kingdom."[26] Other accounts were created by the voluntary charitable societies that appeared in American cities in the first half of the nineteenth century, founded and staffed by middle- and upper-middle-class women. Personal contact with poor and deviant women led these volunteers to perceive these women's human individuality, to see how social forces rather than personal inadequacy had created their poverty, and at length to perceive the "fragility" of their own seemingly secure position. As time went on, they moved further and further from the simplistic devotion to the "worthy" poor with which they had begun to the point of creating institutions to care for prostitutes and female ex-convicts, despite the "vitriolic opposition" of much public opinion.[27] The case histories they wrote are vivid and personal, describing the precarious lives of those who lived in the urban underworld of the destitute.

URBAN POOR AND HOMELESS WOMEN

This underworld contained various levels; its members pursued a range of activities that furnished a bare subsistence sometimes, but not always, one step removed from outright homelessness—activities that were rare in American cities for at least a generation but that began to reappear in the 1980s as the homeless population grew. The woman I once saw selling packets of needles outside Gimbel's department store in Manhattan for "whatever you want to give me" was (like the Dwelling Place woman who sold flowers) following the tradition of past sisters who offered pins, cakes, apples, matches, flowers, and many other commodities on the streets of New York and London.[28] Like hers, their selling was often simply a respectable form of begging.

The poor of London, especially, engaged in an extraordinary variety of ingenious modes of maintaining life. Over centuries an intricately elaborated social structure had evolved in which every occupation, even the most degraded, had its own tradition and sense of its rights. Many people who would otherwise have been forced to become beggars or prostitutes were able instead to take part in this complex street economy. Mayhew's reports of their lives and their feelings about themselves both reveal a style of life undreamt of by those who are comfortably off and allow us to see the incredible sacrifices people will make to preserve their sense of integrity.

The women who existed just this side of total destitution were generally either street sellers or street finders, as they were called. Mayhew explains that selling in the street was the last recourse of women who had failed at charing or needlework or were too feeble for anything else. Widows, "if they are young and reckless, . . . become prostitutes; if in more advanced years, or with good principles, they turn street-sellers; but this is only when destitution presses sharply." Certain categories of items—light to carry and cheap to stock—were reserved by custom for the old and poor. These included "watercresses, lucifers [matches], pincushions, ballads, . . . pins and needles, stay-laces." Irish women sold fruits and vegetables; one branch of this trade consisted of "the sale of 'refuse,'" or damaged pieces, by "middle-aged and elderly" widows and spinsters. Another specialty of old women was sheep's trotters (boiled sheep's feet, eaten by poor people). All these women earned only a few pence a day, enough to pay for a miserable room or part of a room and for a diet of bread and tea, with occasionally a herring. A blind woman who sold tapes, pins, and cotton thread lived in a ten-foot-square room whose rent was one shilling a week; she had a lodger, a woman who sold bootlaces, who slept with her and paid sixpence of the rent. The blind woman's fourteen-year-old son and a dog also lived there.[29]

The finders—forebears of the homeless who today collect bottles and cans for redemption—got their living picking up rags, bones, cigar ends, and "pure" (dog's dung, so called from its use in purifying leather). Although male pure finders had been in existence for twenty to thirty years at the time of Mayhew's investigation, before then the trade belonged exclusively to old women, who carried a covered basket to hold the pure, which they sold to tanyards. An old woman pure finder living in a dark room at the top of a tiny house told Mayhew:

> "I could never bear the thought of going into the 'great house' [workhouse]; I'm so used to the air, that I'd sooner die in the street, as many I know have done. I've known several of our people, who have sat down in the street with their basket alongside them, and died. . . . I'd sooner die like them than be deprived of my liberty, and be prevented from going about where I liked."[30]

Some old women were "mud-larks," finders who scavenged on the bank of the Thames at low tide, collecting pieces of rope, bits of iron, wood, coal, bones, and copper nails to sell.[31] Others might be crossing sweepers, blind musicians, or, if slightly better off, belong to one of many other similar occupations.

For younger women, employment was difficult to obtain, hard to endure, and unreliable. The members of the New York voluntary societies observed that women who could not find work as domestics or needleworkers—or who lost the positions they had—were reduced to begging, prostitution, or the poorhouse. In both countries the lowness of wages (much lower for women than for men) kept most working women close to starvation, especially if they had children to support; the piecework rates for needlework were so low that women working twelve hours a day could not support their families. Many of the younger ones therefore supplemented their earnings with part-time prostitution.[32]

Women might be made destitute by the death or desertion of their husbands; with no means of support, unable to pay rent, they were evicted. Some sent their children out to beg to avoid this. Many immigrant women arrived in New York penniless and often pregnant as well (having been sent over by charities or "public bodies" trying to get rid of them). Unable to find work, they became prostitutes.[33] Alcoholism was responsible for much destitution and homelessness. Margaret Dye, describing the early work of the American Female Guardian Society (AFGS; founded in 1834 as the Female Moral Reform Society), tells how grief after her husband's death led a Mrs. Moore, whom he had introduced to a nightly "social glass," into full-fledged alcoholism. She ran away periodically from the family that employed her as a live-in seamstress to go on binges. At length they refused to take her back, though she showed up occasionally "filthy and sick," "famishing with hunger and cold," to beg for food.[34] Sarah Bennett, in her history of the first forty years of the AFGS, tells of a "girl . . . whose intemperate mother turned her out of doors at 10 o'clock one Sunday night, and told her never to return, because she refused to purchase liquor for her." Other children were abandoned to vagrancy by alcoholic parents; they might then be picked up by the police and sent west to the "Farms," unless the procurers got to them first. Girls as young as twelve were bribed to "frequent the theatre" or induced to enter brothels unknowingly.[35]

PROSTITUTION

The fate a homeless woman in New York could anticipate was a vagrancy arrest, followed by time in prison and then the street again; the poorhouse if she was old; or, if young enough, being shipped out to the poor farms.[36] Thus it is not surprising that desperate girls and women turned to prostitution. Dr. William Sanger, whose 1858 study of prostitution in New York was based on questionnaires answered by 2,000 prostitutes, reports that 525 of them became prostitutes because of destitution. (The rest had jobs and still became prostitutes, presumably because they could make more money that way.) Bad treatment of domestic servants (leading them to run away) and the insufficient wages paid to needleworkers—plus the virtual impossibility of finding any other kind of employment—were the major reasons for the large number of prostitutes in the city. Young country women might wind up as prostitutes either after they had been abandoned by a lover whom they followed to the city or because they were attracted by the independence and financial rewards prostitution offered.[37]

In London similar causes operated, with the addition of great promiscuity in the cheap lodging houses, where children of both sexes slept several couples to a bed.[38] Young girls were thus drawn into lives of prostitution and vagrancy as companions to boy tramps. The Victorian hysteria over prostitution, however much it may have derived from repression and hypocrisy, had some real basis in the extraordinary number of such women, which increased with every industrial depression or financial panic. A New York newspaper article of 1858 described young prostitutes in London: "The streets swarm with drunken and foulspoken young girls—often mere children; and when I say swarm, I mean that you have to push your way to get through them."[39]

Most of these young prostitutes remained on the street only four to five years. In England they were subsequently likely to marry or find a job. Although Sanger asserts that a fourth of the prostitutes of New York died every year, usually in their early twenties, from venereal disease, the effects of alcohol, and abuse from men, other sources indicate that some managed to move back into respectable society. In 1849 the New York City Almshouse commissioners reported that one in five found a "way of earning an honest livelihood." Others married.[40]

Many who survived to become old, however, faced a horrifying fate. Although young prostitutes might be able to lead far more comfortable lives than "honest" workingwomen, unless they were shrewd and saving businesswomen they, like the hetairai of Greece, ended their lives miserably. Mayhew gives a chilling description of one occupant of a small house where prostitutes lived:

> We went into another room, which should more correctly be called a hole. There was not an atom of furniture in it, nor a bed, and yet it contained a woman. This woman was lying on the floor, with not even a bundle of straw beneath her, rapped up in what appeared to be a shawl, but which might have been taken for the dress of a scarecrow feloniously abstracted from a cornfield. . . . She started up as we kicked open the door that was loose on its hinges, and did not shut properly. . . . Her face was shrivelled and faminestricken, her eyes bloodshot and glaring, her features disfigured slightly with disease, and her hair dishevelled, tangled, and matted. More like a beast in his lair than a human being in her home was this woman. We spoke to her, and from her replies concluded she was an Irishwoman. She said she was charged

nothing for the place she slept in. She cleaned out the water-closets in the daytime, and for these services she was given a lodging gratis.⁴¹

Elderly former prostitutes often wound up as servants in brothels, cleaning, sewing, and washing or performing services similar to that of one fifty-year-old woman Mayhew talked to. Her job was to follow the "dress-lodgers," or prostitutes given their fancy clothes by the keepers of the brothels where they worked, to make sure they did not decamp with the clothes or take men to another house. She said, "I'm a drunken old b—— if you like, but nothing worser than that. I was once the swellest woman about town, but I'm come down awful. And yet it ain't awful. I sometimes tries to think it is, but I can't make it so. If I did think it awful I shouldn't be here now; I couldn't stand it. But the fact is life's sweet, and I don't care how you live."⁴²

A number of old women continued as prostitutes, though, like their counterparts in ancient Athens, they had to operate on the lowest level, as streetwalkers. Mayhew, who usually manifests considerable sympathy for the people he interviewed, does not hide his distaste at the thought of sexuality in old women:

> We come now to treat of the lowest class of prostitutes—those old women of the town who prowl about the thoroughfares and main streets, chiefly in the evenings and at midnight. . . . Many of them resort to "bilking" for a livelihood, that is, they inveigle persons to low houses of bad fame, but do not allow them to have criminal dealings with them. . . . While in these houses they often indulge in the grossest indecencies, too abominable to be mentioned, with old grey-headed men on the very edge of the grave. Many of these women are old convicted thieves of sixty years of age and upwards. Strange to say, old men and boys go with these withered crones, and sometimes fashionable gentlemen on a lark are to be seen walking arm in arm with them, and even to enter their houses.⁴³

Similar were the "Park Women," who frequented the parks in the evening when it was too dim to see clearly. One Mayhew spoke to was a curate's daughter who had been seduced by the son of the family for which she worked as governess. She discovered that their marriage ceremony had been false only after her "husband" had killed himself because of debt. She took up with another man and then another, and eventually became a prostitute. After contracting a disease that severely disfigured her face, she was reduced to working in the park at night: "She would not go to the workhouse, and she could get no work to do. . . . No one would take her into their service, because they didn't like to look at her face, which presented so dreadful an appearance that it frightened people."[44]

CHARITY AND "REFORM"

In both London and New York there were institutions for "penitent Magdalens"; but the number of women these could help was insignificant, and their heavy emphasis on repentance and reformation made them unattractive to many besides. Mayhew's park prostitute "knew all about the Refuges. She had been in one once, but she didn't like the system; there wasn't enough liberty, and too much preaching, and that sort of thing; and then they couldn't keep her there always; so they didn't know what to do with her. . . . She could not live long, and she would rather die as she was."[45]

The lack of appeal of being "saved" emerges from the charity workers' own descriptions of their work. The AFGS, for example, spent much time and energy investigating the "worthiness" of those who sought assistance. Worthiness was determined by traditional criteria: Caroline Kirkland, writing of the Home for Discharged Female Convicts, opened in 1845 by the women of the New York Prison Association (founded in 1844), asserts that the former prisoners showed by their willingness to submit "to our strict rules" and by "docility and obedience the sincerity of their desire to reform." An 1846 editorial in the *Advocate of Moral Reform*, the journal published by the AFGS, says that the "misfortune, innocence and helplessness" of "the virtuous poor . . . renders them worthy."[46]

Although one reason for this emphasis on worthiness was the influence of the family ethic, another was the need to reassure a disapproving public. "Fearing their unprecedented activities would call forth hostility and derision, women in early voluntary associations aided the least 'socially offensive' members of their sex."[47] But the imposition of such standards could also have been based—whether consciously or unconsciously—on the additional recognition that it would be virtually impossible for the newly reformed or rescued to get along in nineteenth-century society without meeting them. The options available all required exactly such "worthy" behavior; although there were some small-scale attempts to set up facilities for needleworkers that paid decent wages, generally only domestic service or factory jobs in the country were open to these women. Bennett's description of the AFGS's successes leaves a chilling awareness of what many a young woman's sense of her fate in life must have been. Young widows with children, for example, were helped to find work in "farmers' families at low wages, where they can support themselves and children much more comfortably than in any other way. The accounts from them have been, almost without exception, favorable. Women of this class are more likely to appreciate good homes, and strive to give satisfaction to their employers."[48] One can hardly blame Sarah Bennett for subscribing to this standard, at a time when all women were expected to "strive to give satisfaction"; at the same time a modern reader does not share the volunteers' disapproval in those cases where the object of charity obstinately refuses to recognize the virtues of the situation chosen for her.

Margaret Dye, for example, recounts the history of Ellen, the illegitimate child of an Irish "lady of rank" and a man employed in her father's house. Ellen was brought up by a wet nurse until this woman began to blackmail the father, who then found a man to bring Ellen to New York, where he "placed her with a poor, degraded family, who . . . used her very badly." She was twelve.

At last she ran away and went to an employment agency, which sent her unknowingly to a brothel; but fortunately she was so puny and sick-looking that the madam would not accept her. She then asked help at random in the street of an AFGS member, who got Ellen apprenticed to her own sister as a servant. Patience and careful training resulted in much improvement in Ellen's "many wrong traits of character."

Two years later, Ellen, now quite pretty, cut her hand, which was treated by a neighbor not known by her family. During two weeks of daily visits the neighbor, who though appearing "quiet and respectable" was actually "leading a life of infamy," attempted to lure Ellen into it by praising her beauty and telling her she " 'was *too handsome* to be brought up a servant, and especially as an *apprentice*;' 'that the control of her employer was cruel and oppressive,' and that she had 'better run away,' for her 'face would procure for her the life of a lady.' " Ellen told her employer about this and thus was saved, for the moment. Another time, however, she was accosted in the public garden near her home outside the city by a young woman who, "availing herself of Ellen's unhappiness because she was apprenticed, . . . commented largely upon her folly in remaining so, when by one simple effort she might '*be free!*' " She got Ellen to promise to run away and "meet her in the city." The meeting place was a brothel, but when Ellen mentioned her employer, the madam, afraid of getting into trouble, sent for the police, and Ellen eventually was returned home.

Some years later she was placed with a dressmaker to learn a trade; but instead of training her the woman made her do housework. Her benefactors being away, Ellen had no one to appeal to, so she ran away again—"a step by-the-way which she was partly induced to take by her old unwillingness to remain as a *servant*, a repugnance she could never overcome." An employment agency sent her to a factory in a nearby city. "She learned readily, and in a few weeks could earn considerable more than her expenses, . . . and enjoyed very much the new feeling of independence which her circumstances inspired."

Ellen's story has a fairy-tale ending. She became the maid of a rich French widow who eventually adopted her; in the end she married a rich Frenchman. Dye intimates, however, that this was luck and that Ellen's lack of humbleness and unwillingness to accept her "place," which put her constantly in danger, by rights ought to have brought her to ruin. Dye seems basically to feel that Ellen did not deserve what she got and tries to make it palatable by dwelling on Ellen's subsequent humility in a meeting with her former benefactress.[49]

From this and other cases recounted by Dye and Bennett emerges a sense of constant precariousness: the ever-present danger of losing one's place in society, even one's connection to it, by deviation from a narrow norm. A poor woman who was proud would be automatically close to making herself an outcast. The knowledge that there was indeed no place—in every sense—for nonhumble women in the world around them may well have lain behind the urgency of the volunteers' attempts to "reform" those they helped. But such reform involved denial of basic needs—for affection, for sex, for self-realization. It was natural enough that the upper- and middle-class ladies of the voluntary societies, themselves trained in the self-abnegation mandated by the contemporary ideal of woman as pure, fragile, domestic, and passive, could offer no "place" that would satisfy women like Ellen, in whom consciousness of these needs survived.[50]

Ellen's fate was not typical; a case history from Kirkland's book about the home for discharged prisoners illustrates another possibility. Margaret, aged nineteen when she came to the home, as a child had learned to fight from her parents, who "would hold a handkerchief between her and another girl, and encourage them to beat and bruise each other over it. She worked in the field, and 'did as much work as three boys,' as her father said—and in time became very strong. When she was fourteen, her father advised her to go and get her living without work—instructing her at the same time how she might do so. This she refused, and left home, working out as a servant."

Having beaten another girl badly in a fight, she was sent for two weeks to jail, where she met five men waiting to be sent to prison. Their cell was directly below hers, "and she conversed with them through a stove-pipe."

> Feeling very sorry for them, she was persuaded to assist them to escape, which she accomplished by dislodging a large stone—a feat requiring more than masculine strength. She did not herself accompany them, as she had but a few days to stay;—but a boy who was also confined to the jail, being angry because she would not allow him to go with them, he having but a week or two to stay, betrayed her, and she was tried and condemned to the State Prison for two years. Behaves very well, though of very high temper, and somewhat given to mischief in a small way. Has a good deal of humor and a large share of sensibility, and persists in thinking the helping of five poor fellows "out of such trouble," a praiseworthy deed.[51]

Margaret's case exemplifies a more likely outcome when a strong personality functions according to its own value system without the support of money or social position: it becomes defined as criminal. In fact, virtually the only way a poor woman who was not lucky like Ellen or able to turn a trick like Mary Saxby's could lead an independent life was as a prostitute or a criminal. Of course such an independence was itself circumscribed, and the ultimate consequences were usually ghastly, but the lure of self-determination could be powerful enough to overcome the worst drawbacks.

The Twentieth Century
through the Depression

Living conditions for the poor worsened during the rest of the nineteenth century. Periodic depressions—and, in the United States, continuing im-migration—increased unemployment and kept wages low. Many people who became homeless built shantytowns out of scrap materials on the peripheries of cities.[1] Others lived in slum areas. Jacob Riis's descriptions of the "other half" in New York (1890) and Jack London's of the "people of the abyss" in London (1903) show how the poor, after a life of struggle to survive, were irresistibly doomed to a starving old age.

An account by Riis of a group of New York's female "professional tramps" being routed out of a "stale-beer dive" during a midnight police raid is steeped in revulsion. The squad "groped its way in single file through the narrow rift between slimy walls to the tenements in the rear. Twice . . . we stumbled over tramps, both women, asleep in the passage. They were quietly passed to the rear, receiving sundry prods and punches on the trip, and headed for the station." The police then broke into a cellar room:

> Grouped around a beer-keg that was propped on the wreck of a broken chair, a foul and ragged host of men and women, on boxes, benches, and stools. Tomato-cans filled at the keg were passed from hand to hand. In the centre of the group a sallow, wrinkled hag, evidently the ruler of the feast, dealt out the hideous stuff. A pile of copper coins rattled in her apron, the very pennies received with such showers of blessings upon the giver that afternoon; the

faces of some of the women were familiar enough from the streets as those of beggars forever whining for a penny, "to keep a family from starving."[2]

One "peculiar variety of the female tramp-beggar," Riis says, was the "scrub," who frequented "the low groggeries of the Tenth Ward" and did the Sabbath chores for orthodox Jews forbidden to work on that day. "The pittance she receives . . . buys her rum for at least two days . . . at one of the neighborhood 'morgues.'" For the other four days she begged. One "distillery" was raided "because the neighbors had complained of the boisterous hilarity of the hags over their beer, [and] thirty-two aged 'scrubs' were marched off to the station-house."[3]

Riis does not say where the "scrubs" came from; but Jack London's sympathetic eye discerned one process by which such homeless, unattached women would come to find their only solace in alcohol. He recounts a life history repeated in the thousands in London and that applied equally well to New York; though in both cases a variety of other causes—parental alcoholism, illness, or death—were just as likely to make a child homeless: A couple married and lived in one room. Their income did not increase, but their family did, and the added expense meant they could never move into larger quarters.

> There is not room in which to turn around. The youngsters run the streets, and by the time they are twelve or fourteen the room-issue comes to a head, and out they go on the streets for good. The boy, if he be lucky, can manage to make the common lodging-houses, and he may have any one of several ends. But the girl of fourteen or fifteen, forced in this manner to leave the one room called home, and able to earn at the best a paltry five or six shillings per week, can have but one end. And the bitter end of that one end is such as that of the woman whose body the police found this morning in a doorway in Dorset Street, Whitechapel. Homeless, shelterless, sick, with no one with her in her last hour, she had died in the night of exposure. She was sixty two years old and a match vendor. She died as a wild animal dies.[4]

As a socialist, London laid the blame for the existence of homelessness and prostitution on the organization of society under industrial capitalism. By the late nineteenth century, Progressive-era American reformers had also come to consider poverty the "result of 'social evils'" outside individual control, although their proposals were generally aimed at ameliorating the worst abuses without affecting the economic structure of society.[5] In England Mary Higgs, a Christian missionary who ran a small shelter for destitute women in London, similarly described how economic pressures were creating a new class of homeless men and forcing into prostitution many women who could not find work. However, she remarks, because of "class prejudice . . . all homeless wanderers, from whatever cause, are lumped together as 'vagrants.' "[6]

Higgs based her conclusions largely on her own experiences tramping through various towns and cities to find out what options a homeless woman had. Her account and that of Ada Chesterton, who did the same thing twenty years later in London, are intensely personal, specifically feminine reactions to conditions on the street as no mere observer can understand them—in Chesterton's case constituting a real identification with the homeless prostitutes, match vendors, unwed mothers, occasional charwomen who lived a drifting, outcast street life. While Higgs, around 1905, made a series of three-to-five-day excursions in different parts of the country, Chesterton launched herself penniless from Euston Station into London one night around 1925 "to see what would happen if I started from zero with nothing but my personality to stand on. . . . I proved beyond the shadow of a doubt that for a woman to get employment, in any recognised calling, without reference or status of some sort, is tragically impossible."[7]

FACTORS PERPETUATING HOMELESSNESS

The women Higgs and Chesterton met had become homeless through death, illness, bad luck, or a rent increase that forced them out of their lodgings. A severe housing shortage prevented them from getting a new place even if they had work, and they had to live in cheap lodging houses or charity shelters. The women in a Salvation Army shelter where Chesterton stayed one night were workers in "slop shops" (where cheap, ready-made clothing was produced), street sellers, charwomen, and out-of-work dressmakers or fur workers. All belonged "to a floating population, without home or habitation, living from hand to mouth, sleeping how and when and where they can." The woman in the bed next to her worked in a slop shop. She had rented two rooms with her husband and three children, but he had been killed in the war, and she and the children lost the apartment. The children were "at an institution in the country"; she had believed she would get them back but now had given up hope. Women who lost their husbands but, unlike her, had no way of earning a living turned to professional begging, alternating "between the streets, the cheaper doss [lodging] houses, the casual ward and prison." They too lost their children to the authorities.[8]

One woman Chesterton met at a lodging house typifies the homeless woman's street career. She wore two of everything and told Chesterton she had a flat of her own but had had to leave because her creditors were insisting on payment. Getting up in the morning, she started to cry. "'Aren't you well?' I asked. 'Oh, my dear,' she said, 'it's the walking about, the walking about. Day after day, it's always the same.'" Chesterton thought this woman had been a shop assistant or kept a lodging house. "One seemed to trace her steady declension, slipping from room to room, at a cheaper and cheaper rent, and always leaving something behind, until at last, her whole wealth on her back, she is faced with destitution." She will sell her spare clothes for food or shelter; then her boots will fall apart, the clothes she wears will get dirty, she will be unable to change her underwear and finally will collapse in the street. The police will send her to the workhouse or to prison. Soon she will be on the street again, walking.[9]

Higgs details further the fate of women caught between the conventional expectation that marriage would make their lives secure and the economic changes under industrialism that had weakened "the marriage bond" so that "destitute and deserted wives are common, cast-off sweethearts not a few; women derelicts abound." Once fallen into "the friendless state," finding it "terribly hard . . . to obtain any employment," such women underwent a "silent disintegration."

> By degrees everything that can be turned into money goes for food. What wonder that the poor soul, desperate at losing all that makes life worth having, easily yields to the man ever ready to "treat" her?
> . . . Suppose she resists drink, . . . and lives as a "charwoman," it is a most precarious existence, varying with the "times." Such women are taken "on" and sent "off" without compunction. . . . There are some few trades for destitute women hardly worth calling "trades," yet in some hand-to-mouth fashion thousands of solitary women exist, who are not idle, but try hard to "keep out of the house," so retaining their last possession—liberty![10]

Younger women saved themselves from the hardships of "respectable occupation" on the one hand and from destitution on the other through prostitution. Many prostitutes were former servants who had stayed out too late on their day off and were afraid to go back to face their employers. Others had been abandoned children. "Parents often cast off girls on very slight grounds," Higgs explains. "To turn a child into the street, if the girl is out of work or supposed to be idle or disorderly, is by no means uncommon." In such a case "it is easy to see how a little indecision, and the pressure of hunger, might anchor a girl to sin."[11] Chesterton, less disposed to moralizing than Higgs, rather admired the young prostitutes she met in London lodging houses: "The attitude of these young people toward sex cannot be described as immoral; nor is it immoral. It is the result of the will to live; they are unable to keep themselves in any other manner."[12]

Even more than to the lack of jobs and lowness of wages, Higgs ascribes the prevalence of prostitution to the lack of decent housing for single women. "The harlot," she says, "is the female tramp," her point being that the possibility of becoming a prostitute prevented many women from having to be tramps. This was why there were fewer female than male tramps; a survey in January 1905 found that only 9 percent of the vagrants relieved in casual wards were women.[13] For this reason fewer such facilities were built for women, and fewer lodging houses existed for them; but since it was this very lack of decent shelter that forced them to become prostitutes, the real number of homeless women remained in a sense invisible.

The only place a runaway servant could go was a private lodging house, whose residents were all prostitutes and so tended to lead her, by force of example and the absence of any visible alternative, down the same path. Many towns had no lodging house for women only, which meant that a single woman who needed shelter was exposed not only to prostitutes but also to solicitations or worse pressures from men staying at the same place. The houses ranged from those that were licensed and inspected by the government, where the better-off prostitutes and older women who had poorly paid but regular work stayed, to unlicensed "doss-houses," where the poorest street vendors and prostitutes, never sure if they could raise the few pennies for each night's lodging, could get a dirty bed. Such places were filthy, and the women had lice.

The Salvation Army and various other Christian groups ran private shelters, but the number of beds available was woefully inadequate. In fact there were too few beds of any kind, as Chesterton discovered one night when she had raised the price of a bed but could find one nowhere. At the bottom of the list was the casual ward, whose prisonlike restrictions and imposition of meaningless, tedious work—even more than its physical discomfort—led the homeless to "push endurance to an inhuman limit" before submitting to them.[14]

Furthermore, at the time Chesterton wrote there was only one casual ward for women in London. After World War I the other women's wards had been turned over to men, as "an outcome of the fear of the authorities that an ex–service man should be discovered bedless and starving in

the streets" and provoke tremendous middle-class criticism of the government. "Because no one cares what happens to the woman who is down
and out, . . . she is deliberately and specifically thrown to the dogs, that
Cabinet ministers may escape a whipping," Chesterton concludes indignantly. What was more, although the London County Council provided
excellent civic lodging houses for men, it refused to consider providing
similar ones for women. "Why should a woman, if she can pay, be compelled to sleep in a dirty bed when for the same price a man can get a
clean one?" Chesterton demands.[15]

Beyond aesthetics or comfort, however, the main objection both writers had to all these alternatives was that they were degenerative. Higgs
points out that the casual ward left people so physically deteriorated
(since it was hard to sleep there and the food was insufficient) that they
could not possibly get work, and in that sense it manufactured tramps.
And she and Chesterton lay great stress on the impossibility of staying
clean in lodging houses, a factor that both consider central to the inability to find work. Describing the terribly crowded and dirty conditions at
one house, where there was only one, public sink for both men and
women so that one could not undress to wash, Higgs comments, "Single
women frequently get shaken out of a home by bereavements or other
causes, and drift, unable to recover a stable position if once their clothing
becomes dirty or shabby." The discovery of how differently the world
regarded them once they no longer looked middle-class impressed these
two women deeply. "It is not likely that a woman will get employment
unless she has character [a written reference] and clothes," says Higgs.

> An unemployed man may obtain work at various occupations to which dirt is
> no hindrance, . . . but a woman must "look tidy," or no one will employ her.
> Therefore conditions destructive to cleanliness are for her equivalent to forc-
> ing her down lower and lower into beggary and vice. Once at a certain stage
> she cannot rise, "no one would have me in their house," say, rightly enough,
> poor miserable creatures with scarcely a rag to their back.

"Bedraggled garments," says Chesterton, "not only spell destitution, but
incapacity, dishonesty, and a total lack of sex morals."[16]

This issue may seem trivial, but it has decisively affected many (such
as the residents of the Brooklyn Women's Shelter described in the introduction and the woman Ann Marie Rousseau tried to help, described in
Part 1). Mayhew's informants mention it; a woman of thirty-three deserted by her husband, for example, told him: "I have so parted with my
things that I ain't respectable enough to go after needlework, and they do

look at you so. . . . If I could make myself look a little decent, I might perhaps gets some work."[17]

Higgs remarks on how vulnerable she became once she was dressed like a tramp: "I had never realised before that a lady's dress, or even that of a respectable working-woman, was a *protection*. The bold, free look of a man at a destitute woman must be felt to be realised."[18] Chesterton, who had great self-confidence, was a talented cook and assumed she could land a job as one, even without references, by sheer force of personality. She was outraged to discover that she was as much disregarded and brushed aside as the most pathetically incompetent or self-doubting derelict: "Neither the officials nor the individuals to whom I applied could persuade themselves that I was not a thief." As she and Higgs both discovered, the homeless woman was reduced to the image her clothes presented, in a much more radical way than was true for male vagrants. Chesterton comments that while the sight of a homeless man arouses compassion and the idea that something is wrong with society, a female vagrant arouses "distrust, if not hostility." Higgs adds, "I do not believe that even women from the higher ranks can well help drifting to destitution if from any cause friends and foothold are lost. Most people distrust a friendless woman. Yet in many cases it is a matter of clothes!"[19]

This discovery helps explain the ease with which middle-class women, once they had lost the essentially flimsy supports that maintained their social position, could fall through the holes in the social fabric. Mayhew gives a telling example in which the clothes principle operated in reverse, to save the woman from homelessness. Known as the "Lady Lurker" (a "lurk" was the ruse or trick a beggar used to induce people to give money), this woman was the daughter of a minister. She had been married to a schoolteacher, then a physician; after her second husband's death she "passed through various grades, till she is now a cadger. She dresses becomingly in black, and sends in her card . . . to the houses whose occupants are known, or supposed, to be charitable. She talks with them for a certain time, and then draws forth a few boxes of lucifers, which, she says, she is compelled to sell for her living."[20] Clearly this mode of survival depended entirely on her ladylike appearance. By contrast, women whose appearance and demeanor did not signal that they occupied their proper "place" might be unable to survive. For women, homelessness is not a function only of economics or of class but also of the image of Woman that a society holds, and thus is connected to the full scope of women's condition within that society.

WOMEN ON THE ROAD

Other homeless women were not city-bound. In England they were typified by Kitty Grimshaw, whom Chesterton met in the casual ward.

> Kitty has a strong, handsome face. She is over sixty, but quite upright, with a
> wealth of greyish hair and quick, humorous eyes. She is a most efficient
> woman and, as she told me, can plant a field of potatoes with any man, and is
> first on the list for a number of fruit-pickers. . . . She has been on the road for
> some eight years, driven there by that economic pressure which has dehoused
> so many women. She lived for some time in a room in Kennington, supporting
> herself by daily housework, with occasional incursions into a laundry.

This modern descendant of Mary Saxby lost her room because the landlord wanted more rent, and had been on the road since. She "does a regular round, returning to Southwark [the casual ward] as a central point"
every few weeks, tramping the roads "with her small stock of matches,
hairpins, etc.," refusing offers of sixpence to give a man "a love" because
she had a man in the navy, a bo'sun's mate from whom she was concealing the fact that she was a tramp. He wrote every few weeks, sending a
little money; Kitty paid an old lady sixpence a week to receive his letters.
Meanwhile she "believes confidently that her man is coming home to
marry her."[21]

The group of women Kitty belonged to constituted about a tenth of
the "tribe of men, tens of thousands in number, . . . marching up and
down England," whom George Orwell briefly joined during the twenties.
Originally, in Britain, the tramping system was based on the craft unions,
which provided information about work, as well as food and lodging, to
traveling tradespeople. After two hundred years this system fell apart under the pressures of industrial capitalism, which among other things
made business slumps no longer local but nationwide affairs that could
not be walked away from. Thus the old pattern of purposeful mobility
gave way to the aimless wandering of unemployed workers who could
find no work.[22]

Mixed in with them, however, were people who became tramps for
other reasons. Higgs felt that Pollie, a woman she met in a casual ward,
had chosen tramping, perhaps because her personality could not adapt
to the "docility and obedience" required of factory- or needleworkers:

> She knew the workhouses far and wide, and had had her tussles with the au-
> thorities. She had thrown her bread and cheese at a matron who gave her it
> after hard work, giving another woman a workhouse diet [i.e., a much better

one]. She had been in prison for "lip." She was, in fact, a tramp proper, and with a little drink and boon companions probably foul-mouthed and violent.[23]

More remarkable was a seventy-year-old woman Higgs met at the same ward. After her husband died, her son had supported her, until his workplace burned down, "and she lost her stay and was turned adrift."

> She had mother-wit enough to beg her way; people gave her tea and pence. She "paid her way" in tramp wards, taking in a little tea and sugar and "tipping" officials with a penny for hot water. . . . One thing remained to her—liberty—but to keep this she was forced to walk from town to town, sampling tramp wards. She had not done it long, but it was too much for her. One arm was too painful to be touched [she had rheumatism]; it was hard to put on her tattered garments; she provoked the wrath of officials by dilatoriness. Her legs were a study. Each leg was swathed in bandages, her feet wrapped in old stocking legs and bandaged, and men's boots put over all, a long—long process. . . . The one effect her wanderings had produced in her was a deadly hatred of workhouse officials.[24]

This woman was not unique. The fact that the workhouse, though hardly pleasant, was much more comfortable than the casual ward, and the food better and more plentiful, makes it all the more striking that many aged or handicapped people preferred to endure tremendous physical suffering on the road in order to avoid it. In the 1880s the mistress of the Marylebone workhouse told an old woman in the casual ward that she would "be much better off in the workhouse, to which the old lady replied that 'thank God she hadn't come down to *that* yet.'" A similar feeling must have motivated the solitary woman tramp whom Orwell encountered waiting for the ward at Lower Binfield to open. "She was a fattish, battered, very dirty woman of sixty, in a long, trailing black skirt. She put on great airs of dignity, and if anyone sat down near her she sniffed and moved farther off." One of the men called out to her to "'be chummy.' . . . 'Thank you,' said the woman bitterly, 'when I want to get mixed up with a set of *tramps*, I'll let you know.'" Orwell comments, "She was, no doubt, a respectable widow woman, become a tramp through some grotesque accident." "For freedom they sacrifice much," Higgs remarks; and, reviewing the alternatives facing women tramps—the tramp ward, prison, prostitution, and suicide—she makes their choice seem self-evident: "Yet life is sweet, and it is a pleasant thing to behold the sun. To be a beggar is best—spring stirs already—God opens hearts. Food and shelter may be begged as 'charity.' It is best to fall into the hands of God, not into the hands of man. The vagrant life is sweetest. This is how tramps are made."[25]

Industrialization also created a new type of migratory worker in the United States, but in a context that made him, briefly, a hero. For a long time the hobo tradition colored perceptions of skid-row alcoholic men, even though the hobo proper became virtually extinct by the end of the depression. Although quite a number of women were hobos, homeless women do not possess this tradition as part of a history, either in their own minds or in those of others. Thus, in a continuation of their typical state of existing outside accepted reality, they have always appeared in the United States as a shocking anomaly.

The hobo developed from the itinerant laborers who in the early nineteenth century formed a general-purpose mobile labor gang; they were canal diggers, railroad builders, river roustabouts, lumberjacks, farmworkers. Though the distinction between hobos and tramps was never very clear, in the American context *tramp* was a derogatory term that first came into use in the 1870s in reaction to a sudden increase in the number of mobile young men who lost their employment in the depression of 1873. Though most were simply working-class immigrants looking for work, they were perceived as lazy, dishonest, and menacing to ordered society.[26]

Hobo had more positive connotations. Hobos were flamboyant, aggressive workingmen "with a great sense of pride, self-reliance, and independence," often politically radical. They boosted their image in the literature they produced, including pamphlets, the *Hobo News*, and a number of books describing the lure of the road. This literature sees the hobo as the free man, possessed by a mystical wanderlust, seeking experience and adventure, as well as a hero of labor who built the industries that made America great. Two vignettes illustrate the essential components of his image. The first is by Glen H. Mullin, a middle-class university graduate who hoboed for a few months to see what "the Road" was like:

To the genuine hobo a train is a thing compounded of magic and beauty. . . . It arouses within him a latent mysticism. The rattle and swank of a long freight pulling out of the yards, the locomotive black and eager, shoving hard a snorting muzzle along the rails. . . . As the hobo sits on a tie-pile, perhaps, and watches her go by, there is a lure in the cars themselves individually.[27]

Could a woman have felt this drive to conquer and possess in the same mode of sublimated sexuality? I doubt it, especially since a female hobo needed constantly to control her sexuality in an objectified, externalized way: when she was not fending off rape, her body was often her working capital.

The second vignette is by Thomas F. Healy, a former hobo, who in 1926 described "Bar-Room Bill" for the *American Mercury:*

> Bar-Room Bill is symbolic. . . . He belonged to a more epic period, the classic days of hobodom that are passing. Sixty years old, a gaunt, gargantuan figure of a man, he stood six feet four in his boots, and his biceps were even yet as thick as another man's thigh. When the West was still the far frontier of high emprise, and mighty men were needed to do the deeds of mighty days, it was Bar-Room Bill and his brothers who cut down the forests, built the railroads and made the deserts bloom. But times changed, and Bar-Room Bill fell upon evil days. Big business came out [West]. . . . Thereafter Bar-Room Bill's disintegration was swift and tragic. . . . Today he is just a tramp on the highways.[28]

Through such imagery, whose components of power and positive action contrast sharply with the degraded, destructive sexuality that is the closest the homeless woman comes to having an image of power, the man on the road was elevated into folklore and myth. But women played no part in this mythology. Female hobos did exist but with an invisibility betokened by the habit many had of disguising themselves as men or boys.

Accounts of women on the road before the depression reveal a variety of types and backgrounds. Among the inhabitants of a tramp jungle in Pennsylvania in the 1870s were "old men, abandoned women, the wretchedest of wretched hags, young persons in the heyday of health and strength, and little children, prematurely old and shrewish."[29] But, overall, women were few. Of 4,310 tramps who applied for public aid in New York State in the winter of 1875–76, only 6.3 percent were women, and of these 19.9 percent were unmarried and 28.3 percent widowed or divorced; it appears then that most were on the road with their husbands, looking for work.[30] Before the Civil War, female "drifters" in the Philadelphia prison, house of correction, and almshouse were "foreign-born and in their twenties." After the war, they were "fewer and older, widows or victims of desertion."[31]

No doubt because women tramps were so uncommon, in 1880 the discovery of one was sufficiently noteworthy to rate equal treatment in the *Railway Age Gazette* (under the heading "Tramps") with a report of an attempted holdup by male tramps. The entire item reads: "A tramp, captured at Rahway, N.J., turned out to be a woman in man's clothes, and was handed over to the police." It is possible that the number of female tramps was somewhat larger than reports would indicate since those who were not caught would have been counted as men.[32]

Commentators seem to have been particularly disturbed by women dressing as men. A *New York Times* report from August 1902 pays more attention to this phenomenon than to the spectacular exploits of the woman in question: "'Jimmie' McDougall, the handsome leader of the large and dreaded band of marauders and tramps who have long been the terror of Monroe County farmers, is now safe behind the bars of a jail, and has turned out to be a woman." When discovered by police, "'Jimmie' was attired in white cloth shoes several sizes too large, blue overalls, and a red flannel shirt." It was after being put in a cell that she "broke down, and . . . disclosed her sex. . . . Her real name was Theresa McDougall," and she had been an actress in Cleveland. "Later she was married to . . . a stage carpenter, with whom she led a tempestuous life, finally running away. She adopted man's attire in order to beat her way from Cleveland to Rochester."[33]

In January 1901 the *Railway Conductor* denounced "the escapade of Susan Shelly of York Springs, Pa., who made her way from her home to Chicago, Illinois, disguised as a tramp, and riding in true hobo style in box and stock cars, clad in male attire." The article quotes a Philadelphia newspaper account:

> Miss Shelly . . . has posed variously as a homeless tramp, girl of education and refinement in search of work, a young author on the hunt of material for a book and a detective. Whenever possible she appeared in men's clothing.
> . . . Dressed in a ragged pair of trousers, blue flannel shirt and threadbare coat, she would slouch into a town in the typical hobo gait, and there levy on the citizens for food, clothing and money in the true tramp style. She delighted in having the police on her trail and seemed to get great enjoyment out of their peremptory orders to move on to another town.

The mayor of Harrisburg, having investigated her "queer case," stated that she "has no intention of violating any law, but that she is consumed by a desire to become famous."

The outrage of the *Railway Conductor* arises from a "full knowledge of the possibilities of a fate worse than death, which encompassed her on all sides," a knowledge (the editor chooses to assume) Shelly lacked; otherwise "she would have shrunk in horror from attempting" such an exploit. "We assume she is a lady," the editor says, "from the fact that she has long occupied a prominent place as a teacher and from her candid acknowledgment that the trip was made with the purpose of gathering matter for a book"; but, he points out, by dressing as she did she abrogated the rights and privileges of that status:

> Men in train service cannot, or do not conceive virtue traveling in a garb that would indicate only the lowest of creatures. Pity alone was perhaps the incentive which induced trainmen to permit her to remain upon their trains, but it is safe to say that they felt under no necessity of offering her any protection because of her sex. Thus it will be seen that she was wholly without protection, and, if possible, more obnoxious than the male hobo whom she impersonated.[34]

Note that her extra obnoxiousness lies in her having been "without protection"—that is, alone. Translating "protection" as control, one can see that what male clothing did was release her from the behavioral controls imposed by "ladyhood" and thereby break down the all-important distinction between "real" women and the other kind; this then prompts the familiar accusation that Shelly's act made her no better than a prostitute ("lowest of creatures"). The editor's anger arises from the concealment not so much of her femaleness (especially since it appears the trainmen knew she was a woman) as of her true status as a female. There is real horror behind the self-righteous justification of the likelihood that the trainmen unknowingly imposed their sexual urges on a "lady." When a man can no longer distinguish between ladies and low creatures, society itself is in danger; as the chatelaine in Michelet's Sorceress fable said on seeing that the witch wife had risen to rival her in status, "All rank and order is overset."

Thus men and women may perform the same acts, but to them society attaches radically different meanings. On the one hand, the image of the male tramp or hobo commonly involved forceful action and power (the hobo is a heroic worker, the tramp a menace) and (in the hobo's case) a sexual component sublimed into a form of noble conquest, with his personal erratic mobility blended into the nation's manifest destiny. The female tramp, on the other hand, is immediately and completely defined by her sexuality. Since the definition of *lady* includes passivity, any woman exhibiting power and forceful action (which naturally includes any woman wearing men's clothing) automatically belongs to the sphere of the "lowest creatures," a category that at least threatens society from outside instead of from inside. Thus while a male tramp has a certain place—as the images quoted above demonstrate—a woman has no place as a tramp unless she can be defined as a prostitute—that is, degraded and marginalized.

An insider's perspective on the early American "sisters of the road" is provided by Bertha Thompson—"Box-Car Bertha," whose autobiography was recorded by Ben Reitman. Thompson, who hoboed during the 1920s and 1930s, was a political radical for whom the problem lay in the society, not the hobo; she claims that there is not much difference between vagrants and the rest of us. "The upper classes have all the vices of the sisters of the road," but because they have money, they never have to go on the road or become public charges.[35] Thompson tends to glorify the hobos (she uses this term for everyone on the road); still, her account is a good counterpoint to the individual-pathology approach.

According to Bertha, women hobos "were still few enough in [the 1910s] to cause a little stir, even among the men hoboes." Most of those she met seemed to be agitators traveling on political work, often for the Industrial Workers of the World. But she also tells of "a small wiry grey-haired old woman" she met during the thirties who had been on the road for thirty years. She had grown up in a railroad division town, and "the trains going in and out . . . gave [her] the wanderlust."[36]

The "old hard-boiled sister of the road" was drawn to it by a desire for freedom; like the archetypal male hobo, she was independent and adventuresome. However, her reason for being there most often was less the unemployment or wanderlust that motivated men than a desire to escape some specific imprisoning situation; and she hit the road because poverty made it her only alternative. "At least half the women on the road," Bertha says, were from "broken homes"; the parents were divorced or dead and the girl had had to live with stepparents or with "aunts and uncles and grandparents." Others had been "paroled" from jails and mental institutions (Bertha gives no figures for the 1920s but claims that about 5 percent of the women on the road during the depression were mentally ill), and many others were from orphan asylums. "Shut up and held away from all activity, such girls have dreamed all their childhoods about traveling and seeing the world. As soon as they are released they take the quickest way to realizing their dreams, and become hobos." Others were escaping from the confinement of marriage. Bertha met one woman of forty-five who had been married twenty years and raised three children. "Two years before she had gotten fed up with the regularity of meals and Saturday night band concerts, and going to church, and had started out hitch-hiking." She had not lost her domesticity, however, and would spend a month at a time in a jungle cooking for the men there. Finally, some women were "just seized with wanderlust," like Bertha herself: "I am truly married to the box cars. There's something constantly itching in my soul that only the road and the box cars can satisfy."[37]

Like the men, women hobos congregated in Chicago, "their hobo center":

> They came in bronzed from hitch-hiking, in khaki. They came in ragged in men's overalls, having ridden freights, decking mail trains, riding the reefers, or riding the blinds on passenger trains. They came in driving their own dilapidated Fords or in the rattling side-cars of men hoboes' motorcycles. A few of them even had bicycles. They were from the west, south, east and north, even from Canada. . . .
>
> On arrival most of them were bedraggled, dirty, and hungry. Half of them were ill. There were pitiful older ones who had been riding freights all over the country with raging toothaches. . . . Some were obviously diseased, and most of them were careless about their ailments unless they had overwhelming pain.

While in town, some of these women worked periodically—doing housework or even office work—but most got money "by begging, stealing, and hustling," or from charitable organizations. In good weather, they slept in parks and washed in public restrooms.[38]

After food and money, the major issue for women on the road was dealing with men. Because of this problem women tended to travel in pairs, either with a man or with another woman. Some frankly hustled to get what they needed from men (many prostitutes Bertha knew in Chicago had started out as hobos); others simply "accepted the fact that it was easier for a woman to get along on the road if she was not too particular." Hitching was simple for women if they were willing to sleep with the men who picked them up, and this may be one reason why there were not that many women in the boxcars. Those who would not "come across" had a more difficult time, though a thirty-year-old woman named Sarah, who had been "bumming around the country, just to see things," for ten years, told Bertha that she didn't have to "take nothing off nobody" because she did housework in between trips and so always had money.[39]

WOMEN IN THE CITIES

There were still, of course, many homeless women in cities. Like Mayhew's informants, some aged poor women chose begging over the poorhouse. Others arrived on the street after a gradual descent typified by the history of two sisters from a cotton-mill family. Both married young but returned to live with their parents. One, partially crippled by polio, cared for their invalid mother while the other worked in the mill until the mother's death left them alone with their father, who was old and unable to contribute much support. Both sisters then worked in the mill, though they also needed social service assistance. When the one who was crippled became pregnant, she began using drugs to kill pain; her sister picked up the habit from her. In time neither could work, so the sister who was disabled, using her deformity, began to beg in the street. The other stayed home except to scavenge at the railroad and the dump. Unable to pay rent, they moved frequently; sent to the county asylum to kick the habit, they returned to it when released. They drank and were "suspected of immoral conduct. Finally they drifted into an old, condemned house known as the 'Free Brick.' No rent was charged in this house, and it was a settling basin for dope fiends and worn-out prostitutes of the poorest sort."[40] Almost two centuries had passed since the six women were found in the abandoned house in London.

Another group of women at risk of becoming homeless were those known as "women adrift," mostly young, both black and white, native-born and immigrant single women who migrated from the country around the turn of the century to find jobs in the cities. Living apart from family, they faced "stigmatization and discrimination." Because their aloneness was perceived "as a badge of sexual misbehavior," they were vulnerable to sexual exploitation by men. Their wages were below subsistence, being based on the assumption that all women lived in families; because of this, some became prostitutes.[41] The poverty of those who did not made them vulnerable when the demand for their labor that existed until 1930 dried up in the depression.[42]

The scarcity of accounts of mental illness among the homeless in this and earlier periods is due to the practice of permanently incarcerating such people. One case from Chicago, however, recorded in 1932, shows that a few such women did remain on the street.

> Mary Lou Jones has been sixteen years old since 1917, to our actual knowledge. It may be much longer, for we guess her real age at between forty-five and fifty years, in spite of old-fashioned pigtails over her shoulders, the Peter Thompson sailor-suit with yellow decorations, the low-heeled ankle-tied shoes and her own statement that she wished to earn her board and room in a family where she would have an opportunity to finish her highschool education.
>
> This longing to complete her education is a plea that has amazingly supported Mary Lou for fourteen years. Within the last few weeks it brought in seven dollars from the congregation of a struggling little church in one of our

poorer districts, where she must have made a most appealing talk. It once carried her as far as Tuskegee Institute, whence she was promptly returned to Chicago.

Mary Lou was one of a number of women with psychological problems who had "wandered around the city for years" but had remained invisible partly because they did not constitute a category recognized by social work professionals; in Chicago no provision existed for women over forty until the Service Bureau for Women was established during the depression.[43]

Some women went on and off the street in accordance with economic fluctuations. During a slump in 1914, the unemployed—both women and men—who slept on benches and begged shelter at police stations in Chicago included not only jobless workers arriving on freight trains but former residents of the black and foreign ghettos. When Bertha Thompson spent a night at the New York City Municipal Lodging House she met some of these immigrant and black victims of the economy:

> The bulk of them seemed old women. All about me were sagging, misshapen bodies, stringing grey hair, faces with experience written deeply in them, tired lusterless eyes. The average age . . . was between forty and fifty, but most of the women looked much older. Together they appeared all middle-aged, hardworking housewives. Certainly none of them looked like criminals. The majority were Irish and Irish-American. About ten percent were Negro, and there was a sprinkling of Polish, Lithuanian and English. A few showed signs of drink. A number appeared to be sisters of the road. All bore the marks of poverty.[44]

Half were widows; a fourth said their husbands had lost their jobs and they had been evicted; the husbands were in the men's side of the building. "When they got a job they would leave, and when it failed they came back." The next day Bertha went to a speakeasy with two of them; they joined a group of others, each of whom told how she got money for liquor. One begged from people she knew; one got change from stevedores who had worked with her husband; one did laundry; one was a prostitute; one, who was missing a foot, begged in the streets; and one peddled matches, collar buttons, and shoestrings. A group of professional beggars also in the bar made their livings by counterfeiting pregnancy or various sores and handicaps.[45]

One more type of urban homeless woman—kin to Orwell's "respectable widow woman" unable to accept her fate as well as to several women I met at the Dwelling Place—was described by a reporter "investigating the vagrants . . . young and old, male and female, white and black," who lived in the New York City subway in 1929. He noticed "a middle-aged woman dressed in clothes that were quite the style fifteen years ago. . . . 'I been seeing her a long time,'" an old man told him, "'but she won't talk, she won't. . . . Thinks she's a grand lady. But she's a bum same as we are, and she ain't got no business putting on any airs. At least I don't rummage in paper barrels.'"[46]

THE DEPRESSION

With the onset of the depression, the happy freemasonry of the road—to the extent that it existed—was submerged by a flood of desperate unemployed. In March 1933 a census carried out in 765 cities revealed an estimated total of about 1.25 million homeless people not in families, living on city streets, in shelters, shantytowns, or hobo jungles. (The census did not include people riding trains or hitching on highways.) Among them were perhaps 150,000 homeless women, and these were said to be undercounted by half. Since most cities had no shelters for women, agencies sent them to furnished rooms, so they were not reported to the census.[47]

Many people who became homeless managed to remain in their communities by building shantytowns ("Hoovervilles," as they were called).[48] But others took to the road. The history of most transients involved unemployment, followed by the loss of their home or by going on relief that was so inadequate it meant starvation unless some family members left. Yet although most social workers, public welfare officials, and other experts recognized that transients were no different from the general population, most of the public persisted in the traditional rejection of community responsibility for outsiders and distrust of strangers. Fears of crime and moral danger, associations with child-stealing gypsies, and the idea that transients were "naturally inferior people" combined with resentment in communities already taxed to the limit to support their local poor. Transients were refused relief and kicked out of communities or prevented from entering them in the first place.[49]

Like the hobos—who in their heyday had been heros but were "labeled deviant" once changing conditions on the frontier led to their being considered "unnecessary for the maintenance of the economy"—the transients were perceived not as victims of the economy but as outcasts.[50] Elizabeth Wickenden, who was acting director of the Transient Division of the Federal Emergency Relief Administration, recalled years later that not one of its 350 transient centers opened without violent protest from the community. "It bothered people that they were dislocated," she said. "This was disturbing."[51]

By the late 1930s social service professionals had begun to recognize the damage done by this attitude and its institutionalization in relief programs that isolated the transients from society. In 1937 Wickenden wrote that both the perception of the transient as a defective, needy individual and the romantic notion of the transient as a "'footloose adventurer,' the heir of our pioneer heritage," resulted in transients being branded as a "breed apart" from "other victims of the depression, . . . reinforcing in the public mind the belief that transiency was a 'social evil' requiring corrective 'therapeutic measures,' and adding to the stigma they already bore."[52]

Once they crossed the line into homelessness, the transients—only yesterday ordinary citizens, respectable working and even professional people—suddenly became the Unknown. Even to the social workers, who recognized the sources of homelessness, transients were "clients" who needed "care" and assistance in reintegrating into "regular community life."[53] Separated from society, transients lost their normal standing as citizens and the dignity that goes with it, just as homeless people do today.

Although concern about transients focused largely on men, commentators also expressed alarm at the phenomenon of homeless women outside families. Yet while the family ethic presumed their need for protection, it produced policies that often denied them any help at all. For example, another reason for the undercounting of women was that—in accordance with the fixed notion that women belonged in families—"the standard social work policy of the day" was to send unattached women home. Those who did not want to go avoided the private agencies and were therefore not counted. (Black women were undercounted because agencies would not take them at all; they were either rejected or did not bother to apply.)[54] As a result many women got no relief since most communities relied on the agencies or simply on overnight lodging in police stations to deal with transients; only large cities had municipal lodging houses where homeless women (including blacks, at least in New York) could get shelter.[55]

What was more, women's settlement rights might be tied to those of their husbands. In New York, for example, women who were abandoned or separated or had left their husbands but were not legally divorced were nevertheless considered to be settled wherever the husband was, or to have no settlement if he had lost his. Without settlement, all the agencies could do was try to send them to places they did not want to go to.[56]

Thus might a woman be led to the road. An estimate based on the 1933 census indicated that 5 to 10 percent of homeless people without families were women. Most were under thirty; according to another source, half were under twenty-one.[57] Of ninety thousand people taken off freights in Mobile, Alabama, by railroad detectives during six months in 1933, "some hundreds" were women. "One was an old woman of eighty-odd who had beaten her way from California. Some were young mothers with babies. Many were young girls. Most of them were drifting about trying to keep in a warm climate."[58] Bertha Thompson, who worked at a relief bureau for transient women in Alabama, says that "the applicants were the end-product of unemployment." They had lost jobs, been put off plantations, and cut off relief. They came in boxcars, hitching, walking, or in their own cars, trying to get to relatives in other states or someplace where the relief might be better.[59]

Forty years later a woman named Ellen recalled her own experiences on the road. A Radcliffe graduate unable to find a job, she "felt really suicidal" by the summer of 1934 and "had to get away from home." She hitched from Florida to Chicago. "I was arrested thirty-one times for vagrancy and put in all sorts of places to get me out of sight. Some of the cops, of course, just picked me up and dumped me on the edge of town. . . . They had their own unemployed so they didn't need me." Eventually she encountered a newspaper columnist who wrote about her; the resulting publicity produced offers to lecture around the country, "and I did, taking the line that young people looking for work were treated as criminals." When, six months later, she decided to go home, she had no trouble getting a job.[60]

Observers feared the "degeneration" of female transients—not just the loss of sexual "purity," but the possibility that women might become habituated to the road and turn into chronic bums.[61] Though these fears were not borne out in general, individual women might be shaken from their accustomed place and find an alternative so appealing that they were disinclined to return. One such transformation occurred in the case of a thirty-seven-year-old woman hobo interviewed around 1934 by Walter C. Reckless, a sociologist. Mrs. Metzger, as he calls her, had an eighth-grade education, was separated from her husband, and had worked in a semiskilled job for five years. She had been unemployed for two years before taking to the road, which she decided to do because "her savings were gone, . . . she could live cheaper on the road, . . . she wanted to travel, . . . to be free of her lover, . . . and . . . to be rid of the people who bothered her about her religion (she was a Seventh Day Adventist)."

Her life on the road resembled that of the pre-depression women hobos described by Thompson.

> She never had a female companion on the road. She has slept in the open, starved for days, ridden in box cars with as many as fifty men, camped out at night alone and with men. She has been attacked and raped on several occasions and has given in on several more. She has asked for food, clothes, and a chance to wash. She has shared food and money with men. But she has never begged for money, never stood in bread lines, and never taken money for sex. . . . All told, she has enjoyed her experiences.

"Yes, I am real happy on the road," Mrs. Metzger herself said. "I don't want any assaults, but outside of that I have been real happy. . . . It is pleasant to go from town to town. All my thirty-seven years I have never traveled." She felt that her "mind is more developed" as a result of her experiences. The most difficult part of being on the road, she told Reckless, was "when I can't find any water and want to get clean. . . . Being dirty means more to me than being hungry." Mrs. Metzger liked to wear a dress, although all the other women on the road wore pants so as to pass for men and avoid molestation. A certain female pragmatism enabled her to reconcile her sexual encounters with her religion: "You have to put up on the road with certain things and you got to give in when forced. But that doesn't mean I don't keep up my religion."

So powerful is the value of appearance for women that even this female hobo clung to it. But she did more. By retaining aspects of conventional femininity yet accepting the casual promiscuity required by the road, Mrs. Metzger created a kind of middle ground between the "real" woman and the prostitute—a territory that disconcerted her interlocutor, as did his perception that she inhabited it quite successfully. At the time the interview took place she was headed back east, to her sister's family, and thought she might stay with them: "I can entertain people with travel talk now." But "if I don't like it at home with my sister, I can still go on the road again." In fact, as Reckless commented, "she seems to have the notion that the road is now her career—something on which she can fall back, something at which she had made a success." He looked on this as an indication of a new "social pathology"—the possible "growth of a chronic female hobo class." But even by his own account the changes in her character that the road produced hardly seem pathological: "She likes the independence of the road and the sense of power she gets from making a go of life on the road. I believe she is proud of herself and thinks that she is a much superior person to the one she was previously."

While Mrs. Metzger herself took the conditions of the road for granted and associated the experience of being outside society with independence and a sense of power—without giving up her own standards of femininity—to Reckless this combination could only indicate a movement toward pathology. Indeed, his original purpose in the interview was to gauge "the extent of demoralization among unemployed and homeless women," and the only consolation for his discovery that "women are making pretty good hoboes as hoboes go" was the prerogative of labeling her deviant.[62]

But Mrs. Metzger was an exception. In another case, a "saleslady in a Fifth Avenue shop" was "shocked, but not alarmed" when it failed. "She was an elegant person with a following of wealthy customers and she did not anticipate any difficulty in finding a place." But no place was to be had; so, her savings running out, she went to "Washington, where she had an introduction to the manager of a gown shop."

> For six months she went from town to town finding nothing. She cut down on her food. Then her real wanderings began. She boarded buses and moved from place to place, using up her funds without results. In Florida the curt treatment and sharp looks of hotel men made her realize that she was fast becoming the type of person that every boarding house keeper and proprietor of small hotels dreads—the down and outer—perhaps the potential suicide.[63]

It was particularly disturbing to find people perceived as middle-class in such a plight, and condemning them was a more equivocal matter than assuming that ragged, dirty transients were up to no good. In 1933 a reporter described the difficulties faced by unattached, self-supporting white-collar workingwomen. "The problem of the self-respecting, independent young girl out of work is one of the gravest in the whole tragic picture of unemployment," she says, and goes on to describe the young middle-class women in New York who, "when their landlady wearies of having them stay on without benefit of rent, ride the subways all night. . . . Some girls live in this precarious way for weeks. Some hire out as domestic help for free room and board. Some go on the streets." Their pride makes them

> hate the idea of charity. . . . When they lose their jobs they make every sacrifice, they exhaust every resource, before they turn to society for help. . . . They half-starve themselves. But they do not go to bread lines, nor do they eat at soup kitchens. Any one who has marveled because there are no women in bread lines should realize that it is not because there are no hungry women. It is because they believe that any public parade of poverty is degrading.

And, by instinct, they observe the familiar principle: "Food is the first thing that goes when a woman gets up against it, and appearance and clothes are the last. This is not vanity as much as self-preservation. They know that 60 per cent. of their chances of getting a job depends on their appearance."

What is remarkable is that the very fact of being poor and jobless renders even these young women suspect. After reminding her readers that these "whitecollar girls" are not the same as "the drifting type of woman" who uses the Municipal Lodging House and the Salvation Army shelter, the reporter feels compelled to reassure them that though poor through no fault of their own, these young women are still worthy of sympathy: "The woman out of work in the big city is not merely the ghetto child. She is more likely of good breeding and education. . . . They are not potential Communists and Reds, nor soap-box orators against the civilization which made their new poverty possible. They are not even filled with self-pity. They have the same courage as men, but are more sensitive."[64] The remarkable logic of this rescue operation demonstrates how easy it was for a woman to step over the line into the outsider's oblivion the moment her poverty became a "public parade."[65]

Several themes of female homelessness in the depression come together in Meridel Le Sueur's portraits of the intense and painful vulnerability of destitute women in Minneapolis:

> It's one of the great mysteries of the city where women go when they are out of work and hungry. There are not many women in the bread line. There are no flop houses for women. . . . You don't see women lying on the floor at the mission. . . . They obviously don't sleep in the jungle or under newspapers in the park. . . .
>
> Where do they go? Try to get into the YW without any money or looking down at heel. Charities take care of very few and only those that are called "deserving." The lone girl is under suspicion by the virgin women who dispense charity.
>
> I've lived in cities for many months broke, without help, too timid to get in bread lines. I've known many women to live like this until they simply faint on the street from privations, without saying a word to anyone. A woman will shut herself up in a room until it is taken away from her, and eat a cracker a day and be as quiet as a mouse so there are no social statistics concerning her. . . .
>
> A woman will do this unless she has dependents, . . . going through the streets ashamed, sitting in libraries, parks, going for days without speaking to a living soul like some exiled beast.[66]

In other words, such a woman has internalized the family ethic. Walter Reckless remarks tellingly that women "have never accepted public or private charity to any great extent as individuals, but rather as members of families."[67] A lone woman accepts the suspicion directed at her and feels shamed. Whereas "a man can always get drunk, or talk to other men, . . ." says Le Sueur, "a woman, ten to one, will starve alone." She emphasizes the difficulties of the "lone girl," automatically considered a "moral culprit" and "picked up" if she begs in the street: "When the police see you wandering they always think you are bad if you are a girl."[68]

Even more invisible than young women in cities were needy older ones, as the Philadelphia social workers who in 1933 conducted a study of "women living alone" found out. They had assumed that this group would consist of young women out of work but discovered instead a different kind of recipient of care from social agencies: "Alone, unwanted by kith and kin, she is old and 'poorly' and habituated to a way of life that shifts between occasional diminishing employment and casual increasing charity."

The study discovered "the human content of a category of need which did not fit the routines of relief administration, and which no one knew very much about anyway." These old women needed not temporary unemployment relief—as the researchers had expected to find—but permanent care. "Less than half" said they had relatives, some of whom helped out, usually by providing "a room outside the relatives' own home. This is eloquent testimony on the social problems involved in the care of these women, the relatives did *not* want them to live with them even when the relatives were the women's own children."[69]

Most of the women lived in furnished rooms by the grace of their landladies, to whom they owed back rent. Assuming that there were other landladies who either did put old women out on the streets or were forced to close down their houses, it seems likely that other old women, too infirm to go on the road and perhaps too confused to apply for assistance, lived on the streets in Philadelphia and elsewhere, blending into that very population of "drifting" types whom the spokeswoman for distressed respectability so easily dismissed.

The social workers' astonishment at their discovery is reflected in this comment: "The aloneness of the women led the researchers into many bypaths of fact and even more of conjecture. While now alone and practically friendless, . . . 70 percent . . . had been married."[70] Clearly no one, not even the specialists in human problems, could conceive how totally old women could lose their family attachments and vanish from society.

Since World War II

During the world war, which absorbed unemployed workers into the military and war industries, and in the postwar era, "there was little or no homelessness as we know it today."[1] What homelessness did exist was represented by the familiar image of skid row, the seedy part of town where older white alcoholic men lived in flophouses or at missions, or spent nights in jail after being picked up for public drunkenness; few actually slept on the street.[2] In this classic form skid row persisted until the late 1960s, when a wave of urban renewal swept the country, and skid-row areas in many cities were demolished.[3]

"INVISIBLE" HOMELESS WOMEN DURING THE 1950s AND 1960s

A salient characteristic of skid row was the absence of women. Studies done during the 1950s and 1960s reported that its denizens were almost all men. In 1958 the sociologist Donald Bogue estimated that up to 3 percent of the residents of Chicago's skid row were women; but this figure was based on census figures, not actual contact. Bogue "thought that many were not homeless but were simply living in the Skid Row areas," some as "live-in employees of the hotels" and others renting rooms in "conventional dwellings" that happened to be located in the area. In Philadelphia's skid row, while "men lived in flophouses and small hotels, . . . poor women usually lived in boarding houses."[4]

"Homeless women," wrote the eminent sociologist Theodore Caplow, "have been something of a sociological mystery." Certain facts—including the prevalence of alcoholism, the smaller likelihood that women will remarry after losing a spouse, their lower incomes—suggested that there should be a lot of homeless women. But, asked Caplow, "where are they to be found?"[5] As ever, they remained invisible. "What few homeless women there were in the 1950s and 1960s must have kept out of sight," another investigator concludes.[6]

Nevertheless Ann Geracimos, a *Village Voice* reporter who went looking in New York City in 1967, had no trouble finding them. The women she describes range from "Missouri Marie" and "Boxcar Betty," who "rode the boxcars in her early days"—clearly the "distaff" side of skid row—to a "depressing" woman named Sally, encountered in an unsavory bar on First Avenue, who seemed to have fallen apart after her second husband died. Having nowhere else to go, Sally came to the bar every day, submitting meekly to sadistic mocking from the bartender. She went with men to their rooms but did not take money for it. When Geracimos offered to buy her a drink, "she inexplicably held out her skirt to me, as though she were about to curtsey. 'Look,' she said. 'It's clean. It's clean.'"[7] Homeless women still knew the difference between ladies and low creatures.

During the 1950s and 1960s the number of homeless women using the New York City Women's Shelter remained fairly constant. In January 1950, for example, 158 unattached women were sheltered; in January 1960, 164.[8] Starting in 1947, the city also had a separate family shelter for homeless women with children (the men had to stay at the men's shelter). A study of fifty of these families (twenty-eight white, eight Puerto Rican, and fourteen black) done between 1949 and 1950 by a social worker described a number of unmarried mothers with children and abandoned, separated, or battered wives. One eighteen-year-old ran away with her baby after social workers put pressure on her to give it up for adoption. Another abandoned her baby in the shelter and disappeared. A third worked but had to give up her job after her baby was born, then was evicted for not paying rent. A fourth simply drifted from one man and one furnished room to another, returning periodically to the shelter.[9]

Between 1968 and 1970 Caplow and his associates, Howard Bahr and Gerald Garrett, carried out a study of 383 "disaffiliated" women, which included fifty-two homeless women who lived at the Women's Shelter, then located in the Bowery area. I see these homeless women as the women in the previous study grown older. Largely middle-aged, they tended to be very isolated, even though three-fourths had been married, often several times. Forty-four percent were black, 56 percent white. A number manifested symptoms of psychiatric disorders such as chronic schizophrenia. Over half were thought to be chronic alcoholics. Marital breakups and drinking appear to be the two major factors behind these women's homelessness. One had been a legal stenographer who supported herself and her daughter. Her alcoholism, however, resulted in a complete break between them (and possibly also, as in another case documented, in the loss of her job).[10] To shelter staff, these women were "shelter types": dependent, unable to cope on their own, and needing a protected, supervised environment. At least two staff members saw them as existing "on the borderline between being in the community and being out of the community."[11]

Before 1970, then, the relatively small number of homeless women included female equivalents of the hobo or skid-row bum, women who either could not cope or refused to deal with the welfare system, and a few who had managed to elude incarceration in state mental hospitals.[12] The image of the "shopping-bag lady" did not yet exist. Remarking that "there is some question as to whether stereotypes of homeless women exist at all," Bahr and Garrett report the variety of ways the Women's Shelter residents were perceived by other Bowery people: "Old ladies with shopping bags. . . . bandages on their legs"; "Prostitutes. Every one of 'em"; "pickpockets, thieves, and panhandlers"; "lost souls."[13]

Once again, because there was no conceptual slot for homeless women, they were perceived as bums, drifters, criminals, and (of course) prostitutes. The fact that New York City provided services gave them a place in the record books and gave Bahr and Garrett a population to study, but in this the city was unique. In Boston, for example, though a few women "showed up in the alley" next to the Pine Street Inn for homeless men "late at night, mostly urban Indians of the region's dominant Micmac tribe," they were "generally chased away." It did not seem to occur to anyone that women should be helped, even though—as Kip Tiernan, the founder of Rosie's Place, Boston's first shelter for women, put it—"women were invariably at the back of every line." Yet in 1974, when Rosie's opened, so many women appeared at the door that some had to be turned away.[14]

EVICTED SRO RESIDENTS OF THE 1970s

Some of these older women who had been drifting around homeless since before 1970 showed up at the Dwelling Place. I think Sylvia Prior, the woman described in Part 1 who (like Geracimos's Sally) hung around bars, was one of them. But increasingly we saw another group who for a while constituted the preponderance of homeless women—former SRO residents.

Caplow, commenting that the results of the study of disaffiliated women "are unbelievably sad," refers not to the Women's Shelter group but to the majority of the subjects—hotel and apartment dwellers, "elderly women living alone in dreary little rooms in huge shabby buildings without economic security or emotional response or personal recognition, without the gratification of familiar pleasures or the excitement of new experiences, and without the elementary protections that ought to be offered by a civilized community."[15] Like the old women discovered by the Philadelphia researchers, these women had been invisible and were found by the team of investigators only after intense effort.

Though isolated, these women were not homeless. Many had lived in their buildings for years, even since before World War II. These SROs were generally formerly good hotels or old tenement buildings converted to single-room units that, since World War II, had become cheap living quarters for old people living on pensions, ex-convicts, former residents of demolished skid-row flophouses, and people on welfare.[16] According to hotel managers, many of the women residents had physical disabilities and mental disorders but refused treatment. While some managers and owners said that such women should be kicked out because they were "a detriment to business" in the neighborhood and frightened off potential tenants, by and large rent control protected them.[17] It was only in the 1970s, when large numbers of these buildings were demolished or converted into high-priced units (87 percent of New York City's SRO rooms were lost between 1970 and 1982), that more and more of these women (and men as well) were evicted and did become homeless.[18] Many rang the doorbell at the Dwelling Place when it opened in 1977.

By then the tidal wave of homelessness that broke in the eighties had been building for some time. High unemployment and the disappearance of low-skilled jobs, inflation, rising prices for houses (which forced people to stay in rental units), and a reduction in the real value of benefits received from social programs were among the factors that led to abandonment and gentrification of housing and simultaneously strained many people's ability to cover both rent and other living expenses, bringing them to the brink of homelessness.[19]

Most did not fall over it until the eighties; but the seventies saw the early casualties. Among these were unemployed young minority men and people on welfare whom the state, to save money, transferred to federal disability pensions (SSI). Whereas welfare in New York included a separate rent allowance, SSI's flat rate was so low that rent became a luxury (in 1976, for example, the SSI allowance was $218 a month, while a room cost $150).[20] As described in Part 1, I met women who chose to live on the street for part of the month because their check would not cover both a relatively decent hotel and living expenses.

Perhaps the largest group of homeless people in the late seventies, however, were those evicted from SROs, not only the long-time residents but also many former inmates of state mental hospitals. A nationwide reform movement begun in the sixties involved the "deinstitutionalization" or discharge of thousands of patients from these hospitals to what were supposed to be community mental-health centers offering outpatient services. Deinstitutionalization was made possible by the new "antipsychotic" drugs, such as Thorazine, which did not cure people but did control their symptoms enough that they did not need constant institutional supervision.

The reform was motivated partly by concern for the rights of patients locked up for years in back wards, as well as a consensus that they would be better served by local centers. However in New York, as elsewhere, the money to finance community centers never materialized. And despite increasing numbers of discharges, admissions also grew, leading the state—whose primary motivation for deinstitutionalization had been a desire to save money by turning state charges over to local agencies—to tighten its admissions policy. This produced an ever larger group of people who could not function outside the hospital but were not allowed in. Their presence put pressure on the municipal hospitals, which—even though they provided only emergency and short-term care—tightened their own admissions policies.[21] Thus, for example, unless a woman was virtually comatose from a drug overdose, severely ill, bleeding heavily, or extremely violent, the Dwelling Place staff could not get her into Bellevue.

Since the lack of community-care facilities did not stop state hospitals from discharging patients, they had to be sent somewhere; and many wound up in the SROs. Since these hotels were affordable on a disability pension and fairly tolerant of strange behavior, many former patients managed to remain there (the earliest discharges from state hospitals had in fact occurred during the 1950s). It is true that they were extremely vulnerable.[22] As we saw in Part 1, a variety of events—a late check, an unpleasant caseworker, an assault, failure to renew a prescription—could precipitate eviction or drive someone out on her own; recall Kathleen, who left her belongings in her room and lived on the street because she felt safer there.[23] Nevertheless, someone who left one hotel could generally find a room at another.

It is not, therefore, strictly true that deinstitutionalization itself caused the rise in homelessness, as people often assume. There was actually a "time lag" of some five years between the first major wave of discharges in the late 1960s and the mass appearance on the street and in shelters of former psychiatric patients in the mid-1970s. As Kim Hopper points out, not until the economic changes described above all but eliminated the supply of cheap rooms did large numbers of deinstitutionalized people become homeless.[24]

It was mostly female ex-patients, as well as some former long-time SRO residents, who became the "shopping-bag ladies." Since by the seventies vagrancy had been decriminalized, they could frequent downtown areas without being carted off to jail.[25] Their special visibility derived not only from the way they resonated in people's imagination but, I suggest, from their being more numerous than former male patients (more women than men having been inmates in psychiatric institutions during most of the sixties) and from their having fewer shelters to go to than men.[26]

THE NEW HOMELESS OF THE 1980s

During the Reagan years as in the depression, people more and more like "us" became homeless yet increasingly took on the aspect of an alien "them." As the eighties began, income dropped, unemployment rose, and antipoverty programs were cut even as poverty increased. The housing market grew still tighter, rents rose, and so did evictions (often of tenants on welfare), while federal housing subsidies and construction of low-income units were cut. Fewer benefits than in the past were available for workers who lost their jobs and could not find new ones, and entire families of these "new poor" became homeless, not only in cities but in rural areas. In the Midwest and West, young hobos—including women—once again rode the rails. "One woman told me how she dealt with trouble on the road," reported an observer. "'You just lay down and spread your legs. It's better than getting your head split open.' I see girls—thirteen to fifteen years old maybe—traveling with older men (twenty-five to forty years old). They are usually dressed like boys and very quiet, intimidated." Many of the new homeless had been living "doubled up" with friends or relatives and finally had to leave, either because the landlord threatened the primary tenant with eviction or because of the effect that unbearable stresses of severe overcrowding and a worsening economic situation had on personal relationships.[27]

A frightening development by the late eighties was the intersection of homelessness with drug abuse and HIV infection—and, increasingly, diagnosed mental illness. Not only did addiction lead to homelessness, but many young people who in the past would have been incarcerated in psychiatric hospitals now lived on the street, became substance abusers, were infected with HIV through needle sharing, and infected their sexual partners. Crack addiction also spread HIV by driving users to trade sex for drugs. Although many addicts sought treatment, hardly any was available, and they were forced back to the street community that supported their habit. As of summer 1990, in New York State alone there were an estimated quarter of a million intravenous drug users and one million cocaine addicts, while New York City had an estimated ten thousand homeless people with AIDS or AIDS-related illness, and thirty thousand HIV-positive homeless people.[28]

While these numbers are large, they represent a relatively small minority of all homeless people. In one study, 14 percent of men and women (predominantly men) interviewed in New York City single shelters reported having been hospitalized for a drug problem; in another, only 3.6 percent of men and 1.0 percent of women reported being homeless because of drug abuse.[29] Still the image of the mentally ill and/or drug-abusing homeless person dominated public perception, supporting traditional assumptions of unworthiness that spread like weeds.

In New York City, for example, the principle of less eligibility took the form of the Koch administration's belief that, in the words of one of its critics, "if you made homelessness too good, people would use it as a vehicle for getting an apartment." Thus the programs supposedly intended to help the homeless were deliberately made "terrible."[30]

Similarly, the nineteenth century's moral judgment of vagrants was replaced by diagnosis of their disabilities, which generally did not involve blame but was no less marginalizing in effect. The professional literature analyzed the psychiatric problems, domestic violence, alcoholism, drug use, and social isolation of the homeless.[31] While most of the writers acknowledged lack of housing and jobs as major causes of homelessness, their reports nevertheless portrayed "the homeless" as a distinct, deviant population whose deficits made them appropriate targets of service providers.[32] Although estimates of the proportion of homeless people who were mentally ill ranged from 91 percent to 15 percent, only a few writers suggested that in most cases "antisocial behavior" and symptoms of psychiatric impairment were simply adaptations to homeless life, not causes of it.[33]

As late as summer 1990, Sister Connie Driscoll, the head of the Mayor's Task Force on Homelessness in Chicago, in an interview with the *New York Times* berated advocates who focused on housing as the primary cause of homelessness instead of "mental illness, drug abuse and a lack of personal responsibility."[34] Such pronouncements by experts gave credence to assertions by nonspecialist pontificators like Michael Novak of the American Enterprise Institute, who was quoted as saying, " 'Homelessness is a misnomer. It really refers to people who are publicly dependent. A lot of these people have homes or a place to live' but are just looking for a handout."[35]

The image of homeless people as deviant outsiders persisted at least partly because it was useful. Diminishing the credibility and confirming the subordinate position of this group, comprising largely people of color, it furthered social control by fostering the model of relief as a charity, not an entitlement. Like the nineteenth-century female convicts who had to accept help on the donors' terms while showing "docility and obedience," homeless people in the eighties had to prove their own worthiness by being "properly deferential" and grateful for what others chose to give, instead of asserting their right to define their own needs and desires.[36]

Indeed the major subtext of homelessness in the eighties, which underlay most public assumptions about homeless people although it was rarely enunciated, was the increasing proportion who were people of color. Peter Rossi gives figures indicating that 45.8 percent of homeless people nationally were African-American, 11.8 percent Hispanic, and 4.9 percent Native American. In New York City in 1987, 69 percent of the women in single-adult shelters were black, 8 percent were Hispanic, 2 percent Asian, Native American, or other groups, and 21 percent white.[37] "Neglect of New Yorkers without homes is racism pure and simple," charged the Coalition for the Homeless in June 1990, although "the senseless murders and benign neglect of homeless people over the past several years were characterized not as racism, but as actions against the undeserving poor."[38] Certainly a hidden (sometimes overt) assumption behind many questions directed at me as an "expert" for years was that "they" (understood: black people) have all been on welfare for generations, are unmotivated, irresponsible, and don't deserve any help.

For all these reasons, it is impossible to stress too much that homelessness was not the result of a particular set of pathologies that suddenly appeared in certain defective people around 1980; rather, problems that had always existed were forced out into the street and thereby exacerbated. With the exception of drug use, the disabilities noted in homeless people today closely resemble those reported in 1950 among the poor families at the Women's Shelter.[39] Yet those families did not remain on the street broadcasting their problems in public—not because they were less "sick" but because they could find cheap rooms.

Certainly there was clear evidence by the end of the 1980s that the primary cause of homelessness was lack of housing. A 1989 study of homeless families in New York City concluded, to the surprise of the investigators, that inability to find affordable housing was a more important cause of homelessness than drug addiction, mental illness, or family violence. Although these problems substantially increased the risk that people would become homeless, they were present in only a "small percentage" of homeless families. What was more, poor education, health problems, unemployment, and teenage pregnancy were not predictors of homelessness; rates of these factors were the same among families on welfare who were not homeless. The study also found that 93 percent of the families had "close relatives" in the city. "It isn't that people are socially isolated," said one of the researchers. "They'd used up their social ties."[40]

For most of these families, then, the cause of homelessness was not personal failure but what I would call a failure of the housing market. Forty-four percent became homeless through eviction or harassment by landlords. Another 44 percent consisted of women in their twenties and their children who had never been able to find a home of their own; they had lived doubled up with parents, other relatives, or friends. "Conflict" was the "most frequently cited reason" for their showing up at a shelter.[41]

THE NEW HOMELESS WOMEN

As the foregoing suggests, female homelessness in the eighties was distinguished by its family nature: the disturbing single woman without a home was joined by the disturbing single mother without a home. Indeed they were sometimes the same person since many women in single-adult shelters were mothers who had either lost their children to foster care or, not wanting to take them into a shelter, left them with relatives. Once they entered the shelter they were stuck, for they could not get housing until they had their children with them and could not get their children back until they had housing deemed appropriate.[42]

These new, young homeless women included those we saw coming to the Dwelling Place, plus others: mothers who had been evicted from their own or others' apartments or had to leave a doubling-up situation when they became pregnant; some who had grown out of foster care; battered women who had to leave a violent man; many who were mentally ill; and those who lost a job and could not find another that paid enough to enable them to keep their apartment. And although women were less likely to be homeless because of drug use than men, there were also the drug users.[43] Despite the persistent image of the bag lady, far fewer older women were homeless than young ones; 61 percent of women in the New York City single shelters in 1987 were under forty.[44]

Old issues still conditioned the experience of these new homeless women. They faced some gender-associated difficulties with work, like the Brooklyn Women's Shelter residents' inability to go to interviews because they lacked decent clothing (as described in the introduction). Now, however, when a woman could get the same job in a fast-food restaurant as a man (if they were lucky), the main issue was less gender discrimination in employment (although the woman might be hindered in working a late shift by the danger of traveling alone at night) than the fact that neither could afford housing on a minimum-wage salary.

Primarily, though, issues of sexuality still distinguished female homelessness. A study carried out in "a moderately sized community" found that while unemployment was the major cause of homelessness for both women and men, women were far more likely than men to become homeless because of domestic violence; another study by the New York City Victim Services Agency found that, in 1988, 35 percent of the women in the shelter system were homeless because they had been battered.[45]

Similarly, life on the street was harder for women than for men. Women were more easily victimized physically; they were raped, and they could get pregnant. Because their lives were so uncertain, homeless women who reported rapes frequently could not get adequate counseling or medical care, or follow through on pressing charges against their attacker. And often they had no safe place to go to afterward but had to return to the site of the assault (Penn Station, for example).[46]

A host of small indignities also bore harder on homeless women, such as having to relieve themselves in public. A man can perform this act more efficiently and hide it relatively easily, saving himself some pride. Men are also used to less privacy (stalls in men's restrooms frequently lack doors); but for women privacy assumes great significance in the struggle to maintain the basic integrity of the self. At a large women's shelter, an old woman asked a visiting politician for a shower curtain because she was embarrassed to shower in front of everyone else.[47] Any woman can imagine the potential for agonizing humiliation in having one's period on the street; the source of the agony is precisely the charged feelings that surround women's sexual functions in our culture.

Though homeless people of both sexes were blamed for their condition, the extent to which that blame was loaded with sexual connotations in the case of women was astonishing.[48] Colleen McDonald, director of a drop-in center for homeless women in Manhattan, described the constant need to educate her male staff. "They have difficulty understanding why women are homeless," she said, especially when the women are young and attractive. The men assumed that if only a woman could "find a good man," she would be all right, and they tended to see themselves in the role of savior. Further, they were likely to pay more attention to younger, more attractive women than to older ones. Given the persistence of such attitudes in a small private shelter, the reports of sexual assault in the large public ones are hardly surprising.

The assumption that homeless women were fair game was shared by men out on the streets. Many workers in the fur district surrounding this drop-in shelter made sexual advances to its clients. "They feel the women belong to them because they're on the streets," said McDonald. While a woman who looked homeless was harassed, businesswomen and shoppers were left alone. The issue was complicated by the fact that many homeless women, like their predecessors, relied on prostitution to get money. While some identified themselves as prostitutes and had pimps, others traded sex for money when they wanted coffee or cigarettes, though they would never have thought of themselves as prostitutes. Once they got entitlements, they stopped.[49]

The ambivalence that combines fear and distaste with attraction toward single women's sexuality explains why these women were so disregarded by the public that the city could treat them like animals in its shelters. Dreadful as conditions were for homeless women with children in welfare hotels, they were better off than women in many of the single shelters; residents of the notorious Brooklyn Arms hotel were shocked to discover, at a meeting with Brooklyn Women's Shelter residents, how much worse the shelter conditions were than their own.[50]

However, a certain ambiguity also attached to homeless women with children. On one hand, as mothers they represented the sanctity of the family ethic. The impact of Jonathan Kozol's book *Rachel and Her Children*, as well as advocates' success in getting homeless families out of the hotels, was due, I think, to an insistent focus on the importance of those homeless women as mothers, emphasizing the necessity of preserving families and the destructiveness for children of growing up in the hotels. On the other hand, however, these women partook of the derogatory and racist stereotype of the young black "welfare mother," irresponsibly having one illegitimate baby after another. Thus the solution proposed by one caller to a New York City radio talk-show discussion of homelessness was to "sterilize all the women."[51]

As the nineties began, then, the age-old set of preoccupations with unsocialized sexuality in homeless women persisted, given particular viciousness by racism. These preoccupations were overt with respect to young women seen as promiscuous; but they also underlay the general perception of older women as "bag ladies." I think the main reason this remained the dominant image of "the homeless woman" among much of the public (though not among service providers), long after these women were vastly outnumbered by others who were not bag ladies at all, was that it provided the first real—and compelling—conceptual category for homeless women.[52] Its power, as Part 5 will show, derived from the fact that it harked back to ancient perceptions of mysterious, implicitly sexual power possessed by old women.

This persistence of the bag lady in people's minds suggests that Michelet's witch did not disappear with the dawn of the modern age; she survived for a long time, though always outside. While her changing personae have acquired a variety of negative qualities, one constant has been her association with some form of illicit sexuality. In reality, each of the traits for which she was condemned had its origin in some economic or social feature within society itself; but she took them on as a kind of service, the payment for which was the magical powers that possession of them endowed. Associated (and sometimes identified) with her over the centuries have been a variety of other outcasts who, like her, embodied anarchic, asocial forces: the vagrant, the criminal, and, of course, the mental deviant.

As we saw, deinstitutionalized mental patients have played a role in perceptions of the homeless out of proportion to their actual numbers. In one of those revolutions that simply turns up a new version of the past, the late twentieth century urban scene has witnessed a peculiar return to the medieval condition where the insane freely circulated face to face with the sane. More helpless, but also more fearsome, to the degradation of poverty these homeless added the mystery of madness—a quality particularly potent in women (as the continuing fascination with the bag woman indicates) since for a long time madness has been particularly women's business.

PART 4

In Praise of Folly

There was an old woman
  And nothing she had,
And so this old woman
    Was said to be mad.
She'd nothing to eat,
    She'd nothing to wear,
She'd nothing to lose,
    She'd nothing to fear,
She'd nothing to ask,
    She'd nothing to give,
And when she did die
    She'd nothing to leave.
—*English nursery rhyme*

The Relativity of Madness

Margery, the daughter of a leading citizen in a small but prosperous town, was married when she was twenty to a prominent merchant and local official. Trouble started for her when a severe illness following the birth of her first child made her decide to confess to her priest a matter that had been on her conscience for a long time. But before she had gotten far, he rebuked her—so sharply that she was afraid to continue. It was no doubt her guilt over this matter, intensified by the priest's reaction, that led to an outbreak of madness—involving hallucinations, self-laceration, and suicide attempts—that lasted seven months.

After her recovery she became interested in dress and set herself to outdo all the other women in town. Her clothes were always in the latest fashion and made of brightly contrasting fabrics, to the point where people stared at her in the street and her husband pleaded with her to be moderate, though in vain. At the same time, and motivated by the same desire to demonstrate her preeminence, Margery embarked on a series of business ventures that, though at first successful, eventually failed.

She thereupon concluded that she was being called to spiritual things and now, in her mid-thirties, decided that she wished to take a vow of chastity and dress in white as a sign of purity. She entreated her husband to agree to live a celibate life. He refused, but she increased her own religious observances, which included fasting and spending eight hours a day in church. Around this time she began to experience extraordinary attacks of weeping and sobbing—very loud and lasting for long pe-

riods—to which she remained prone for years. She saw visions, fluctuated between exaltation and despair, and was tortured for a while by
sexual desire, but at length achieved a clear sense of a vocation to serve
Christ. She then left her husband and children in order to travel from
place to place in accordance with instructions she received from the
Lord, talking endlessly about the love of God, making quite a spectacle
of herself with her crying and the convulsions that accompanied it, and
occasionally getting into trouble for her outspokenness. This remained
her pattern for most of the rest of her life; over time the habit of receiving
direct communications from God strengthened her self-assurance, so
that she became increasingly difficult to live with.

Margery is unusual only in combining a number of symptoms, each
common in itself. Quite a few women at the Dwelling Place behaved in
exactly the same ways, although I never saw all these traits in a single
person. One regular member of the coffee hour had a habit of turning
every minor incident into an excuse for an impromptu sermon on the
love of the Lord; her constant interruptions infuriated the others. Another woman once shaved her head as "penance" for her "sins," which
turned out to be her sexual feelings for her husband. Like Margery, she
alternated between intense experience of her sexuality and equally intense revulsion and self-castigation in the name of religion. Still another
woman had a mission from God that provided a rationalization for constant traveling about. Her access to privileged information from on high
involved her in continual disputes with other women since her sense of
being isolated and superior made her unwilling to acknowledge that anyone else's point of view could be valid. Finally, there were many women—
like Millie, for example—prone to sudden, violent fits of crying.

Unlike them, however, and despite her perpetual traveling, Margery
never became homeless—not so much through any virtue of her own as
because she was lucky. That is, it was her good fortune to live in fifteenth-
century England, where her particular obsessions could be defined in
terms of a recognized vocation: religious mystic. All her life Margery
Kempe (c. 1373–c. 1438) was supported by food and gifts from people
who believed in her divine inspiration; she accomplished pilgrimages to
Jerusalem and to Compostela in Spain and eventually became renowned
as a minor mystic and spiritual healer, invited to converse with bishops
and doctors of theology.[1] She died peacefully at about sixty-five in her
native town of Lynn.

Was Margery mad? Even in the fifteenth century, many people objected to her. On a purely practical level, she was so hard to put up

with—because of her constant preaching and extravagant displays of crying—that her fellow pilgrims frequently deserted her en route. In itself this behavior was not unusual. Women commonly acted as if possessed at pilgrimage sites; an account from later in the fifteenth century of a pilgrimage to Jerusalem that was essentially the same as Margery's describes how, on their first sight of the city, "the women pilgrims shrieked as though in labour, cried aloud and wept."[2] As previously in the matter of dress, Margery's distinction in this respect was largely in outdoing everyone else; her cryings did not restrict themselves to special occasions but came—sometimes—every day, and once fourteen times in one day.

There were, moreover, differing opinions about the cause of the crying. " 'She never knew the time or the hour when [her cryings] would come, and as soon as she found that she would cry, she would suppress it as much as possible so as not to annoy people. For some said it was a wicked spirit vexed her: some said it was a sickness: some said she had drunk too much wine: . . . and thus each man had his own thoughts.' "[3] "Sickness" here means physical illness, which some thought caused her convulsions.

For her contemporaries, however, the basic issue was not medical but theological. In response to the insecurity and social unrest produced by the gradual dissolution of the feudal order in the late Middle Ages, various heretical groups had arisen whose mystical doctrines attacked the established Christian church, which eventually set up the Inquisition to counter them. An eccentric, outspoken individualist like Margery naturally fell under suspicion, and in her travels she was frequently accused of being a heretic, threatened with the stake, and haled before various churchmen who questioned her closely. Only because she convinced them that her religion was orthodox was she able to continue her career.

The three possible causes suggested by Margery's contemporaries for her crying—possession by an evil spirit, too much wine, and physical illness—reflect the Middle Ages' different approaches to the various behaviors that we would class together as "mental illness." There were also some who, through certain conventional gestures, expressed an idea of what was wrong with her that resembles our modern concept of insanity. During the pilgrimage to Jerusalem her fed-up companions "rounded on her . . . and cut her gown so short that it came but little below the knee, while at the same time they gave her a piece of white canvas cut in the shape of an apron so that she should be thought a fool and despised." Some time later, back in Lynn, " 'a reckless man, little caring for his own shame, with will and of set purpose, cast a bowlful of water on her head as she came along the street.' "⁴ Nevertheless, despite such implied accusations of folly, or madness, Margery was treated primarily as a person possessing genuine spiritual power. Today, on the other hand—science having replaced religion as the major organizer of our perceptions of human phenomena—women who not only behave the same way Margery did but give the same explanations for it are considered to be not theologically but physically out of line (that is, "ill") and so are dealt with medically.⁵

To me this contrast suggests that our ideas about insanity are more relative than we generally recognize. The kinds of behavior we now think of as "mental illness" have been part of human experience for millennia, and it is as experience, not as illness, that I would like to discuss them. The current widely accepted hypothesis that psychiatric disorders have an ultimately organic basis in structural or physiological brain pathology does not make the experiential meanings of these conditions irrelevant. Looking at the meanings other ages have given madness can provide a perspective that will help us establish a connection with "the homeless mentally ill" instead of fencing them off in the category of "special-needs populations." One of the biggest surprises for me at the Dwelling Place was learning that even after someone has been diagnosed mentally ill, she's still a person with whom you can have a relationship.

As the example of Margery Kempe suggests, mental illness—or rather madness, a word I prefer since it denotes a recognized experience without necessarily associating it with disease—has been conceptualized differently in the past, and the treatment of people considered mad has varied accordingly. In the ancient Near East "abnormal behavior" was generally attributed to possession by demons or evil spirits. This connection between unusual mental states and supernatural powers was not necessarily negative; the Bible, for example, uses the same words to describe the behavior of people considered mad and that of the prophets. But although prophets too heard voices, saw visions, and dressed oddly, a distinction was made between the trances they induced deliberately for specific occasions and similar behavior that was both chronic and unrelated to external reality as defined by social norms.⁶

It was, however, necessary to distinguish between true and false prophets. In ancient Palestine people considered insane were left to themselves or the care of their families unless they were violent or otherwise a threat to public safety. Similarly, a prophet could act as he chose "even if some mocked him and others considered him mad, as long as what he said and did were not sufficiently threatening." But if his revelation opposed a powerful interest group, he had to be discredited as a threat to the community. Thus, for example, the priests and prophets of Jerusalem demanded Jeremiah's death when he prophesied the destruction of the temple.[7]

The tradition that madness was caused by a supernatural power persisted in ancient Greece and Rome. Although the contemporary medical view of madness rejected this explanation, holding that mental imbalance was due entirely to physiological causes involving an excess of one of the four humors, this was the view only of an educated elite. The popular belief in possession as punishment for sin developed in the classical period into the idea that specific deities inflicted madness on people who had angered them. This association of madness with divinity meant that mad people were considered special, sometimes even sacred, but also were shunned; indwelling in them was a "damaging power" resulting from a divine curse, which could pollute others.[8]

The Middle Ages perceived both mental and physical disorders primarily in a moral context; both were thought to be the result of behavior that departed from the rule of reason. Thus even madness for which a physiological cause was demonstrated could be interpreted as a cosmic or divine punishment for sin. Possession, too, "was almost always associated with sin in that the devil seldom could have power over a man unless he had consented to it in some way, usually by sinning."[9] But madness was also a mode of knowledge. Unreason—the entire nonrational side of life—was seen as an integral part of the universe and therefore of humanity. As a transgression against reason, it was catalogued among the vices; but the reality of its existence was recognized, and a mad person, having knowledge of it, spoke a truth. At the same time, madness was a condition of those who had received a revelation of ultimate religious truth and in this case did not imply sin. These holy fools seemed mad to the world; but "what society deems madness may be sanity to God."[10]

The actual treatment of mad people reflects these contradictions. Although people did not automatically take Margery Kempe's cryings as evidence of holiness, doubt combined with suspicion that her claim to be a mouthpiece of the Lord might be true; thus the same companions who ridiculed her by dressing her like a fool later precipitously left the ship they had intended to sail in because Margery's "voices" had warned her against taking it.[11] On the one hand, homeless mad people without families or from poor classes were left to live in the streets and wander about, ridiculed and abused by children, unless they were dangerous, in which case they were dealt with by local authorities. Those not native to a locality were often expelled and transported to wherever they were from. But they might also be given assistance. Town or church officials sometimes paid for an exorcism or a pilgrimage to a shrine where madness was said to be cured. On the other hand, the centuries-old notion that mad people partook of the superhuman led to their being treated as less than human: the practice of throwing stones at them in the street dates at least from the ancient Near East and persisted in Europe for centuries. Only as butts that could these witnesses to the prevalence of unreason be tolerated.[12]

Renaissance humanism reinterpreted madness; it was no longer a "cosmic phenomenon" but a human defect identified with irrationality and stupidity. Yet madness was still morally, philosophically meaningful and could still reveal truth—human, now, rather than divine; Shakespeare, for example, makes Lady Macbeth's madness a signal of her guilt, and his fools are wise. Unreason still had a place within the human world.[13]

From this place the seventeenth century removed it, as it removed all other undesirables from its midst. By the century's end a new view of human nature based on reason had drawn a sharp separation between reason and unreason, shutting out all forms of the nonrational from the notion of what was human. Since all possessed reason, all were expected to make the choice to behave rationally—that is, according to accepted social norms.[14] Irrational behavior was therefore considered a failure of will, an error subject to correction. Further, if reason was the essential attribute of the human, its absence rendered someone nonhuman. Thus "a certain image of animality . . . haunted the hospitals" of the eighteenth century. Failure to follow the dictates of the social order was "conceived in terms of an animal freedom"—except that "the animal in man no longer [had] any value as the sign of a Beyond" as it had had in the medieval period.[15]

Such was the rationale behind the widespread confinement that began in the late seventeenth century, described in Part 3. Not only were the insane and the vagrants no longer to wander the countryside; all social deviants were to be locked away. Those who transgressed the limits of their "place" were assumed to have lost their senses and were sent to the houses of correction (a significant word) to regain them. This is why the insane were not distinguished from criminals or political prisoners; their offense was the same.[16]

Thus the exile of unreason from thought paralleled the exile of mad people from society. The age of reason, having denied that the nonrational existed, enforced the denial by hiding it from public view, at the same time dismissing the experience of madness as meaningless. This dismissal was inherent in the transformation of madness into mental illness, which, beginning in the eighteenth century, corresponded with the disconnection of conscious experience from what Foucault calls the "Beyond."

During the Enlightenment, madness became the subject of medical investigation, and one disorder after another was brought under the umbrella of mental disease. Hysteria, for example, which previously had been considered a bodily ailment—a disease of the uterus, which left its place and wandered through the body, or a disorder of the "animal spirits"—by the end of the eighteenth century was associated with nervous sensibility. Mental disorders were attributed to the nervous system rather than to the humors or animal spirits; but no clear distinction was made between the physiological irritability of the nerve fibers themselves and the psychological irritability that characterized people who suffered from "nerves." Thus those individuals considered most prone to nervous disease were not only those with the most delicate, weakest fibers, but those whose emotional sensitivity was great too: idle women, that is, with a too-lively imagination, "an unquiet heart." "From now on one fell ill from too much feeling"; and madness acquired "a new content of guilt," for the degree of irritation one experienced was determined by the type of life one led. Activities ranging from too much novel-reading to "immoderate thirst for knowledge" to immoderate sexual desire created unnatural stimulation of the nervous system, leading to their own just punishment. Since Enlightenment thought celebrated the virtue of life in accord with nature, madness resulting from an unnatural life was now seen as the punishment of a moral fault.[17]

This concept inspired major reforms in the early nineteenth century; Enlightenment ideals affirming the worth of the individual resulted in a liberation of the insane from the chains and dungeons of the houses of correction. A new system of care called "moral treatment" involved compassion, gentleness, rest, activities, and a cheerful, pleasant environment, all intended to reeducate the patient into compliance with the bourgeois moral values centered in the virtue of work and the patriarchal family. In this setting mad people were reduced to the status of minors, while reason, says Foucault, had for them "the aspect of the Father."[18]

The ideal of moral treatment broke down as the nineteenth century progressed. The earlier idea that madness was caused by overexertion of mind or body in a society become increasingly artificial had developed by mid-century into the concept that mental disorder was an inevitable effect of progress, the price paid for civilization. The theory of degeneration, developed in France at this time, assumed that deviations from the "normal" were hereditary; each generation of a degenerate family would be worse until they became idiots and died out. The ease with which this theory could be assimilated to Darwinism made it popular, especially since the stresses created by the industrial revolution were causing many breakdowns among the urban poor, and the asylums, overcrowded in the second half of the century with people for whom middle-class psychiatrists felt little sympathy, once again became hellish places where people were locked up for life. It was therefore convenient to be able to blame people themselves, or at least their heredity, for their condition.[19]

The dominant positivist thinking of the late nineteenth century reduced madness to an entirely organic phenomenon. Psychiatrists who believed that madness was "brain disease" attempted, without success, to localize specific psychological states in specific areas of the brain. In the early twentieth century Freud rescued madness from this biological determinism and restored psychological causation—not to mention the Beyond, in the form of the unconscious.[20] By the end of the century, however, psychiatric thinking had largely swung back to the disease concept. Sophisticated diagnostic techniques revealed that specific abnormalities of brain structure or function were associated with particular symptoms, leading to the hypothesis that the fundamental cause of mental illness was some form of biologically based predisposition or vulnerability to stress. Actual clinical disorder was then triggered by psychosocial factors in a person's environment, which also determined the particular form the disorder took.

Whether brain abnormalities were the ultimate cause of mental illness or an effect of that cause, however, remained unknown; and treatment, whether involving antipsychotic drugs, creation of supportive environments, or psychotherapy, often could provide at best amelioration of symptoms, not cure.[21] For me this raises the question: If we cannot cure the "mentally ill," how are we going to live with them? Being able to do this (as opposed to returning to the era of confinement, which some experts were advocating in the late 1980s) depends on some appreciation of how, even within our own culture, madness can be relative.

Mental Illness and
Sex Roles

Until the mid-1980s, while the average person would say that homeless women must be "crazy," the average social service professional would tell you that most of them were schizophrenics. Even later, much popular writing still stressed their "mental illness" to explain why they were on the street.[1] But at the Dwelling Place we discovered that in practice it is not always easy to draw a line that clearly demarcates the ill from the not-ill. Two people with exactly the same "symptoms" may be defined and treated in quite different ways; or, as Part 1 showed, a person may be defined differently if her circumstances change, although her behavior is the same.

For these reasons some sociologists have highlighted the social context by treating chronic mental illness as a form of deviant behavior—that is, behavior that breaks certain generally agreed-on rules or social norms. This perspective sees mental illness not as a quality inherent in the individual but as a label applied by others.[2] It allows us to take into account the fact that there exists among the general population an enormous amount of the same behavior that in the "mentally ill" is taken as "symptoms" of "illness." "Apparently, many persons who are extremely withdrawn, or who 'fly off the handle' for extended periods of time, who imagine fantastic events, or who hear voices or see visions, are not labeled as insane either by themselves or others." One writer remarks on "the incredible amount of trouble a person may cause for himself and others before anyone begins to think about him psychiatrically, let alone take psychiatric action against him." A 1951 study of attitudes toward mental illness in a small Canadian town found that the "only consistent criterion for mental illness was admission to a mental hospital. Once it was known that this had taken place, the same behaviour that formerly was judged 'normal' would be considered as 'abnormal.'" The authors concluded: "Mental illness, it seems, is a condition which afflicts people who must go to a mental institution, but until they go almost anything they do is normal." Thus a great deal of deviant behavior that might easily be characterized as mental illness is either ignored or rationalized away.[3] For example:

> Napoleon-fever is an absolutely certain sign of insanity. A neighbor once had a bout of the disease, dressed up in imperial uniform, mounted a cow and dashed about the paddock hurling curses at the Duke of Wellington. In the England of those days, this was regarded as merely eccentric behaviour, and therefore not requiring mandatory doses of ECT, a straitjacket and enough tranquillisers to turn him into a cabbage. Health costs were lower then.[4]

Two factors turn eccentricity into insanity. First, as one sociologist explains, "the deviations of the psychotic person from customary role expectancies . . . increase his social visibility and put strains upon others."[5] The other factor is the amount of power the person possesses. Since the norms on which the judgment is based have been created and are enforced by those in power, to flout them with impunity one must possess some power of one's own.

Historically women have been subject to different "expectancies" and had less power than men. Defining specific women as insane had to do not only with what was "wrong" with them but with the social norms that dictated how women ought to behave, in a context where someone else had the power to enforce those norms. As we saw, for example, in an age that disapproved of sensuality and learning in women, hysteria was seen as the fate of women who were too fond of sex or knowledge.[6]

In the case of Norma (whose husband had her committed), the fact that the husband controlled the situation was responsible for her being defined as mentally ill; his interest was to dispose of his troublesome wife in a manner that enabled him to marry someone else. The fact that his definition was supported by two psychiatrists and a judge means only that, among three representatives of those who made the norms against which her behavior was judged, there was a clear consensus that she violated them. Looking at the case in this way lets us see Norma's behavior in terms of her position within her social situation, instead of solely as a personal problem. Did she, originally, simply fail to fulfill a set of expectations that (perhaps) ran counter to her nature? Was she then afraid to express as much anger as she felt at their being imposed on her, because of the tremendous weight of authority—economic, psychological, physical—that lay behind them? And might she then have discovered that being "crazy" relieved her of the obligation?

ROLE STEREOTYPES

I begin with the expectations from which "mentally ill" women have been thought to deviate. But actually I have to begin with the proposition that those expectations constitute an impossible injunction—a double bind, as it were, guaranteeing failure since they impose two contradictory standards at once. In an often-cited study Inge Broverman and others related concepts of mental health to sex-role stereotypes. A group of male and female psychiatrists, psychologists, and social workers responded to a questionnaire asking them to indicate for each item in a list of pairs of opposite stereotypical personality traits (such as "very subjective—very objective") which trait in each pair would more closely describe the behavior of a mentally healthy man, mentally healthy woman, or mentally healthy adult of unspecified sex. The researchers found that, while the concepts held by these professionals of a healthy man and a healthy adult were the same, their concept of a healthy woman was significantly different; she was perceived as (to take just a few examples) less aggressive, less independent, more emotional, more easily influenced, more submissive, more passive, less logical, knowing less "the way of the world," less able to make decisions, less self-confident, and more dependent than the healthy man or adult. Not only—as the researchers comment—does this set of attributes seem "a most unusual way of describing any mature, healthy individual"; it also leads to the conclusion that in order to be considered normal, healthy women, women must be unhealthy adults. This is the double bind: they must "decide whether to exhibit those positive characteristics considered desirable for men and adults, and thus have their 'femininity' questioned, that is, be deviant in terms of being a woman; or to behave in the prescribed feminine manner, accept second-class status, and possibly live a lie to boot."[7]

Although this study was published in 1970, its results appear still to be valid. A 1981 article reviews evidence that sex-role stereotyping continued to exist among mental-health professionals and that "these biases are especially prominent in the treatment of women who reject traditional role constructs of women's place." In 1984 a review of various earlier reports concluded that "community-based programs for the chronically mentally ill" had "lower performance expectations" for women than for men, "based on societal role definitions" and the expectation that women will not "become economically productive." Finally, a 1988 report cites a string of studies, as well as new results, all indicating "that females, relative to males, tend to be seen by professionals as intrinsically more maladjusted."[8]

Certainly Broverman's results throw light on a phenomenon I described in Part 1—the woman whose dependency was quite acceptable while she was married suddenly being categorized as defective ("mentally ill") when the marriage ended. That is, during her marriage she was expected to conform to the portrait of the "mentally healthy female," but when she was thrown into a position of having to take care of herself, the "mentally-healthy-adult" expectations suddenly applied. Again the implication is that the defective concept of female is the standard one. The reason, I think, is the tendency, pointed out in Part 3, to think of women not as single self-related individuals but in terms of their connection with a family. Thus to specify "female" is automatically to imply a kind of contingent existence, one based on relationship to other rather than to self and in which dependency and passivity are natural. That is why in the study the concept "adult," which implies autonomy, resembled "man" but not "woman," and why "adult" expectations apply only to women in nonstandard situations: specifically, when they are no longer in a family.

Two traits of the "mentally healthy woman," passivity and dependence, were constant themes in the lives of the homeless women I knew. A good example of passivity in action (so to speak), of a kind that we encountered over and over at the Dwelling Place, is Alice, who lost her apartment but continued to return to her old block on the first of the month to wait for the mailman, who knew her and would hand her her SSI check. At length he said she had to file a change of address, and she did, but only with the post office, not with Social Security; the next month her check did not come to the new address. After some calls to SSI, I learned that no check would be forthcoming for another two weeks.

Meanwhile Alice needed a place to stay; she had been on the street for several months. She talked and worried a great deal about not having a place, but it was hard to get her to do anything. She finally called Mary House because I was standing over her; and then I saw at least part of the reason why simple acts were so difficult for her: she couldn't see. She was farsighted and badly needed glasses (which she could have gotten with Medicaid but only after great perseverance); without them she had trouble seeing the numbers on the dial and needed a magnifying glass to see written numbers. Making the call involved manipulating earphone, dial, magnifying glass, and slip of paper in turn, all with her head bent low so she could make out which hole to put her finger in. The whole procedure took ten minutes; when she finally spoke to someone, she was told they had no bed.

At this point Alice's mind stopped working. If I said, "Alice, you have to decide to do something because if not you'll wind up spending the next two weeks in Penn Station" (where she had been), she answered, "Oh no, I'll die before I spend the night in a station." However, she wouldn't make any positive choice. She could also have gone to SSI and gotten certification of a missing check, which at that time would have enabled her to go to welfare and ask for emergency money, and she said she would do that; but she didn't. Her mind simply hopped around all sides of the issue, refusing to land on it. It is frustrating even trying to describe this because in her center I sensed an emptiness that is hard to put into words. Her sense of purpose evaporated; it didn't last past when you spoke to her. She was grateful for my caring and wanting to help but quite unable to take the action that the help required. For such women, when I or someone else took their problems in hand we became—like a husband—the filler of the void with our will and purpose. They could act for us or for each other (they were all eager to help out in the shelter and quick to give each other advice on how to deal with welfare), but not for themselves.

It turned out, further, that the new address Alice wanted her check sent to was that of a man in Brooklyn whom she had met "in the park." Who was he? She didn't know him well but kept saying he had a good job, a nice apartment, so he must be honest because how could he risk losing all that? She assumed that bad people didn't have good jobs—that is, they lost them because they were bad. Alice had been married for years and had a teenaged daughter (who was staying with a friend), but whatever experience of living this had given her had not dented her extraordinary naiveté. I had to assume that marriage had completely protected her from ever having to act in the world. Now she behaved almost as if she resented the fact that some external force was no longer setting her life in order for her.

This same feeling, I suspect, also lay behind the episode of Lydia's breakdown, described in Part 1, in which she was so clearly asking to be babied. It is important, however, to examine precisely what was involved. In Lydia's case it was not exactly an inability to act in the world; she had worked all her life and had told me she always liked to work hard and therefore had trouble adjusting when arthritis compelled her to stop. Her breakdown had to do with her husband's sudden desertion. At issue, then, is not so much a physical requirement of action—work, let us say— as the psychological stance required in being alone, or living for oneself. More than merely being the caretaker (which in many marriages is debatable anyway), the man functions as the *image* of the caretaker and especially as the locus of primary existence. Thus to Alice the stranger in the park *was* the man who should receive her money—that is, he was not himself, whoever he was; he was the MAN who takes care of you.

Virginia Woolf said, "Women have served all these centuries as looking-glasses possessing the magic and delicious power of reflecting the figure of man at twice its natural size."[9] I suggest that at the same time man has served the inverse function for woman: no matter how large her actual size—that is, how capable, solvent, intelligent, strong, or whatever she might actually be—having that man there has enabled her to avoid the agony of perceiving herself as such and therefore separate in herself, not part of someone else (which is to say totally at odds with the standard expectations and thus terrifyingly separate from the entire social context). Instead everything she does gets transferred magically over to him so she no longer has to own it. While many women in society also function this way, seeing homeless women do so had a particular starkness, because they had achieved that condition which for those inside is only a shadow haunting the imagination: as "unaccommodated woman," they walked unclothed through an ultimate aloneness that revealed what often is left when the images that dress women up in society are stripped away—nothing.

The fact is that women like Alice and Lydia have gotten a raw deal— or, to be precise, suffered a breach of contract; they had (implicitly) agreed to settle for passivity in return for being taken care of. After years of carrying out their end of the agreement, for which they gave up their (potential) capacity for autonomy, they were suddenly left with no caretaker and, to add insult to injury, found themselves expected (by social service agencies, for example) to be able to function on their own. Naturally enough they resented this, and resisted, in their way; so although it was irritating to sit there and coax Lydia to sip some orange juice as though she were a child, I could hardly blame her for acting like one.

But the image of the man as caretaker is not just an image; it is embedded in expectations and norms that shape the objective conditions of women's lives. For example, another group of researchers who in the early 1960s compared female former mental patients with "normal"— that is, never-hospitalized—women from the same neighborhood came up against the problem of what criteria to use for the comparison. They felt that the central criterion used for men—their ability to hold a job and support a family—was not applicable to women, who had to be evaluated on the basis of how they functioned as wives, mothers, and homemakers. Even so this criterion was not equivalent to the one used for men because of the different circumstances of women's lives, which both cushioned failure and hid it. "Female roles tend to 'mask' female aberrance. . . . As mother, wife, and as woman, the female functions in settings which shield her misdeeds from public view." At the same time female deviance when it does occur is easier to put up with: "In middle class America, at least, it is easier to tolerate and carry a poor housewife and mother and an inadequate wife than a sick breadwinner." A "considerable number" of the so-called normals were found to have symptoms ranging from mild to severe: one, for example, heard voices; another saw people who weren't there.[10]

The idea that female roles mask female aberrance involves more, however, than just being sheltered. Such a role can act as a mask because the role itself is so close to the aberrant behavior that to some degree they overlap. If normal ("healthy") women are supposed to be dependent, where do you draw the line beyond which dependency should be considered pathological?

This question is not confined to those middle-class women studied in the sixties. Tremendous social changes have occurred since this research was done, but the cultural attitudes most women—on all socioeconomic levels—internalize do not seem to have shifted accordingly. "Since men hold the power and authority, women are rewarded for developing a set of psychological characteristics that accommodate to and please men," wrote three psychiatrists in 1981. "Such traits—submissiveness, compliance, passivity, helplessness, weakness—have been encouraged in women."[11]

Certainly, reports by service providers who worked with or studied women in homeless shelters during the 1980s repeatedly note the women's "helplessness training," the problems posed by their having been "socialized to be dependent," and their lack of self-esteem, self-confidence, and "the social and vocational skills and ego strengths that might permit them to move into other circumstances."[12] The authors of a statewide study of homeless people in Ohio stress women's "economic dependence

. . . on parents or partners" and conclude that "the problems of homeless women" are "extremes of the normal lack of social, emotional, and economic resources of women in general."[13] The intensity of the pressures women feel to conform to conventional sex roles is evident from the extreme situation of battered women, who often seek help from family and community for leaving a violent man, only to be told (depending on which culture they belong to): "marriage is holy"; "you must keep the family together"; "you married him, now you have to put up with him."[14]

THE MEANING OF SCHIZOPHRENIA

Passivity and dependence can be connected with mental illness in a number of ways.[15] Here I want to relate them to schizophrenia. Most of the Dwelling Place women whose psychiatric histories we knew had at some point been diagnosed schizophrenic. What is more, while studies—some relying on self-reported histories of psychiatric hospitalization, some on clinical judgments by interviewers—differed on the extent of mental illness among homeless people (as described in Part 3), researchers generally agreed that a larger proportion of women than of men had such disorders and that a major one was schizophrenia.[16]

The predominant psychiatric view of schizophrenia sees it not as a single entity but as a group of diseases with different etiologies, in each of which several factors may combine to produce the disorder. Although specific genetic, endocrine, immunological, and biochemical factors have been associated with schizophrenia, no ultimate cause has been identified. Diagnosis must be based on a complicated set of criteria describing symptoms that vary widely, from delusions and hallucinations to lack of emotion and inability to feel pleasure. Broadly speaking, however, the essence of this condition can be described as "loss or distortion of the self as a meaningful entity."[17]

Whether or not schizophrenia has a biological cause, its extreme variability from one person to the next has led to a consensus that environmental stresses play an important role in determining whether it will develop and what form it will take. One hypothesis, the "vulnerability-stress model," sees schizophrenia "as a product of interacting forces, some genetic or biological and some psychological, and some innate or constitutional and some learned through experience. . . . Both a disturbed rearing environment and an innate vulnerability to schizophrenia are necessary to generate the syndrome."[18]

Although older theories that attributed schizophrenia solely to early childhood experiences are no longer widely accepted, they retain value as descriptions of the role of psychodynamic factors in "facilitating and preventing the disease process." Some of these theories describe irrational family milieus that "profoundly influence the onset or course of schizophrenia."[19] One such "family-transaction" theory, developed by Theodore Lidz, offers a useful paradigm for seeing how socially sanctioned female passivity intersects with socially condemned female pathology. The parallels between Lidz's portrait of the distorted and disrupted schizophrenic personality and the characteristics listed above of the "mentally healthy woman" are striking.

According to Lidz, the essence of the problem is that the child's self is not her own but is given over to the parent. Because the child's energy goes "into giving meaning to [the parent's] life," she never learns to separate her own needs and feelings from those of the parent (of either sex, but, often with daughters, the father). In some cases both parents are involved in creating "a strange family milieu filled with inconsistencies, contradictory meanings, and denial of what should be obvious," which the child is required to validate.[20] To do this the child must repress not only her perception of reality but the awareness of her own feelings that is the foundation of a sense of self.

The effect is to "distort the child's meanings and reasonings"—that is, her thinking. She never learns—or learns inadequately—to distinguish what is real from what is not; lacking even the confidence that something dependably real exists, she lacks as well the firm sense of the place she herself occupies that is essential to the most basic functioning in relation to the external world and other people. For someone with no sense of her self as a separate entity, the need to become independent of parents and begin to live her own life that arises in late adolescence is overwhelming and impossible to fulfill. Similarly, the prospect of developing relationships with other people is terrifying: "Intimacy for one who has such fluid self-boundaries threatens engulfment and loss of any semblance of individual identity."[21]

This description of the family setting that facilitates schizophrenia overlaps remarkably with the conventional version of their role that so many women have internalized. Living their lives for another person is the norm, while the list of traits of the "mentally healthy woman" seems to constitute a fair description of the damaged personality produced by the schizophrenogenic family. Herein too lies an explanation of the abrupt disintegration even of women with no psychiatric history when they lose their husbands or other caretaking relatives. A wife just divorced or widowed who suddenly has to function on her own is in the same position as an adolescent never allowed to develop an autonomous self who must suddenly launch herself into the world.

I think this may also be the condition of many young homeless women suddenly forced to leave their families, whether because of eviction or drugs. Colleen McDonald, the director of the Olivieri Center for Homeless Women, which reaches out especially to psychiatrically impaired women, told me she saw the center's role as not only providing basic services but also giving women "some sense of themselves back. I don't get that need as much from men." Men, she thought, had a sense of identity that women did not start out with—more expectations of themselves—and, despite drugs and mental illness, they could deal better with being homeless. But, she concluded, in this paternalistic society set up to take care of women, they became used to being taken care of and needed more support, including reassurance and encouragement even on the basic level of believing they had a right to make any simple statement about their feelings or opinion.[22]

I myself observed this incapacity for self-assertion in another form at the Brooklyn Women's Shelter demonstration described in the introduction. A group of women martial artists demonstrated simple self-defense techniques, and several then went among the crowd holding up mitts, which they encouraged the shelter residents to punch at. Though these young homeless women lived daily with violence, none that I saw could strike out with the full force of their shoulders. In fact the vision of female empowerment represented by these practitioners of karate brought out on their faces a soft, almost childish wonderment.

The inability to hit out provides a good point of contrast with men. Gender stereotypes help determine the nature of mental illness for men no less than for women, though of course both the stereotype and the "illness" will be different. Indeed different personality disorders tend to be distributed along gender lines, reflecting the stereotypes that men are active and aggressive and women passive and sick. Many researchers have found, for example, that women are more often diagnosed with Dependent Personality Disorder, while men are more often said to have Antisocial Personality Disorder.[23] Correspondingly, a number of studies of homeless people have reported that women have more and severer psychiatric disorders than men, who are more often said to be drug or alcohol abusers and to have criminal records.[24] However—as Elmer Streuning, the director of a study by the New York State Psychiatric Institute that evoked criticism for reporting a similar result, pointed out—this difference does not necessarily mean that women have more psychological problems than men. More likely, it represents the different ways men and women express their problems.[25] An analysis of how social context shapes male mental illness would presumably have to take into account the role stereotype that sanctions men getting drunk and belligerent, plus the likelihood of such behavior's being defined as mental illness or as something else.

For women, at least, the loss of self that characterizes schizophrenia appears to be a function of both real and perceived powerlessness. Much research has connected the development of mental illness in women to their "disadvantaged status." Not only do their "legal and economic" disadvantages make them effectively helpless, but "the expectation of powerlessness and inability to control one's own destiny . . . prevents effective action on one's behalf." Powerlessness then plays a role "in the development of psychological distress and clinical illness." Since low-income women have less power than middle-income women, it is not surprising that they have been reported to have higher rates of mental illness.[26]

Such women are often unable not only to assert themselves but to act. Consider another finding of the study of former mental patients. Although—based on ratings by the people they lived with—the "normal" women carried out their domestic activities better than did the patients, one item on the list does suggest the extent to which inability to act in the world has been institutionalized as an aspect of "normal" femininity. This item was doing the grocery shopping, which involved handling money. Only 34 percent of the former patients could do this without help; but only 67 percent of the normals could either.[27] In our society, money is a token of the selfhood that derives from power to act in the world; and were these helpless "normal" wives (whose husbands, perhaps, preferred them that way) not the same in that respect as the deviant homeless I described in Part 1 who spent their checks right away to avoid the disconcerting sense of owning money? What would happen to these normal wives if they suddenly had to negotiate a welfare application— or to the ones with symptoms if, during the application process, they made remarks that led a caseworker to refer them for psychiatric evaluation?

Another parallel with the schizophrenic child involves the fact that someone who is unable to act has a distorted perception of reality. Reality becomes known through action, and those whose sphere of action is narrow necessarily acquire narrow ideas of it. What is more, the self develops through action—that is, by making decisions about life and acting on the basis of them; the less such responsibility a person is permitted the less developed the self will be. Survival skills such as compliance and passivity "are antithetical to the use of *active* psychic mechanisms for coping." Many homeless women who had been sheltered in their homes or marriages never learned how the world works and never developed the ability to deal with it. Beyond this, only through acting does one acquire a personal history, and only when one has a history does one have a meaningful sense of the future.[28]

Not only have homeless women been socialized into passivity and dependence; they also live in an environment to which passivity is not an inappropriate response. Studies of the psychology of poverty have shown that because very poor people's environment is itself unpredictable and inconsistent, logical, rational thinking is not effective in coping with it; planning for the future, for example, is useless.[29] One cannot be confident that the same people or institutions will respond consistently to the same situation—witness the arbitrariness of welfare decisions and procedures—and therefore one can have no confidence that one's own actions will have consistent (or any) effectiveness. So one tends to act on impulse, to be ruled by emotion—again, a characteristic of the "mentally healthy woman" on the same order as the "improvidence" with which the poor have been charged. And when one's situation is such that "getting better" could not improve it but would only make one unbearably conscious of how awful it is and how painful one's feelings about it are (especially by contrast, often, with a happier past), self-preservation actually dictates total refusal.[30]

This was explicitly illustrated for me one evening at the Dwelling Place. I went upstairs to get my coat from the office (which was kept locked) and found standing before the door a white-haired, tattered but still quite elegant woman whom I knew of but had never spoken to. On the floor at her feet were a shopping bag and a battered animal case in which she kept her cat. She simply stood, facing the padlocked door. Thinking she must want something from the office (where we kept supplies that the women were always requesting), I asked, "Can I help you?" At first she did not respond at all; then she picked up her things and went down the hall. This woman was European, I found out later, and had been a professional until her sister broke down and was diagnosed schizophrenic. This apparently triggered something in her; she worried that it ran in the family, went to psychiatrists, and wound up on the street. Only her fear that the cat was too cold induced her to seek shelter;

she was proud, hostile, and extremely hard to deal with. Hearing all this, I realized that she had not wanted to enter the room; she had wanted to face the locked door. Rather than wishing doors would open for her, she preferred to feel sure they would stay closed.

SYSTEMS OF PERMANENT CARE

I do not mean to present a picture of homeless, poor—or any—women as totally, or even essentially, incompetent and pathetic. The same writers who describe the negative effects of women's socialization also affirm that homeless women are "resourceful, determined, courageous, and self-reliant" and point out that "much of their plight is due to socioeconomic circumstances pitted against which the best individual coping skills will fail."[31] I saw myself that the depth of the Dwelling Place women's inner resources could be measured by how creatively they managed to function despite the obstacles created by their socialization. In fact perceiving these obstacles was one reason for my feeling that so many women with psychiatric diagnoses "weren't really crazy." They seemed to have the same problems all women had, only intensified by homelessness.

I say this not to contest the existence of mental illness but to suggest that to the extent its nature is socially determined, social factors can prevent or ameliorate it. In particular, this means shifting away from the tendency to categorize mentally ill homeless women (and men) as a needy, dependent population. Many do need caretaking, but the conceptual constructs through which we view them will affect the form that caretaking assumes, as past caretaking institutions have demonstrated.

For a long time, one such institution was marriage, which spared many women the need to become autonomous.[32] In the past, in fact, the wife's dependency and inability to function on her own rendered her analogous to the schizophrenic; they even had a similar legal status. In 1860, for example, Mrs. Elizabeth Packard was committed by her husband, a minister, to a state mental hospital in Illinois because she disagreed with him on certain questions of faith. In her account of her incarceration Packard asserts that even the hospital director, by his own treatment of her and remarks he made to others about her, tacitly admitted that she was not insane; this, however, was not relevant, for Illinois law at the time provided that married women could be committed at their husband's or guardian's request "without the evidence of insanity required in other cases."[33] Why should wives be thus equated with insane persons? Because—so I read the implication—their essential relation to society was the same.

Although wives are no longer subject to legal control by their husbands, the question of what to do with troublesome, dependent people remains. For a long time, as we saw, the answer was institutionalization. By the end of the nineteenth century, most Americans who could not work were in prisons, hospitals, and mental asylums, all of which constituted a system of permanent care. In the twentieth century, in response to objections to the state mental hospitals, control of their inmates came to be carried out medically, using drugs.[34]

Among these dependent people, unattached women, as we saw, were particularly disturbing. Thomas Szasz has made the provocative assertion that schizophrenia represented a solution to the social problem of what to do with dependent people—which, in the case of women, generally meant those who did not marry or whose marriages ended. Until recently (and still today except in a few rather special realms) women were not supposed to live alone. They were required to be subject to the control of some male figure—if not father or husband, then Christ—so in past centuries a standard solution for such women was commitment to religious life. In the modern period this was replaced by commitment to a "permanent-care facility" as madness largely replaced religious life as an alternative "career" for women who did not marry (as well as for men who threatened to be perpetually dependent).[35]

The shift from the theological to the medical framework is noted by Packard herself:

> Had I lived in the sixteenth instead of the nineteenth century, my husband would have used the laws of the day to punish me as a heretic for this departure from the established creed—while under the influence of some intolerant spirit he now uses this autocratic institution as a means of torture to bring about the same result—namely *a recantation of my faith*. In other words, instead of calling me by the obsolete title of heretic, he modernizes his phrase by substituting insanity instead of heresy as the crime for which I am now sentenced to endless imprisonment in one of our Modern Inquisitions. . . . Much that is now called insanity will be looked upon by future ages with a feeling similar to what we feel toward those who suffered as witches in Salem, Massachusetts.[36]

We came to take the solution of psychiatric commitment so much for granted that in the 1970s, as deinstitutionalization effectively canceled it and increasing numbers of solitary women appeared on the street, people were shocked and horrified to discover that they even existed. The breakdown of our two systems of permanent care—that is, of the stability and permanence of marriage and of the state hospital system—by creating such numbers of visible homeless women, betokens real structural flaws in a society where the childish dependency of women has its complement in the parental authority of men.

Daddy's Good Girls

According to popular legend, Saint Dymphna, who lived around the sixth century, was the daughter of a pagan (probably Irish) king and a Christian mother who died when Dymphna was young, though not before she had been taught Christianity and baptized. As the girl grew older, her father developed an illicit passion for her because she closely resembled her dead mother, whom he had adored. On her confessor's advice Dymphna fled, but her father pursued her and caught her at Gheel, in what is now Belgium. When she persisted in refusing to submit to him, he beheaded her, and at that moment regained his sanity. In the thirteenth century her relics were discovered and said to have cured "a number of epileptics, lunatics and persons under malign influence."[1] She thus became the patroness of the insane; her shrine became a place of pilgrimage, and the town of Gheel itself assumed a collective vocation of caring for the mentally ill, which it still pursues today.

The legend does not make any very clear connection between the particular events of Dymphna's martyrdom and the curing of insanity, but I can offer one. A suggestion of it came from the Dwelling Place woman who informed me one day at lunch that in a former life she had been Saint Barbara, whose story remarkably resembles Dymphna's. The daughter of a rich Roman pagan, Saint Barbara was martyred in the third century by her father. To prevent her from marrying and being taken away from him (or, in another version, to hide her so no man would see her great beauty), he built a luxurious tower to shut her up in. Nevertheless, she became interested in Christianity and was secretly baptized. When she confessed her faith to her father, his fury at having, despite his precautions, lost her to another man (since her conversion meant accepting the superior authority of Jesus) led him to denounce her to the authorities. As was customary, he carried out her execution himself.[2]

Both these saint's tales are concerned with the control of women in a society where men hold power. If those in power define who is mad, Saint Dymphna's association with the insane seems to reflect some awareness of how this dynamic operates when a woman defies the authority of the father. It is true that the story exalts Dymphna's rejection of her father; but that is only the Christian overlay. Sexual morality is not the issue here; power is, for one must remember that both these stories are told from the perspective of the winning side in the struggle between the pagan and Christian fathers for the daughters' allegiance. Thus Dymphna's father's madness (possession by the devil) is simply the sign that he belonged to the enemy, while the curative effect of her martyrdom on him and, later, on others who fell away from the true authority is a demonstration of that authority's power working through her. These daughters chose the right side in the conflict, and that is why they appear as saints. (Those who chose wrong were, as we will see in Part 5, the witches, undutiful daughters who were accused of having taken Satan—the pagan father—as their master; his supposed copulation with them is exactly parallel to the two saints' fathers' incestuous desires. As always, the accusation of illicit sexuality surfaces in reaction to women who do not submit to the proper authority.) The stories make clear how vital the control of women was felt to be and suggest what powerful weapons could be marshaled against those who showed reluctance to stay in line.

To me the choice by the woman I met at lunch of Saint Barbara as her previous incarnation reflects an unconscious perception of this same relation, which persists today, between people (but especially women) labeled insane and the structures of authority, still overwhelmingly male. One can look at it from two perspectives: that of an objective reality consisting of courts and judges, hospitals and doctors, who define, dispose of, and treat people; or that of a subjective reality, which consists of the women's own perceptions of and responses to the objective situation. It is this second perspective, and the women's images, that I want to use. The individual psychology behind these images is less important here than the way they reveal a specifically female version of the dynamic in

which passivity becomes necessary, suffering required, and action inter-
dicted. Understanding this will, in turn, explain certain behaviors that
seem mysterious, quaint, or plain crazy.

It is perfectly logical that most of the homeless women I knew were
obsessed by images of all kinds of powerful men, for in the United States
the authority of government is conceptualized as male and represented
by male images, from the local policeman to the black-robed judge to the
president to the male deity to whose ultimate authority the whole operation supposedly subordinates itself. Nor were the Dwelling Place women
the first to have been impressed by this power relation. In the 1840s Father Isaac Hopper, a prison reformer, described the case of J., who had
been convicted of perjury and sentenced to Sing Sing prison for fourteen
years. "She was confined in ――― jail about two years *before* conviction, the jury not being able to agree on the first trial. She had been in
Sing Sing but a short time, before it became evident that her mind was
giving way under the weight of her sufferings."

She became severely depressed, then violently deranged, and was
transferred to a "lunatic asylum," where Hopper visited her.

> We took her [for] a walk through the yard and garden, and . . . one of the
> company remarked what a pleasant place it was. She looked around and re-
> plied, "Yes, it is a very pleasant place, but chains are chains, if they are made
> of gold, and mine grow heavier every day I wear them." After this visit she
> seemed for a short time to be much worse—she used vulgar and profane lan-
> guage, and tore up her blanket and made pantaloons of it. It was found diffi-
> cult to keep her in her room: she several times picked the lock of the door and
> escaped, but was soon re-captured and returned to her old quarters. Some
> weeks afterwards I made her another visit, and found her attired in her new
> costume. As soon as she saw me, she made an effort to get out of my sight, as
> she did not wish me to see her with her pantaloons on; but I called her, and
> she came to me. I took her kindly by the hand, and said, "J., what does all this
> mean?" She replied, "It is military; I am an officer of state."

After getting her to change her clothes, he took her for a walk, during
which she wept and said that "she had not a friend in the world—that
she was forgotten by every body."

Hopper himself thereupon undertook to be her friend; he wrote to her,
visited, and brought her on trips to New York City. She improved considerably; and at the same time Hopper was told by a state senator that she
was innocent of the crime she had been imprisoned for. Having assured
himself that she was no longer "deranged," he procured a pardon for her
from the governor and found her the best situation an ex-convict could
hope for—placement with a family in the country.[3]

J.'s rapid recovery as soon as she encountered a kind person who gave her a sense of human connection indicates that her period of madness was essentially the result of the desperate circumstances that made her feel entirely helpless and alone—and angry. Her symbolic behavior in making herself the pants (quite improper at the time, as we know) might have seemed deranged but actually makes sense. In taking on male attributes (including the use of "vulgar and profane language," a male prerogative)—that is, in identifying herself with the power that had (unjustly) imprisoned her—she was implicitly identifying her femininity with powerlessness and rejecting it. Her anger was a perfectly rational response to her situation, and her mode of expressing it appropriate, given her captivity, for even the kind Father Hopper would have been shocked if he had understood the message of her pantaloons.

What is more, the *kind* of power J. attributed to herself exactly matches that which absorbed the homeless women I knew: the power of men who control what happens in society—or, more specifically, what happens to *them*. Like J., they wanted to be on its side, which in their case involved a kind of sentimental attachment to individuals who embodied it. Thus, for example, during coffee-hour discussions of celebrities the women talked about female movie stars, but the men they brought up tended to be politicians, whom they discussed as if they had been movie stars. Nelson Rockefeller was one who evoked this kind of response. When he died in February 1979 there was a scandal over his relationship with his young secretary, played up for all it was worth by the *New York Post*. At one coffee hour the women, passing the newspaper around, agreed that it was a shame, he was such a good man; he left someone forty-five thousand dollars, let Henry Kissinger and others borrow money and never asked for it back, and on and on. At length I had had enough. "Rockefeller was a *bad man*," I exclaimed. "Why are you wasting all this sympathy on him?" Astonished silence greeted me, until one woman said wonderingly, "I always thought he was terrific." I began to explain that Rockefeller was the representative of the rich who cared nothing for poor people like themselves, but no one really heard. They were all swept away by sentimentality, as though Rockefeller's life were a bad movie.

Another day, one of the same women did let slip a hint of anger when she ventured a criticism of the mayor of New York and of President Carter. They had both done a bad job, she said, and wouldn't be reelected; politicians say anything before the election but then break their promises. Several of us agreed with her, but she was evidently uncomfortable and,

to my surprise, kept justifying herself. Whereas I took saying negative
things about politicians for granted, doing so made her anxious and
therefore defensive—although she never thought twice about criticizing
the sisters or the volunteers or the other homeless women. Similarly, she
was proud of her good relationship with the manager of the hotel and
always took his side when someone else complained about him. In fact
her self-righteousness on these occasions inevitably brought out my own
tendency to want to feel like Daddy's good girl, and each time I had to
fight down the automatic assumption that the man in authority was right
and the woman in conflict with him wrong.

At the top of the hierarchy of male authority, of course, was God himself; and many women had a complicated, ambivalent relationship with
him that was a paradigm of what occurred at every point down the line.
The Lord for them was both lover and judge. As lover, he entrusted them
with secret knowledge or a special mission or, most important, bestowed
approval and a sense of being good, justified; as judge, he punished them
for their sins.

Judith, a young Jewish woman on bad terms with her parents, had
been influenced by the Jehovah's Witnesses who handed out literature in
the Port Authority bus terminal; her talk about the Christian god had
upset her parents, and she felt very guilty. What was she doing at the
Dwelling Place as a Jew, she asked herself; her father had told her she was
a freeloader in that Christian place. Her parents hated her, she went on,
except she thought her father liked her a little. She had transferred this
same paradoxical attitude to the Christian father. She was a Jew, she
said, so how could Jesus love her? Besides she was bad. But did I know
that Jehovah loved a whore? I said yes, and so why didn't he love her?
"You just said I was a whore," she responded. Then she asked if I loved
Jesus; I said I had no relationship with him. She couldn't understand this;
her own connection to this father figure (good or bad) was so central to
her being that the idea of my having none at all was more frightening
than if I had said I hated him. She began again to abuse herself: she was
evil, she was a blasphemer, she ought to kill herself because she was no
good. In fact she threatened suicide, so I wound up taking her to the
emergency room at Saint Vincent's, where she paused beside a man lying
on a stretcher and informed him that he should be happy because since
he was suffering Jehovah would send him to heaven. Apparently the best
way to escape Jehovah's hatred was to suffer a lot.

In fact, the necessity or validity of suffering (or being punished) was a
constant theme in many homeless women's ideas about life. While Judith

fluctuated between the conviction that she was evil and the hope that Jesus could love her, some women identified with the Lord entirely and only had him punishing other people (on whom they were quick to pass judgment in his name); others, like the woman who shaved her head, carried out his punishment on themselves. But for all of them the necessity of suffering and the expectation of punishment (as well as the ambivalence between lover and judge) remained constant and constituted the foundation of their perceived relationships with other male figures, especially those who embodied the powers of state.

To some degree the government controls all of us, but the homeless women, who depended on its checks, were interned in its hospitals, pushed around by its policemen, and disposed of by its judges, had a far more immediate experience of its power over their lives. Thus certain power relationships that for women inside society are discreetly veiled by social gratuities operated stark naked in the world of the homeless; and this was perhaps the source of the menacing imaginings of some, fantasies of violence and persecution by powerful, impersonal authorities possessing secret knowledge. In particular, institutions that conduct clandestine operations turned into shadowy figures inhabiting many women's minds. Thus Fran, the woman mentioned in Part 1 who believed she was followed by an entourage of "intelligence," informed me that the men she went out with had always turned out to be CIA or FBI; quite a few others also believed the FBI was after them.

Some women associated all these feelings with the police. Emily, who had been a maid but had to stop working because of a heart condition, received an SSI pension and did well enough until her sister died and she started menopause. At that time, it seems, the police siren began. As far as I could gather, Emily began to hear the siren every time she had a place to live—an SRO, an adult home in Queens—everywhere but in one of the railroad stations, which was where she lived when last I saw her. Whatever inner compulsion it was that forced her to leave any shelter she found, it quite naturally took the form of a police siren warning her to move on.

Other government agencies were also perceived as male powers that both gave and destroyed. Ellen, the woman who had lost her fingers, was obsessed by all the workings of legal authority, though her thoughts centered on the Treasury, the source of her check. Ellen had long before retreated into a world of metaphor whose safety lay in indirectness, which is to say that without real effort it was impossible to understand much of what she said. She not only expressed herself in metaphor but also acted symbolically; her constant care to ward off the destructive powers of state took some odd forms. One day as I handed her coffee she asked me for an extra Styrofoam cup. It was for a mouse that had come out of a hole in her room at the hotel. She was going to give the mouse water in it, or coffee or milk, because if the mouse had something of its own (I managed to make out) it would leave her alone. When I discovered later that Ellen's check was late, I realized that she was experiencing the mouse as a kind of spy sent by the Treasury, an intrusion related to the absence of her check.

Hers was indeed a spy-novel world, permeated by invisible threats that had to be defended against by perpetual precautions against letting vital information slip out unawares. She once told me it was better not to use people's names in my writing because of "the State." Another time I asked her if she spoke other languages besides English, and she answered with a long speech about how "they" made it difficult. "It's better not to," she concluded, and I saw how her whole life was fenced in by the ever-present *they* which exerted over her an ominous control.

Yet her fantastical construction had a solid base in reality. When we first knew her, she had asked me if I was a legal stenographer because she needed one, adding something I couldn't understand about forms and "the Treasury." I had assumed this was a delusion based on her legal obsession (one many other women shared). But months later it developed that she had a disability pension that had gotten tangled up in the bureaucracy; as a result, her checks were going to the wrong person—a man. She did indeed need a legal stenographer: someone to take her words and turn them into language someone in "the Treasury" could read. It was sheer terror at the danger of stating the naked fact that necessitated an indirection that may have been pathological but was hardly meaningless.

A few women named the Mafia as their persecutor, an interesting variation on the perception of patriarchal authority. Others, especially older ones, invoked the Nazis. Rose, a European Jewish refugee in her seventies whose family had been killed by the Nazis, did not refer to them directly, but her experience informed her behavior. In response to suggestions or offers of help she would avert her eyes and say, "Let the United States come and arrest me." If you said, "Rose, what do you want to do?" she answered, "I have not betrayed . . . What I wonder is why the Jewish people have not come, and what is going on behind the curtain." Rose, in fact, gave me my first hint of the connection between homeless and "normal" women. She was exactly like my own grandmother (a victim not of the Nazis but of the Cossacks), who also acted as if punishment was all she expected from the world. My grandmother had her family and was not homeless; but behind the curtain, I thought, she and Rose must have had much the same feelings.

The opposite of the Nazi was a male figure perceived as not destructive at all but benevolently paternalistic and often romantic. Nelson Rockefeller, as we saw, was one such figure. What made him so was not only his political power and his glamorous personal life but also his connection to the Rockefeller millions, for money, both symbolically and really, is power, and men are the ones who have it.

While most women I knew used one or two or three of these images to express their perceptions of male/female and social-power relationships, Mimi had a set of ideas that included almost every one of them. She too had a legal obsession and would often walk into the Dwelling Place with an announcement that she had just come from "the judge," or leave saying she had to go see him. Pulling from her handbag a pamphlet from the Jehovah's Witnesses, she would point to it significantly, informing me that all the details or the revealing evidence was in there; once she showed me a legal form related to her "case." It was the right one, but it was blank.

While Mimi's ideas were clearly delusional, they were also quite meaningful. Mimi was a black woman with very light skin who always wore a blond wig. Her father had been white, she said, her mother black; and her system of ideas was a composite of dualities, based on this condition of being two contradictory things at once. She was obsessed by the figure of the transvestite, a good emblem of such a problematic state of being. Whereas to Fran all men were CIA, to Mimi they were all gay. A gay man she had found in the women's room at her hotel threatened to rape her and throw her out the window. She talked of a husband who was a gay and had an operation to make himself a woman. She identified him with Satan and the "gays" with the demons who were taking over America. One day, however, she announced triumphantly that her husband had died—"the bad one." She claimed she never wanted to get married again but told me in the next breath that she was engaged to Rockefeller. (After Rockefeller died she became engaged to his brother.) Another time she came in saying she had been to court, and it had gone very well; she had had a woman judge who agreed with her and said it didn't matter if they were black or white, they were all gays.

Mimi evidently had organized a whole set of issues into dualities expressed through the one of gay/straight: good/bad, black/white, man/

woman. Although her obsession with homosexuality (and it was not restricted to men: she once told me that her sister had died and turned into
a transvestite—or the other way around; I couldn't get it straight) was
unique in my experience, like Ellen's with "the State" it signals a basic
issue. Many of the women—who as their histories suggest tended to have
quite traditional, conservative social attitudes—felt great fear and distaste toward homosexuality, though usually directed at the idea of lesbi-
anism. I think that these feelings (which did not prevent friendships with
individual gay men and women; many of the volunteers were homosex-
ual men, and the women adored them) arose because their extremely
weak sense of themselves made the blurring of basic categories that homosexuality suggests threatening. A woman whose own hold on her female identity is under great stress needs a firm and uncomplicated sense
of the man/woman distinction, which is dangerously compromised by
the idea of the transvestite or of homosexuality in general.

For in fact all of Mimi's various dualities boiled down to a single fundamental one, which I discovered on the day in 1979 that the Israel-
Egypt peace treaty was signed. Waving the *Daily News* with its front-
page photo of Anwar Sadat and Menachem Begin, Mimi announced that
she was going to Egypt to make a business investment with Sadat. However he wanted her only as a blond because that was the way he saw her,
although it wasn't her true self. Her husband, who was a millionaire, did
want her as her true self; and she had no intention of losing her true self
but was going to appear to Sadat the way he wanted her—for a time—
because of this investment, by dyeing her hair.

I thought: Mimi's delusions are deep. For she had put in a nutshell the
whole traditional power dynamic between individual men and women,
as well as the more general one that lies behind the elaborate delusions of
spying, secrecy, privileged information: the need for women to appear
the way men (husbands, the government) want them to in order to get
what they need (support, welfare). Thus is created the central duality of
true self and false; and, like Mimi, most of the Dwelling Place women no
longer knew which was which, for after years of hiding the true self from
the intelligence operatives, they had lost sight of it themselves. But this
was the secret that the CIA sought, the judges passed judgment on, the
Rockefellers wanted to buy, and the Nazis tried to stamp out. As the
study of sex-role stereotypes, Lidz's theory of schizophrenia, Mrs. Packard's incarceration, and the two saint's tales all suggest, the true self is
not wanted: a woman who acted according to its dictates would step
outside the power structure and be free—and therefore dangerous.

Yet the metaphoric aptness of Mimi's images must not tempt us to lose sight of their literal meaning: one day she actually was attacked by a man in her hotel. Unlike a previous occasion when she claimed to have been hit by a bus but had no bruises, this time she had two black eyes and a broken arm. The "gay" man's threat to rape her, which had seemed to us a fantasy, now appeared to be an actual incident that had gotten incorporated into her fantasy system. Similarly, her earlier judge stories now melted into what sounded like the real story of the rapist being brought to trial; she said he had pleaded guilty and would be sentenced. (We never found out what had happened because Mimi did not live at the Times Square and told us little about her daily life.)

Thus while the homeless women's images of powerful male figures symbolized their perceptions of power relations in society, they also derived directly from experience and on that level were not symbolic at all. The essential ambiguity of the male figure as both punisher and lover (perfectly expressed by Mimi's alternation—from one sentence to the next—between her bad gay husband and her rich Rockefeller fiancé) reflected a real-life double bind: the person who punished the homeless woman was also the only source of what she needed. As a result, not only did she accept the punishment, but it became intertwined with gratification: a situation that constituted the essence of powerlessness because it prevented her from seeing other possibilities—strength, self-reliance. In fact the idea of being strong herself was frightening, less because it invited more punishment, which after all she was used to, than because it threatened the loss of the little she might have. So she devalued whatever real strengths she had in order to avoid even approaching this conflict.

The results of such a training were demonstrated in the fall of 1981, when the Reagan administration cut the food stamps of the women living in the Times Square from thirty-eight to seventeen dollars a month. It was possible to request a hearing with a reasonable chance of getting the cut restored because real need was easy to demonstrate (aside from the food stamps the women had only three dollars a day to spend on all their needs after paying rent). But few could be persuaded to go for the hearing, even with a volunteer along to support them; they were afraid that everything would be taken away.

Looking at homeless women's mental illness in a context that takes their lack of power into account provides an explanation of the bizarre behavior of women on the street: it is an instance of the traditional choice of oppressed people to go underground in order to carry out certain activities that do not simply maintain life but preserve its meaning. Thus writers circulate suppressed manuscripts, and political activists communicate in code. The homeless women, concealing their messages within mystifying speech and action, similarly engaged in strategic self-defense within a powerless situation. Ellen, after getting a huge back payment from SSI for the checks she never received, told me an incredible story, impossible to follow, about how her money had gotten tangled up in the government—something about a "crypto——." "You mean cryptogram?" I asked. "Like a code?" "Yes," she said. In her case what had to remain clandestine was the fact that, whatever she had been through, she had managed to retain her self or at least some essential piece of it. The paradox that one has to both hide the self and express it at the same time lies behind those mythified activities of collecting and hoarding and heterogeneous dressing, which it is now time to look at once more.

The Modern Margerys

I have used the metaphor of political oppression deliberately, because the question of identity—which is at the heart of a decision that someone is mentally ill—is at least partly a political one. Just as people who oppose a government identify themselves with certain ideas—about, say, the freedom to act and speak according to individual needs—that may put them in danger, many homeless women learned early in their lives that danger arose from simply being who they were (that is, acting and speaking according to their needs). In certain family or institutional situations this constituted a subversive act. The strategy, therefore, involved finding a way to enable the outlawed self still to exist, but in disguise.

A psychiatrist told me that his mother, after several years of having delusions about being persecuted and about sex, among other things, and taking odd trips for what seemed to be no reason, was put in a mental hospital but would not stay there. She was willing to be in a regular hospital for her organic complaints but, as he put it, "played a game of tennis"; in the mental hospital she developed physical problems, but then in the regular hospital she needed psychiatric care. At length he refused to have anything to do with her until, after some months, she developed a new pattern. She put her things in bags, went out and walked the streets, and finally, when she was cold, hungry, and physically deteriorated, called him. "As a doctor," he said, "I couldn't allow her to be in such a physical condition"—that is, he could not handle this difficult relationship with the feelings of a son; he had to switch into his doctor role.

On some level his mother had figured that out and so approached him as a patient. In that way she could have the connection with him, though she had to lose the special quality of the parent/child relationship. The contact was kept, but neither of them was happy with it, which is typically the price paid for the safety of the disguise. Note, however, that this woman could have chosen any number of ways to damage herself physically but wound up walking the streets with bags.

For women especially, bags resonate with meaning. The possessions we choose to own and the clothing we choose to wear are basic means of defining ourselves as apart from anyone else; this is why Terry snapped at me for trying to get her to take a pair of secondhand jeans. According to Erving Goffman, everyone's personal belongings, and the place or places where they are kept, "represent an extension of the self and its autonomy," while their privacy and inviolability represent the self's integrity. He describes the way mental hospitals and other such "total" institutions systematically strip inmates of their selves—among other means by refusing to permit them personal possessions or private places to keep them in—and the inmates' corresponding strategies (often clandestine) for acquiring and holding onto various objects. Having no place to store things, patients in the hospital Goffman studied developed ways to carry their belongings around with them. One such "portable storage device was a shopping bag lined with another shopping bag."[1]

According to one Dwelling Place staff member, the practice in some mental institutions was to give each patient a bag to keep her things in. One hospital where she had worked eventually acquired small cabinets that were placed by the women's beds. It was considered an achievement when someone gained the confidence to leave her things there instead of carrying them with her. The staff member claimed that the phrase *shopping-bag lady* came out of the mental hospitals, where it was used by staff to refer to such patients.[2]

Holding on to possessions was mandated partly by the threat of theft in the hospital; but as the staff member's account suggests, there is a psychological component as well. Someone whose sense of self is shaky to begin with and whose hold on private space and personal belongings in the material world is perpetually insecure is likely to feel exposed, vulnerable, threatened. The shakier you feel inside, the more you need something external to hold on to, and a bag with its handle is very satisfying—witness the comments I quoted in Part 2; while the emptier you feel, the more you are led to compensate by filling the bags up. At the same time, if you possess only a few objects, they acquire great importance, no matter what they are or whether they have any practical value. This is why street people tend to collect and hang on to things they clearly have no "use" for.

A woman in her early thirties had been diagnosed schizophrenic in her late teens and spent years in and out of institutions. One day, during a period when she had her own apartment, she showed up at her aunt's house carrying all her clothes in shopping bags, saying she was afraid that if she didn't keep everything with her it would be stolen by someone who would get into her apartment by breaking down the walls. Although in New York City it is perfectly rational to fear that one's apartment will be broken into, it is not through the walls that thieves are likely to enter. But for this woman the apartment represented her self, and its walls *were* threatened; she habitually heard voices, broken-off parts of her own psyche that she refused to admit were products of her own mind but insisted had an objective existence outside her—that is, she experienced her self as fragments, which did not even belong to her but were alien beings. Filling the bags with clothes and holding on to them became a symbolic substitute for keeping the parts of herself together in one container and owning them.

Hearing voices is an extreme instance of psychic disintegration, but the feeling of falling apart—to a less pathological degree—is not uncommon, and I suspect that the enthusiastic involvement of ordinary women with their bags derives from this. In the early stages of working on this book, I went through a phase in which I suddenly stopped on the street and clutched at whatever bags I was carrying (usually a briefcase and handbag), out of a momentary panic that I was missing something. When I realized that this anxiety was not really about bags but came from feelings inside me, I began to experiment with not carrying any bags, and gradually the need to hold on so literally passed.

Some people extend this form of symbolic behavior well beyond the limitations imposed by even many bags, for lacking a stable self often makes you feel empty to an extreme that no mere bag can compensate. A regular Dwelling Place visitor, a charming, intelligent woman, had an unstable temper but seemed nevertheless to be functioning well, although we knew relatively little about her. One day the manager of her hotel called, shaken. Having entered her room while she was out because the tenant next door complained of a smell and said she had seen worms crawling out from under the door, he had discovered it was piled with garbage, "over my head," he said. He warned us that if it wasn't cleared out that day he would evict her, so I went over to find her and tell her this.

On seeing me the manager insisted that I go up and look at the room; he evidently thought that otherwise no one would believe his account of it. But it was exactly as he had said: not only over his head, and mine, but over the head of anyone less than seven feet tall. The room's entire area— it was about ten by twelve—was piled with junk, except for a small space that allowed the door to open. The bed was not visible. There were old papers, bags and boxes full of unseen items, pieces of cardboard, match-books, clothes, and no doubt bits of food stuck in the mass here and there (I saw a mayonnaise jar on the floor) that were producing the smell. She had to have taken months to accumulate such a pile; it took my breath away, especially since she herself was less than five feet tall.

Even more stunning, though, was the idea that she had *needed* this mountain of trash and was keeping up the room just for the sake of her hoard. Clearly she did not live there, though she lived somewhere, for she changed her clothes and was clean and rested. I had the sense that the extraordinary fullness of the room was a measure of how empty she felt inside; and then I recalled her inquisitorial nature, her intense driving interest in other people's lives and habit of asking insistent questions about personal subjects, getting answers because her manner virtually hypnotized her victims. It came from the same sense of worthlessness that made her need the room stuffed full of garbage: a feeling that other people were full and she wasn't.

It turns out that the "hoarding habit" is common among inmates of mental institutions, who collect and hold on to a great variety of objects, "generally of no practical use," including "papers of any kind, . . . pieces of wood, stones, leaves, sticks, soap, spoons, strings, . . . wires, cups, feathers." This effort to assert their existence is not surprising considering the drastic loss of self that the hospital makes them experience.[3] Another account of institutional hoarding demonstrates its defensive function. A "chronic schizophrenic" at a midwestern state hospital collected large numbers of towels, which she kept in her room, and also wore an extraordinary amount of clothing: six dresses, sweaters, shawls, two dozen pairs of stockings all at once, plus "sheets and towels wrapped around her body, and a turban-like headdress made up of several towels"—a total of twenty-five pounds of extra clothing; in a photo she looks startlingly like a bag woman. The hospital staff considered this excessive dressing a form of hoarding, but the fact that she wore the clothing (plus the sheets and towels) instead of just keeping it in piles in her room suggests that all those layers constituted a psychological barrier, a shield

against the destructive invasiveness of the institution. Someone less vulnerable might erect a purely psychological barrier, but she needed something tangible. In Part 2 I quoted a comment that women wrap themselves in fatness or words or silence to keep others at a distance; this
inmate's behavior is just an extremely literal version of the same thing.
She apparently only began to wear so much clothing "shortly after [she]
had been admitted to the hospital"—that is, in reaction to the tremendous threat it posed, she created a virtual shell to protect her empty center.[4]

Hoarding, then, is not the rare outlandish aberration of a small mysterious street subculture but a common and rather logical response by
many people to extreme deprivation or threat of a particular sort. Many
undiagnosed among us who live in less extreme situations also have the
collecting habit, though in more moderate ways. A Long Island subur-
banite had a neighbor in her seventies who had cared for her old father
until he died. During this time she acquired the habit of leaving her house
at six every morning to go through the neighborhood garbage cans before the collection was made, returning around eight with a loaded cart.
She had been doing this for years, and my informant was sure that her
house was full to the rafters. Here one might speculate on the emptiness
of a life sacrificed to that of the father, which needed to be compensated
for. There was also the woman (writer, mother, and wife) who revealed
to me the existence of a secret hoard of old shopping bags that she *could
not* throw out—flinging open the door of her kitchen cabinet with the
ambivalent glee of confession; or the well-dressed woman I passed on
Madison Avenue in the mid-1970s who carried a small shopping bag
that I recognized as a design last used by Bloomingdale's at least ten years
before.

I also found another, less tangible form of collecting among the Dwelling Place women. Only the richer minds practiced it. One of these was
Richards, who had a habit of imputing other people's experience—whatever it might be—to herself. In a conversation about the Black Muslims,
for instance, she said she had been one herself, but when questioned got
vague and walked away. On another occasion she was wearing a bro-
caded skullcap; I asked about it. "Of course I'm *not* the Pope," she responded, in the tone of one who has to say the obvious to a child (though
it was she who brought up the Pope; I had thought it was a yarmulke).
Then she informed me that the word *pope* meant head, the Pope being
the head of the church. But it was in fact Richards (the possessor of a

thousand Ph.D.'s) who felt herself to be a container of everything—or, one could say, the place where everything came to a head. She collected the universe.

Or there was Patty, who was twenty-three and had spent her entire life in foster homes and an orphanage. She told a group of us one afternoon that she had been in every state in the country and traveled to every country in the world. She mentioned Africa, and I asked what it was like. She rolled her eyes and told me there were cannibals. I said I thought that was just a superstition. She said no, there were cannibals, and she herself had seen people cut up into pieces. This made me so uncomfortable I dropped the subject. Although at the time I was not sure just who was being cut up, it seems to me now that she was expressing what she felt had been done to her plus a fearful reaction to her own impulse to incorporate— that is, her needs were so fierce that she experienced herself not only as taking in everything in the world but as eating everyone else up. If one's own self is fragmented, one cannot see others as complete persons either. They also are reduced to bits and pieces—objectified and cannibalized, in the sense that one sees them only in terms of one's own needs and treats them as objects to satisfy these—much in the manner of the hospital hoarders, who seem "almost to have a desire to incorporate" the objects they hoard, which they put into their "mouth, nostrils, vagina, anus, and so on."[5]

But the crazed universality that Patty and Richards both claimed was also an effort to reconstruct their selves through a kind of imaginative power. In appropriating to themselves all kinds of experience, they were reaching toward an enlargement of the self through connection with the outside world. Similarly, Richards transformed the castoffs she used— the shower curtain, for instance—into creations peculiarly her own. The problem was that these appropriations and transformations achieved no integration; they were only additional bits and pieces.

Yet the attempt to reach toward universality has always been a highly respected undertaking, carried out, often enough, under conditions that to the naked eye would not be easy to distinguish from those of today's SRO hoarders. The painter Albert Pinkham Ryder lived for years in a two-room apartment in New York City that was cluttered with waist-high piles of "every conceivable kind of object" from painting materials to old newspapers to food to clothes. Ryder maintained paths to the door, easel, and fireplace; "being unable to keep his cot clean, he slept on a piece of carpet on the floor." But, he told a friend, he never saw the rubbish; he was aware only of the view from his windows of an old garden and of "the eternal firmament with its ever-changing panorama of mystery and beauty." Intensely absorbed in an inner vision, he too was quite cut off from the external world. But while Ryder was a kind of holy fool, venerated for his special vision, Richards was just a crazy lady on the street. "On all who knew him, he made an impression of inner harmony and peace," while the impression she made was quite the opposite.[6] Yet the connection between them bears investigating.

We begin by considering further the fragmented, heterogeneous nature of the hoarder's collection. A passerby on Upper Broadway in Manhattan was once stopped by a bag woman who asked her to watch her bags while she went to buy some fruit. "I don't want anyone to get them," she explained, "because they're all matching—they all came from Sloan's." The humor of this anecdote lies in the idea that a woman in such a situation should still feel so typical a "feminine" urge. But beyond that, it signals organization: unlike others I have described, she felt her*self* held together by some unifying principle, expressed naturally by an assertion of that correct mode of self-presentation on which so many women have been brought up: that things should "match."

Despite the exigencies of street life, I discovered at the Dwelling Place, most homeless women did exercise some control over their appearance, so that even women just in off the street often had distinctive "looks" of their own. Even more than her possessions, a woman's mode of dress reflects the state of her self; and, given the fervent belief of so many homeless women in the traditional female stereotype, it was not surprising to find them taking the effort to make things match. Matching is a prime attribute of that conventionalized, rule-abiding style of femininity of which appearance is so essential a component. The female identity it dictates may be inauthentic but does keep a great many women in one piece by providing them with a structure on which to hang a definition of themselves. Concern for one's appearance presumes some kind of relationship with others, simply because it implies being looked at; and indeed, as I said in Part 1, women who had lived isolated street lives often dressed in strangely assorted ways that became less strange as their growing connection to the other people in the shelter strengthened their sense of being unified individuals themselves.

With this in mind, consider the appearance of Leah, who was perhaps the apotheosis of the nonmatcher. Leah looked fierce; she was the most impressive figure I ever saw at the Dwelling Place, largely because of her clothing, which gave her an aura of archaic power that I associated with biblical epics like *The Ten Commandments*. She wore more layers than one could imagine, although there seemed to be more than there were because every bit of them was sewn together in patches by hand in crazy-quilt style. All the edges were tattered, giving her (to switch images) a medieval look enhanced by her leggings, which were of heavy woolen cloth wrapped with string at the bottom. Her outer coat was made partly of some kind of fur worn bald in places; her inner one, of various fabrics taken from heavy garments like bathrobes. Around her head were wrapped rags, pieced together with large knots. This headdress, which resembled several rounds of rope, did not appear to be intended for warmth; strands of Leah's rather long gray hair stuck through it. She wore, finally, three pairs of glasses all bound together very solidly with wire at the bridges and temples. Half of the outermost pair had broken off, though, so she had three lenses in front of one eye and two in front of the other.

The variety and irregularity of real crazy quilts is limited and controlled by their rectangular shape. Accordingly, although Leah gave evidence of a certain interior disorderliness, she was externally well directed and self-sufficient. She had lived on welfare in an apartment in the East Village until the building was destroyed by fire and she was placed in a hotel that she hated because she felt the other tenants were out to murder her (not an unrealistic idea: she still had an incompletely healed scar on her lip from the last time she had been mugged). She had come to the Dwelling Place because she wanted to be placed in a foster home. Clearly much experienced in the ways of the bureaucracy, she had little patience for any situation that made demands on her without producing results. After a few days, one of the sisters asked if she could wash Leah's clothes. Leah turned over her two inner shirts, but when the sister found a bug on one of them and said she must be deloused, she left. Evidently she was willing to give us a chance, but only a limited one, and no assistance had been forthcoming that was worth the indignity of the delousing.

Part of the reason for this failure, however, was that we couldn't get her story straight; although she told different (and occasionally contradictory) pieces of it to different staff members, questioning her was difficult. The moment you said one thing to contradict her or asked one question hinting that you didn't take everything she said as pure truth, she flew off the handle and raised her voice into a kind of keening that effectively ended that topic. She was intelligent, resourceful, and creative; nevertheless, all the fragments of her self, though held together in one conglomeration, were too badly assorted to cohere fully; and their fragile cohesion was threatened by questions likely to elicit certain facts—such as, for instance, that she had been in Manhattan State Hospital (something we suspected from the way she had mentioned it in one angry outburst). Her layers too, I think, were protective.

Leah's brief encounter with the Dwelling Place was no different from hundreds of others, but her outfit had such a strong effect on me that I felt there was something special about her. Perhaps it was only that some creative power had enabled her to put together a costume that expressed her self-reliant withdrawal from a bureaucratic system that would have turned her into a matched object and disposed of her without consideration of her individual needs; yet in using that creativity she had tapped a vein of imagery that went far beyond herself as an individual. My vague associations to biblical epics and medieval pictures turned out to be absolutely accurate, and the costume I had thought was determined by her specific circumstances belonged to a tradition that traverses not only centuries but cultures as well. In the context of this tradition she may be compared to the visionary painter Albert Ryder.

Since earliest times there has been much speculation about the relation between genius and madness, for both seem to derive from someplace beyond ordinary conscious life—the Beyond, the realm of the divine or the unconscious—which has universally been recognized as mysterious, for in it divinity and degradation meet and are hard to distinguish. Different cultures have drawn the line between genius and madness at different places; but ours goes to an extreme in the number of people it puts into the mad category. In the late twentieth century Leah's costume was a signal that she too belonged there; but in previous ages it would have been a badge of her membership in the same category as Ryder: that of the fools, those possessed by unreason, or folly.

For centuries, and across cultures, the essential element of the fool's costume was its being made up of particolored bits and pieces. The most familiar example is the motley worn by medieval court fools; but motley was not unique to the Middle Ages. "Traditionally associated with lunacy," motley survived from Roman times (the Romans kept fools too). Like folly itself, medieval motley had a double meaning. "The fact that the fool's dress was sometimes imposed on offenders as a peculiarly degrading form of punishment is only explicable on the assumption that it was no mere carnival costume, but a badge of madness and servitude." Yet at the same time it signaled the special insight that made the fool or mad person special; the court jester was "the 'sage-fool,' . . . the truth-teller whose real insight was thinly disguised as a form of insanity."[7] The coat of patches was also the standard dress of holy fools throughout the Middle East; another example is Joseph's coat of many colors.[8]

The chasm between the modern Western mentality and a culture for which the fool represents a meaningful aspect of reality emerges in the following description, written by an Englishman in 1871:

> Most of the reputed saints of Egypt are either lunatics or idiots. Some of them go about perfectly naked. . . . Others are seen clad in a cloak or long coat composed of patches of various coloured cloths, adorned with numerous strings of beads, wearing a ragged turban, and bearing a staff with shreds of cloth of various colours attached to the top. Some of them eat straw. . . . Whatever enormities a reputed saint may commit, such acts do not affect his fame for sanctity; for they are considered as the results of the abstraction of his mind from worldly things; his soul, or reasoning faculties, being wholly absorbed in devotion.[9]

Just like Ryder (who, by the way, was "a big man, with unkempt grizzled hair and full beard, and the face of a seer" and "wore the clothes of a workman or a tramp"; when he went for evening walks on Eighth Avenue people gave him money because he looked destitute).[10] The ambiguity associated with these earlier fools survives today only in the common attitude toward the artist—a mixture of reverence and contempt. Still, visions are permitted the Ryders, but the modern-day Kempes must join the ranks of the mentally ill and, no longer either holy or evil, be dismissed as meaningless—that is, "sick." We retain only a piece of the motley tradition, in the familiar image of the clown dressed like Harlequin (when not dressed like a tramp), a considerably diluted version of the negative aspect of the fool.

No doubt Leah created her costume not according to this culturally institutionalized model but out of her own psychology. Yet that only demonstrates our modern lack of connection to a universal of human nature. When Margery Kempe, after recovering from her breakdown, dressed in brightly contrasting fabrics, her fool's dress expressed her own sense that her conscious, rational self had broken into fragments—thus letting in the Beyond—but also symbolized her assumption of a social role that other people recognized. Margery was never able to shake the ambiguous quality of that role; for most of her life there were always those who called her a plain fool, not a holy one, like the fellow pilgrims who forced her to assume other elements of the fool's costume. Margery herself, having once recognized her vocation, wanted to wear pure white—in a sense wiping out the discordant aspects of her behavior that made people doubt her—a symbolic act whose importance is evident from the fact that permission to do so was denied her by the churchmen to whom she applied until after her pilgrimage to Jerusalem.

Despite the traces that remain of the former meaning of the fool's dress, which were probably behind the strong impression Leah's outfit made on me, for Leah there could be no such ambiguity as Margery had benefited from. Even at the Dwelling Place, attempts to help her were conditioned by her probably being a former mental patient. Deinstitutionalization had released mental patients to a "community" for which madness represented not a meaningful aspect of the universe but a stigmatized medical defect. This made it easier to get such people out of the way by shipping them off to an appropriate institution "for their own good" than to imagine ways of creating connections that could keep them integrated with society as much as possible. By the end of the eighties calls were being heard for "reinstitutionalization"—which to my mind, despite the humane intentions behind most proposals, amounts essentially to restoring the practice of confining people considered socially useless.[11]

Yet unavoidably, people who become marginal remain connected to the rest of us, as we construct fantasies to explain their equivocal position, try to put them out of our minds by hiding them away, cross the street to avoid them, or get involved in attempts to help them. The intensity of this connection, and the strength of the feelings involved, are manifest in the violence of the response particularly to those women who set themselves, culturally and sometimes physically, out of bounds.

PART 5

At the Margins

I believe that men are generally still a little afraid of the dark, though the witches are all hung, and Christianity and candles have been introduced.

— *Thoreau*, Walden

The Dangers of the Margin

Some years ago I got a call from a friend who had just encountered a homeless woman named Sally in a church on Madison Avenue. Sally had recited a monologue that strongly affected my friend, who repeated it to me in what she said were very nearly Sally's actual words. This is a condensed version:

> I've been on the street for nine years. I can't help myself. I've kept myself down. Everything that can happen to anybody has happened to me—I've been beaten, I've been kicked, they've spit on me, I've been mugged, I've been raped, they stabbed me two times in the stomach, they took me into the hospital and put me on a table, and I died. They cut into me and I died. Then they put me in a box but it wasn't my time. I hadn't finished with what I was here to do. The Lord sent me here to do something and I hadn't finished it yet. But now I'm ready to die. I pray for death every day.
>
> The world is full of filth. The church is full of filth. When they took me in and they gave me that room, they gave me a room full of filth. There were rats and filth all over the place—vomit and dirt and rats. I lay there on a filthy pile of rags—they didn't give me a bed. I lay there with my mouth open and two cockroaches went in. They went into my mouth and went down to my stomach. I went to the father and he had to give me some liquor to kill them. And I told him I couldn't stay in that horrible filthy place any more. And the woman who ran it she kicked me out anyhow because I said a filthy word.

"She sees herself as the Christ figure," said my friend; "she takes in the filth of the world." To her, Sally's monologue was a remarkable evocation of a deep and specifically female self-hatred that she herself identified with. (I later discovered this feeling to be quite common among the homeless women; Terry, for example, once told me she felt that a black cloud was coming out of her mouth whenever she spoke—not so different from Sally's roaches.) For my friend, then, Sally was an archetypal figure of a certain aspect of women's psychology.

But to others she looked quite different. It turned out that Sally was (relatively speaking) famous, for the previous year the *New York Times* had covered the story of how she finally came in "out of the cold" after the staff of a nearby social service center wooed her off the streets. To the *Times* reporter (also female), Sally was a figure of high comedy: "The chief thing about Sally, the former 'shopping bag lady,' is that she has personality. What a loss to the world of theater when Sally decided to go on the bum," her article begins. And here is the same monologue my friend heard as rendered by the reporter:

> "I have suffered, oh, no one knows what I have suffered," moaned Sally, holding her head with a gesture that would have brought Sarah Bernhardt to her knees.
>
> Sally says she has been beaten, robbed, mugged and stabbed. She also once swallowed a cockroach, an experience of unrelieved horror, except that a priest had enough presence of mind to give her a long slug of wine to wipe out the taste. Sally is not alcoholic, but, she confides with an air of candor that would do Mary Pickford proud, "I do like apricot brandy."
>
> When asked why she had stayed with The Bum ["her late consort"] for so long, particularly after he jumped on her stomach and she had to be taken to Beth Israel Hospital, where they gave her up for dead and all the doctors were so darling to her, she replied, "Well, I was young and I was stupid."

The reporter spoke to Leona Feyer, director of East Midtown Services to Older People, the center whose staff succeeded in getting Sally on SSI and placing her in a nearby hotel, but only after a three-year effort. "These people are outlaws, you know," Feyer is quoted as saying; "they are outside society and want no contact with it."[1] She said the same thing to me when I interviewed her a year later. She thought the bag women had been inadequate and dependent their whole lives and "basically want to be homeless" because they "really can't tolerate the minimal structure that is involved in living with people."

As it happened Sally had left her hotel just as the *Times* article appeared, probably in order to avoid being kicked out for abusing other tenants and screaming in the night. This pattern was familiar to us at the Dwelling Place; we found that about half the women eventually would settle into the Times Square, helped by the presence of the community there, although sometimes it took three or four tries. Feyer's staff, however, was not set up for homeless women and had little experience with them, and I got the impression that she was irritated at Sally for not recompensing all the effort they had expended on her. Sally was "self-centered and infantile," she told me, and predicted that the Dwelling Place (which was just about to open) would never succeed. Although her exasperation was understandable, I felt that underlying it was the professional's negative judgment of people who were not properly responsive to professional services.

Thus, while to my friend, Sally represented a great negative element of the female psyche, to the *Times* reporter she was a clown—assimilated right into the fool figure—and to Feyer she was a bad client, whose refusal to accept the solution to her problems offered by those who knew best cast her in the light of an ungrateful child.[2] While my friend identified with Sally, the reporter and the social service professional distanced themselves from her. These responses typify the basic dynamic between any social group and the people who fail to fit its norms and therefore become marginal. In essence, the people inside society see the outsiders not as the outsiders are but as the observers need them to be. Although consciously identifying with outsiders may seem a more humane response than putting them in a separate category from oneself, much experience finally taught me that identification dehumanizes no less than distancing, for when they become representations of someone else's idea, they cease to be just who they are. It is surprisingly difficult to get past all the images to see them simply as individual people. Why that should be has to do with why there are marginal people at all, and always have been.

THE FUNCTION OF MARGINAL PEOPLE

Not long ago, New York papers reported that seven old ladies had been found who lived in the rest rooms at Pennsylvania Station. They had lived there for three months. The judge who heard their case and the reporters who wrote about it seemed surprised that such a thing was possible.

This is the opening of *Subways Are for Sleeping*, published in 1957, an account of "a group of people who live, by and large, by their wits, . . . people of ingenuity who do not conform to the patterns of life which 'sound' people prescribe." The author, Edmund Love, felt compelled to cite the case of the seven old ladies because, he said, "in writing this book,

I came to realize a long time ago that some persons may not believe that my people exist either. . . . In an age protected by Social Security and unemployment insurance, by prosperity, and organizations like Alcoholics Anonymous, it seems inconceivable that a person can still be lost."[3]

I have shown that people can get lost, and how, and who; now I am interested in the disbelief of the others. It works in two ways: first as a denial that there are many such people, and then, once their existence is forcibly demonstrated, as a refusal to admit that they are real people like the rest of us. This is because they violate certain assumptions about life that are so important to our basic sense of who we are that we must preserve them at the cost of the other people's humanness. These assumptions define, as one sociologist puts it, what is "decent" and what is "real"; the social norms based on them are so taken for granted that for most people violating them is unthinkable, and those who do are perceived as "bizarre and frightening." One example particularly relevant to homeless people is a complex of norms based on the feeling that in a public place a person ought to be "involved" in something or have a purpose (indeed loitering is specifically forbidden by law).[4]

Anyone who has ever had to wait too long for someone else outside a restaurant will have felt the psychological, if not legal, pressure of these norms: one feels a need to look ostentatiously at one's watch, glance up and down the street, and so forth, to let the world know why one is there. Thus homeless women who sat up all night in Penn Station made great efforts to look like travelers. They and other vagrants who made an art of getting by through hiding their condition had learned the hard way how such norms operate. One of Love's subjects, for example, informed him that the police in Grand Central Station were intolerant of book readers after seven in the evening but that "even the seediest vagrant" could sit there all night if he read a newspaper. In 1978 homeless women in another city described exactly the same newspaper/book distinction to a nurse who encountered them at a skid row hospice.[5] It is the person who does not take these norms into account who appears to us to be mentally ill.

So a woman who sits in a niche just off the sidewalk, completely exposed to the stares of passersby but obviously "off in her own world," as we say—clearly not part of ours—has to be "crazy" or she would do something to disguise herself. But I suggest that, beyond this, the acute discomfort she creates in many people arises from a violation of another, perhaps more fundamental norm: the idea that an essential attribute of humanness—a basic distinction between the human and the animal—

involves living under shelter, and further that because she is a woman, her violation of it is more disturbing than it would be were she a man. As we saw, not only is there no tradition of vagrancy to which she can be assimilated as the male vagrant can, but the very idea of female humanness depends on being part of a family. The homeless woman is far more anomalous than the homeless man, for since there is no category to which she can be said to belong, she is indefinable; she has no recognized status. If one thinks of society as a pattern of social forms that create categories into which its members fit, her lack of category makes her marginal, in the sense that because she fits into the pattern nowhere she has to exist at its edge—not completely cut off from society (she may get SSI checks or at the least soup on a bread line or garbage from a can), but at the same time also belonging to the realm outside its borders.[6]

"Danger lies in transitional [or marginal] states, simply because transition is neither one state nor the next, it is undefinable," says Mary Douglas.[7] Being in such a state, or place, puts one in contact with the power that inheres there by virtue of its lack of the order and structure on which social control depends—the power of the formless to break down forms. Old people, for example, while still part of the mortal, human world, are also close to death and the world beyond, at the same time that their loss of social functions detaches them from the categories they have belonged to.[8] All excluded people are charged with such power; and for this reason the frequent practice of putting different categories of deviants together in the same facility is quite logical.

The power that inheres in the spaces between categories also explains the marginality of the "mentally ill." Theodore Lidz says that while cultures have tabooed certain areas of experience that lie between categories to "foster formation of firm ego boundaries," the schizophrenic, having never learned to separate self from other or to form other essential categories, "becomes preoccupied with material that *lies between* categories" and with "other such thoughts and feelings that are eliminated from awareness by socializing repression as a child grows up, and that have little conscious representation because no clear-cut categories for such ideas exist."[9]

This mental marginality explains the fear and suspicion of former inmates of mental hospitals. The parallel between the spatial or physical apartness implied in vagrancy or homelessness (or the old woman living at the edge of the forest) and the psychological alienation of those who go beyond rational thought and perception into "the disordered regions of the mind," as Douglas puts it, becomes an identity in the inmates' case because they are physically segregated just for their psychological divagation. The study described in Part 4 which found that behavior was not defined as abnormal until someone was known to have been in a mental hospital may therefore be interpreted as showing that the physical separation was what formalized the classification; it constituted a move outside society and into the margin. Once there a person is automatically regarded as dangerous and unreliable.[10] But despite this distrust—or perhaps one might say through it—the marginal person remains connected to society. The function she serves emerges when we consider another marginal person, the scapegoat.

The ancient practice of scapegoating was a religious sacrifice in which the sins and suffering of a community were ritually transferred to a selected victim, who was then driven out and, often, put to death. By casting out evil, the community preserved its integrity and ensured its survival. In ancient Greece the chosen victims were ugly, deformed, poor, or otherwise outcast already.[11] Here the idea of magically transferring one's own guilt or pollution to someone else who will do the suffering for it operates quite literally. Similarly the medieval fool, by always ridiculing others, was thought to take their bad luck on himself; he also functioned as a scapegoat at fertility festivals and in acting as a mock king who was abused in place of the real king.[12]

But it is not always so clear that a magical transference is occurring; more often the transference is unconscious, a function of projection, and expulsion or abuse is justified by supposed personal characteristics of the scapegoat. In medieval legend the Wandering Jew, who represented "the concept of the Jew as eternal exile and wanderer, outside society and apart from it," acquired supernatural qualities—being "unlimited in space, age, time, location and size"—which were then ascribed to real Jews. "Alleged physical features" signaled their separateness. "In medieval folk tradition, and later, the Jews, much like witches, were held to be ugly, malodorous, animal-like, blind, deformed or malfunctioning in some respect." They were turned into ghosts and bogeys to frighten children and were thought to practice sorcery, to be able to turn themselves into cats, to summon demons, possess the Evil Eye, cause earthquakes, raise storms, and spread plague—all attributes also accorded witches.[13]

Apparently people need certain others to be set apart because they need to feel a distance between themselves and some specific thing the others represent. Thus the Jews after 1215 were required to wear special badges or hats, just as prostitutes and poor people had to wear distinguishing signs.[14] Although the badges of the poor had the practical function of preventing unauthorized people from receiving alms or relief, this practice also indicates a need perpetually to experience the distinction between an *us* and a *them*. The qualities attributed to the outcasts (so often the same, no matter which outcasts were in question) are in fact a clue to what the people inside society do not want to acknowledge in themselves.

It turns out, further, that when someone winds up outside, *all* kinds of antisocial attitudes, qualities, and behavior are easily ascribed to her. Once she makes that move outside the human community (as defined by those inside it), the rules and regulations that govern normal humanity appear to fall away from her so that she seems "fundamentally different, . . . perhaps even a different species," and therefore capable of anything.[15]

The perceived characteristics of marginal people are therefore a set of paradoxes; in these people opposites coexist. As we saw in Part 4, during the classical era mad people might be considered sacred but were also shunned; "contact with holiness, like contact with its opposite uncleanness, was perilous and to be avoided."[16] Later, the fool was seen as both an imbecile ("natural man") and a wise person; and in our own day there is the notion that the person who thinks in between categories may be not a schizophrenic but a sage or artist. As we saw, too, bag women have been perceived either as animals or as superhuman creatures. Finally, since sex roles are a basic prop of any social structure, marginal people are often perceived as sexually indeterminate.

In the past the connection between these marginal attributes and the society that excluded them was explicitly recognized through ritual. Medieval society, for example, not only briefly exalted the fool as mock king but institutionalized cross-dressing by both women and men during the great seasonal carnivals as part of a temporary suspension of social norms and structures, including sex roles, and even of the human/animal distinction: "Men on New Year's Day clothed themselves in the skin of a stag, with its horns upon their heads, and were accompanied by other men *dressed in woman's clothing*."[17] This transvestism, which is a kind of clowning, exemplifies the fool's function of keeping people in touch with the indeterminate marginal realm (the Beyond). Though it has lost its religious meaning, transvestism is still typical of the modern-day fool, the clown. At the Halloween parade in Greenwich Village one year, I saw three men dressed as bag women, prancing and singing in front of a crowd; they quite eclipsed the singing trio of three real women who had been trying to perform in the same space.[18]

What makes transvestism a virtue in fools, however, is exactly what makes it a sin in women, for such blurring of categories is tolerable only in someone who is marginal. In ancient Rome the distinctive clothing prostitutes had to wear was specifically not the standard women's garment but the toga—men's dress; it signaled their status as not-really-women.[19] The act that ultimately triggered the execution of Joan of Arc, who wore male dress to preserve her virginity and thereby her divine inspiration, was her insistence on once again putting on men's clothes after having been ordered to wear a woman's dress. The question for Joan's contemporaries was whether she was a saint or a witch; but in either case she would remain marginal.[20] The superhuman power of the margin is also manifest in the nineteenth-century belief that the prostitute could destroy society, as well as in the terror inspired today in a passerby by a homeless woman's anger.

"Real" women who violate the boundaries of their category but cannot easily be defined as marginal (like Susan Shelly, who to the horror of the *Railway Conductor* turned out to be not a bum but a lady) are even more threatening. The attempt to introduce the "bloomer dress" in the United States in 1851, for example, evoked outraged associations with prostitution, criminality, and madness, as the image of the trousered woman blurred into those of other creatures at the margins. For the rest of the century, long pantaloons were worn only by young girls (who, being sexually immature, were no threat), dancers, and—of course—prostitutes.[21]

Remember, though, that the power that inheres in the realm outside social control is a perceived quality originating in the experience of those inside society, who inevitably fail in their perpetual struggle for a kind of psychic resting state; the more they fight to keep their categories intact, the more these become contaminated with their opposites, so that the unacknowledged parts of the insiders' own psyches create a hidden identity between them and the outsiders. This unconscious secret relationship, so vigorously denied by the very act of scapegoating, lies behind the seeming duality of the outcast. The scapegoat seems evil because we project that part of ourselves that we cannot face on her; but she also seems supernaturally wise because concurrently we project on her our own unconscious knowledge of what we are doing, so that *she* appears conscious that she and we share a hidden connection. Looked at psychologically, her power comes from this (supposed) knowledge of our identity—identity in the sense not only of sameness but of knowledge of one's true self, of who one really is. Such a truth is precious; it is in fact the treasure that the homeless women are rumored to carry in their bags.[22] But since it is a truth we have chosen to hide from ourselves, those who possess it appear to pose a severe threat.

These people, as we saw, comprised at various times the poor, crippled, blind, unemployed, criminal, and insane, as well as vagrants and prostitutes. They also included certain women, and sometimes men, who for various reasons were called witches. Most of these outcasts have in spired fears of contagion or contamination, either medical or moral, a symbolic expression of the fear that the evil they carried would reinfect society if they were not physically removed.[23]

Since one deviant looks much like another once relegated to that undefined area outside, any given deviant can fit into almost any category of deviance that happens to be convenient. The person chosen as fool, for example, was often already deformed either physically or mentally. Furthermore, the categories themselves change according to the needs of the time, so that deviants are continually being redefined. While the witches' contemporaries accused them of being in league with evil, twentieth-century psychiatry diagnosed them retroactively as hysterical or psychotic, and has dealt with contemporary prostitutes not as bad women but as sick ones. Despite such changes, however, deviants still function as scapegoats, which is why the change from evilness to illness has made no real difference in how they are treated. A contemporary psychologist laments that although the term *mental illness* was coined by people "who wanted very much to raise the station of . . . the psychologically disturbed from that of witches and 'crazies,'" people still hate and fear the mentally ill, who "are society's lepers."[24] Their name has changed, but not what they are.

WOMEN AT THE MARGIN

Homeless women, however, violate an additional, sex-based norm: that women should not be alone. For a woman, being alone equals being outside because she is not in a relationship to a man. This rule was laid down early; as far back as Euripides' *The Trojan Women*, Andromache, waiting with the others after the fall of Troy to be apportioned out as a slave to one of the Greek conquerors, laments:

> But I, who aimed the arrows of ambition high
> at honor, and made them good, see now how far I fall,
> I, who in Hector's house worked out all custom that brings
> discretion's name to women. Blame them or blame them not,

> there is one act that swings the scandalous speech their way
> beyond all else: to leave the house and walk abroad.
> I longed to do it, but put the longing aside, and stayed
> always within the inclosure of my own house and court.[25]

Twenty centuries later, the prohibition still stood; it supplies the answer to Ada Chesterton's question as to why the London County Council refused to provide lodging houses for women as it did for men. The women, being more anomalous than the male outcasts, were more disturbing; giving them beds would make them visible and acknowledge them as belonging to society in a way that could not be tolerated.

When to aloneness a woman adds other unacceptable traits, the reaction is intense. For example, the volunteers of the nineteenth-century American charitable societies were violently attacked when they broadened their efforts to include not just the "worthy" poor but prostitutes and female convicts. The Female Moral Reform Society, crusading during the 1830s against the double standard whereby prostitutes were treated as outcasts while the men who bought their services suffered no discredit, earned "abuse and scorn" in numerous vehement newspaper editorials, and postmasters were "instructed to 'suppress or destroy'" the society's journal.[26] The Women's Prison Association had to overcome objections to its program of helping female ex-prisoners that were based on the ideas that any woman once degraded by imprisonment was incurable and that such assistance would encourage crime. Caroline Kirkland spends much of her book trying to convince her readers that female ex-prisoners have normal human feelings that make them amenable to rehabilitation.[27]

Prostitutes and female convicts were indeed not seen as real human beings, for they had stepped outside the category of femininity. The equation of womanliness with goodness meant that a female who was "bad" was not truly a woman and by extension could hardly be called human either. "A degraded woman is proverbially lowest in the scale of humanity," says Kirkland. "When we would attempt to plead for the female convict, we are ready to ask a feather from an angel's wing! . . . How [could we] expect to gain the attention and sympathy of those, who . . . find it hard to believe that the poor, disgraced wanderer, to whom a prison atmosphere has become natural, . . . is still a woman and a sister?" Female prisons "are, in fact, *oubliettes*, . . . places in which to be forgotten, lost; stricken from the rolls of humanity."[28]

The requirement that women belong to a home made any transgression of other norms that kept them out of one worse than men's transgression of the same norms. "By some strange fallacy of social arbitration," Kirkland comments, "a man who has outraged all laws, divine and human, is still a subject of hope; he may serve out . . . his prison life, and enter upon a new one afterwards with fresh opportunities and unbroken spirit; while a woman once fallen is renounced by her kind." A typical comment of people the prison association approached for support was: "But there is something so disgusting in the idea of meddling with convicts, and above all with *female* convicts!"[29]

Ada Chesterton encountered the same distinction when she could not find a bed and had to spend the entire night in the streets. Sometime after midnight she found a food stall still open, but the proprietor refused to serve her. "The most abject specimen of man is quite welcome if he has the pence to pay. . . . But in the case of women there is the rooted belief that they must be bad lots or they would have a home; if they are not thieves they are prostitutes, and either way, even a commercial connection with them might cause trouble with the police." The public is indignant if a shabby man is refused beer in a bar. "But no one seems to think it unjust or even strange that a coffee stall keeper should 'shoo' off a woman who wants to buy food or drink in the watches of the night." The same man who said he didn't serve women when she was destitute was quite friendly when she came back well dressed. "Dirt, in a man," she comments elsewhere, "not infrequently suggests romance—in a woman it implies degradation, neglect and an obstinate refusal to undertake the obligations of her sex."[30]

In the twentieth century "welfare mothers" have replaced prostitutes as scapegoats for the sexual "sins" of society. Already deviant by virtue of their poverty and singleness, women on Aid to Families with Dependent Children are made to bear the punishment from which other women's socioeconomic position protects them. This punishment has ranged from man-in-the-house rules and other moral-fitness criteria created in the fifties to the imposition in the eighties of mandatory work programs. Connecting welfare to work penalized recipients considered undeserving of remaining at home like "good" women, forcing them into the lowest-paid, dead-end jobs.[31] The intense discomfort with nontraditional families that such measures exemplify indicates the extent to which issues of women's place are still with us. It is no surprise that they pop right up when we come face to face with homeless women.

Modes of Distancing

The *Soho Weekly News*, a now-defunct arbiter of trendiness, once devoted the first page of its "Style" section to a photo layout of two bag women and two high-fashion models. Originally, the copy explained, the intention was to print just the homeless women—one wrapped in a blanket, one wearing a babushka. But when Giorgio Sant'Angelo opened his fall collection "with blanket wrappings and babushkas, we thought you might enjoy seeing the 'High Side of Fashion,' too." So the models got added. The bag women, be it noted, look quite miserable and pathetic.[1]

This macabre conjunction, offensive though it might be, yet has the virtue of exposing the same unpalatable truth as the well-known drawing of the beautiful woman looking into a mirror that on second glance turns into a picture of a skull. Whether we like it or not, the women outside share at least our humanity and, in the case of half of us, our femaleness too. What that makes of humanity, or femaleness, is something most people don't want to consider, and that is why we have invented so many ways to make the homeless women other than they are. We place them in a category that allows us to distance them and make them Other; and as soon as that happens, they can also become the scapegoats for whatever we need to reject in ourselves.

For this purpose the "shopping-bag lady" has been a potent image. Even after homelessness had received a great deal of media attention, I still met quite a few people who were astonished to hear that bag ladies were usually just women who had been released from mental hospitals or kicked out of SROs. Even once they knew this, the idea that these women were somehow special and different died hard. Widely different people shared the notion that the women were all right out there because that was what they *wanted*. In 1974 the feminist newspaper *Majority Report* editorialized (only partly tongue in cheek), "No institution worth its requisition forms can give these women what they want, namely: the freedom to live where and how they desire, the right to the pursuit of the necessities and luxuries of life in other people's garbage, the precious liberty of remaining dirty, and the courage to smell."[2] In 1979 the director of New York City's Human Resources Administration's office of psychiatry told a *New York Times* reporter, "They're a very special kind of person. . . . Many are surprisingly resourceful. . . . They value their life style."[3]

The writer Brian Kates, tracing the life of Phyllis, a Dwelling Place woman who was murdered in 1981, spoke to a woman who had been Phyllis's neighbor. "Well, that's a shame," she commented when he told her what had happened. "But you know what they say. Them people don't want a real place to live. They actually prefer to live outside. That's a fact."[4] As late as 1987, a housewife from Washington State named Beulah Lund, who after seeing a homeless woman thrown out of a museum in Washington, D.C., went on the street to "quench this horrible need in myself" to see "who they really were," told *People Weekly* she had "always thought that most of the homeless 'wanted to be where they were. I wanted to believe that.' "[5]

The corollary of this belief was that unlike "us," the homeless women had no needs that would make them feel as bad as *we* would in such a situation. For many people homeless women therefore had a magical quality that was particularly strong around the question of how they managed to survive outside. A Manhattan patrolman offered a reporter this theory: "Their bodies are strong and can take more than ours. You'd die if you ate what they do."[6] As we know, they did die; but nobody thought of them dying, only surviving. And the ability to survive physically apart from shelter (including not minding being filthy) was the source of their perceived animal quality, much as the old woman in the goose-girl fairy tale, who also possesses strength beyond what one might expect, is associated with a kind of bestiality. A 1979 CBS News report on New York's homeless women, for instance, stressed how we look away from them because they are like gargoyles or lepers—images evoking not even a real but a magical grotesque animal and a human whose humanity is revoltingly decaying.[7] A *New York Times* "About New York" column similarly invoked bag women's "special" quality: "They seem to work at fashioning a leprous silhouette."[8]

It was therefore appropriate that an early study of street people was done by Alan Beck, director of New York City's Bureau of Animal Affairs, and published in *Natural History* magazine. Beck and his co-author Philip Marden observed the homeless much like animals in a habitat, counting the varying numbers who appeared at different temperatures and before and after garbage collections, and describing the different "home ranges" of women and men. Although the study did include taped interviews with three of the people they observed, the researchers' orientation toward them was essentially as a different species.[9]

While some people were tolerant and even admiring of homeless women, others were not. "You scum bag! Why don't you go to the Department of Welfare? To the Salvation Army? Why don't you live like anyone else! You pig! Why don't you become a citizen?" shouted a woman wearing a fur coat and walking her dog as she passed photographer Joan Roth talking to a bag woman on a city street.[10] I doubt that this angry woman habitually called out to the homeless; what provoked her on this occasion was Roth's treating this woman like a regular person.

Still others turned bag women into a kind of joke, a form of denial that hit a peak in 1983. That year the "street look" became fashionable—clothes designed in layers with mock rags and tatters, explicitly imitating the garb of homeless people as the "layered look" of a few years before had not. Bloomingdale's, the apotheosis of trendiness, featured a boutique displaying expensive "street couture" that, according to a store employee, sold well. "Bag ladies are in," she remarked. Despite much criticism and protest, only a few months later a window at the elegant jeweler Tiffany's displayed figurines of a bag woman and a homeless man as background for a fifty-thousand-dollar diamond necklace. A sign above the man said, "Enhance your life." After many protests the store removed the display but would not admit that there was anything wrong with it. An official said that no street people had come into the store to complain about it, adding that he "likes bag people, particularly bag women." And some weeks after that, Holiday Inn franchise owners visiting Chicago were entertained at a party by an actress whom the hotel corporation hired to dress up as a bag woman and wander around, providing "an authentic Chicago scene."[11]

The utter contempt revealed in these incidents is not even conscious and indeed could not have been expressed so openly if it were. To those who could design and wear the Bloomingdale's clothes or create the Tiffany's window the homeless woman must have been so remote she had absolutely no reality as a human being. Certainly to the official who "liked" bag women she was just a little doll like the figurine in his window, who provided entertainment. People who are economically insecure, to whom the implications of homeless women's existence might be more present and frightening, deny or blame them with vehemence. It is those who represent not just wealth but power who can afford light-hearted dismissal.

So strong is the need to distance the homeless, however, that even people trying actively to help them, who knew them personally, could still fall into it. At a meeting in 1981 of the Coalition for the Homeless, an advocacy group, a man who ran a shelter in Brooklyn reported that he was getting as clients working-class people who had lost their homes. This shocked him; the great discovery he wanted to share was that he was servicing not the people he had expected but "our brothers and sisters" who work, as he put it, unaware of the distinction he was making. He thought it would make a real impression if the public discovered that it was others like themselves who were homeless (the implication of course being that the others were not like "us"). He was right, too; what finally galvanized large-scale efforts to provide food and shelter was the appearance of large numbers of newly homeless families. This man was reacting just like the advocate of "whitecollar girls" quoted in Part 3; and so was the editorialist in a Brooklyn community newspaper who in 1986 chided local residents for opposing the creation of a shelter for homeless families in a neighborhood armory. "No longer are [today's homeless] exclusively society's failures, those who have spent a lifetime sponging off the rest of us," the editorial argues. "The new breed includes recent victims of arson, unemployment, illness, or loss of a loved one. These are real calamities that each and every one of us can relate to."[12] Almost all the women I had met at the Dwelling Place years before were victims of one of those calamities. But clearly people feel that somewhere a line needs to be drawn.

And the one they still draw is the old line between worthy and unworthy. Nor have the criteria for worthiness in poor women changed much. As part of a search for places to refer Dwelling Place women to, I once called a private halfway house we had heard of to find out if it would be suitable. An extremely unpleasant man answered, who was instantly unwilling to accept anyone from the Dwelling Place but didn't want to say so directly. Instead he told me that one of our nuns could describe his operation much better than he could. I said she was away for several weeks. He said he hoped she was getting a good rest, since he had predicted long ago that the sisters would just burn themselves out if they kept going as they were. His principle, he said, was helping people to help themselves, and he wasn't interested in anyone who wasn't willing to put in the effort. He knew the kind of people we got and he didn't want them because these old women, once they got rested up, became hostile. I said we had some who weren't; but he assured me he didn't work "on panic"—that is, I couldn't call him up and say I had to send someone over in three hours. I said I certainly would never place someone permanently like that. Then he asked if I had emotional problems, or had ever used drugs. I said no; and suddenly he became friendlier.

This man was basing his category of worthiness on the old idea that angry women are bad women (and old angry women—the ones on his mind—are even worse).[13] Even more interesting is his anger at me for blurring the distinction between hostile women and good ones, which I did simply by being at the Dwelling Place, which was notorious not only for helping the undeserving but for breaching the essential line between service provider and client. To preserve it he needed to reassure himself that I was not one of *them*—and to believe me, even though he must have known how often people who use drugs lie about it.

There are still other ways of distancing the homeless. I once called the Veterans Administration for Evelyn to find out why her pension check had stopped coming and spoke to a woman who was friendly and helpful but had trouble at first understanding what the problem was, because, it turned out, she couldn't imagine how Evelyn could be a veteran. When I told her the Dwelling Place was a shelter for homeless women, she had assumed we were all young and pregnant. Yet she must have passed old homeless women on the streets near her midtown office. Evidently to her, as to the man just described, young pregnant homeless women were much less disturbing than old ones, so she had simply erased the old ones from her mind.

Magical projections flourish in the space left open by such distancing. And, deriving not from the poorly seen object to which they attach but from within the observer, they provide some interesting clues about that observer. At the Dwelling Place one afternoon, Bertha, a woman who was on the "not welcome" list because of her potential for violence, was let in by mistake. The next minute a man on duty at the parking lot next door rang the bell to say that Bertha had a huge knife on her and had said something about killing everyone in the house. One of the nuns called the police for help in getting her out but had trouble convincing them to come. Two sisters kept Bertha calm while we waited. She had had a legitimate reason for coming: we had her welfare identification card, without which she couldn't cash her check. But she had bitten someone badly a few days before, and the sisters knew she could "pop" (as they said) at any minute. When the police arrived, ten or fifteen minutes later, they treated the whole thing as a big joke, paying no attention to the nuns' explanation of how potentially dangerous Bertha was, even though they did take a knife from her. It was not huge, though, but small, and possibly just a table knife; they dropped it into a street-drain grating so we never got a look at it.

The contrast between the reactions of the parking-lot man and the police to the phenomenon of a big, powerful, angry black woman is interesting. The parking-lot man saw her realistically as dangerous, but blew her up in his mind as worse than she was—indicated by his seeing the knife as larger than it was. But the policemen, denying that she was dangerous at all by acting as though they were humoring a bunch of overexcited women (and, perhaps, by getting rid of the knife so completely), were also overreacting, possibly to cover up an equal amount of fear. Neither saw the actual woman; in both cases what they saw came from inside themselves.

The question then is: What inner experience gets projected on homeless women? It seems to be different for women and for men. Women, lacking social and economic power as they do, have a particularly acute sense of the fragility of the social apparatus that keeps those who are economically dependent inside, and their identification with homeless women is frequently passionate. Even after bag women had become a minority among the homeless, they still represented the primary mode of female homelessness to many. In 1990 a writer for *Moxie*, a magazine for women over forty, called to interview me about "bag ladies." I told her I would talk about bag ladies, but on the understanding that they were only a small proportion of the women who were currently homeless. Although her article does make this point, its emphasis and emotional focus—as well as that of the editor-in-chief's essay on homelessness in the same issue—are entirely on the question "What are the chances a respectable, middle-aged, middle-class woman will end up on the street" as a bag lady?[14]

The editor, Kathy Soverow, concludes that homelessness is really about "giving up" and "relinquishing yourself willingly to a state of helplessness, despair, and friendlessness," and that she herself will never be homeless because "I have too much hope and far too many friends for that." The passion of her need to affirm this leads her to deny the socio-economic dimensions of homelessness. The writer, Jo Giese, more willing to explore both these factors and her own fears, punctuates her article with vignettes of Jeanie, a homeless woman living on the beach of Venice, California, with whom Giese had "identified so fully" while going through a divorce "that I'd check to see how she was doing to gauge how *I* was doing." She quotes Jill Halverson, founder of the Downtown Women's Center, a shelter in Los Angeles, describing the "fear of going over the edge" that women feel "as we enter our middle years" and "realize how vulnerable we are. I suspect we also realize there's no great value placed on the middle-aged or older woman."[15] The same intense identification was expressed by actress Mary Stuart, who in describing for *New York* magazine her year-long relationship with a homeless woman in Central Park called her "my little shadow."[16]

Some women writers have delved deeper, using the image of the bag lady to examine the meaning and function of the established category of acceptable femininity. Women, being so constrained by role stereotypes, are often close to terror when they feel the call of an inner self that wants to violate them. If they follow that path, their training tells them, the homeless woman's fate will be theirs. This is the moral of Cynthia Macdonald's poem "The Kilgore Rangerette Whose Life Was Ruined," which is a cautionary tale, a nightmare fantasy of retribution on the order of "Little Red Riding Hood." The narrator, one of the famous line of cheerleaders who perform at half-time in the Cotton Bowl, "kicked with the wrong leg" and caused half the line of girls to go down. "Maybe I should have known—there had been / Problems of appearances before," she says—incidents in her childhood that demonstrated a suspicious inability to conform to the type of convention of which one hundred perfectly synchronized kicking girls is an apotheosis. Feeling there is no place for her anywhere in society, she becomes the only bag lady in Dallas. "It's not a bad life. No one expects grace or precision."[17] As such she is the perfect inverse of the perfect Southern girl she was before; the assumption (ironic on Macdonald's part) is that once a woman is knocked out of place she falls like Lucifer, all the way. And being knocked out is easy, for keeping oneself in step requires split-second timing.

Once lodged in the psyche, this message—that if you go out into the woods alone the wolf will get you—carries the corollary that when you do venture beyond the boundaries, you cross an absolute gulf and make a total sacrifice, for freedom can be achieved only by giving up everything. I think that many women do believe, unconsciously, that such radical deprivation is the awful price they must pay for demanding selfhood. Again the homeless woman appears to the imagination as the emblem of such a condition; she provokes terror and rage because the sight of her summons all the feelings surrounding this dreadful conflict to the surface.

Such a confrontation is depicted in "Opus," a play by Cynthia Belgrave. Three women sitting in an employment-agency waiting room hate each other on sight: the white woman hates the younger black woman because she's tall and a model; this black woman hates her because she's white and blond; and both hate the other black woman because she's old. They exchange vicious slurs, based on the stereotypes of race, class, and age that they incarnate. But when a bag woman appears, all three are terrified that the agency will associate them with her and refuse them jobs; they unite in focusing their fury on her, screaming at her to get out. "Angry Angry Angry," mumbles the bag woman. "They hate BEING." She slips down on the floor, and they realize she has died; they begin to kick her. "You hag!" screams the older black woman. "Dying is being old! I'm not old. I'm not! . . . Wake *up* you hag . . . you failure . . . you garbage dump—you pus bag—you . . . *vomit* you." Then, horrified by their own behavior, they stop and "really look at [the] woman for the first time." Their identification with the stereotypes falls away, and genuine feeling rushes in, especially awareness of their fear of age, which makes women useless to society and from which the stereotypes provided an illusory protection. Individually they must now confront death—or what they equate with it, the loss of their feminine roles. Yet with that loss comes—as the bag woman put it—"BEING" and the ability to feel for each other. As the play ends the two younger women take the older one in their arms to comfort her.[18]

The area of inner experience that the homeless woman evokes in other women, then, involves profound fears about "being"—about the virtual right to exist apart from role stereotypes or the social category of femininity. Men do not respond so strongly. Jo Giese reports that her boyfriend found it inconceivable that a woman like her could worry about becoming a bag lady. Over the years I worked on this book, I found men might be interested in my subject, particularly if it fit in with some political or intellectual interest of theirs, but just as often simply looked blank when they heard what it was. Others associated homeless women with their mothers and felt guilt arising from a deep-rooted assumption that women should be taken care of—by men (that is, themselves). One man explained to me that having been "softened" in childhood by the Christian ethic of caring for one's neighbor, he felt society's failure to care for these people as his own personal failure. His Christian upbringing, he thought, had given him strong reactions to the bag women, out of proportion to their presence in his life.

I also encountered an interesting variation of the classic arrangement whereby the woman serves as object for the man's self-gratification. *New York Post* columnist Murray Kempton, discussing a 1979 report on homeless women, appears to have convinced himself that they are all Irish, the evidence for this notion being the report author's discovery that many of the women called themselves Mary. To Kempton this has "a marked ring of the convent school." He evokes sheltered Irish Catholic women who upon being widowed could not cope with the outside world and became homeless but are now "struggling and, in their way, heroically enduring the whole force of [the city's] rawness. And yet they know their road so intimately and contend with it in ways so subtle," he continues, "that we cannot say that the Irish identity is not in itself a mask and a strategy"—thereby setting up Irishness as the necessary model for their heroic virtues.[19]

Mostly Kempton is right on target. Many homeless women *were* previously sheltered and could not cope with the world, and the practice many had of calling themselves Mary (as I myself found them doing) *is* a mask and a strategy. But surely it derives from the pervasiveness of Christianity in general, for plenty of black women called themselves Mary, and one can hardly assume they were pretending to be Irish. Kempton has simply wrapped up the image of the homeless women's heroism in a sentimental vision of Irish ethnicity, as though all the African-American and Latina bag women did not exist. The reason he could miss them is that he was too involved in constructing the image of homeless women in a way that would let him feel good about his Irishness.

Kempton at least managed to relate the homeless women to human society. Many others seemed to share what one social worker refers to as "long-held beliefs that homeless women are even more derelict and eccentric than homeless men, and thus the most socially undesirable of all marginal people."[20] *Zappers and the Shopping Bag Lady*, a play by P. J. Gibson and Aishah Rahman produced in 1979 by the Black Theatre Alliance of New York City, is a science-fiction fantasy based on the idea that New York will be "zapped" by three supernatural figures unless they are shown something good in the city. This is the heroine's job, and she does it by impersonating a bag lady. When she is mugged in Brooklyn's Prospect Park, people come to her aid and chase the muggers away. The fact that New Yorkers would help a bag lady is what finally saves the city, the assumption being that since she is the lowest of the low, the most revolting, least human type of creature, a willingness to help her *has* to demonstrate goodness. This assumption was not explained but taken for granted, as though the writers never questioned that everyone feels this way about bag ladies.

And to a remarkable extent everybody does. A homeless woman used to sit in Times Square in the company of four healthy, playful cats, which she kept on leashes and would introduce by name to the many passersby who stopped and talked to her. But one day the cats disappeared (she said men in uniforms came and took them away), and from then on she became "anonymous, or worse," since those few who noticed her did so only to be disgusted by her "island of squalor." It was having the cats, concluded an editorialist in the *Times*, that "made their mistress look, to the world, like a human being."[21]

Otherwise, who would have noticed? After the first major report on the homeless came out in 1981, Ellen Baxter, one of its authors, was interviewed on WINS, a New York City all-news radio station. The interviewer's take on the homeless-people issue was that it was so depressing he couldn't understand why a person "with your background" was involved in it. He had been a newsman thirty years, he said, and they always told him, "Don't get involved or you won't be able to do your job." But though he thought he had seen everything, he still found things that could shock him—like Baxter's inexplicable dedication. In accordance with the bland sentimentality characteristic of WINS, in this reporter's eyes her "background" consisted primarily of having gone to Bowdoin College and being a Ph.D. candidate at Columbia University—plus one other thing. "You look like a debutante," he added, implying that pretty young girls like her had no reason to be interested in depressing things.

Actually Baxter's background was perfectly suited to her work. She had worked in and around mental hospitals since 1971, she said, and had done research in Gheel for five years. Nevertheless the reporter kept stressing her "idealism"—he must have used that word fifteen times to express the idea that it was only her youthful idealism that kept her in such work since adults wouldn't sacrifice themselves in that way or think they could really make a difference. His use of the word was reductive, putting her in a category that diminished her judgment ("youth") and also provided a reassuring explanation of her commitment—that "young people" don't understand the world as well as their elders. She is only doing this while she's young, until she *finds out*.

The interview, in short, was not so much about homeless people as about why Ellen Baxter should mess with them. Why should this hardened newsman find her involvement with the homeless "shocking"? Perhaps if she had not been so pretty, he would not have been so shocked. I have a feeling that his response was rather like what the *Soho News* hoped we would feel when it put the models and the bag women on the same page. The need is to keep the two separate; beautiful bright creatures must have no truck with ugly dim ones, for if the best can mix with the worst, nobody in between is safe. Even more flagrantly than Joan Roth, or me at the Dwelling Place, Ellen Baxter had violated the boundary between "us" and those who do not "live like anyone else."

The Witch Image:
Subversive Female Power

For women, living like anyone else means living within the set of conventions that define femininity—a category that, as we saw, is drastically limited. Frequently at the Dwelling Place I was startled by depths of feeling, of intuitive wisdom or clear thinking I perceived in the homeless women, or by their coherence of expression in crafts or painting—startled because their appearance, incoherence, and emotionality were such good disguises that I had forgotten that these women for the most part had to be strong and smart to survive the experiences they had had. But these disguises could not be put off; they were the result of the abnormal existence of the self that has been driven underground, distorted manifestations of powers that could not get used positively. Virginia Woolf, having invented the parable of Shakespeare's sister, who had Shakespeare's genius but was not allowed to exercise it and wound up killing herself, concludes:

> Any woman born with a great gift in the sixteenth century would certainly have gone crazed, shot herself, or ended her days in some lonely cottage outside the village, half witch, half wizard, feared and mocked at. For it needs little skill in psychology to be sure that a highly gifted girl who had tried to use her gift for poetry would have been so thwarted and hindered by other people, so tortured and pulled asunder by her own contrary instincts, that she must have lost her health and sanity to a certainty.[1]

And Margaret Mead, describing the way cultures institutionalize certain activities as the province of one sex or the other, remarks, "It is always possible for society to deny to one sex that which both sexes are able to do; no human gift is strong enough to flower fully in a person who is threatened with loss of sex membership."[2] Not just "gifts," though, but the self itself is nipped in the bud, stunted or deformed. Or, as Adrienne Rich puts it: "For centuries women have felt their active, creative impulses as a kind of demonic possession."[3] Notice she says "active" as well as "creative"; she means not only specific talents but the positive energy of simply being oneself, which implies action. Throttled, such energy goes bad: it makes you sick; it makes you mad, in both senses. This we have seen. But I want now to talk about the way this thwarted energy has peculiar effects on other people as well, which get you into trouble.

For example, people I interviewed often commented on bag women's angry muttering or shouting at passersby. Some women were so terrified that one might shout at them that they crossed the street to avoid her. The man mentioned in the introduction who was hit on the back by the woman Valerie admired took it personally. Was it his arrogance that angered her, he wondered—because he was young, decently dressed, not "conquered by the world" as she was? Much later I learned that such shouting and even violence usually had nothing at all to do with their ostensible objects. These were responses not to external reality but to voices inside the women's heads, or perhaps just excited thinking or visual images. Still, it took me a long time not to feel personally attacked when someone at the Dwelling Place began shrieking at me on being asked whether she wanted another sandwich—to understand that I (like the man who was hit) was only a blank outline into which she projected the real object of her anger, which might go back years (like Pamela's rage at psychiatrists).

However, the fact that this man searched within himself for the cause instead of brushing the attack off as the act of a crazy person suggests a certain psychological power that the women have. Another incident demonstrates a different manifestation of it. An artist told me about a friend of hers, a woman in her seventies who had a great deal of money and was rather eccentric in her behavior. This woman, carrying some bags full of paint and other supplies for renovating a building she owned, stopped in at the artist's Soho gallery to pick out a print to buy. The gallery owner thought she was a bag woman but decided to humor her and let her choose a print. She gave her name and address and left; whereupon he went to look her up in the phone book and was astonished to discover that she existed.

This woman was not dressed shabbily; the artist said she favored Danish silver jewelry. If the man had really looked at her, he would have known instantly that she was not homeless. But what with the bags, and whatever peculiarity there was in her behavior, the bag-woman image was so powerful for him that it blotted out reality. This is a concrete example of what so many of my interviewees feared: the bag woman actually did contaminate the "normal" one. And note that—just as with the woman in the Fanny Farmer store in Part 2—the bag woman had her effect without being there. That, I would say, is magic. In both cases described here the bag women—real and imagined—had an effect on other people that I can best express as casting a spell. The man on the street felt guilty even though he had no reason to; the one in the gallery was blinded by a false seeing, as bewitched people are said to be. Of course, I could also say these were personal psychological and emotional reactions and analyze them in terms of these men's individual personalities (if I knew anything about them); however, most people do not seek the reason inside themselves when someone else "makes" them feel uncomfortable but attribute their response to the other person and—this is the point—treat her accordingly.

I suggest, then, that this "power" of the bag woman is identical to the suspected "witching" of the old woman in the goose-girl fairy tale. What is more, both are the result of the women's true nature having gone into hiding. In the story, the magical old woman only appears evil because the kingdom has fallen into a wrong attitude toward femaleness, and all the female qualities it is unwilling to acknowledge have been attributed to her. The bag women bear a similar load of negative projection and have, moreover, acquired the power that goes with it: the same uncanniness that marginal people possess. And this power tends, as I discovered, to be perceived and expressed in terms of witchiness. In fact, remarkably little of the content of these projections on old women has changed from the time of the fairy tale down to the present.

Discussing the witch craze of the sixteenth and seventeenth centuries, for example, the historian H. R. Trevor-Roper remarks that in "times of panic . . . we see the persecution extended from old women, the ordinary victims of village hatred," to judges and clergy.[4] Persecution of old women, that is, is a normal phenomenon that belongs to ordinary conditions of life. An account from two centuries later provides a hint of how the role old women often played in village life could generate feelings that made them the standard scapegoats. Mrs. Cummings, "an ancient housekeeper" of Herefordshire, recalling her youth in the 1820s for a folklorist in 1895, described an old woman named Mary Phillips "as thin, with a large wen on her neck and a dreadful cough, and sitting up in her press bedstead night and day. Mrs. Cummings's mother would scold when she knew her children had been to see her" to hear her stories of "fairies and ghosts." Mary Phillips was evidently a suspicious character from whom children should be kept. But she was also the "wise woman" to whom, at a time when doctors were scarce, expensive, and not very effective, people went for healing. "I could not doubt Mary," said Mrs. Cummings; "she knew the use of all herbs, charmed burns and cuts, and cured nearly all who went to her, but she could not cure herself. . . . My mother would say she was suffering for her sins; Grandmother said 'nonsense.' "[5]

These conflicting opinions reflect an ambivalence that is still typical, as is the children's fascination. Although in the 1820s witchcraft beliefs still survived in rural England to give credence to people's distrust of Mary Phillips despite (or because of) her power to cure, the conviction that old women have peculiar and malevolent powers seems to have little to do with literal belief in witchcraft, for it persists even in our secular present. A survey done in 1966–67 of college students in Newfoundland discovered that as children they had been afraid of certain "witches"— old women of the neighborhood who were reclusive, behaved oddly, or resembled pictures of witches in the children's school readers. One account says the children believed that one such old woman would catch them and turn them into animals if they walked on her stoop; china dogs and cats in her window were thought to be "children she had changed." In another town the grownups too feared a certain "witch." They thought she could cast evil spells and often "blamed illnesses" on her. Witches were said to live in "all the old, deserted, run-down houses around the community. Children were told that if they went near these places they might be caught by a witch and stewed."[6]

These stories awakened personal echoes. A childhood friend of mine, who grew up in Queens, New York, had told me that in a big old house on the water lived an old woman whom all the children in the neighborhood called "witch"; they thought that if she caught you she would pop you in the oven and roast you for dinner. In my own suburban community, there were certain houses that I was scared to pass; and the same was true for city kids. In the early 1960s a woman known as "Ole Lady Brown" (though she was actually only about forty) lived with her cats in an unheated storefront in a Brooklyn neighborhood. All the small children and even teenagers were scared of her. Teenage girls used to pound on her door, taunting her to come out (terrified, but not admitting it to each other), and when she did would turn their backsides to her and roll their hips. Interestingly, the adults in this traditional Irish community did not share this attitude, but—evidently feeling the ancient reverence for the holy fool—treated her "like a saint," saying "Hail Marys and Blessed be to Gods in her honor as she passed."[7]

While it is easier for children than for adults to express their sense of an old woman's uncanniness by saying she is a witch, the adults still sense the power; they just do not know what to call it. What to call it is exactly what I am working out here; and the way to do it is through the witch image. Years ago I started my thinking for this book with the single idea that the bag woman is the modern witch. Subsequent ideas plus the encounter with brute fact made it clear that this concept was too simplistic; but now, having created a context for it, I can take it up again.

THE HISTORICAL WITCHES

There has been much debate about the European witch-hunt; who the accused witches were, whether they actually engaged in practices that could be called witchcraft, what those practices were are unresolved questions. It is impossible to enter this debate here, let alone extract answers from it; but it does provide a context into which can be fitted the individual experiences described above.

Although theories differ, there is a consensus among historians that witchcraft beliefs and the concomitant accusations are related to strains in a society. The European witch-hunt, in this view, came out of the Catholic Church's attempt to establish hegemony by eradicating first paganism, then heresy. Its struggle against the heretical sects went on in the context of great social tensions arising from the shift from feudalism to modern society and from the religious conflicts generated by the Reformation.[8] Church authorities developed the ideology of witchcraft as an instrument for attacking and discrediting a whole range of enemies— from organized sects that could not be assimilated into medieval Christian society to individual village wise women, whose function as healers and diviners challenged church authority in other ways.

The idea of "witch" is an old one. Folk beliefs about certain people's possession of magical powers and ability to harm or help others with them derived from the pagan past. These magical practitioners—variously called wise women, cunning men, wizards, conjurors, and white witches—filled important functions in peasant society: "divination and the finding of lost objects, disclosure of thieves, healing through folk-medicine and enchantments, love magic, protective magic, and often midwifery."[9] Individual accusations of witchcraft—involving personal wrongs such as killing someone's cow or making someone sick—were made among peasants for centuries.

Another, classical tradition involved the belief that certain women had the ability to change into animals, fly through the air at night, cast spells and make love potions, raise storms, and make people and animals ill.[10] The ancient Germanic peoples had similar beliefs. In both cases, although male sorcerers were recognized, "women, or particular types of women, were believed to have more special powers."[11] The idea of "a creature which flew about at night, screeching, and lived on the flesh and blood of human beings"—particularly babies—which the Romans called a *strix*, became an essential part of the church's witch ideology. "*Striges* were indeed thought of not as ordinary birds but as beings into which certain women could transform themselves. . . . The *strix* is a witch who is a woman by day but at night flies through the air on amorous, murderous or cannibalistic errands." In the Middle Ages the idea of night flying was attached to the pagan goddesses Diana, Hecate, and Holda, who were thought to ride at night, accompanied by a train of female spirits.[12]

In the fifteenth century, secular and ecclesiastical authorities elaborated these and other ideas into the concept of an organized heretical sect of witches flying at night on broomsticks or on the backs of animals to a great meeting called a sabbat. Still, only eminent or rich people, mostly men, were accused.[13] Only when this concept was applied in the sixteenth century to the local peasant accusations of witchcraft did the search for witches become a mass phenomenon; and when the officials came to a village, people asked to name the source of evil always knew who she was. Poor elderly women were almost always the first ones accused, although the accusations would next spread to their families and then move at random as people accused each other.[14]

At this point a complex of feelings about women interacts with a social and political power struggle. The church in its battle against paganism opposed all forms of magic, whether for harm or healing, for magic invoked a power other than that of the Christian god and was in fact identified with the "demon-worship" of the pagan religions.[15] This was the basis of church opposition to peasant healers, even—or especially—when they were successful. Their success—involving as it did (as with Mary Phillips) a combination of empirical knowledge of the properties of herbs and other substances and personal magical powers—naturally threatened both the spiritual and material authority of the church, Protestant as well as Catholic.

On top of this, most of these healers were women. Woman, the representative of the flesh, was considered more susceptible than man to the lure of Satan, the Adversary, who through her sought to undermine the foundations of society.[16] If, however, we look at this issue in terms of the scapegoat dynamic, we see that "adversary" is only another name for that which we refuse to recognize in ourselves. To the Christian ideology, identified so strongly with the male logos principle of spirit and the Word or idea, the Adversary was necessarily embodied in female flesh; which means that the witches were simply scapegoats to whom was attributed everything that official Christianity defined itself as not being.

It was certainly no coincidence that midwives, so closely associated with the quintessential operation of female flesh, were among the most suspect of women, at least in the eyes of the authorities. According to one scholar, "the demonologists and ecclesiastical officials were absolutely obsessed with the potential evil which they believed midwives could perform. *Malleus Maleficarum* and other learned Christian demonological treatises provide lurid sketches of 'Satan's whores' dedicating unbaptized babies to devils or killing them and using their fat to make flying ointment." In fact "an intensive campaign to control the practices of midwives" coincided with the church's persecution of witches. The political nature of this attack is confirmed by the fact that the peasants themselves did not share these ideas and did not accuse local midwives of being "instruments of the Devil."[17]

Thus a certain population consisting mostly of women was accused of being enemies of Christian society, just at a time when that society was undergoing unsettling changes that made people anxious and insecure. Under such circumstances, scapegoating comes in handy. People can reestablish their sense of certainty by blaming some specific group for their troubles instead of having to accept responsibility themselves, blame someone in power who can retaliate, or—worst of all—accept the idea that the cause is unknown or under no one's control. At the same time, those in power—who generally are benefiting at everyone else's cost from the status quo—want those others not to blame *them*. The solution is to blame a third party who cannot retaliate and who has always looked rather suspicious anyway.

Accordingly, the many official trials of accused witches transformed "the people's witch beliefs . . . into a highly effective means of social control. . . . Through a period of great tensions, as Europe made the difficult transition from one economic-political system to another, the peasants were induced, through the witch trials, to blame much of their malaise on their local witches and were able to rid themselves of social elements which appeared burdensome or troublesome." These "elements" were mostly outcast and deviant old women (although records of peasant accusations between the fifteenth and seventeenth centuries show that along with female—and sometimes male—magical practitioners, "marginal male figures such as beggars" were also accused).[18]

AGE, ANGER, AND THE POWER OF WITCHES

What was it about old women that so persistently generated such a response? "At least in Europe, the image of the witch as a woman, and especially as an elderly woman, is age-old, indeed archetypal. . . . As far back as the records go, people had always been apt to imagine troublesome or eccentric old women as being linked in a mysterious and dangerous way with the earth and the forces of nature, and as themselves uncanny, full of destructive power."[19] It is these feelings we must investigate.

We begin with the question of age. There were young witches, as there are young bag women, but the popular image of both is primarily of an old woman.[20] For example, certain physical characteristics made people likely to be accused of witchcraft. Any kind of physical abnormality left a person of either sex open to suspicion. But other characteristics that made women suspect were not anomalies but simply the normal features of old age. "Accusations might be levied against the 'old woman with a wrinkled face, a furr'd brow, a hairy lip, a gobber tooth, a squint eye, a squeaking voice, or a scolding tongue.' "[21]

Apparently old men did not fall under such suspicion; it was old women who were frightening and mysterious.[22] Mrs. Cummings, remembering other "witches" of her youth, said, "A great many old women, thin, brown, wrinkled old crones bent nearly double and wearing long cloaks, went about by night carrying walking sticks. How they lived no one knew. They inhabited the old houses deserted by the forgemen, and were supposed to have dealings with His Satanic Majesty."[23] Even in this small community of the 1820s, old women could get lost. No one, apparently, wanted to know "how they lived," perhaps because they sensed the knowledge would be unpleasant. This reaction, so like our own tendency to look away from bag women, suggests that old women's homelessness partakes of something old and universal.

"Men look no further than unto ye witch," said a sixteenth-century writer arguing against belief in witches. "They fret and rage against her: . . . they looke not to the cause why ye devil hath power over them: they seeke not to appease God's wrath. But they fly upon ye witch: . . . shee is made the cause of all plagues & mischiefes."[24] What is it that is so awful about old women? There is a quality of deep physical revulsion, of nausea even, in the expressions of hatred for the witches. In Robert Southey's poem "The Witch" (1798), a father, watching his son nail a horseshoe to the threshold "to keep off witchcraft," complains about the old woman they fear:

> Look at her,
> And that's enough; she has it in her face! . . .
> A pair of large dead eyes, sunk in her head,
> Just like a corpse, and pursed with wrinkles round;
> A nose and chin that scarce leave room between
> For her lean fingers to squeeze in the snuff;
> And when she speaks! I'd sooner hear a raven
> Croak at my door!

The tone here recalls the hatred of old prostitutes expressed by classical authors and echoed by Mayhew and Riis. Less vehement—but more telling for its very casualness—is a comment by South African novelist J. M. Coetzee in a reminiscence of his years in the United States studying "the syntax of exotic languages." Marveling at their complexity, he says, he asked himself whether a new ark bearing "the best that mankind had to offer" should not leave behind Shakespeare and Beethoven "to make room for the last aboriginal speaker of Dyirbal, even though that might be a fat old woman who scratched herself and smelled bad"—presumably the most repellent form of humanity he could think of.[25]

Why should the figure of the old woman—and her near twin, the witch—be informed by such loathing? I think it is grounded in obscure feelings about women's connection with sexuality and conception. "The witch figure . . . recurs with dreadful monotony over the entire world," says Margaret Mead.

It is not without significance that we have no such recurrent monotonous image of the male who does evil magically. . . . The figure of the witch who kills living things, who strokes the throats of children till they die, whose very glance causes cows to lose their calves and fresh milk to curdle as it stands, is a statement of human fear of what can be done to mankind by the woman who denies or is forced to deny childbearing. . . . She is seen as able to withhold herself from men's desire, and so to veil the nexus with life itself.[26]

If women control this nexus, in order for men to feel safe in a society where men are supposed to hold all the power, women's powers must be "domesticated," to use Adrienne Rich's word. Michelet's fable of the Sorceress allying herself with the power of Nature and upsetting the medieval order is thus particularly apt. "Through control of the mother," Rich says, "the man assures himself of possession of his children; through control of his children he insures the disposition of his patrimony and the safe passage of his soul after death."[27] That is why mothers are supposed to be married. A nonmarried woman who exercises her powers freely and without giving credit to the proper authorities is dangerous—and so is one who has gone past motherhood.

While old people in general occupy an ambiguous position, old women are perhaps the most anomalous of normal human creatures, for age destroys female roles more totally than male ones. Old men have more chance to exist as active subjects with meaningful functions than old women, who, having originally suffered an objectifying reduction to sexual and maternal functions, once these are gone no longer fit the category "woman"; in women, age *is* deviance. And just because woman's ability to conceive makes her the representative of the life force, if she denies or outlives it she becomes the representative of death: a horrifying negation, an emptiness on the order of a dead animal or a broken object. Only such an extreme formulation can explain the intensity of the revulsion old women evoke. And it is the near impossibility of looking into such a void that causes people to fill it up with projections of evil—that is, once no longer defined by the limited function society assigns it, woman's mysterious connection with nature becomes a blank on which people can inscribe all their own fears about death and the source of life (the source of power); it thereupon appears actively destructive. The old woman acquires the familiar paradoxical quality of the marginal person, in this case of being both inhumanly empty and full of inhuman power (interestingly, the older a magical practitioner was, the more power she was assumed to have). As such, she is no longer human but mythic.[28]

Projections of destructive malevolence on old women are more than pure fantasy, however; they are also valid on the human level. They express unconscious recognition of a common psychological reality: when you take away someone's human dignity, she is likely to get angry at you. In fact the thing that made (and makes) these projections easy to believe in was (and is) the old women's anger. The Southey poem makes it clear that the source of trouble was the father's abuse of a poor old woman gathering firewood on his land to keep herself warm, in accordance no doubt with the traditional system of neighborly relief, under which she was quite within her rights.[29] Her angry reaction, though perfectly justified, only confirmed the bad character attributed to her, allowing the father retroactively to rationalize his original harshness, for anger was a standard aspect of the witch character. Recall that the list of characteristics making an old woman suspect included, along with physical traits, "a scolding tongue." "Many of those accused" of witchcraft "were solitary, eccentric, or bad-tempered; amongst the traits most often mentioned is a sharp tongue, quick to scold or threaten."[30] In Tudor and Stuart England, "social harmony" was highly important, and the angry woman who created discord with her sharp tongue was considered a deviant and punished, frequently on the cucking (ducking) stool.[31] One does not read about men who displayed such nonconforming behavior; the "scold" is by definition a woman. This suggests not that men never got angry but that anger in a woman was considered much more of a problem.

"The existence of an angry person in an interstitial position . . . is dangerous," says Mary Douglas (referring here to someone who does not fit into any social categories and must exist uneasily in the cracks between them, a condition she equates with marginality). "When such unhappy or angry interstitial persons are accused of witchcraft it is like a warning to bring their rebellious feelings into line with their correct situation." Such people's anger is dangerous because they can call upon what Douglas terms the "anti-social psychic power" that inheres in the unstructured place they occupy—and which is antisocial simply by virtue of the fact that it derives from that place, the essence of society being structure.[32] The old woman, marginal by definition, who expresses anger is automatically assumed to be ready and willing to deploy that power against anyone who gets in her way. And in her case the power is that same female force that the church had set out to suppress, which certainly was "antisocial" in the sense of being inimical to the social structure of Christian Europe.

These same themes recur in the seventeenth-century New England witchcraft trials. "The accused were from the start primarily women who had violated gender norms," writes historian Carol Karlsen. First, they often lacked male family members and therefore stood to inherit property, which made them "aberrations in a society with an inheritance system designed to keep property in the hands of men." Second, they were seen as "discontented, angry, envious, malicious, seductive, lying, and proud women"; for the Puritans, too, "anger, no matter how mild, was viewed with deep suspicion when the person expressing it was a woman." Third, the accused witches were "almost all over forty" and thus "no longer performing what Puritans considered to be the major role of women: they were no longer bearing children." The Puritan fear of witches stemmed from the belief that witches had power "to disrupt the social and natural order. These more general powers carried an implicit sexual content."[33]

The objection to women's anger is based on fear of their power; anger is threatening only where power backs it up. Indeed witchcraft, so called, is nothing other than the self-ruled exercise of female power (or, the unimpeded pursuit of female modes of being) without regard for the conventions ordained for women. The horrific nature of the witch image reflects not the innate character of this power but the tremendous threat it represents to a male-dominated society; to the Puritans, for example, "disorderly women posed a greater threat than disorderly men because the male/female relation provided the very model of and for all hierarchical relations."[34] At the same time the witch image functions as a bogey to scare "real" women into behaving (that is, into bringing "their rebellious feelings into line with their correct situation").

Even today, this image packs a wallop. "We still live with witches in our culture, however much their shape may have changed over time," Karlsen concludes, citing "respected writers, not to mention Hollywood and the advertising industry," who produce images that "attest to the continuing power of woman-as-witch in our collective imagination."[35]

This power is intriguingly demonstrated—in reverse—by an item that appeared in the sensational tabloid *Sun* in July 1986. "BAG LADY IS MOM OF 217 TRASHCAN BABIES," says the page 1 headline. The story concerns "beloved bag lady Hildy Brunson," "a mysterious woman" in her seventies "who roams the streets" of London digging through trash cans for food. In these cans she finds newborn infants who have been abandoned by their mothers, either because they are illegitimate or because they are deformed and the mothers "fear the devil had a hand in the baby's birth." She then brings the babies to a police station, hospital, or church, stopping to baptize them in a puddle if she thinks they are close to death. The story is accompanied by an obviously phony photo of this legendary lady, "another Mother Theresa." She is, of course, the absolute inverse of the witch who dedicated unbaptized newborns to the devil or murdered them. The *Sun* seems to be concocting a new witch legend that contains all the ancient themes and indeed underlines their persistence by its very attempt to reassure its readers with this portrait of a white witch, whose power over life and death is used for good.[36]

As late as 1980, however, the old legend was still very much alive in the city of Amarillo, Texas, which, "buffeted by the winds of social change that accompany rapid growth," embarked on a minor witch-hunt. Three years before, according to the *New York Times*, a teenager had been killed by a shotgun on the property of a couple who belonged to the Church of Wicca, modern-day practitioners of a witchcraft tradition that goes back to an ancient Celtic nature religion. The couple was charged with murder but acquitted. However, the public became aware of their church just at a time when the city was experiencing an unprecedented crime wave that was due to its "leap into latter-day urbanity. . . . So it was that the difficulties of modernity and the presence of self-professed witches came to be linked in the minds of some of the many Amarillo residents who adhere to the fundamentalist Christianity of their forebears." When the Church of Wicca scheduled a national convention at the local Holiday Inn, fundamentalist church leaders protested. "We have seen an outbreak of demonic power recently in Amarillo—child rapes, murders and the like—and we don't need to have the witches meeting here," an evangelist couple proclaimed. The San Jacinto Baptist Church threatened to cancel a marriage-encounter seminar that had also been scheduled for the Holiday Inn and did cancel it when the motel refused to cancel the witches. A statement issued by the Church of Wicca said that the purpose of its own meeting was "to illustrate that witches, male or female, do not always have long, warty noses, wear pointed hats and brew evil-smelling concoctions in a cauldron."[37]

Again the pressures of social change had produced an anxiety that made people seek a scapegoat, and that scapegoat, after four centuries, was still the witches. While the Church of Wicca embraces both sexes, it practices a form of nature worship that belongs to the same pre-Christian tradition that the medieval church fought so vigorously to suppress—a tradition in which, as Michelet says, female power was given an importance that Christianity could not tolerate. So these twentieth-century Americans were condemning much the same witches as their forebears, and for the same reasons. It might be objected that because the protesters were fundamentalists who believed literally in the devil, their reaction is atypical today. But in fact the reaction itself is not, only that it took so literal a form. Since the essential issue behind the witch image is not magic or religion but female power, the image can still function even in an entirely secular context as a focus for exactly the same fears and accusations that prevailed three and four hundred years ago, as has been demonstrated by no less an institution than the U.S. Air Force.

In 1972 Lieutenant Erika Uehlinger was discharged from the Air Force under a regulation allowing an "officer with less than 3 years of tenure to be ousted without a hearing." She was charged with "having a 'defective attitude toward the Air Force and with adversely affecting the morale and efficiency of other personnel.'" These difficulties were said to stem "from her alleged belief and practice in witchcraft and devil worship." A captain who had trained her asserted "that her emotional problems and severe extremes in behavior was caused by her clinging faith in the Satan she claimed to see and intimately know. I am convinced," he added, "that she should be processed out of the Air Force for her own and the benefit of the Air Force before she does something dangerous to the Air Force or herself."

Uehlinger, filing suit for reinstatement, denied this charge, claiming that she was really discharged because she had "filed a long report to the inspector general alleging security violations" at the missile base where she was stationed—including a charge that personnel were "'stealing secret documents and selling them'"—as well as "improper management and unsanitary conditions." It was after the filing of this report that a psychiatrist who initially had "determined that she suffered from occupational maladjustment characterized by nervousness, depression, weight loss and irritability" but had seen nothing "impairing her judgment or reliability" changed his evaluation to conclude that she had a personality disorder that made "her future in the Air Force . . . doubtful." She was reevaluated, he said, "because of 'the way she wrote the report,' not because she had written it"; by then, it seems, the inspector general had confirmed that most of her allegations were accurate. Uehlinger contended further "that the Air Force has told her husband that he 'must dump me' if he is to continue his career as a pilot." The base commander, asked to comment on her charges, would only say, "It was generally known here that she professed witchcraft."[38]

The New York Times article that reports Uehlinger's case does not say what activities, if any, she engaged in that might be construed as witchcraft. But in any case the ancient pattern is all there: an upstart woman challenges the power of the "authorities," and they accuse her of being a witch—that is, of the familiar list of sins: wrong emotions, off-color sexuality ("intimately know"), and unsavory powers ("does something dangerous"). Her self-assertive action is translated into "personal problems," and the threat she poses is countered by attacking her credibility as a woman. And in a sense, as far as the Air Force was concerned Uehlinger really was a witch. Within such an Ur-patriarchal institution any act of individualism is a threat; how much more so a woman invoking a power that belongs to her and not the Air Force? If witchcraft means female power, from the Air Force's point of view Uehlinger's original complaint did constitute an act of witchcraft (indeed one might think that a woman setting herself to buck the military power structure would *have* to be assisted by occult forces). But most important is that the Air Force's charge of witchcraft had exactly the same function as all the earlier such charges: to punish the deviant and keep the others in line.

Bringing Them Inside

The accusations of witchcraft made in response to the old-time wise woman's power to heal derived from the principle that, it not being female to have power, this ability had to come from somewhere outside her; and since power in women threatened to overset society, its source must therefore be the enemy of society—the Adversary. Satan is also the master of the young alluring witch, who is just as destructive as the wicked old one—is, in fact, her former self. The idea of women's "devilishness" so perfectly expresses the fear of female power that, as with the witch image, its meaning goes far beyond the original context. Modern fictional portraits of women continue to make capital out of this old association.

THE ATTRIBUTION OF DEVILISHNESS

In a poem by Robert Frost, "The Pauper Witch of Grafton," the narrator's witchiness is her wicked sexuality—hostile, controlling, and destructive. Significantly the context is that she is now old and poor, and two towns are fighting over which one is legally obligated to give her relief. The poem is a monologue describing her relationship with her husband, who had started courting her by disproving a story that she was a witch who had ridden an old man of the neighborhood all over the county, leaving him hitched in front of all the town halls. But after they were married, "something" changed his mind and he decided he wanted her as a witch. The "signs" of her witchiness that she showed him, she says, were "woman signs to man" that gave her such power over him that he would do whatever she asked, even foolish, dangerous things. "And he liked everything I made him do," she concludes, evidently relishing this male masochism and submissiveness—although she now suspects that if she had known, when she was young, what degradation she would come to, she would not have had "the courage / To make so free and kick up in folks' faces." In effect Frost punishes her for "making free"—that is, exercising her evil (in his eyes) power—by leaving her old, homeless, and unwanted: a form of retribution that I think is not accidental when I recall the number of people who asked me whether many of the homeless women were not former prostitutes.[1]

In popular writing ideas of "witchiness" are more explicit. Romantic novels, for example, frequently use the word *witch* in the title, generally to suggest that the heroine has unusual and dubious qualities of strength, independence, or both. Even in the relatively mild forms most of these novels describe, witchiness is definitely a threat to society and so must be punished, sometimes horrendously.[2] By contrast *The White Witch of Rosehall*, by Herbert de Lisser (1929), is a full-scale horror story of female anger, sexuality, and power run amok, an object lesson in the ultimate of female evil. And since the author explicitly links this evil to the nature of the surrounding society, it appears as not just the aberration of one bad woman but the consequence of a failure of social control. Annie Palmer, mistress of a plantation in slave Jamaica, has lived a suspiciously solitary life since her last husband's death; she dresses in men's clothes to ride around her estate at night; violent sexual desires lead her to make unwomanly advances to Robert, the handsome hero, who is younger than she; still young and beautiful herself, she is suspected of having murdered her three husbands—perhaps by occult means, for it is whispered that she has strange powers and can, for example, make herself invisible and suck the blood of babies until they die. But her greatest feat is to call up apparitions of monstrous animals that terrify not only her slaves but the other white people as well. This ability leads Annie to "believe that she possessed the power of a god"; she remains in semibarbarous Jamaica because there she can live, "almost unfettered, the life she loved, a life of domination and of sensuality"—including intense pleasure in watching her slaves being whipped. In other words, female power unchecked by civilized restraints turns monstrous.[3]

In Annie Palmer sex and anger are clearly linked with demonic power. Violent feeling—sexual and other—has always been associated with animality, reflecting the perception that being wholly taken over by feelings means losing a share of humanness since consciousness (the prime trait distinguishing human from animal) is dimmed.[4] Annie's sexuality is scarcely worse than her anger; they seem in fact hardly distinguishable, and equally inculpating. Violent feeling of any kind is objectionable in women; and the notion that such feeling is not merely subhuman but actually fiendish is old, much older than the witch craze. Going very far back, we find that the necessity of discrediting and punishing angry women by damning them to hell is illustrated quite literally by the fate of Hecuba, queen of Troy, who, though a model and devoted wife and mother, forgot herself in the end and therefore was not spared.

After the fall of Troy and the deaths of her husband Priam and all but two of her children, Hecuba was being taken home as a slave by the Greek conquerors when these last two children were also murdered. In one version of the story she cursed the Greeks with such furious invectives for having sacrificed her daughter at the request of the ghost of Achilles that they put her to death, after which her spirit was changed into a black bitch that leaped into the sea. In another, she took horrible vengeance on Polymestor, a Thracian king who had killed her son for gold; as the Thracians tried to stone her in retaliation, she began snapping and growling at the stones, then turned into a bitch and ran off howling through the wilderness. Her anger is clearly pictured in the snapping and growling and howling of the dog—not an ordinary dog but, as one commentator says, "a sort of Hell-hound."[5] The image is so close to the customary characterization of a bad-tempered woman as a "bitch" that I am tempted to take it as a general judgment on women who allow their anger to get the better of them, even when it might be justified. Hecuba was an old woman, too, and had lost her place in society; as Ovid remarks, in her wrath she "forgot her years but not her courage" and planned her revenge "just as if she was still a queen."[6] Her horrible fate was the price she had to pay for being angry out of place.

Age (whose power may be thought of as the successor to sexual power) and anger come together with animal and devil attributes in one terrific creature that connects the witch accusations to modern bag women: "a strange apparition that was seen in the Canton of Schwyz [Switzerland] in 1506. According to a contemporary chronicler, [it] was in the form of an old woman, dressed in dirty old clothes and outlandish headgear—but in addition it had great long teeth and cloven feet. Many, we are told, died of terror at the sight of it; and plague swept through the land."[7] How could our own image of the bag women (not excluding the animalism—recall the television commentator who called them gargoyles) still accord so exactly with this ancient superstition? Because Satan represents a psychological and sociocultural constant that, externalized and literal centuries ago, is largely internalized and figurative today as a metaphor for the rejected parts of woman's nature. Women who display anger, sexuality, or sometimes any strong feeling are still for us creatures of the devil, although we express our objections in modern language; "anger in women is often labeled as pathological rather than understood as a consequence of a devalued position" because therapists "share the dominant cultural fear of anger in women."[8]

As with the witches, too, those of lower socioeconomic status receive more condemnation, so that with us the homeless are primary targets for this projection. But in addition the women themselves appear to confirm it as reality by readily accepting it. Creatures of the same socialization as everyone else, they have been punished far more severely than most for expressing anger or sexuality or too much of any feeling (think of Millie, who said, "I have this trouble that I get emotional"); so they learned to hate and condemn these qualities in themselves. Having internalized the image, they believe in their own devilishness.

I first became aware of this at the Dwelling Place, whose traditional religious atmosphere encouraged a rather literal expression of it. One afternoon a television crew came to do a spot for the evening news. They went into the kitchen and filmed a pot of soup while one of the women stirred it and everyone cracked jokes about its being a witches' brew that was good for you though it looked bad. It was a joke, but a self-conscious and uncomfortable one, arising from a certain defensiveness based on the expectation that—presented with the spectacle of women whose lot had been punishment (deserved, as they and society both agreed) suddenly coming together to be fed, clothed, and made comfortable—the outside world might not feel so sympathetic as to preclude some form of retaliation. Sure enough, only a month later, a *New York Times* reporter in a "human"-interest article about the shelter described one woman, by name, as having a "witch's grin."[9] She was quite upset. Not much of an attack, perhaps, but enough to remind the women of where they really stood.

Often individual women expressed a deep self-hatred in terms of a witchlike identity or complicity with the author of evil. Angela, a woman in her twenties, came in one afternoon but would give no information about herself. Devoured by tension, preternaturally alert to every stray glance in her direction, she was barely able to sit in a chair. When asked her name by one of the sisters, she fled the room. It turned out that she carried two switchblades, and one night her behavior became so threatening that she had to be taken to the hospital. She left behind some writing, in which she said that the end of the play was near, the actors almost done: "I am walking the dark streets and meeting the darkness which is my friend, in which I find the evil that is inside me."[10]

These devils were present only by implication. Not so with another woman who called herself Sandra when she came to the shelter but told me a few days later that her real name was Lorelei Scheherazade Marie, attributing to herself thereby a full range of female sexuality: destructive siren, soul queen seducing the king to transcend his own destructiveness, asexual virgin wedded only to spirit. The aspect that dominated in her mind, however, was revealed by a spectacular remark she made one afternoon during a conversation about apartments and hotel rooms. She stood up in the middle of the living room, stretched, and announced: "I know the devil. He's going to let me stay in *his* apartment." The room was thrown into pandemonium—literally, since the other women were so tuned in to this mode of expression that all their demons jumped up and hollered in sympathy. This was Sandra's version of the witches' reported claim to have intercourse with the devil.

The alleged witches actually confessed to this act, it now appears, only after they had been tortured, so that their confessions—all recorded by the witch hunters—represent merely what they were forced to say to confirm their persecutors' preconceptions.[11] And something not dissimilar had also happened to Sandra. Her three personae are images not of female states of being that arose out of female experience but of men's experience of women; all three represent women whose significance lies in some relation they had to men. Sandra, that is, was defining her own experience of herself in terms provided by a culture that never took her experience into account. What I want to do now, then, is precisely to take women's experience into account and reexamine this entire question of devilishness from their point of view. It will look rather different.

THE GOD OF THE NATURAL WOMAN

I begin with the accused witches themselves. They were always the poorest members of society, Keith Thomas reminds us, suggesting that they could have been afflicted by a "combination of religious depression and material poverty. . . . For persons in a state of hopelessness attachment to the Devil symbolised their alienation from a society to which they had little cause to be grateful. In this sense the idea of devil-worship was not a total fantasy. . . . When she saw herself as going over to the Devil, the witch was surrendering to passions with which everyone was familiar and on whose repression society depended." These passions were not necessarily sexual feelings but anger, hatred, and the desire for revenge; the witch went over to the devil because he promised to gratify them—to provide food, money, or the means of revenge, as well as "sexual satisfaction to compensate for spinsterhood or a husband's death."[12]

In a similar way the possession experienced by female witch accusers in New England, thought by the Puritans to be caused by a witch's attempt to seduce them to go over to Satan, expresses a power struggle involving "the legitimacy of female discontent, resentment, and anger." The violent fits of Elizabeth Knapp, a servant of the clergyman Willard, "spoke of a deeper resentment that was so fundamentally a part of her being that she could not acknowledge it, even to herself. Only when taken over by the Prince of Evil could she express the full force of her feelings—her *desire for* the independence and power embodied in the symbol of the witch and her rage at the man who taught her that independence and power were the ultimate female evils. When possessed, she could assert the witch within."[13]

From the witch's point of view, then, the devil is the one who gets you what you need, who supports and feeds your antisocial tendencies; and antisocial tendencies for a woman, remember, cover a great deal of ground since there are so few "social" tendencies included in the definition of acceptable femininity. It should therefore be no surprise to find a few women who (for whatever reason) operate outside the restricted area thinking of themselves as "witches" quite positively, or talking about the "devil" as a friend.

Lolly Willowes; or, The Loving Huntsman, a 1926 novel by Sylvia Townsend Warner, tells how Miss Laura Willowes, a mild, passive spinster who has lived with her brother's family in London since the death of her father, suddenly at the age of forty-seven decides to move to a small country village and live by herself, to her family's outrage. Months later, when her nephew comes on a prolonged visit, she feels the possessive power of the family about to take her over again and, in terror and desperation, calls out for aid. Satan, appearing as a quiet man dressed as a gamekeeper, answers; she makes a compact with him for her freedom.

But this Satan is not the possessive lord imagined by the witch hunters, nor is Laura a stereotypical witch. "When I think of witches," she explains, "I seem to see all over England, all over Europe, women living and growing old, as common as blackberries, and as unregarded." They lead dull, dependent lives: "Nothing for them except subjection and plaiting their hair." One becomes a witch, then, not to be harmful (nor helpful, either) but "to escape all that—to have a life of one's own, not an existence doled out to you by others." And one has one's freedom, and owns one's life, for this witch's master is not a lover who possesses her; he leaves her alone, for he is the impersonal spirit of Nature, who is her master only as Nature is the ruler of humanity: belonging to it, we follow its laws. As in acting with Nature instead of against it we achieve the greatest freedom, Laura finds that under Satan's "undesiring and unjudging gaze, his satisfied but profoundly indifferent ownership," she is finally herself.[14]

This novel, set largely in the 1920s, is fantastical, but it raises a real issue. The disturbance of the family over Laura's seemingly simple act of going off on her own signals that for a woman in the marginal position of aging spinster to act as though she were a person in her own right is a big thing indeed. How big is suggested by Laura's ruminations about her family after she has been some time in the country and realized how miserable she was for years.

> There was no question of forgiving them. She had not, in any case, a forgiving nature; and the injury they had done her was not done by them. If she were to start forgiving she must needs forgive Society, the Law, the Church, the History of Europe, the Old Testament, great-great-aunt Salome and her prayerbook, the Bank of England, Prostitution, the Architect of Apsley Terrace [where her brother's family lives], and half a dozen other useful props of civilisation.

It was, that is, the entire structure and value system of Western civilization that reduced the self-chosen spinster (for Laura had refused chances to marry) to a piece of property that the family "disposed of" as they thought best—just as it created the prostitute as an object whose function was also related to the system of property.[15]

Laura's Satan, then, is on her side; he is the adversary only of Western civilization. Within that restrictive society he provides a free space in which Laura can experience and act on her own feelings—that is, can be who she really is. One might say then that Satan is the deity of the true feminine self, an association that holds as much today as it did for Michelet's Sorceress. In Margaret Atwood's 1972 novel *Surfacing*, for example, the narrator's trip to a remote Canadian island, where she lived as a child, to search for her missing father becomes a search for a lost self of her own. It is a real vision quest, which Atwood conceives of in specifically female terms as the opposite of the traditional male grail quest, whose object is an exalted spirituality attainable only by one who is physically pure. Atwood's narrator goes in the opposite direction, toward pure animality, spending several days in the woods without clothes, refusing to eat anything not wild until she has had her vision, a process presided over by a familiar figure. He appears first in a rediscovered childhood drawing of a man with horns and a barbed tail, who, she explains, is God—"if the Devil was allowed a tail and horns, God needed them also"—and then as a horned animal-like figure in copies her father made of ancient rock paintings. Finally she sees him herself, in the woods: "It gazes at me for a time with its yellow eyes, wolf's eyes. . . . Reflectors. It does not approve of me or disapprove of me, it tells me it has nothing to tell me, only the fact of itself. Then its head swings away."[16]

This figure is the god of what Atwood calls the "natural woman" and is, in fact, the same creature that the medieval peasants dressed up as during festivals—that is, it evokes not Satan so much as his ancestors, the pre-Christian nature gods. Under its aegis, the narrator rediscovers a part of herself that had been left out in the woods with it since her childhood. In the process she nearly turns into an animal herself: "a creature neither animal nor human, furless, only a dirty blanket, shoulders huddled over into a crouch." Once she accepts that this creature is also her, however, she is ready to return to civilization, only not as she was before: "I have to recant," she concludes, "give up the old belief that I am powerless."[17]

This change is the key, for the social problem of marginality and the individual question of a woman's true self are both issues of power. As we saw, the woman who went over to Satan was accused of having acquired unlawful power that (it was assumed) would be wielded destructively against the institutions of Western society. But as Atwood's narrator realizes, this power does not come from Satan at all. It is her own and is based on a conviction of the validity of her own perceptions of reality that enables her to act on them; "Satan" is just a mental construct to which she can attribute it since she is not prepared to acknowledge it as hers. Not surprisingly, actions based on such perceptions are likely to take her beyond the limits of woman's conventional role.[18] Lt. Uehlinger is a good example because she illustrates what I mean in concrete and unmythic terms. The "natural woman" is not simply she who possesses the mysterious connection to nature and the source of life that was perhaps the original form of female power and source of male fear, but more broadly she who possesses the original *self* that would exist if women's own feelings and needs were not distorted by dictates based on the needs of Western civilization. This female self is equally a source of male fear because, being undomesticated, it disregards rules that do not agree with it.

The concept of the witch, then, comes out of a great power struggle of which the social conflicts that produced the historical witch-hunt were only one version. For nearly as far back as we can go, Western civilization has always won, which is why the witches have such a bad name. Unwilling to share their opprobrium, most women refuse to take action that might evoke it and thus remain powerless. But as so often when some element of an individual personality appears negative and intractable, hampering effective functioning in life, I think also for the sake of the collective female self we need to go back to origins—to what happened initially to put female power eternally on the defensive—in order to release the fear and regain what we lost. To do this I turn again to myth—to the legend of Lilith, the original witch.

ORIGINAL FEMALE POWER

In the Zohar, one of the mystical works of the Jewish Cabala, Lilith's origin is said to be a quarrel between the sun and the moon, which originally were "equal in dignity." God intervened and "caused the Moon to diminish herself." The result was the birth of Lilith, who is said to be "flaming fire" from the navel down, her energy deriving from resentment of this diminishment.[19] According to another myth, Lilith was the female half of the original androgynous Adam, made of dust. Then, however, God "severed the female from Adam's side" and made Eve to be his bride and the mother of humanity. Unwilling to be domesticated and humiliated by this diminishment of the primordial freedom of the feminine spirit, Lilith fled into the wilderness, where she consorted with demons. Her "vengeful murderous rage" led her eternally to wander, seeking to harm men and children. In still another version she is said to be the female half of the devil.[20]

Lilith represents exactly the aspect of femininity that, being rejected and cast out, as in the goose-girl tale becomes the witch. She appears not just in the Hebrew tradition but all over the ancient Near East as the night hag, a seductress who though exiled still desires Adam and visits men at night, causing nocturnal emissions; she endangers children and women in childbirth; she is the demon of screeching, associated with owls—all, of course, witch attributes.[21]

Lilith is simply the original "bad" woman, cast out at the beginning of patriarchy for asserting unacceptable needs for equality and independence; the association with demons emphasizes how what was powerful and active in women was always literally damned. In real life this has meant that women who experienced these forbidden needs have themselves felt evil, as though they had a secret demon lover. Yet the legend shows clearly that Lilith's uncouth and frightening aspect was no more than the effect of her anger and despair at being outcast. Her refusal to be subordinate contrasts with Eve's acceptance of the conditions of patriarchy. Lilith, it is said, was so jealous of Eve that "a single drop of Lilith's menstrual blood is laden with sufficient bitterness and poison to kill the population of an entire town." Eve is safe and comfortable but in exchange must accept being subordinate and lose much of her instinctual life; she "feels fettered to the earth by men and children and mirrors Lilith's jealousy."[22]

Looking at the homeless women's behavior in terms of this conflict between Eve and Lilith, we can see their passivity and dependence as the result of their having learned and conformed to the terms of life in society, and their angry and desperate outbreaks as the Lilith part of them breaking through. Like her, they were cast out; and the longer they stayed outside, the stronger that part became and the more they grew to resemble her. On a broad social level, the split between Eve and Lilith is the split between the respectable woman and the prostitute, the sane woman and the mentally ill, and between the homeless and the woman going home. Eve's jealousy of Lilith appears as idealization of the bag women's strength, independence, and so on; though at the same time the very fact that such women exist raises the specter of our own inner Lilith of unacceptable needs, a creature who seems dirty, bestial, fiendish, and mad. All our roots and connections within society give us a stake in denying her.[23]

But like those Dwelling Place women who came in off the street incoherent, then slept for three days and woke up with changed personalities, Lilith or the "natural woman" has only run wild through being cast out in the first place; once she is brought back inside, she will again start to comb her hair and dress in clothes that match. And as Atwood's narrator discovered, bringing the "natural woman" inside involves a change in ourselves: specifically, an acceptance of power.

One reason women (not only the homeless) have had such difficulty owning their own power is just that it was always thought of as coming from the devil. Not only did this make it a negative thing in itself, but one's entire process of development was conceptualized in terms of being *against* something. Besides, even where Satan is imagined as a friendly sort, as in *Lolly Willowes*, one still remains eternally secondary to an external male power. It would be much better to think of female power as primary and positive—that is, originating within oneself and acting inherently for oneself—and it would also be historically more accurate, for originally female power was primary, personified in the many forms of the Great Goddess, in relation to whom the male was a son or consort.[24]

Despite the triumph of Christianity, a sense of the significance of this female power lasted in European folk culture until relatively recently, embodied in a whole series of local female divinities. These mother-goddess figures, drawn from both the pagan Germanic and classical traditions, have come down to us through the fairy tales of the Grimms and others. Among them were Diana, Hecate, and the Germanic Holda, all believed to ride at night with a train of followers. Holda, for example, was "a supernatural, motherly being. . . . [She was] originally . . . a pagan goddess associated with the winter solstice and the rebirth of the year." If angered she could "turn into an ugly old hag with great teeth and a long nose, the terror of children," but she also did helpful things for the households she visited by night.[25]

Different localities had their own versions of this goddess, all associated with the devil but also conferrers of supernatural benefits on humans.

> On the Virgin Mary's birthday—the festival of maids, as it was still called at the beginning of [the nineteenth] century—the maidens in Thüringen used to rise before daybreak and bathe with the water of a sacred spring, which made them beautiful. In Hesse bathing in Frau Holle's pond, or in various sacred wells, makes barren women fruitful. Here we have the same notion of fertility due to the sacred water of the goddess; but in later days she has been replaced by the Virgin Mary.[26]

Comparing this ritual with the one the princess in our fairy tale performs, it becomes clear who the old woman in that story is.

Another version of the Goddess was the medieval Mother Folly, or the Mother of Fools, who reigned during church fool festivals when the social hierarchy was symbolically turned upside down, in direct contrast to the Virgin, that paradigm of woman under patriarchy. The "devil's dam," or devil's grandmother (that is, *great* mother), also appears in many fairy tales: "The devil . . . lives with the old woman, i.e., his own mother, the Great Mother Earth."[27] The devil, if we recall his origins as a nature spirit, is, like the fool, a "natural man" or son of Mother Nature. Indeed the kinship of devil and fool was recognized in medieval folklore that represented the devil as a clown, a "'simpleton' who is 'fooled' or 'cheated.'"[28] Both violate the categories by which society operates, letting in the Beyond, which for Western society is the domain of the Great Mother that it has so rigorously excluded. Her appearance as Mother in the folk tradition is a survival of her earlier preeminence, while the perspective that sees the devil as the woman's master is the product of the patriarchal state of mind, whose need is to deny her power.

Descended by way of the fairy-tale witch from these medieval figures, the Great Mother is still among us—that is, people still make images of her that others find compelling—although, not surprisingly, she is today a marginal person. In Kurt Vonnegut's novel *Jailbird*, for example, she appears as Mrs. Jack Graham, the mysterious majority stockholder in RAMJAC, the world's largest conglomerate; living in hiding as a shopping-bag lady on the streets of New York, she carries out a grand scheme to save the country from capitalism by buying up the economy and leaving it "to its rightful owners, the American people." In keeping with the scope of this mission, she has distinctly divine characteristics. She issues instructions by phone and mail but never appears in the flesh; asked if he has ever seen her, one employee responds: "That's like asking me if I've seen God." On the crown of her head is "a bald spot the size of a silver dollar" fringed by a white "tonsure"—the symbol of being given to God. Even her maiden name, Mary Kathleen O'Looney, evokes Mother Folly. Her scheme fails in the end because, says Vonnegut, capitalism by its nature is "indifferent to the needs of the people." Or, one might say, in modern society Goddess power is in eclipse, allowing the Goddess to be degraded and her power coopted and made negative.[29]

The Goddess's degradation is further elaborated in Mary McCarthy's novel *Birds of America*, where she appears symptomatically split in two. Peter, the teenaged protagonist, has constructed a philosophy of life based on a belief in a "universal moral faculty" that keeps human beings in harmony with Nature, "his other mother." He has made his real mother Nature's stand-in in the human realm and keeps close watch on the ethical foundations of her actions in order to enforce sufficient purity of motive to justify his faith. The novel traces the destruction of this faith through a series of incidents whose climax is a shattering encounter with a Parisian *clocharde*, or female tramp. Peter more or less forces her to spend the night in his room in a misguided attempt to prove the viability of his ethic by redeeming her into the form of femininity that fits it. But she fails completely to respond to his overtures and remains revoltingly alien, evoking in him "a nauseous repulsion." She disappears while he sleeps, having, however, first destroyed "everything he cared about." When, a few days later, he sees his mother, he realizes that "she had no authority for him any more." Finally he has a little vision in which the shade of Kant, his philosophical mentor, visits him to announce, "Nature is dead, *mein Kind*"—which is to say Peter's idealization of Nature, involving a refusal to acknowledge the full spectrum of female reality on the same order as the one that produced the witches.[30] Peter's attempt to make his mother be perfect called up the *clocharde*, just as in our fairy tale the king's insistence that his daughter have only sweet feelings produced the goose-girl.

INTEGRATING THE OUTCASTS

The fact that she gets herself embodied in characters by mainstream writers indicates that the Goddess still holds a measure of power, even in her marginal position.[31] During the 1980s, moreover, efforts were made to bring her inside and rehabilitate her fully. Writers, artists, social critics, and feminist "thealogians" began using her image consciously to redefine women's experience and create new paradigms of personal relations that could free us to evolve nonhierarchical patterns of social organization and practice. Their work runs the gamut from explorations of how archetypal Goddess images function within the individual psyche, to the creation of new principles of power and their application to specific political actions, to large-scale visions for restructuring culture and society.[32]

My own experience—encounters with women like Leah as well as the research I did to create a context for understanding them—also brought me to the Goddess image, which seems to underly the complex of tangled responses that homeless women evoke. The way in which Goddess and witch still constitute the two sides of a single figure, with the witch today taking the form of a homeless woman, is demonstrated by two dreams of a contemporary woman.

This woman had been involved in an intense love affair in which she acted out a Lilith side of herself—being "fiery" and "seductive"—but which she ended abruptly and unreasonably when her lover made her angry. A few weeks later "she fell into a dark and heavy depression. She felt cold and sick, stopped bathing and wore the same clothes day after day." Then unexpectedly she saw her lover, who looked "clean and obviously happy and healthier since the end of their affair." That night she had the following dream: "A large, heavy, dirty, dark skinned derelict woman fell upon me as I emerged from a doorway. She pinned me to the ground, almost suffocating me, and would not let me up until I negotiated with her." In an attempt to revisualize the dream, the dreamer "learned that the dark, heavy derelict woman was named Seraphina. Seraphina said she would not let the woman up unless she promised to take her home with her, bathe and anoint her, clothe her in beautiful garments, and allow her to live in her house forever. The dreamer accepted Seraphina's terms and realized she must seek the inner meaning of her great love affair, and the two began to dwell together." In another dream some weeks later, Seraphina "was a wise woman and oracle, dressed in a rich heavenly blue robe and seated upon a throne in an underground realm which she ruled."[33]

Although this woman had allowed herself to act out her Lilith-like desire for power (sexual in this case), she was nevertheless possessed by the patriarchal attitude toward Lilith and thus literally cast herself out—following, in her exiled state, the pattern of real homeless women who gave up the struggle to stay clean when their sense of self weakened. Thus in the dream the cast-out self assumes the shape of a bag woman whom the dreamer must take into her home—that is, the dwelling place of her true or complete self. When she does this the derelict turns into a queenly wise woman—rather like the one in the fairy tale, whose house was also transformed into a palace.[34]

For the dreamer these dreams were a vehicle for bringing the outcast inside. Her facility for interpretive imagination provides an unusually clear model of how the image of the homeless woman functions as a living and intense presence in the contemporary female psyche. Although the image had a wholly personal meaning and function for the dreamer, her use of it in a way completely parallel to (though, be it said, entirely independent of) my own signals its general significance.

Nor does the process of integrating the homeless woman depend on a specialized analytic technique. For me it happened largely through my experiences at the Dwelling Place. It was the daily dealing ("dwelling") with the women there that got me started disentangling my projections from who they actually were—for you cannot deal effectively with people whom you see largely through your own fantasies. Eventually the experience becomes so painful that you either withdraw from it or start to think. In my case I wrote this book, following, as it turned out, a precedent I discovered only after I had begun.

For the women of the nineteenth-century voluntary societies, as we saw, the prostitute and the criminal were the figures on whom their own Lilith side was projected. One can therefore imagine what a tremendous revolution of feeling and belief it was that led them ultimately to identify with these women, to a degree that enabled Caroline Kirkland to write:

> Whatever we are able to do . . . for the hapless subjects of our care, is done, in literal truth, for ourselves; . . . we actually learn as much from them as they learn from us. . . . In reading these souls, often truly laid bare before us under the influence of helplessness and despair, we learn human nature in a way and to a degree which opens to us the recesses of our own hearts, and forces us to recognize the consequences which ensue from carrying out to their extremes the very faults which in our smoother lives look like trifling offences.[35]

Kirkland's book, while primarily a plea for support for the work of the Women's Prison Association, is also a record of this same process of integration.

For me, suddenly to see back 130 years to an experience exactly like my own was an enormous affirmation not only of my personal feelings but of my sense that the issue of homelessness must be dealt with on the level of consciousness as well as that of social action. For many, including myself, the one is a bridge to the other, and the bridge is built with an image: here, the double image of the old woman outcast/goddess. It represents a state of individual powerlessness that translates into a political condition, one of whose signs is the demarcation between "us" and the women outside. I have tried to break down that distinction by showing what connections do exist between us and them. Once we embrace these connections, the obstructions to bringing them inside will at least not arise from within ourselves.

In New York City in the 1980s, although there was money to fund residences for the homeless and buildings were available for renovation, there was frequently strong, and successful, community opposition to such facilities, even when intended for women only. Unlike homeless men, decrepit women were not feared as physically dangerous; as we know, they had other powers. If they looked peculiar, or smelled bad, or acted strangely, people with money to spend would find an area where a shelter was sited unattractive; merchants would suffer, and the price of real estate would drop.[36] We take the validity of such an equation for granted; but in fact it is only a modern version of the ancient dynamic of giving relief, based no less on an ethic of money and power. Indeed the idea that an old woman can drive down the value of your property by peeing on the sidewalk in front of your house is a piece of magical thinking exactly on a par with the belief that she can make you wither and die by casting a spell on you. Where could she possibly get such a power? From you, of course: if you believe it, it will happen. Or, to put it another way, if you gave her alms, she would not curse you; if you gave her a home, she would relieve herself inside it. After all, the power is not hers— it is yours.

Notes

INTRODUCTION

1. Information on conditions at BWS comes from statements made at the demonstration, conversations with monitors for the Coalition for the Homeless, and from Homeless Women's Rights Network, "Victims Again."

2. "Municipal Shelters under Attack Again." *Safety Network/NY: The Newsletter of the Coalition for the Homeless*, July 1990. Later in 1990 the city moved to open new assessment shelters in several boroughs but only because it was under a court order to do so as a result of action by the Coalition. (Interview with Kristin Morse of the Coalition, October 21, 1990.)

3. Interview with Widney Brown, a Tae Kwon Do black belt and experienced self-defense teacher, May 22, 1990.

4. I heard these sentiments expressed at a workshop, sponsored by several advocacy groups, intended to resolve differences between advocates and grass-roots homeless activists (New York City, May 12, 1990). "Rage and suspicion about the system rightfully exists when we all know that the suffering of the poor is *no accident*," wrote a commentator in *Voices to and from the Streets*, "a newsletter written by NYC homeless, for NYC homeless." Annie Q., "The Homeless Movement," 2.

5. For example, in June 1990 the Long Island Rail Road began an effort to evict homeless people from Penn Station in New York City, in response, a spokesman said, to complaints from commuters no longer willing to encounter panhandlers and homeless people sleeping on the floor. Clara Hemphill, "LIRR to Boot Homeless Sleeping in Penn Station," *New York Newsday*, June 1, 1990, p. 4. This eviction had both symbolic and practical importance. For years the station had been a central resource homeless people had used to meet needs ranging from sleep to warmth to money (begging, finding dimes in pay-phone coin returns).

The attempt to "sweep" them from the station represented a significant change in attitude on the part of both authorities and the public.

REAL LIFE OUTSIDE

The Dwelling Place

1. In changing the names of the women described in this book, I had to use far more names than they actually possessed among them because so many were called Mary. In addition to names, details about their lives and circumstances have been altered.

Why They Were Outside

1. My unsystematic observations are supported by the results of a research project that studied a similar group of women about ten years before the Dwelling Place opened. See Bahr and Garrett, *Women Alone*, 135–36: "for women the dominant process leading to homelessness was the marital experience, as opposed to the occupational history for men." For further comments on this distinction, see Part 3.

Alexandre Vexliard, who studied the tramps (*clochards*) of Paris in the mid-1950s, also concluded that among the women (*clochardes*), in general, deaths and family ruptures played a "dominant role." *Le Clochard*, 142. The women Vexliard describes—most of them feeble-minded or physically disabled or both, and one given to violent rages—all originally led normal lives. In explaining their homelessness he points out that other people with the same disabilities and personality problems were able to lead conventional lives because they happened to have a supportive "social framework" ("family, profession, employers," although for women it would most often be family) that held them inside society, while the *clochardes* did not (pp. 145–46, quotations from 146).

2. Although this figure of "about half" is largely subjective, it coincides with a New York State Office of Mental Health estimate "that 45 to 50% of the homeless are 'mentally ill'" (Baxter and Hopper, *Private Lives*, 10). In December 1982 Mary Ellen Hombs of the Community for Creative Nonviolence testified at a Congressional hearing, "By 1981 it was estimated that nearly one-third to one-half of the more than 2 million homeless men and women in America were ex-mental patients." Quoted in U.S. Congress, *Homelessness in America*, 13.

3. A striking parallel to the stories of these women is that of a woman in totally different circumstances. She was an artist, married to another, famous artist; I heard her story from someone who knew her during the 1950s. After a trip she made to Europe by herself, their marriage deteriorated, and eventually they separated. When he died, she broke down and wound up at a state mental hospital. When she was discharged, she was supposed to go to a quiet place to recuperate. Someone suggested an island that was not just quiet but desolate and primitive. While she was there, my informant heard her say some "disturbing" things, such as that she'd like to take her pants off and sit on the moss in the woods. After a month-long bout of fog she left the island and went to the Hamp-

tons, where she was thrown out of her hotel for taking off all her clothes and lying in the lobby (a woman I knew at the Times Square did exactly the same). This episode brought her back to the hospital.

When she got out next, she had no money and was placed in an SRO. She left it, putting all her clothes on her back and carrying everything else in shopping bags. However, she still had rich friends on Park Avenue, and every few months she showed up at one of their apartments (shocking the maid!) to take a shower, eat a meal, and perhaps stay overnight. Finally someone contacted her son, who lived out West; he arranged for her to go there, where she remained.

4. Although at present the law prohibits involuntary hospitalization unless a person is considered dangerous to herself or others, many women I knew were old enough to have been incarcerated under the previous law, which made it much easier to commit someone involuntarily.

5. The recruitment systems are described in Baxter and Hopper, *Private Lives*, 87.

6. Such discharges were said to occur largely at the private hospitals, which were not bound by law as were the municipals to provide discharged patients with a place to live.

7. Beverly Burlett, "Four Days in the Women's Shelter," *Majority Report*, October 17, 1974; Baxter and Hopper, *Private Lives*, 64–67; Baxter and Hopper, "New Mendicancy," 400–401. The gynecological-exam requirement was dropped in 1981. As the introduction indicates, conditions in city-run single-women's shelters were by 1990 generally much worse than in the original Women's Shelter.

8. Kim Hopper, who did ethnographic research among New York City homeless people during approximately the same period that I was at the Dwelling Place, comments, "It was my considered impression that even the severely disabled who refused to use the public shelters did so after a careful weighing of the personal costs involved. To be sure, some of these deliberations could entail seemingly unreal factors—suspicions of threats to one's life, . . . for example. But the evidence of direct observation offers little support for dismissing these as the unfounded concerns of hopelessly addled minds. On the contrary, . . . the deterrent effects of public shelter [may well] have been keenest for those whose afflictions left them unusually sensitive to traces of menace in their surroundings." "More Than Passing Strange," 157.

Life on the Street

1. This study, carried out in 1979 for the Manhattan Bowery Corporation, is cited in Baxter and Hopper, *Private Lives*, 80. Beulah Lund, a housewife from Washington State who went on the street for six weeks in Washington, D.C., to find out who homeless people "really were," also told a reporter that "many so-called bag ladies are loners who are deliberately filthy or act deranged solely to protect themselves" from men. Acting deranged is a well-known trick even among the nonhomeless, but for the reasons given in the text I doubt that many women choose to be really dirty even to deter attackers. Arias, "Posing as a Bag Lady," 32, 37.

2. A 1978 description of homeless women observed at a hospice in another city also reports that "only a few women, notably the women who were reported to be severe alcoholics, appeared unclean. Many showed great resourcefulness with regard to personal hygiene measures." Strasser, "Urban Transient Women," 2078.

3. This woman appears in Rousseau, *Shopping Bag Ladies*, 135ff.

4. Reported in "What's in the Bag?" *Majority Report*, October 17, 1974, p. 1.

5. Ada Chesterton, an English journalist who investigated homeless women in London in the 1920s, had a similar reaction: "Even in the meanest London street you feel the effects of the open sky and the lack of space within the four walls of a building tries you very heavily. . . . I found the confines of a building pressed very hardly on my spirits after but a short period of life in the streets. And if this was the effect on me, . . . what must the influence of the open air be to those who can remember no other form of existence?" *In Darkest London*, 210.

6. Quoted in "Street Level."

Mary Higgs, a Christian missionary who made several investigative trips as a tramp in early-twentieth-century England, describes the similar demoralization she experienced—even though she was only pretending to be down and out—when she was bullied by the admitting official of a tramp ward: "Then he proceeded to insinuate I was a woman of bad character; my eyes fell and my face flushed, and I suppose gave colour to his statement. Reply or justification was worse than useless. I grew so confused I could not state correctly the number of my children, but said I had 'one or two.' Evidently a bad character, leaving children up and down the country." *Glimpses into the Abyss*, 142.

7. Chesterton, *In Darkest London*, 168. Exactly the same effect is described by Orwell in *A Clergyman's Daughter*, 202. His comments go far to explain some homeless people's lack of interest in coming inside:

> She had come, like everyone about her, to accept this monstrous existence almost as though it were normal. The dazed, witless feeling that she had known on the way to the hopfields had come back upon her more strongly than before. It is the common effect of sleeplessness and still more of exposure. To live continuously in the open air, never going under a roof for more than an hour or two, blurs your perceptions like a strong light glaring in your eyes or a noise drumming in your ears. You act and plan and suffer, and yet all the while it is as though everything were a little out of focus, a little unreal. The world, inner and outer, grows dimmer til it reaches almost the vagueness of a dream.

"Few people realize how quickly a new-comer to 'the road' becomes demoralized," wrote an English government official not many years before Orwell's novel takes place. "In six weeks—some witnesses say a fortnight—character is broken down, and the victim is 'in it' for life." Quoted in O'Connor, *Britain in the Sixties*, 81.

8. "Prolonged periods of sleep deprivation have sometimes led to increased ego disorganization, hallucinations, and delusions in individual cases. Some investigators have assumed that a long enough period of sleep deprivation will produce a psychosis in normal subjects, but this cannot be stated with certainty." Hartmann, "Sleep," 158.

Women who used the Olivieri Center for Homeless Women in Manhattan, a drop-in center that reached out specifically to those considered mentally ill, went through the same transformation. After they rested, saw the medical team, and got used to the staff, many of their apparent psychiatric symptoms disappeared. Interview with Colleen McDonald, director of the center, November 12, 1987.

A homeless man described the effects of lack of sleep to Kozol: "The lack of sleep leaves you debilitated, shaky. You exaggerate your fears. If a psychiatrist came along he'd say that I was crazy. But I was an ordinary man." *Rachel and Her Children*, 171. See also Snow et al., "Myth of Pervasive Mental Illness," 421, for a discussion of so-called symptomatic behaviors as "adaptations to the trying exigencies of street life."

9. Vexliard, *Le Clochard*, 62.

10. Ibid., 62, 145.

11. Interview with Ann Marie Rousseau, February 6, 1981.

The Effects of the Relief System

1. Though a few younger women had children in foster care, they were considered single for welfare purposes because the children were not with them.

2. Piven and Cloward, *Regulating the Poor*, 148, 166, 169. See the last two sections of Part 3 for a discussion of the historical development of relief in this country and the first section of Part 3 for the pauper's badges.

3. Piven and Cloward, *Regulating the Poor*, 147–61, gives many examples of such procedural mechanisms.

4. Ibid., 166.

5. Orwell, *Down and Out*, 184.

Ten Years Later

1. The following information is based on a July 23, 1990, interview with Sr. Nancy Chiarello, the director of the Dwelling Place. This change in the shelter's residents reflected a general shift in the homeless population that occurred during the 1980s; it is described in Part 3 of this book. I emphasize that since the Dwelling Place now took only single women over thirty, its residents were not representative of homeless women in general. In particular, only a small minority of all homeless women are drug users (see the section "Since World War II" in Part 3).

2. A study of shelter residents in Philadelphia in the winter of 1981–82 found that "young adult chronic patients constitute roughly 43 percent of all undomiciled individuals who currently live on the street." These people (43 of 193 studied were women) had "fallen between the cracks of a care system that has neglected their needs." Arce et al., "Psychiatric Profile of Street People," 816. In using the term *mental illness* here I follow the terminology of service providers, although, as Part 4 explains, I question some of the implications of this categorization.

Community

1. Two social workers who created a "dinner group" among mentally ill homeless women in a group residence similarly report that the "diagnostic infor-

mation . . . had limited value in predicting how the women would function within the group or . . . how each member would contribute to the character of the group as a whole. Furthermore, diagnostic formulations served to underscore the psychiatric disabilities of group members and raise questions in the [social] workers' minds as to the ability of members to handle the responsibilities entailed in group participations." After five years, group members could plan, shop for, cook, eat, and clean up after dinner almost completely on their own. Berman-Rossi and Cohen, "Group Development and Shared Decision-Making," 65.

In *Faces of Homelessness*, Hope and Young quote Erna Steinbruck, director of a Washington, D.C., group home: "I've seen women move from being terribly chronically ill to managing on their own. We have to needle them often, keep them to their plans. We *are* patient, because we know they need supports all along. But the progress of some women—they're miracle stories" (82).

See also Hoch and Slayton, *New Homeless and Old*, which reports research on the skid-row community of Chicago, past and present. The authors demonstrate that the SRO residents were not incompetent at living but succeeded in creating heterogeneous communities based on mutual helping, which allowed them to retain their autonomy.

2. Interview with Ellen Baxter, director of The Heights, March 29, 1988. In *The Heights*, she describes her philosophy that housing for the homeless should be integrated and permanent rather than transitional and specialized for different groups. See also Stephanie Golden, "A Home Heals Most Wounds," *New York Newsday*, July 13, 1988, p. 58. Baxter has since developed several other permanent residences.

3. Interview with Conrad Levenson, December 13, 1990; Dean, "A Balancing Act," 15. See also Levenson, "Designing Homes for the Homeless."

4. "Somewhere inside," commented a friend of mine who came that day, "they sense that men are where all the power resides and that you have to get what you need through a man. So the important thing about Elizabeth Taylor is how she gets husbands."

5. By 1990 Ellen had moved out of the Times Square into a much nicer community residence; she was on medication and "looking great." Interview with Sr. Nancy Chiarello, July 23, 1990.

6. Baxter and Hopper, *Private Lives*, 31. Apparently similar to the Dwelling Place in philosophy is the Downtown Women's Center in Los Angeles, where "a sense of community is fostered" and "there is a sense that no rules apply to therapy with homeless women except that they will respond positively when they have a sense that they are in a supportive environment where staff are patient, caring, and respectful." Stoner, "Plight of Homeless Women," 287.

7. Vexliard, *Le Clochard*, 273, quoting Boris Simon, *Les Chiffoniers d'Emmaus*.

MYTHMAKING

1. See von Franz, *Introduction to the Interpretation of Fairy Tales*, chaps. 1 and 2.

2. This summary is based on the version in *The Complete Grimm's Fairy Tales*, 725–34.

3. "The Princess Who Loved Her Father Like Salt," 66–67.

4. *Encyclopaedia Britannica*, 6th ed., s.v. "salt." The salt trade was of major economic importance in the ancient world.

5. "You shall burn no leaven nor any honey as an offering by fire to the Lord" and "You shall season all your cereal offerings with salt; you shall not let the salt of the covenant with your God be lacking from your cereal offering; with all your offerings you shall offer salt" (Leviticus 2:11, 13). May and Metzger, *Oxford Annotated Bible*, 123–24.

6. Jung, "Study in the Process of Individuation," par. 575.

7. Briar Rose (the Sleeping Beauty) is also fifteen when she pricks her finger on the spindle (*The Complete Grimm's Fairy Tales*, 238).

8. Neumann, *Great Mother*, 139–40 and fig. 25. These mysteries are depicted in *The Golden Ass* of Apuleius.

9. von Franz, *Shadow and Evil*, 105.

10. von Franz, *Problems of the Feminine*, 81; Jobes, *Dictionary of Mythology*, s.v. "apple," "pear."

11. Neumann, *Great Mother*, 217–18. In the ancient Egyptian religion the Nile goose was said to have laid the cosmic egg and thus been the mother of all creation. Neumann also reproduces a terra-cotta figure of Aphrodite standing on a goose (plate 137).

12. von Franz, *Shadow and Evil*, 270.

13. It is also interesting that geese have a connection with devils and witches, who are often supposed to have duck or goose feet. Ibid., 224.

14. For example, Lilith, the Mesopotamian goddess of "night, evil, and death," is represented as "winged, bird-footed, and accompanied by owls" (Neumann, *Great Mother*, 272 and plate 126). The connection with wisdom also occurs in the Christian context, where an owl appears in paintings with Saint Jerome. Ferguson, *Signs and Symbols*, 8.

15. In the same vein, Isabel Canovas, an accessories designer, told a reporter that "a bag is like a little house in which you put everything that you can't live without." La Ferla, "Right Stuff," 81.

16. Barth, *Rag Bag Clan*.

17. Beck and Marden, "Street Dwellers," 78.

18. Robert Garrett, "Bag Ladies: Alone among the Crowd," *New York Post*, November 16, 1977, p. 40; Roberts and Pappas, "Shopping-Bag Ladies," 17. As late as 1984 it was still being reported that "even the most deranged bag ladies . . . are vulnerable because of rumors that they keep money in their bags." Alter et al., "Homeless in America," 14.

19. Francesca Drane, "A Bag Lady Fights for Her Life," *News World*, October 13, 1978, p. 1A; Mark Liff, "Boys Set Fire to Bag Lady in IRT with 20G," *New York Daily Press*, October 13, 1978, p. 3. These two temporary papers were published during a newspaper strike. The incident was also reported on radio and television.

20. One example is a children's play called *Jennifer and Her Bag Lady* by Lee Frank, which I saw produced in 1981. This bag lady carried loose pearls that had been a necklace, which she refused to sell.

21. Garrett, "Bag Ladies."

22. Many people who have embarked on various forms of service to others

have reported this experience. A number of such stories are collected in Ram Dass and Gorman, *How Can I Help?*

23. Doug Tsuruoka, "New Commander of 72nd Precinct Is Linked to Burning of Homeless Woman's Possessions," *Prospect Press* (Brooklyn), August 19–September 2, 1982, p. 1 (quotation on p. 20).

24. Michelet, *Satanism and Witchcraft*, 6–7.

25. Ibid., 52, 42.

26. Ibid., 52.

27. Ibid., 59, 71, 87–88.

28. Ibid., 120–22, 127.

29. Anderson and Zinsser, *A History of Their Own*, vol. 1, 140–43.

30. Ibid., 162, 163.

HOMELESS WOMEN HAVE ALWAYS EXISTED

The Ancient World through the Eighteenth Century

1. Mayhew, *London Labour and the London Poor*, vol. 4, xl; Bahr, *Skid Row*, 7, quoting an article from the *Village Voice*.

2. Gilmore, *Beggar*, 2–3.

3. Vexliard, *Sociologie*, 99.

4. Between the thirteenth and eighteenth centuries, vagabonds constituted about a sixth and at times a third of the urban population of Europe, and over a tenth of the population as a whole (Vexliard, *Le Clochard*, 36; Vexliard, *Sociologie*, 25). One historian estimates that in France in 1789 poor people (including both the homeless and those who had homes but lived at or below subsistence level) "formed something above a third (and, speculatively, perhaps as much as a half) of the total population." Hufton, *Poor of Eighteenth-Century France*, 24.

In 1814 a British government committee reported that there were thirty thousand mendicants in London out of a population of just over a million. These were people who had no permanent lodging but stayed, when they could, in cheap lodging houses. George, *London Life in the 18th Century*, 329, n. 5; Ribton-Turner, *History of Vagrants*, 217.

5. Sjoberg, *Preindustrial City*, 163; Fensham, "Widow, Orphan and the Poor," 139.

6. Fensham, "Widow, Orphan and the Poor," 131; *Encyclopaedia Judaica* (Jerusalem, 1972), s.v. "widow."

7. Otwell, *And Sarah Laughed*, 129–30; Bullough and Bullough, *Prostitution*, 18.

8. Bullough and Bullough, *Prostitution*, 29.

9. Sjoberg, *Preindustrial City*, 157.

10. Vexliard, *Sociologie*, 103.

11. Pomeroy, *Goddesses, Whores, Wives, and Slaves*, 202.

12. Bullough and Bullough, *Prostitution*, 33, 34; Henriques, *Stews and Strumpets*, 58.

13. Anderson and Zinsser, *History of Their Own*, vol. 1, 48–49; see also Pomeroy, *Goddesses, Whores, Wives, and Slaves*, 114.

14. Gilmore, *Beggar*, 14.

15. Foucault, *Madness and Civilization*, 8.

16. Thomas, *Religion and the Decline of Magic*, 562.

17. Gilmore, *Beggar*, 11; Vexliard, *Sociologie*, 107–9.

18. Komisar, *Down and Out*, 1.

19. I would like to thank Alice Kessler-Harris for making this point to me.

20. Komisar, *Down and Out*, 3; Ribton-Turner, *History of Vagrants*, 42–44.

21. Komisar, *Down and Out*, 3–6.

22. Ribton-Turner, *History of Vagrants*, 45–60, quotations from 52, 56.

23. Ibid., 80, 102.

24. Bullough and Bullough, *Prostitution*, 68, 67.

25. Ibid., 13.

26. Sjoberg, *Preindustrial City*, 134; Bullough and Bullough, *Prostitution*, 44; Henriques, *Stews and Strumpets*, 131; quotation from Mayhew, *London Labour and the London Poor*, vol. 4, 185.

27. Bullough and Bullough, *Prostitution*, 131.

28. Ibid., 174; Hufton, *Poor of Eighteenth-Century France*, 311; Henriques, *Prostitution and Society*, 55–56.

29. Sanger, *History of Prostitution*, 162.

30. Bullough and Bullough, *Prostitution*, 258.

31. Ribton-Turner, *History of Vagrants*, 61.

32. Vexliard, *Sociologie*, 34, 64, 67, quotations from 104.

33. Thomas, *Religion and the Decline of Magic*, 554–64.

34. Komisar, *Down and Out*, 6.

35. Ibid.

36. Quoted in Ribton-Turner, *History of Vagrants*, 170.

37. Piven and Cloward, *Regulating the Poor*, 33.

The harsh treatment of those who had no alternative except to fall back upon the parish and accept 'the offer of the House' terrorized the impoverished masses. That . . . was a matter of deliberate intent. The workhouse was designed to spur men to contrive ways of supporting themselves by their own industry, *to offer themselves to any employer on any terms*. It did this by making pariahs of those who could not support themselves; they served as an object lesson, a means of celebrating the virtues of work by the terrible example of their agony. (34)

38. Foucault, *Madness and Civilization*, 56, 58, 57, 6.

39. Ribton-Turner, *History of Vagrants*, 133, 174.

40. Piven and Cloward, *Regulating the Poor*, 169; quoted in Ribton-Turner, *History of Vagrants*, 175.

41. Komisar, *Down and Out*, 17; Abramovitz, *Regulating the Lives of Women*, 85–86.

42. Marshall, *English People in the Eighteenth Century*, 148; Laslett, *World We Have Lost*, 30, 32.

43. Piven and Cloward, *Regulating the Poor*, 17–18; Marshall, *English People in the Eighteenth Century*, 242–46.

44. George, *London Life in the Eighteenth Century*, 94, 91.

45. Ibid., 172, 113, 171.

46. Ibid., 215, 232, 223.

47. Saxby, *Memoirs of Mary Saxby*. I would like to thank Alix Kates Shulman for telling me about this pamphlet.

The Nineteenth Century in Britain and the United States

1. Marshall, *English People in the Eighteenth Century*, 247, 249.

2. Komisar, *Down and Out*, 10–11.

3. Higgs, *Down and Out*, 48.

4. Crouse, *Homeless Transient*, 16; Rossi, *Down and Out in America*, 18; see also Crouse, 17–19.

5. Abramovitz, *Regulating the Lives of Women*, 3. According to Abramovitz, the family ethic has been more important than the work ethic in shaping the relation between women and the welfare system.

6. Ibid., 84–85.

7. Jones, "Strolling Poor," 28, 34, 41. The earliest transients in Dutch New Netherland were bond servants escaping from their indentures in the English colonies (Crouse, *Homeless Transient*, 25).

8. Abramovitz, *Regulating the Lives of Women*, 76, 80–81, 54, 58, 99; quote on 81. See Abramovitz's chap. 3 for a detailed description of how colonial poor laws affected women.

9. Ibid., 80.

10. Jones, "Strolling Poor," 44–45.

11. Abramovitz, *Regulating the Lives of Women*, 86–87; Komisar, *Down and Out*, p. 16.

12. Komisar, *Down and Out*, 16–17.

13. Katz, *Poverty and Policy*, 3, 56; Piven and Cloward, *Regulating the Poor*, 46, quoting Robert H. Bremner, *From the Depths: The Discovery of Poverty in the United States* (New York: New York University Press, 1956), 16.

14. Quoted in Allsop, *Hard Travellin'*, 88.

15. Katz, *Poverty and Policy*, 132, 136, 135.

16. Komisar, *Down and Out*, 17.

17. Katz, *In the Shadow of the Poorhouse*, 17–18.

18. Abramovitz, *Regulating the Lives of Women*, 155, 151.

19. Komisar, *Down and Out*, 34, 37.

20. Komisar, *Down and Out*, 30; Katz, *Poverty and Policy*, 101; Abramovitz, *Regulating the Lives of Women*, 154, 161, 201; Giddings, *When and Where I Enter*, 72.

21. Riis, *Battle with the Slum*, 169.

22. Peiss, *Cheap Amusements*, 7, 165–66; Berg, *Remembered Gate*, 65–71; Stansell, *City of Women*, xii, 41, 155–56, 191. For a full description of the construct of domesticity, see Cott, *Bonds of Womanhood*, chap. 2.

The centrality of "home" to the concept of "woman" is further illustrated by Susan B. Anthony's 1877 speech "Homes of Single Women," which assails those who might doubt that single women as much as the married possess "the true womanly home instinct." DuBois, *Elizabeth Cady Stanton/Susan B. Anthony*, 151. Despite her success as a novelist, Catharine Maria Sedgwick associated "inferiority & dependence" with her single state, wishing for "a home of my own," which she saw as giving her "independence." Quoted in Cott, *Bonds of Womanhood*, 193.

The term *family ethic* is Mimi Abramovitz's. I use it here in preference to *cult of domesticity* or *true womanhood* because it suggests a broader concept whose relevance persists past the nineteenth-century enshrinement of the middle-class woman in the home into our own day.

23. Stansell, *City of Women*, 173, 97; see also Peiss, *Cheap Amusements*, 114. Stansell describes an incident in which a group of workingmen assaulted a solitary young seamstress dressed for an evening out, calling her a "Goddamned vagabond." Although she could not have looked like a vagabond, Stansell says, "it was this image, with its evocations of sexual profligacy and prostitution, that shaped their perceptions of a young woman out alone" (p. 97).

24. Peiss, *Cheap Amusements*, 166; quote from Stansell, *City of Women*, 171; Walkowitz, *Prostitution and Victorian Society*, 4.

25. Higgs, *Glimpses into the Abyss*, 248. See also Meyerowitz, *Women Adrift*, 49, and Abramovitz, *Regulating the Lives of Women*, 153, quoting Josephine Shaw Lowell, an American charity-reform leader: "'The unrestrained liberty allowed to vagrant and degraded women' was 'one of the most important and dangerous causes of the increase of crime, pauperism, and insanity.'"

26. Mayhew, *London Labour and the London Poor*, vol. 1, xv.

27. Berg, *Remembered Gate*, 173, 178.

28. See, for example, Mayhew, *London Labour and the London Poor*, vol. 1, 134ff., 145, 392; [Dye], *Wrecks and Rescues*, 9.

29. Mayhew, *London Labour and the London Poor*, vol. 1, 459, 117, 462, 394.

30. Ibid., vol. 2, 142–45, quotation from 145.

31. Ibid., 155.

32. Ibid., 334; Sanger, *History of Prostitution*, 345.

33. Sanger, *History of Prostitution*, 459, 465–66.

34. [Dye], *Wrecks and Rescues*, 183, 191, 190.

35. Bennett, *Woman's Work*, 167.

36. [Dye], *Wrecks and Rescues*, 120; Sanger, *History of Prostitution*, 565, 633.

37. Sanger, *History of Prostitution*, 525; Stansell, *City of Women*, 188–90.

38. Mayhew, *London Labour and the London Poor*, vol. 1, 414.

39. Quoted in Sanger, *History of Prostitution*, 663.

40. Walkowitz, *Prostitution and Victorian Society*, 18–19; Sanger, *History of Prostitution*, 455–56; Stansell, *City of Women*, 179–80.

41. Mayhew, *London Labour and the London Poor*, vol. 4, 232.

42. Ibid., 248.

43. Ibid., 360. Sanger gives a similar picture of the aged New York prostitutes, "those truly wretched beings, the outcasts of the outcasts" (*History of Prostitution*, 565).

44. Mayhew, *London Labour and the London Poor*, vol. 4, 363, 245.

45. Bennett, *Woman's Work*, 124; Mayhew, *London Labour and the London Poor*, vol. 4, 245.

46. Kirkland, *Helping Hand*, 83; quoted in Bennett, *Woman's Work*, 129, 125.

47. Berg, *Remembered Gate*, 148.
48. Bennett, *Woman's Work*, 429.
49. [Dye], *Wrecks and Rescues*, 29–36.
50. For a description of this ideal see Berg, *Remembered Gate*, 86.
51. Kirkland, *Helping Hand*, 104–5.

The Twentieth Century through the Depression

1. Rossi, *Down and Out in America*, 19–20. Central Park in New York City, Grant Park in Chicago, and the Back Bay area of Boston were all constructed on the sites of shantytowns considered eyesores.
2. Riis, *How the Other Half Lives*, 72.
3. Ibid., 249.
4. London, *People of the Abyss*, 163. "Nowhere in the streets of London," he comments, "may one escape the sight of abject poverty, while five minutes' walk from almost any point will bring one to a slum" (19). London adds that there were at that time thirty-five thousand homeless women and men in the city (54). Under such conditions homeless women would have attracted no special notice. London describes one he saw in a park: "As we entered the garden, an old woman between fifty and sixty, passed us, striding with sturdy intention if somewhat rickety action, with two bulky bundles, covered with sacking, slung fore and aft upon her. She was a woman tramp, a houseless soul, too independent to drag her failing carcase through the workhouse door. Like the snail, she carried her home with her. In the two sacking-covered bundles were her household goods, her wardrobe, linen, and dear feminine possessions" (47). But she was only one of the many homeless, including whole families, who slept in Spitalfields Gardens by day, not being allowed by the police to sleep anywhere at night.
5. Abramovitz, *Regulating the Lives of Women*, 183.
6. Higgs, *Glimpses into the Abyss*, 15.
7. Chesterton, *In Darkest London*, 11.
8. Ibid., 204, 43, 202–3, 152. At the same period Orwell also described "that curious tribe, rare but never quite extinct—the tribe of women who are penniless and homeless, but who make such desperate efforts to hide it that they very nearly succeed; women who wash their faces at drinking fountains in the cold of the dawn, and carefully uncrumple their clothes after sleepness nights, and carry themselves with an air of reserve and decency, so that only their faces, pale beneath sunburn, tell you for certain that they are destitute." *A Clergyman's Daughter*, 201.
9. Chesterton, *In Darkest London*, 77–78.
10. Higgs, *Glimpses into the Abyss*, 321–22, 188–89.
11. Ibid., 320–21, 221.
12. Chesterton, *In Darkest London*, 64.
13. Higgs, *Glimpses into the Abyss*, 312.
14. Chesterton, *In Darkest London*, 115.
15. Ibid., 117, 118, 44.
16. Higgs, *Glimpses into the Abyss*, 106, 250; Chesterton, *In Darkest London*, 220.

17. Mayhew, *London Labour and the London Poor*, vol. 3, 417.

18. Higgs, *Glimpses into the Abyss*, 94.

19. Chesterton, *In Darkest London*, 92, 120; Higgs, *Glimpses into the Abyss*, 189–90.

20. Mayhew, *London Labour and the London Poor*, vol. 1, 246.

21. Chesterton, *In Darkest London*, 138–39, 155, 157.

22. Orwell, *Down and Out*, 200; Allsop, *Hard Travellin'*, 56–58.

23. Higgs, *Glimpses into the Abyss*, 161.

24. Ibid., 156–58.

25. Ribton-Turner, *History of Vagrants*, 328; Orwell, *Down and Out*, 194; Higgs, *Glimpses into the Abyss*, 267.

26. Katz, *Poverty and Policy*, 157, 162, 166. Not until the 1890s did a more sympathetic literature picture the tramp as a colorful figure out of folklore (Katz, *In the Shadow of the Poorhouse*, 92).

27. For a description of the hobo, see Rooney, "Societal Forces and the Unattached Male," 13–18, quote on 33; Mullin quoted in Allsop, *Hard Travellin'*, 249.

28. Healy, "Hobo Hits the Highroad," 334.

29. Pinkerton, *Strikers*, 60.

30. Katz, *Poverty and Policy*, 166–69.

31. Hoch, "Brief History," 18–19.

32. "Tramps," 217.

33. "Tramps' Leader Found to Be a Woman," *New York Times*, August 7, 1902, p. 1.

34. "An Unsophisticated Hobo," 26–27.

35. Reitman, *Sister*, 281.

36. Ibid., 15, 234.

37. Ibid., 254–55, 70, 281, 233, 16, 274.

38. Ibid., 68–69, 70–72.

39. Ibid., 39, 230.

40. Gilmore, *Beggar*, 107–8, 111.

41. Meyerowitz, *Women Adrift*, xvii, 41, 21, 33, 39. For black women wages were even lower than for whites, and black women were excluded from the more desirable "women's" jobs (p. 36).

42. Crouse, *Homeless Transient*, 110.

43. Baker, "Home for Mary Lou," 669, 670.

44. Allsop, *Hard Travellin'*, 171; Reitman, *Sister*, 134.

45. Reitman, *Sister*, 135, 136–40.

46. "Breakfast, Bedroom and Bath," 54.

47. Rorty, "Counting the Homeless," 692; "Forgotten," 142. Some estimated as many as 1.5 million homeless (Rossi, *Down and Out in America*, 22), while estimates of the number of homeless women ranged from 14,482 to 250,000 (Crouse, *Homeless Transient*, 108).

48. Crouse, *Homeless Transient*, 100; Rossi, *Down and Out in America*, 25.

49. Crouse, *Homeless Transient*, 49, 92, 225, 226; quote on 92.

50. Rooney, "Societal Forces and the Unattached Male," 21.

51. Elizabeth Wickenden, speaking at "On Being Homeless in New York: A

Historical Perspective, 1700–1987," symposium at the Museum of the City of New York, January 28, 1987.

52. Elizabeth Wickenden, "Transiency—Mobility in Trouble," *Survey* 73 (October 1937), quoted in Crouse, *Homeless Transient*, 260.

53. Crouse, *Homeless Transient*, 133–41; quotation, from a Travelers' Aid social work manual, on 140.

54. Ibid., 109, 9.

55. Ibid., 69, 88.

56. Ibid., 232. Except between 1933 and 1935, there was no federal relief program for transients, so they depended entirely on whatever assistance states and localities chose to provide. Ibid., 5.

57. Rorty, "Counting the Homeless," 692; *The Nation*, 143; Allsop, *Hard Travellin'*, 184.

58. Ripperger, "Going Places," 51.

59. Reitman, *Sister*, 245. Thompson claims that in 1934 only 4 percent of women transients were on the road for adventure (p. 254).

60. Westin, *Making Do*, 154–57.

61. Crouse, *Homeless Transient*, 116–17. Particular alarm was occasioned by teenage transients. In an editorial the *Ladies' Home Journal* warned, "Unless some action is taken . . . , these girls, many of them only fifteen or sixteen years old, are on the way to becoming habitual wanderers" (p. 20).

62. Reckless, "Why Women Become Hoboes."

63. Ripperger, "Going Places," 53.

64. Johnston, "Woman Out of Work." The general idea that it was degrading for women to accept public charity was shared by the Salvation Army, which in 1931 established a "free food station" that enabled women to "avoid the 'harrowing experience of having to eat the bread of charity in public' and the humiliation of standing in line with the general Salvation Army clientele, that is, men." Crouse, *Homeless Transient*, 84; quote is from a 1931 Salvation Army pamphlet.

65. The importance of appearance for these young city women is echoed by another depression account that describes "as many as half a dozen girls crowded into one room apartments, sleeping in relays, and pooling their clothes to assemble one outfit presentable enough to pass muster with a prospective employer." Agnes V. O'Shea of the New York City Central Registration Bureau for Women, quoted in Crouse, *Homeless Transient*, 111.

66. Le Sueur, "Women on the Breadlines," 140–41.

67. Reckless, "Why Women Become Hoboes," 175.

68. Le Sueur, "Women Are Hungry," 144, 156, 149.

69. Harrison, "Women without Work," 73.

70. Ibid. During the depression "no adequate relief measures were taken for the homeless older men and women, who did not fit into the programs designed for young people." Wood, *Paths of Loneliness*, 73.

Since World War II

1. Hopper and Hamberg, *Making of America's Homeless*, 63. Most of the following description of the forces that created the massive homelessness of the eighties, which for reasons of space can be only very sketchy here, is based on

their thorough, clear analysis. For a similarly penetrating structural analysis, see Marcuse, "Neutralizing Homelessness."

2. Rossi, *Down and Out in America*, 34, 38. At this time, homelessness was defined not as lack of a roof over one's head but as "living outside family units" (p. 30). It was closely associated with disaffiliation, the state of lacking social ties. For years social scientists continued to assume that homelessness involved a personal pathology that resulted in social isolation.

3. Hopper and Hamberg, *Making of America's Homeless*, 19. In *Songs from the Alley* Kathleen Hirsch describes the destruction wrought on the seedy but socially cohesive South End of Boston by urban renewal starting in the late 1960s. The loss of "the old sense of community," she says, "would bear directly on the problem of homelessness ten years later" (98).

4. Rossi, *Down and Out in America*, 29, 39; Jones, "Street People and Psychiatry," 810.

5. Caplow, "Foreword," xv–xvi. Caplow is referring to a study completed in 1970, not the situation in 1976.

6. Rossi, *Down and Out in America*, 35.

7. Ann Geracimos, "Where Do the Ladies Go? Distaff on Skid Row," *Village Voice*, June 15, 1967, pp. 17, 39–40.

8. Department of Welfare, City of New York, *Monthly Statistical Reports* for January 1950 and January 1960. The numbers fluctuate month by month (although the warmer months do not necessarily show lower numbers). By contrast, in January 1950 the men's shelter took in 6,196 individuals, and the city's upstate facility for men, Camp Laguardia, 594.

9. Herrmann, "Study of 50 Cases."

10. Bahr and Garrett, *Women Alone*, 116, 92, 100, 104.

11. Ibid., 94, 101.

12. Geracimos ("Where Do the Ladies Go?") describes several women who at that period would normally have been sent to psychiatric hospitals, such as "Broadway Rose," whose turf was the theater district during the 1940s, and a woman "found sleeping in the hallway of a Brooklyn building wearing ten dresses, to which were sewn small bags of money containing $964 and a savings account book with a balance of $2,666." In 1971 a reporter described a group of women who had been sleeping in recessed doorways on Lexington Avenue between Forty-second and Forty-fourth Streets for at least eight years (John Darnton, "Alone and Homeless, 'Shutouts' of Society Sleep in Doorways," *New York Times*, October 26, 1971).

13. Bahr and Garrett, *Women Alone*, 119.

14. Hirsch, *Songs from the Alley*, 110–11; Tiernan quoted on 111.

15. Caplow, "Foreword," xvi.

16. Shapiro, *Communities of the Alone*, 148–50; Rossi, *Down and Out in America*, 33.

17. Bahr and Garrett, *Women Alone*, 12, 10–13, quote on 10.

18. Hopper, Susser, and Conover, "Economies of Makeshift," 201. This article gives a detailed analysis of how the restructuring of New York City's political economy during the 1970s and early 1980s lies at the root of homelessness there.

19. Based on Hopper and Hamberg, *Making of America's Homeless*, 21–39.

20. Ibid., 4; John L. Hess, "Vagrants and Panhandlers Appearing in New Haunts," *New York Times*, August 6, 1976, p. B1.

An extremely prescient 1975 article by James David Besser documents the appearance in midwestern skid rows of women, large numbers of men between eighteen and twenty, recently laid-off workers, elderly pensioners caught by inflation, and entire families. Reporting the skid-row old-timers' prediction of "a series of mass dislocations that will eventually rival the wrenching migrations of the 1930s," Besser describes how skid row's "residents are simply written off, shoved into a conveniently invisible corner of our society, and branded as incapable bums." "Skid Row Explosion," 51–53, quotes on 53.

21. Baxter and Hopper, "Pathologies of Place," 3; Koenig, "Problem That Can't Be Tranquilized."

22. Hopper and Hamberg, *Making of America's Homeless*, 35; Hopper, "More Than Passing Strange," 162.

23. Darnton ("Alone and Homeless") quotes one of the women who slept out on Lexington Avenue as saying her room on Delancey Street, "paid for by welfare, is frightening . . . because it is so rundown and without an adequate lock."

24. Hopper, "More Than Passing Strange," 160. Hoch and Slayton, comparing the residents of the old skid row with the new homeless, assert that the central factor in contemporary homelessness is not greater individual pathology but the loss of the SROs, which enabled the "old homeless" to "maintain their autonomy and avoid dependence on the formal caretaking system." *New Homeless and Old*, 7.

25. Rossi, *Down and Out in America*, 34; Hess, "Vagrants and Panhandlers."

26. For the relative numbers of women and men in psychiatric institutions, see Chesler, *Women and Madness*, 310–18.

27. Based on Hopper and Hamberg, *Making of America's Homeless*, 39–56, 58, 60–61. Report on hobos quoted in Hope and Young, *Faces of Homelessness*, 33. Roth and Bean, "New Perspectives on Homelessness," includes a report on rural homeless people.

28. "Meeting the Treatment Needs of Homeless Drug Users," 3; Anthony Scro of the New York State Division of Substance Abuse Services, speaking at a New York State AIDS Institute conference, "Sub-acute Care Needs of AIDS Patients," New York Academy of Medicine, July 19, 1990 (appearance of mentally ill, substance-abusing homeless people who are also HIV-positive, figures for drug users statewide); "AIDS Commission Shocked by Visit to City Shelter" (figures for homeless people with AIDS and HIV infection); interview with Sr. Nancy Chiarello, director of the Dwelling Place, July 23, 1990.

29. Struening, "Study of Residents," vi; Hagen, "Gender and Homelessness," 315.

30. Councilman Abraham Gerges, speaking on WNYC-AM's program "On the Line," November 11, 1989. He was then chair of the City Council's Select Committee on the Homeless. In *Rachel and Her Children* Kozol also describes the city's "deterrence" policy (15).

31. See, for example, Bassuk, Rubin, and Lauriat, "Is Homelessness a Mental Health Problem?"; Stefl, "New Homeless," 46–63; Arce et al., "Psychiatric Pro-

file of Street People"; Hagen, "Gender and Homelessness"; and Rossi, *Down and Out in America*, chap. 6.

As Marcuse puts it, "Much research connected with homelessness focuses on ascertaining the precise characteristics of the victims rather than the causes of their victimization." "Neutralizing Homelessness," 88.

32. A typical comment: "Another expression of the troubled existence of the homeless is their antisocial behavior." Bassuk, Rubin, and Lauriat, "Is Homelessness a Mental Health Problem?", 1548. Rossi, after describing the disabilities that make people especially vulnerable to homelessness, does add that this picture of poor physical and mental health, social isolation, and so forth must not make us "lose sight of the fact that the essential and defining symptom of homelessness is lack of access to conventional housing. . . . If conventional housing were everywhere abundant and without cost, there would be no homelessness except for those who preferred to sleep in the streets and in public places"—of whom, he asserts (and I agree), there would be very few (*Down and Out in America*, 181 and note). However, the real impact of his book is its massively detailed portrait of overwhelmingly disabled and hopeless people. In his and other reports, as Kim Hopper puts it, "homelessness remains locked with the conceptual brace of 'deviancy' " ("More Than Passing Strange," 164).

33. The 91 percent figure is that of Bassuk, Rubin, and Lauriat ("Is Homelessness a Mental Health Problem?"); however, they interviewed only seventy-eight people. Other studies have reported prevalence rates of 30.8 percent, 25 percent, and 15 percent (Roth and Bean, "New Perspectives on Homelessness," 718; Struening, "A Study of Residents," v; and Snow et al., "Myth of Pervasive Mental Illness," 410).

For comments on psychiatric symptoms as adaptive behavior, see Hopper, "More Than Passing Strange," 158, and Snow et al., "Myth of Pervasive Mental Illness," 421: "Our field observations indicate that many of the behaviors from which psychopathology is inferred might be better understood as behavioral adaptations to the trying exigencies of street life rather than as symptomatic of psychiatric impairment."

See also Chamberlin, "An Ex-Patient's View," an attack on the psychiatric profession's practice of defining certain people "as 'needing' psychiatric services" (p. 11).

34. Jason DeParle, "Homeless Advocates Debate How to Advance the Battle," *New York Times*, July 6, 1990, p. 14. The article also quotes Stuart Butler of the conservative Heritage Foundation as saying that "these are seriously ill people."

35. As reported by Corn and Morley, "Beltway Bandits," 296.

36. Stern, "Emergence of the Homeless as a Public Problem," 120. The federal government's focus on what Stern calls the "gift relationship" as embodied in voluntarism to solve the homelessness problem was reflected in the large number of heartwarming newspaper stories detailing the gratitude of individual homeless people and the gratification experienced by volunteers serving in soup kitchens and shelters. For example: Josh Barbanel, "Homeless Find Humanity at Private Shelters," *New York Times*, March 13, 1988, p. 1, and Merle English, "Shelter Rescues Tenants' Christmas," *New York Newsday*, December 26, 1989,

p. 18. On the usefulness for social control of defining homeless people as deviant, see Hopper, "More Than Passing Strange," 164–65.

37. Rossi, *Down and Out in America*, 123; Commissioner William J. Grinker, New York City Human Resources Administration, testimony at a hearing on shelters for single women, held by the New York City Council Committee on Women and Select Committee on the Homeless, October 7, 1987 (photocopy, p. 2).

38. "Perspective." A particularly gruesome example of what I consider racist assumptions is the response of Henry Kusjanovic, a resident of the suburb of Greenburgh, New York, to the prospect of a transitional facility for homeless families being built behind barbed wire on wooded property, 400 feet from his home. "Someone got these women pregnant," he told a reporter. "What happens when the men come around and they can't get in? They'll come through the woods. They'll rape our children." Kusjanovic claimed he objected not because most residents would be black but because they were poor. Michael Winerip, "The Homeless Head for Suburb and Suits Follow," *New York Times*, July 24, 1990, p. B1. See also my comments in "The Dangers of the Margin" (Part 5) about the "welfare mother."

39. Herrmann describes unstable employment, family violence, psychiatric problems, fathers and husbands in jail, and alcoholism among the families she studied ("Study of 50 Cases"). Two contemporary social workers writing about homelessness also concluded that "the multiproblem families of previous decades may be the homeless families of the 1980s." Hagen and Ivanoff, "Homeless Women," 30.

40. Clara Hemphill, "Study: Housing Too Costly for Homeless," *New York Newsday*, November 17, 1989, p. 19. These findings contradict a statement by the psychiatrist Ellen Bassuk that "substance abuse and family violence—not unrelated pathologies—are the main cause of family homelessness throughout the country" (quoted in Levitas, "Homeless in America," 88). However, another *Times* article cited studies that "have found that families that become homeless are surprisingly similar to other low-income families" (Josh Barbanel, "New York's Shelters: Who Uses Them and Why," *New York Times*, January 26, 1988, p. B2).

41. Hemphill, "Study"; interview with Beth Weitzman, professor of public administration at New York University and coauthor of the study, on "On the Line," WNYC-AM, November 29, 1989.

42. Hopper and Hamberg, *Making of America's Homeless*, 58; Grinker testimony, 3. According to Kristin Morse of the Coalition for the Homeless in New York City, once a woman entered a single-adult shelter, she was officially considered single and thus ineligible for federal Aid to Families with Dependent Children, with its larger rent allowance, which might have enabled her to find an apartment she could live in with her children. Interview, October 22, 1990.

43. Weitzman, "On the Line" interview; testimony of Beth Gorrie, associate director of the Coalition for the Homeless, at the City Council hearing on single homeless women, October 7, 1987, quoting the Human Resources Administration's statistic that "over 10% of the women in city shelters are foster care 'graduates'" (photocopy, p. 3); Chiarello interview. According to Weitzman, "Preg-

nancy in a public-assistance family greatly elevates the risk of becoming homeless," presumably because it adds too much stress to an already difficult living situation.

Women's lower rate of drug use as a reason for homelessness was reported by
Hagen, "Gender and Homelessness," 315; according to Dr. Elmer Struening of
the New York State Psychiatric Institute, men in the city shelters in 1987 reported
twice as much alcoholism and substance abuse as women (interview, November
19, 1987).

44. Grinker testimony, 2.

45. Hagen, "Gender and Homelessness," 315. According to Stoner ("Plight
of Homeless Women," 281), "Many homeless women and adolescent females
report that they left their homes after repeated incidents of abuse by their
spouses, rape, incest, and desertions."

The Victim Services Agency study is reported in Arias, "Beyond Shelters," 18.

46. Interview with Gayle Raskin, program manager of the Rape Crisis Program of St. Vincent's Hospital, New York City, May 30, 1990.

47. Interview with Colleen McDonald, director of the Olivieri Center for
Homeless Women in Manhattan, November 12, 1987; the story about the old
woman was told by City Councilman Abraham Gerges at the City Council hearing on homeless women, October 7, 1987.

48. In Britain, too, "sexuality, ignored in relation to men's homelessness, was
once again [i.e., in the late 1960s] considered central to definitions of homeless
women, although the focus had changed from 'moral concern' to one where
women's need to prove sexual attractiveness was considered paramount." Watson, Housing and Homelessness, 59.

49. McDonald interview.

50. The two things that particularly shocked them were the BWS residents'
being subject to curfew and the level of brutality they endured. Interview with
Rita Kingkade of the Homeless Women's Rights Network, May 18, 1989. According to the Coalition for the Homeless, the line between the deserving and
undeserving poor is today being drawn between single homeless people and families, with the families being the worthy ones ("Home Relief Survives the Budget").

The astonishing invisibility of single homeless women is perfectly illustrated
by a New York Times article on aid to the poor, which in explaining the state
home-relief program describes it as providing "grants to childless couples and
single men." The single women without children have simply vanished. Kevin
Sack, "Slump Forcing Up Albany's Aid to Poor," New York Times, January 28,
1991, p. B3.

51. On attitudes toward "welfare mothers" and assumptions about African-
American women's sexuality, see Wilkerson and Gresham, "Racialization of Pov-
erty"; Gresham, "Politics of Family"; and Abramovitz, Regulating the Lives of
Women, 321–28.

Stern points out the ironic reversal of the distinction between worthy and unworthy poor that had occurred by the 1970s. In the nineteenth century "the single mother (assumed to be widowed)" was worthy and "the vagrant and tramp"
were unworthy; whereas today "the single mother (assumed not to be married)"

is unworthy and "the docile and appreciative homeless . . . [have become] the image of the worthy poor" ("Emergence of the Homeless," 120).

The caller's remark was recounted by Councilman Abraham Gerges, speaking at a Coalition for the Homeless forum in Brooklyn, May 21, 1988.

52. An example of the power and persistence of the bag-lady image is the June 1990 issue of *Moxie*, a magazine (now defunct) for women over forty. It contained a "special report on homelessness" that—despite some acknowledgment that there were other types of homeless women—focused almost exclusively on bag ladies and the question of whether a middle-class woman could ever become one. See the discussion in the section "Modes of Distancing" in Part 5.

IN PRAISE OF FOLLY

The Relativity of Madness

1. Bennett, "Margery Kempe," 124–50.

2. Rosen, *Madness in Society*, 147–48; quotation from Bennett, "Margery Kempe," 139.

3. Bennett, "Margery Kempe," 139 (quoting from Margery's autobiography).

4. Ibid., 132, 144 (quoting from Margery's autobiography).

5. In Samuel Butler's utopian novel *Erewhon*, physical illness is punished as a crime, whereas moral lapses evoke sympathy and attempts at cure.

6. Rosen, *Madness in Society*, 33, 35–36, 63.

7. Ibid., 63; Jeremiah 26.

8. Rosen, *Madness in Society*, 73–75, 86.

9. Doob, *Nebuchadnezzar's Children*, 17.

10. Rosen, *Madness in Society*, 155; Doob, *Nebuchadnezzar's Children*, 31–32n.

11. Doob, *Nebuchadnezzar's Children*, 33; Bennett, "Margery Kempe," 133.

12. Rosen, *Madness in Society*, 139–40, 87–88.

13. Ibid., 156.

14. Ibid., 165.

15. Foucault, *Madness and Civilization*, 72, 73–74.

16. Rosen, *Madness in Society*, 162–69.

17. Foucault, *Madness and Civilization*, 156, 157, 158, 148; Rosen, *Madness in Society*, 182.

18. Bockoven, "Moral Treatment," 167; Foucault, *Madness and Civilization*, 257, 252, 261, 254.

19. Rosen, *Madness in Society*, 183, 188; Ackerknecht, *Short History of Psychiatry*, 55–56; Bockoven, "Moral Treatment," 307.

20. Ackerknecht, *Short History of Psychiatry*, 72–75; Foucault, *Madness and Civilization*, 198.

21. Charles A. Kaufmann, "Implications," 201–36; Gudeman, "Person with Chronic Mental Illness," 719.

Mental Illness and Sex Roles

1. See, for example, Deirdre Carmody, "The Tangled Life and Mind of Judy, Whose Home Is the Street," *New York Times*, December 17, 1984, pp. B1, B10; Pia McKay, "My Home Is a Lonely Bed in a Dreary D.C. Shelter," *Washington Post*, February 16, 1986, pp. C1, C3.

2. See Becker, *Outsiders*, 9.

3. Scheff, *Being Mentally Ill*, 47–48; Goffman, *Asylums*, 128, n. 3; Carstairs, "Social Limits of Eccentricity," 380; Goffman, *Asylums*, 128, n. 2.

4. Alexander Cockburn, "Press Clips," *Village Voice*, October 1, 1979, p. 28.

5. Lemert, "Legal Commitment and Social Control," 371.

6. For a description of this Enlightenment attitude toward women, see Anderson and Zinsser, *History of Their Own*, vol. 2, 112–22.

7. Broverman et al., "Sex-Role Stereotypes," 6.

8. The first article quoted is Carmen, Russo, and Miller, "Inequality," 1325. The second is Bachrach, "Deinstitutionalization and Women," 1172, 1171, 1175. This article also discusses the possibility that "protection" by their families, based on the stereotype of women as passive and dependent, is one reason women generally enter the psychiatric-care system at later ages than men (1175; see also the discussion of the Angrist et al. study later in this section). The third article is Waisberg and Page, "Gender Role Nonconformity," 15.

Although I am necessarily generalizing here, it is important to remember that, as Carmen, Russo, and Miller ("Inequality") point out, sex-role stereotypes vary and have different effects among different age, racial, and ethnic groups, as well as for lesbians and disabled women (1326).

9. Woolf, *A Room of One's Own*, 35.

10. Angrist et al., *Women after Treatment*, 10, 11, 151.

11. Carmen, Russo, and Miller, "Inequality," 1321.

12. These quotations are from, respectively, Breton, "Need for Mutual-Aid Groups," 50; Roth, Toomey, and First, "Homeless Women," 16, 17; and Bachrach, "Homeless Women," 379–80.

Similarly, Parsons describes a program designed to empower "low-income minority girls"—from her description, a group at considerable risk of future homelessness—by changing their perception that they had no control over their lives as well as giving them alternatives to the traditional female roles that led them to get pregnant "as an entry to womanhood." "Empowerment for Role Alternatives," 28.

13. Roth, Toomey, and First, "Homeless Women," 16, 17.

14. Statement by Susan Lob at a meeting sponsored by the Coalition for the Homeless in Brooklyn, New York, May 21, 1988. Lob was then advocacy coordinator of the Park Slope Safe Homes Project, a battered-women's shelter in Brooklyn.

15. Carmen, Russo, and Miller ("Inequality") discuss this connection in terms of the prevalence of depression among women, 1322.

16. Bachrach, "Homeless Women," 377; Kaufmann, "Implications," 202.

17. Tsuang, Faraone, and Day, "Schizophrenic Disorders," 260, 286; Kauf-

mann, "Implications," 204–5, 211; Wyatt, Kirch, and DeLisi, "Schizophrenia," 717; quotation from McGlashan, "Schizophrenia," 756.

18. McGlashan, "Schizophrenia," 753.

19. Ibid.

20. Lidz, *Origin and Treatment of Schizophrenic Disorders*, 48, 68.

21. Ibid., 69, 81.

22. Interview, November 12, 1987.

23. Landrine, "Politics of Personality Disorder," 325. Diagnoses in such studies are based on the standard criteria of the American Psychiatric Association's *Diagnostic and Statistical Manual of Mental Disorders*, 3d ed.

24. Reported in Hagen and Ivanoff, "Homeless Women," 20–21, and in Hagen, "Gender and Homelessness," 315.

25. Interview, November 19, 1987.

26. Carmen, Russo, and Miller, "Inequality," 1323, 1322.

27. Angrist et al., *Women after Treatment*, 151.

28. Haggstrom, "Power of the Poor," 78; quote from Carmen, Russo, and Miller, "Inequality," 1321.

29. Roman and Trice, *Schizophrenia and the Poor*, 63–64.

30. To put it another way: "Lower class patients who have an insoluble reality situation often have little desire to get better." Hollingshead and Redlich, *Social Class and Mental Illness*, 348.

31. Roth, Toomey, and First, "Homeless Women," 12; Breton, "Need for Mutual-Aid Groups," 49.

32. This function of marriage appears clearly in Mary Higgs's response to the notion that women do not have to be homeless because they can always work: "There are . . . quantities of semi-'unemployable' women, women who would—after a fashion—succeed in looking after their own home and rearing children; but who, divorced from home, are not 'worth their salt.'" *Glimpses into the Abyss*, 191.

33. Packard, *Modern Persecution*, 83, and *Marital Power*, 101. Quote is from Szasz, *Manufacture of Madness*, 15.

34. Katz, *Poverty and Policy*, 154, and Katz, *In the Shadow of the Poorhouse*, 181–82.

35. Szasz, *Schizophrenia*, 148–49, 154–55.

36. Quoted in Szasz, *Manufacture of Madness*, 130–31.

Daddy's Good Girls

1. Quote from *Butler's Lives*, vol. 2, s.v. "St. Dympna"; Baring-Gould, *Lives of the Saints*, vol. 5, 207–10; Ellen Baxter, "Geel, Belgium: A Radical Model for the Integration of Deviancy," in *The Community Imperative: Proceedings of a National Conference on Overcoming Public Opposition to Community Care for the Mentally Ill* (Philadelphia, 1980), 67, quoted in Hombs and Snyder, *Homelessness in America*, 59.

2. Ferguson, *Signs and Symbols*, 64; *Butler's Lives*, vol. 14, s.v. "St. Barbara."

3. Quoted in Kirkland, *Helping Hand*, 105–9.

The Modern Margerys

1. Goffman, *Asylums*, 248–54, quotes on 248, 251.
2. Describing her incarceration in an Irish insane asylum, Kate Millett says, "Like all the other women here, I have adopted a shopping bag that goes with me everywhere and is guarded all the time from the guards but left about continually among the women" inmates. Her bag contained forbidden attempts to communicate with the outside world that asserted her real, noncrazy self—letters written on toilet paper like those of the Irish political prisoners in Armagh. *Loony-Bin Trip*, 222.
3. Arieti, *Interpretation of Schizophrenia*, 416.
4. Ayllon, "Intensive Treatment of Psychotic Behaviour," 58.
Street women do wear layers to keep warm, and some younger women who became homeless in the eighties told a Dwelling Place staff member that they dressed in layers specifically to avoid rape; men apparently were put off by having to go through several pairs of pants to get at them. Nevertheless, layering also has a psychological component.
5. Arieti, *Interpretation of Schizophrenia*, 419.
6. Goodrich, *Ryder*, 27, 19, 30. I thank Barbara Novak for this reference.
7. Welsford, *Fool*, 124, 239.
8. Willeford, *Fool and His Scepter*, 16.
Although the Revised Standard Version calls Joseph's coat a "long robe with sleeves," the King James "coat of many colors" is supported by other renderings that suggest strips or small bits of material of different colors. The coat is a sign of Joseph's special quality, which is his relationship with the Lord, signaled by his power to interpret dreams; this power convinces Pharaoh that the "Spirit of God" (Genesis 41:38) is in him and results in his being made ruler of Egypt. In his case the particolored costume is a badge of the positive aspect of communication with the Beyond. *Interpreter's Dictionary of the Bible*, s.v. "cloth"; Orlinsky, *Notes on the New Translation of the Torah*, 118–19.
9. Quoted in Briffault, *Mothers*, 609.
10. Goodrich, *Ryder*, 27–28.
11. For one such proposal and a description of others, see Rossi, *Down and Out in America*, 198, and Dear and Wolch, *Landscapes of Despair*, 187, 190, 252. See also Chamberlin, "An Ex-Patient's View." "Segregating people according to psychiatric labels," Chamberlin asserts, "can only lead to inferior and unwanted 'services' being provided to this subgroup, rather than to an attack on the basic economic and social causes of *all* homelessness" (p. 11).

AT THE MARGINS

The Dangers of the Margin

1. Molly Ivins, "After Long Years on Streets, Sally Is Out of the Cold," *New York Times*, September 30, 1976, p. 43.
2. As Bahr explains, "The rehabilitators reserve compassion for the 'worthy'—those whose situation is not their own fault, who respond in 'acceptable' ways, and who manifest some improvement ('success') as a result of the help. The

skid row men reserve gratitude for those helpers who give them gifts, as opposed to services which are theirs by right. . . . Each feels betrayed by the other; the skid row man because he is promised therapy or charity when there is none, and the rehabilitator because he is cheated and conned by an apparently insincere client." *Skid Row*, 47.

3. Love, *Subways*, 11–12, 13.

4. Scheff, *Being Mentally Ill*, 34, 32, 34–35.

5. Love, *Subways*, 28; Strasser, "Urban Transient Women," 2078: "When resting in transit terminals, reading a newspaper rather than a book seemed to discourage harassment by security guards."

6. This idea of marginality is based on Douglas, *Purity and Danger*, 94–95.

7. Ibid., 96.

8. de Beauvoir, *La Vieillesse*, 59, 91, 220.

9. Lidz, *Origin and Treatment of Schizophrenic Disorders*, 85–86.

10. Douglas, *Purity and Danger*, 95, 97–98.

11. Szasz, *Manufacture of Madness*, 260, 263–64; Rosen, *Madness in Society*, 84–85.

12. Welsford, *Fool*, 73–74; Willeford, *Fool and His Scepter*, 158.

13. Newall, "Jew as a Witch Figure," 101, 103, 105, 108, 111, 115.

14. Ibid., 104.

15. Scheff, *Being Mentally Ill*, 77.

16. Rosen, *Madness in Society*, 86.

17. Dekker and van de Pol, *Tradition of Female Transvestism*, 6–7; quote is from Pearson, "Woman as Witch," vol. 2, 19 (italics in original).

18. The fundamental tension between the transvestite (and other marginal figures) and the basic principles that hold society together is described by Willeford, *Fool and His Scepter*. See, for example, page 86: "The transvestism so common in ceremonial clowning and in saturnalian festivals has deep roots in fertility magic. . . . The reversal of sex roles activated the demonic . . . since these roles are fundamental to the cultural life that holds the demonic at a distance."

19. Henriques, *Stews and Strumpets*, 131.

20. Anderson and Zinsser, *History of Their Own*, vol. 1, 156–59; Dekker and van de Pol, *Tradition of Female Transvestism*, 43. Joan followed in the tradition of a long line of female saints who adopted male dress to preserve their virginity and thereby their saintly state (p. 45).

21. Banner, *American Beauty*, 94–96.

22. Similarly, Willeford refers to "the hidden treasure the fool bears as a social outcast. . . . The fool has seen and heard the transcendent value that, according to St. Paul and Erasmus, is only available to fools." *Fool and His Scepter*, 138.

23. Katz describes the social function of lumping such people together and segregating them: "By its inattention to differences between individuals and groups, the social construction of deviance turns the victims of misfortune and exploitation into objects that deserve, at best, pity and charity rather than respect, dignity, and an equitable share of social resources. This was the function of assembling the blind, insane, criminal, deaf-mute, idiot, pauper, insane, and homeless children" into a "metaclass that is despised." *Poverty and Policy*, 136.

24. Rosenhan, "On Being Sane in Insane Places," 254.

25. Euripides, *The Trojan Women*, ll. 643–50.

26. Berg, *Remembered Gate*, 185.

27. Kirkland, *Helping Hand*.

28. Ibid., 37, 43, 44.

29. Ibid., 44, 73. Even the judicious and clear-sighted Mary Higgs cites the additional "moral danger" involved in female (as opposed to male) tramping. "I think it is a great evil to recognise that woman has the right to go about from place to place in that unattached kind of way," she told a government committee. And, describing the struggles of the down-and-out woman to avoid prostitution, she comments, "the 'pit' lies just beneath them, that terrible pit, where honour, love, and womanhood are swallowed up"—implicitly equating womanhood with honor and love. *Glimpses into the Abyss*, 80, 313, 189.

30. Chesterton, *In Darkest London*, 170–71, 120–21.

31. Abramovitz, *Regulating the Lives of Women*, 323–26, 349–58. Abramovitz explains the apparent contradiction between the family ethic and the attempt to force women to work by showing how poor and immigrant women and women of color came to be defined as "undeserving" and channeled into the labor market to meet the need for cheap labor (pp. 36–40). See also Cerullo and Erlien, "Beyond the 'Normal Family,'" 248–61, for an analysis of how issues of race have shaped the distinction between "good" (worthy) and "bad" (unworthy) women.

Modes of Distancing

1. *Soho Weekly News*, April 28, 1977, p. 14.

2. *Majority Report*, October 17, 1974, p. 2.

3. John Kifner, "Hospital at Last Identifies Its 'Shopping-Bag Lady,'" *New York Times*, January 10, 1979, p. B7.

4. Kates, *Murder of a Shopping Bag Lady*, 117.

5. Arias, "Posing as a Bag Lady," 32.

6. Beverly Burlett, "Who Are the 'Shopping Bag Women'?" *Majority Report*, October 17, 1974, p. 9.

7. A considerable print ad campaign, as well as television spots promising indescribable horrors, preceded this "Special Report" consisting of two brief segments aired on February 19 and 20. But the only women shown were cheery, reassuring souls, grateful to the wonderful passersby who gave them change. Playing on viewers' fears to lure them to watch, the report wound up reassuring them that homeless women were just harmless eccentrics or mentally ill.

8. Francis X. Clines, "About New York: Sidewalk World of the Shopping-Bag Women," *New York Times*, December 16, 1976, p. 44.

9. Beck and Marden, "Street Dwellers," 81.

10. Roth, "If I'm Not on My Milk Crate," 75.

11. "Bloomingdales' 'Street Look' Fashions"; "Tiffany's Display"; "Holiday Inn."

12. "Compassion Should Come First," *Prospect Press* (Brooklyn), February 20–March 5, 1986, p. 20.

13. He resembled the hotel managers who complained to investigators for

the Bahr and Garrett study (discussed in the section "Since World War II" in Part 3) of the trouble caused by elderly women lodgers who were "destructive, loud, angry, upset" (*Women Alone*, 10).

14. Giese, "Bag Lady," 40–45, 120, and Soverow, "Creating a Safety Net," 17.

15. Soverow, "Creating a Safety Net," 17; Giese, "Bag Lady," 44.

16. Stuart, "My Shadow," 75.

17. Macdonald, *W(h)oles*, 15–16.

18. Cynthia Belgrave, "Opus," typescript, 1978. I am grateful to the author for allowing me to read and quote from this work.

19. Murray Kempton, "Marys of the Wilderness," *New York Post*, January 31, 1979, p. 24.

20. Stoner, "Plight of Homeless Women," 284.

21. David C. Anderson, "The Off-Broadway Cats," *New York Times*, December 6, 1983, p. A30.

The Witch Image: Subversive Female Power

1. Woolf, *A Room of One's Own*, 51.

2. Mead, *Male and Female*, 375.

3. Rich, *Of Woman Born*, 54.

4. Trevor-Roper, "European Witch-Craze," 144.

5. Murray-Aynsley, "Scraps of English Folklore," 382; Leather, *Folk-Lore of Herefordshire*, 45.

6. Widdowson, "Witch as a Frightening and Threatening Figure," 210, 211, 217.

7. Georgie Lee, "Old Lady Brown . . . ," *Brooklyn Affairs*, February 1984, p. 24.

See also O'Brien, *Woman Alone*, 71: "When I was a little girl, it seemed every neighborhood had a witch. Ours was an old, bent woman who appeared outside her dark and (we thought) cobwebby house once a day to water plants and tidy her porch. I had to walk by on my way to school, excited and fearful. Would she be outside? Usually when I reached the hedge that divided her property from the house next door, I would run as fast as I could, quickly glancing over to see if she was there. If she wasn't, I would be both relieved and disappointed."

8. See Trevor-Roper, "European Witch-Craze," 131, 141.

9. Horsley, "Who Were the Witches?" 697.

10. Baroja, "Magic and Religion in the Classical World," 72–73.

11. Baroja, "Witchcraft amongst the German and Slavonic Peoples," 89.

12. Cohn, *Europe's Inner Demons*, 206, 207, 213.

13. Ibid., 229, 239.

14. Judith Zinsser, personal communication; see also Anderson and Zinsser, *History of Their Own*, vol. 1, 168.

15. Cohn, *Europe's Inner Demons*, 155, 157, 159; Szasz, *Manufacture of Madness*, 86.

16. Anderson and Zinsser, *History of Their Own*, vol. 1, 164–66.

17. Horsley, "Who Were the Witches?" 709.

18. Ibid., 713–14 and 707, n. 37.

19. Cohn, *Europe's Inner Demons*, 251, 262.

20. Thus Macdonald's Dallas bag lady says of the ones in New York, "But all of them are old and I am not." *W(h)oles*, 16.

21. Thomas, *Religion and the Decline of Magic*, 567.

22. "Why are old women alone cast so often as witches?" asks O'Brien in *Woman Alone*. "When I think back to the images of my childhood it seems old men were always kindly creatures who pulled children into their laps, told Br'er Rabbit stories, and fixed bicycles. They grew bright rose gardens, and when I walked past to go to school, they waved to me and I would wave back. I knew, absolutely, their houses had no cobwebs" (p. 71).

23. Murray-Aynsley, "Scraps of English Folklore," 383.

24. Quoted in Macfarlane, "Witchcraft and Conflict," 298.

25. Coetzee, "How I Learned about America," 9.

26. Mead, *Male and Female*, 231–33.

27. Rich, *Of Woman Born*, 48.

28. Cohn, *Europe's Inner Demons*, 248. This analysis illuminates further the gallery owner's reaction to the artist's friend. An old woman who behaved oddly—even an obviously well-to-do one—had so little reality for him as an individual that he easily superimposed his fantasy on her. Or, to put it another way, old women are naturally so suspect—even uncanny—that anything they do outside narrow limits evokes doubt or uneasiness that translates into false assumptions or misperceptions.

29. The same situation occurs in *The Witch of Edmonton*, a play of 1621 by William Rowley, Thomas Dekker, and John Ford, based on the execution of a real woman named Elizabeth Sawyer for witchcraft. The play says explicitly that the witch is no more than a scapegoat for other people's sins; see act II, scene i; act IV, scene i.

30. Cohn, *Europe's Inner Demons*, 249.

31. Thomas, *Religion and the Decline of Magic*, 526, 527–29.

32. Douglas, *Purity and Danger*, 102.

33. Karlsen, *Devil in the Shape of a Woman*, 196, 101, 152, 71, 130, 134.

34. Ibid., 181.

35. Ibid., xiii.

36. Daniel Peters, "Bag Lady Is Mom to 217 Trashcan Babies," *Sun*, July 8, 1986, p. 13. This slightly different version of the headline appeared on the page with the story.

37. William K. Stevens, "A Convention of Witches Is Viewed Darkly by Some in Amarillo," *New York Times*, September 27, 1980.

38. "Witchcraft Issue in Ouster Battle," *New York Times*, June 15, 1972, p. 15.

Bringing Them Inside

1. *Poetry of Robert Frost*, 207–10, quoted lines on 209, 210. In this poem Frost picks up on an old image. A source of 1669, describing Swedish witches' trip to their sabbat, says, "For their journey they said they made use of all sorts of

Instruments, of Beasts, of Men, of Spits and posts"—just as the witch of Grafton rode a poor old man all around the countryside. Quoted in Murray, *Witch-Cult in Western Europe*, 103.

2. Two examples are McIntyre, *River Witch*, in which the heroine's child dies; and Wilkins, *Fanfare for a Witch*, whose heroine, although a good witch, remains firmly marginal, never inheriting the fortune to which she is entitled. At the end she is left penniless, stateless, and virtually identityless, about to embark on a course of adventuring.

3. de Lisser, *White Witch of Rosehall*, 137.

4. Among the Greeks and Romans "she-wolf" was one of many terms for a prostitute. In Rome these *lupae* "frequented parks and gardens and attracted custom by wolf-cries." Bullough and Bullough, *History of Prostitution*, 32; quote from Henriques, *Stews and Strumpets*, 121. These women's explicit marginal status (including the blurring between human and animal) neutralized their power. At the same time, the fact that wolf cries could *attract* customers demonstrates once more the paradoxical quality of marginal people and puts in a nutshell their whole relation to society.

5. Avery, *New Century Classical Handbook*, s.v. "Hecuba." Quote from Murray, *The Trojan Women*, 86.

6. *Metamorphoses of Ovid*, 300.

7. Cohn, *Europe's Inner Demons*, 249.

8. Carmen, Russo, and Miller, "Inequality and Women's Mental Health," 1325.

9. Francis X. Clines, "About New York: A Haven for Shopping-Bag Ladies," *New York Times*, December 13, 1977.

10. This is a paraphrase, not a quotation. I never saw Angela's notebook; one of the nuns described it to me.

11. Anderson and Zinsser, *History of Their Own*, vol. 1, 170–71.

12. Thomas, *Religion and the Decline of Magic*, 521–22.

13. Karlsen, *Devil in the Shape of a Woman*, 246, 247.

14. Warner, *Lolly Willowes*, 234, 235, 239, 247.

15. Ibid., 150, 6.

16. Atwood, *Surfacing*, 185, 218.

17. Ibid., 222.

18. See also Emily Dickinson's poem beginning "I think I was enchanted," asserting a heroic rebellion in which she relies on "witchcraft" to set up her own version of reality in opposition to God's entire creation. *Complete Poems of Emily Dickinson*, poem 593.

19. Koltuv, *Book of Lilith*, 2, 3, 4.

20. Ibid., 8, 19, 16, 17, 6, 34.

21. Ibid., 27, and *New Century Cyclopedia of Names*, s.v. "Lilith."

22. Koltuv, *Book of Lilith*, 83.

23. Like Satan, though, Lilith has admirers; thus Ida Cox sang, "Wild Women Don't Have No Blues."

24. See Rich, *Of Woman Born*, 80, 88, 96, and Neumann, *Great Mother*, especially 309–16.

25. Cohn, *Europe's Inner Demons*, 213.

26. Pearson, "Woman as Witch," 37.

27. von Franz, *Shadow and Evil*, 105.

28. Jung, "On the Psychology of the Trickster-Figure," 135. See also Willeford, *Fool and His Scepter*, 79, 81, 86.

29. Vonnegut, *Jailbird*, 86, 139, 219, 231.

30. McCarthy, *Birds of America*, 279, 139, 278, 287, 288.

31. Other works in which bag ladies appear with archetypal resonance include Elizabeth Hardwick's novel *Sleepless Nights*, Jean-Claude van Itallie's *Bag Lady Play*, first produced in 1979, and Mark Alan Stamaty's comic strip *Mac-Doodle St.*, which ran in the *Village Voice* and was then published as a book. I have also found short stories, plays, poems, and art works by lesser-known artists, both male and female, in which homeless women have great psychological importance.

32. Examples of these three types of projects are, respectively: Downing, "Artemis," 119–27; Starhawk, *Truth or Dare*; and Eisler, *Chalice and the Blade*. Orenstein, *Reflowering of the Goddess*, surveys the international expression of Goddess images in contemporary writing and visual art.

33. Koltuv, *Book of Lilith*, 118–19, 121.

34. The dreamer's locating this female angel (seraph) underground emphasizes her Goddess-like wholeness in contrast to the Western tendency to split off and separate the good (heavenly) and bad (hellish) aspects of femininity.

35. Kirkland, *Helping Hand*, 85–86; see also Berg, *Remembered Gate*, 218.

36. Decline in property values seems to be the most common fear among residents of communities where shelters and other programs for homeless people are planned. Other fears are of crime, the spread of disease, children being frightened, increased littering, and general decline in the quality of life. See Hopper et al., *One Year Later*; Alter et al., "Homeless in America"; Ritzdork and Sharpe, "Portland, Oregon," 190–91; and Anello and Shuster, *Community Relations Strategies*. See also Michael Winerip, "The Homeless Head for Suburb and Suits Follow," *New York Times*, July 24, 1990.

Bibliography

Abramovitz, Mimi. *Regulating the Lives of Women: Social Welfare Policy from Colonial Times to the Present*. Boston: South End Press, 1988.

Ackerknecht, Erwin H. *A Short History of Psychiatry*. Translated by Sula Wolff. New York and London: Hafner, 1968.

"AIDS Commission Shocked by Visit to City Shelter." *Safety Network/NY: Newsletter of the Coalition for the Homeless*, April 1990.

Allsop, Kenneth. *Hard Travellin': The Hobo and His History*. London: Hodder and Stoughton, 1967.

Alter, Jonathan, Alexander Stille, Shawn Doherty, Nikke Finke Greenberg, Susan Agrest, Vern E. Smith, and George Raine. "Homeless in America." In *Housing the Homeless*, edited by Jon Erickson and Charles Wilhelm. New Brunswick, N.J.: Center for Urban Policy Research, 1986.

Anderson, Bonnie S., and Judith P. Zinsser. *A History of Their Own: Women in Europe from Prehistory to the Present*. 2 vols. New York: Harper & Row, 1988.

Anderson, S. C., T. Boe, and S. Smith. "Homeless Women." *Affilia* 3 (1988): 62–70.

Angrist, Shirley S., Mark Lefton, Simon Dinitz, and Benjamin Pasamanick. *Women after Treatment: A Study of Former Mental Patients and Their Normal Neighbors*. New York: Appleton-Century-Crofts, 1968.

Anello, Rose, and Tillie Shuster. *Community Relations Strategies: A Handbook for Sponsors of Community-Based Programs for the Homeless*. New York: Community Service Society, 1985.

Arce, A. Anthony, Marilyn Tadlock, Michael J. Vergare, and Stuart H. Shapiro. "A Psychiatric Profile of Street People Admitted to an Emergency Shelter." *Hospital and Community Psychiatry* 34 (September 1983): 812–16.

297

Arias, Maria. "Beyond Shelters: Making Homes for Battered Women." *City Limits*, August/September 1988, 18–20.

Arias, Ron. "Posing as a Bag Lady, Housewife Beulah Lund Finds Fear and Love in the Homeless Netherworld." *People Weekly*, February 16, 1987, 32–37.

Arieti, Silvano. *Interpretation of Schizophrenia*. 2d ed. New York: Basic Books, 1974.

Atwood, Margaret. *Surfacing*. 1972. New York: Popular Library, 1976.

Avery, Catherine B., ed. *The New Century Classical Handbook*. New York: Appleton-Century-Crofts, 1962.

Ayllon, T. "Intensive Treatment of Psychotic Behaviour by Stimulus Satiation and Food Reinforcement." *Behaviour Research and Therapy* 1 (1963): 53–61.

Bachrach, Leona L. "Chronic Mentally Ill Women: Emergence and Legitimation of Program Issues." *Hospital and Community Psychiatry* 36 (October 1985): 1063–69.

———. "Deinstitutionalization and Women: Assessing the Consequences of Public Policy." *American Psychologist* 39 (1984): 1171–77.

———. "Homeless Women: A Context for Health Planning." *Milbank Quarterly* 65 (1987): 371–96.

Bahr, Howard M. *Skid Row: An Introduction to Disaffiliation*. New York: Oxford University Press, 1973.

Bahr, Howard M., and Gerald R. Garrett. *Women Alone: The Disaffiliation of Urban Females*. Lexington, Mass.: Heath, Lexington Books, 1976.

Baker, Helen Cody. "A Home for Mary Lou." *Survey* 67 (March 15, 1932): 669–70.

Banner, Lois W. *American Beauty*. New York: Knopf, 1983.

Baring-Gould, S. *The Lives of the Saints*. Rev. ed. 16 vols. Edinburgh: John Grant, 1914.

Baroja, Julio Caro. "Magic and Religion in the Classical World." In *Witchcraft and Sorcery: Selected Readings*, edited by Max Marwick. Harmondsworth: Penguin, 1970.

———. "Witchcraft amongst the German and Slavonic Peoples." In *Witchcraft and Sorcery: Selected Readings*, edited by Max Marwick. Harmondsworth: Penguin, 1970.

Barth, Richard. *The Rag Bag Clan*. New York: Dial Press, 1978.

Bassuk, Ellen L., and Alison S. Lauriat. "The Politics of Homelessness." In *The Homeless Mentally Ill: A Task Force Report of the American Psychiatric Association*, edited by H. Richard Lamb. Washington, D.C.: American Psychiatric Association, 1984.

Bassuk, Ellen L., Lenore Rubin, and Alison S. Lauriat. "Is Homelessness a Mental Health Problem?" *American Journal of Psychiatry* 141 (December 1984): 1546–50.

Baxter, Ellen. *The Heights: A Community Housing Strategy: A Report of the Community Service Society of New York on a Successful Community Model to Create Permanent Housing for Homeless People*. New York: Community Service Society, 1986.

Baxter, Ellen, and Kim Hopper. "The New Mendicancy: Homeless in New York City." *American Journal of Orthopsychiatry* 52 (July 1982): 393–408.

———. "Pathologies of Place and Disorders of Mind: 'Community-Living' for Ex-Mental Patients in New York City." *Health/PAC Bulletin* 11 (1979): 1–12, 21–22.

———. *Private Lives/Public Spaces: Homeless Adults on the Streets of New York City*. New York: Community Service Society, 1981.

———. "Shelter and Housing for the Homeless Mentally Ill." In *The Homeless Mentally Ill: A Task Force Report of the American Psychiatric Association*, edited by H. Richard Lamb. Washington, D.C.: American Psychiatric Association, 1984.

———. "Troubled on the Streets: The Mentally Disabled Homeless Poor." In *The Chronic Mental Patient: Five Years Later*, edited by John A. Talbott. Orlando, Fla.: Grune & Stratton, 1984.

Bean, Gerald J., Mary E. Stefl, and Steven R. Howe. "Mental Health and Homelessness: Issues and Findings." *Social Work* 32 (1987): 411–16.

Beck, Alan M., and Philip Marden. "Street Dwellers." *Natural History*, November 1977, 78–85.

Becker, Howard S. *Outsiders: Studies in the Sociology of Deviance*. New York: Free Press, 1973.

Bennett, H. S. "Margery Kempe." In *Six Medieval Men and Women*. New York: Atheneum, 1968.

Bennett, Mrs. S. R. I. *Woman's Work among the Lowly: Memorial Volume of the First Forty Years of the American Female Guardian Society and Home for the Friendless*. New York: American Female Guardian Society, 1877.

Berg, Barbara J. *The Remembered Gate: Origins of American Feminism*. New York: Oxford University Press, 1978.

Berman-Rossi, Toby, and Marcia B. Cohen. "Group Development and Shared Decision Making: Working with Homeless Mentally Ill Women." *Social Work with Groups* 11 (1988): 63–78.

Besser, James David. "The Skid Row Explosion." *Progressive* 39 (October 1975): 51–53.

Bingham, Richard D., Roy E. Green, and Sammis B. White, eds. *The Homeless in Contemporary Society*. Newbury Park, Calif.: Sage, 1987.

Bockoven, J. Sanbourne. "Moral Treatment in American Psychiatry." Parts 1, 2. *Journal of Nervous and Mental Disease* 124 (August, September 1956): 167–94, 292–321.

"Bloomingdales' 'Street Look' Fashions." *Safety Network/NY: Newsletter of the Coalition for the Homeless*, June 1983.

"Breakfast, Bedroom and Bath in the Subway." *Literary Digest* 101 (June 8, 1929): 54–56.

Breton, Margot. "The Need for Mutual-Aid Groups in a Drop-In for Homeless Women: The *Sistering* Case." *Social Work with Groups* 11 (1988): 47–61.

Briffault, Robert. *The Mothers: A Study of the Origins of Sentiments and Institutions*. 3 vols. New York: Macmillan, 1927.

Broverman, Inge K., Donald M. Broverman, Frank E. Clarkson, Paul S. Rosenkrantz, and Susan R. Vogel. "Sex-Role Stereotypes and Clinical Judgments of Mental Health." *Journal of Consulting and Clinical Psychology* 34 (1970): 1–7.

Bullough, Vern L., and Bonnie L. Bullough. *The History of Prostitution*. New Hyde Park, N.Y.: University Books, 1964.

Butler's Lives of the Saints. Revised and supplemented by Herbert Thurston and Donald Attwater. New York: P. J. Kenedy, 1956.

Caplow, Theodore. "Foreword." In *Women Alone: The Disaffiliation of Urban Females*, by Howard M. Bahr and Gerald R. Garrett. Lexington, Mass.: Lexington Books, 1976.

Carmen, Elaine (Hilberman), Nancy Felipe Russo, and Jean Baker Miller. "Inequality and Women's Mental Health: An Overview." *American Journal of Psychiatry* 138 (October 1981): 1319–30.

Carstairs, G. M. "The Social Limits of Eccentricity: An English Study." In *Culture and Mental Health: Cross-Cultural Studies*, edited by Marvin K. Opler. New York: Macmillan, 1959.

Cerullo, Margaret, and Marla Erlien. "Beyond the 'Normal Family': A Cultural Critique of Women's Poverty." In *For Crying Out Loud: Women and Poverty in the United States*, edited by Rochelle Lefkowitz and Ann Withorn. New York: Pilgrim Press, 1986.

Chamberlin, Judi. "An Ex-Patient's View of *The Homeless Mentally Ill*." *Psychosocial Rehabilitation Journal* 8 (April 1985): 11–15.

Chesler, Phyllis. *Women and Madness*. New York: Avon Books, 1972.

Chesterton, Mrs. Cecil [Ada E.]. *In Darkest London*. New York: Macmillan, 1926.

Coetzee, J. M. "How I Learned about America—and Africa—in Texas." *New York Times Book Review*, April 15, 1984.

Cohen, Neal L., Jane F. Putnam, and Ann M. Sullivan. "The Mentally Ill Homeless: Isolation and Adaptation." *Hospital and Community Psychiatry* 35 (September 1984): 922–24.

Cohn, Norman. *Europe's Inner Demons: An Enquiry Inspired by the Great Witch-Hunt*. London: Chatto, Heineman, for Sussex University Press, 1975.

The Complete Grimm's Fairy Tales. New York: Pantheon, 1944.

Corn, David, and Jefferson Morley. "Beltway Bandits." *Nation* 248 (March 6, 1989).

Cott, Nancy F. *The Bonds of Womanhood: "Woman's Sphere" in New England, 1780–1835*. New Haven and London: Yale University Press, 1977.

Crouse, Joan M. *The Homeless Transient in the Great Depression: New York State, 1929–1941*. Albany: State University of New York Press, 1986.

Crystal, Stephen. "Homeless Men and Homeless Women: The Gender Gap." *Urban and Social Change Review* 17 (Summer 1984): 2–6.

de Beauvoir, Simone. *La Vieillesse*. Paris: Gallimard, 1970.

de Lisser, Herbert G. *The White Witch of Rosehall*. London: Ernest Benn, 1929.

Dean, Andrea Oppenheimer. "A Balancing Act: Conrad Levenson Rehabilitates Housing to Shape New Lives for the Homeless." *Historic Preservation* 42 (November/December 1990).

Dear, Michael J., and Jennifer R. Wolch. *Landscapes of Despair: From Deinstitutionalization to Homelessness*. Princeton, N.J.: Princeton University Press, 1987.

Dekker, Rudolf M., and Lotte C. van de Pol. *The Tradition of Female Transves-*

tism in Early Modern Europe. Translated by Judy Marcure and Lotte C. van de Pol. Basingstoke and London: Macmillan, 1989.

Dickinson, Emily. *The Complete Poems of Emily Dickinson*. Edited by Thomas H. Johnson. Boston and Toronto: Little, Brown, 1960.

Doob, Penelope B. R. *Nebuchadnezzar's Children: Conventions of Madness in Middle English Literature*. New Haven and London: Yale University Press, 1974.

Douglas, Mary. *Purity and Danger: An Analysis of Concepts of Pollution and Taboo*. London: Routledge & Kegan Paul, 1978.

Downing, Christine. "Artemis: The Goddess Who Comes from Afar." In *Weaving the Visions: New Patterns in Feminist Spirituality*. San Francisco: Harper & Row, 1989.

DuBois, Ellen Carol, ed. *Elizabeth Cady Stanton/Susan B. Anthony: Correspondence, Writings, Speeches*. New York: Schocken, 1981.

[Dye, Mrs. Margaret]. *Wrecks and Rescues*. 2d ed. New York: American Female Guardian Society, 1859.

Eisler, Riane. *The Chalice and the Blade: Our History, Our Future*. San Francisco: Harper & Row, 1987.

Estroff, Sue E. "Medicalizing the Margins: On Being Disgraced, Disordered, and Deserving." *Psychosocial Rehabilitation Journal* 8 (1985): 34–38.

Euripides. *The Trojan Women*. Translated by Richmond Lattimore. In *Euripides III, The Complete Greek Tragedies*, edited by David Grene and Richmond Lattimore. Chicago: University of Chicago Press, 1958.

Farina, Amerigo. "Are Women Nicer People Than Men? Sex and the Stigma of Mental Disorders." *Clinical Psychology Review* 1 (1981): 223–43.

Fensham, F. Charles. "Widow, Orphan and the Poor in Ancient Near Eastern Legal and Wisdom Literature." *Journal of Near Eastern Studies* 21 (April 1962): 129–39.

Ferguson, George. *Signs and Symbols in Christian Art*. New York: Oxford University Press, 1959.

Fischer, Pamela J., and William R. Breakey. "Homelessness and Mental Health: An Overview." *International Journal of Mental Health* 14 (Winter 1985–86): 6–41.

"Forgotten—and Scrapped." Editorial. *New Republic* 75 (June 21, 1933): 141–42.

Foucault, Michel. *Madness and Civilization: A History of Insanity in the Age of Reason*. Translated by Richard Howard. New York: Random House, Vintage Books, 1973.

Frost, Robert. *The Poetry of Robert Frost*, edited by Edward Connery Lathem. New York: Holt, Rinehart and Winston, 1969.

George, M. Dorothy. *London Life in the 18th Century*. 1925. New York: Capricorn Books, 1965.

Geracimos, Ann. "Where Do the Ladies Go? Distaff on Skid Row." *Village Voice*, June 15, 1967.

Giddings, Paula. *When and Where I Enter: The Impact of Black Women on Race and Sex in America*. New York: Morrow, 1984.

Giese, Jo. "Bag Lady." *Moxie*, June 1990.

Gilmore, Harlan W. *The Beggar*. Chapel Hill: University of North Carolina Press, 1940.

Goffman, Erving. *Asylums: Essays on the Social Situation of Mental Patients and Other Inmates*. Garden City, N.Y.: Doubleday, Anchor Books, 1961.

Golden, Stephanie. "Lady versus Low Creature: Old Roots of Current Attitudes toward Homeless Women." *FRONTIERS: A Journal of Women Studies* 11, nos. 2–3 (1990): 1–7.

———. "Single Women: The Forgotten Homeless." *City Limits*, January 1988, 12–16.

Goodrich, Lloyd. *Albert P. Ryder*. New York: Braziller, 1959.

Gresham, Jewell Handy. "The Politics of Family in America." *Nation*, July 24/31, 1989, 116–22.

Gudeman, Jon E. "The Person with Chronic Mental Illness." In *The New Harvard Guide to Psychiatry*, edited by Armand M. Nicholi, Jr. Cambridge, Mass., and London: Belknap Press, 1988.

Hagen, Jan L. "Gender and Homelessness." *Social Work* 32 (July-August 1987): 312–16.

Hagen, Jan L., and André M. Ivanoff. "Homeless Women: A High-Risk Population." *Affilia* 3 (Spring 1988): 19–33.

Haggstrom, Warren C. "The Power of the Poor." In *Poverty American Style*, edited by Herman P. Miller. Belmont, Calif.: Wadsworth, 1966.

Hardwick, Elizabeth. *Sleepless Nights*. New York: Random House, 1979.

Harrison, Earl G. "Women without Work." *Survey* 70 (March 1934): 73–74.

Hartmann, Ernest. "Sleep." In *The New Harvard Guide to Psychiatry*, edited by Armand M. Nicholi, Jr. Cambridge, Mass., and London: Belknap Press, 1988.

Healy, Thomas F. "The Hobo Hits the Highroad." *American Mercury* 8 (July 1926): 334–38.

Henriques, Fernando. *Prostitution and Society*. Vol. 2, *Prostitution in Europe and the Americas*. New York: Citadel Press, 1965.

———. *Stews and Strumpets: A Survey of Prostitution*. Vol. 1, *Primitive, Classical and Oriental*. London: MacGibbon & Kee, 1961.

Herrmann, Lucie. "A Study of 50 Cases Known to the Municipal Family Shelter in N.Y.C. from June 1st, 1949 to June 1st, 1950." Master's thesis, New York School of Social Work, Columbia University, 1950.

Higgs, Mary. *Down and Out: Studies in the Problem of Vagrancy*. Rev. ed. of *My Brother the Tramp*. London: Student Christian Movement, 1924.

———. *Glimpses into the Abyss*. London: P. S. King & Son, 1906.

Hirsch, Kathleen. *Songs from the Alley*. New York: Ticknor & Fields, 1989.

Hoch, Charles. "A Brief History of the Homeless Problem in the United States." In *The Homeless in Contemporary Society*, edited by Richard D. Bingham, Roy E. Green, and Sammis B. White. Newbury Park, Calif.: Sage, 1987.

Hoch, Charles, and Robert A. Slayton. *New Homeless and Old: Community and the Skid Row Hotel*. Philadelphia: Temple University Press, 1989.

"Holiday Inn." *Safety Network/NY: Newsletter of the Coalition for the Homeless*, November/December 1983.

Hollingshead, August B., and Fredrick C. Redlich. *Social Class and Mental Illness: A Community Study.* New York: Wiley, 1958.

Hombs, Mary Ellen, and Mitch Snyder. *Homelessness in America: A Forced March to Nowhere.* Washington, D.C.: Community for Creative Non-Violence, 1986.

"Home Relief Survives the Budget." *Safety Network/NY: The Newsletter of the Coalition for the Homeless,* July 1990.

Homeless Women's Rights Network. "Victims Again: A Report on the Conditions of Homeless Women in the New York City Shelter System." New York. January 1989. Photocopy.

Hope, Marjorie, and James Young. *The Faces of Homelessness.* Lexington, Mass.: Heath, 1986.

Hopper, Kim. "More Than Passing Strange: Homelessness and Mental Illness in New York City." *American Ethnologist* 15 (February 1988): 155–67.

Hopper, Kim, and Jill Hamberg. *The Making of America's Homeless: From Skid Row to New Poor, 1945–1984.* New York: Community Service Society, 1984.

Hopper, Kim, Ezra Susser, and Sarah Conover. "Economies of Makeshift: Deindustrialization and Homelessness in New York City." *Urban Anthropology* 14 (1985): 183–236.

Hopper, Kim, Ellen Baxter, Stuart Cox, and Laurence Klein. *One Year Later: The Homeless Poor in New York City, 1982.* New York: Community Service Society, 1982.

Horsley, Richard A. "Who Were the Witches? The Social Roles of the Accused in the European Witch Trials." *Journal of Interdisciplinary History* 9 (Spring 1979): 689–715.

Hufton, Olwen H. *The Poor of Eighteenth-Century France, 1750–1789.* Oxford: Clarendon Press, 1974.

The Interpreter's Dictionary of the Bible. New York and Nashville, Tenn.: Abingdon Press, 1962.

Jobes, Gertrude. *Dictionary of Mythology, Folklore and Symbols.* New York: Scarecrow Press, 1962.

Johnston, Marlise. "The Woman Out of Work." *Review of Reviews* 87 (February 1933): 30–32.

Jones, Douglas Lamar. "The Strolling Poor: Transiency in Eighteenth-Century Massachusetts." *Journal of Social History* (Spring 1975): 28–54.

Jones, Robert E. "Street People and Psychiatry: An Introduction." *Hospital and Community Psychiatry* 34 (September 1983): 807–11.

Jung, C. G. "On the Psychology of the Trickster Figure." In *Four Archetypes: Mother, Rebirth, Spirit, Trickster,* translated by R. F. C. Hull. Princeton, N.J.: Princeton University Press, 1970.

———. "A Study in the Process of Individuation." In *The Archetypes and the Collective Unconscious,* vol. 9, pt. I of *Collected Works of C. G. Jung.* Princeton, N.J.: Princeton University Press, 1968.

Kamber, Michael. "Going into the Shelters." *Z Magazine,* April 1990, 30–36.

Karlsen, Carol F. *The Devil in the Shape of a Woman: Witchcraft in Colonial New England.* New York: Vintage Books, 1989.

Kates, Brian. *The Murder of a Shopping Bag Lady*. San Diego, New York, London: Harcourt Brace Jovanovich, 1985.

Katz, Michael B. *In the Shadow of the Poorhouse: A Social History of Welfare in America*. New York: Basic Books, 1986.

———. *Poverty and Policy in American History*. New York: Academic Press, 1983.

Kaufmann, Charles A. "Implications of Biological Psychiatry for the Severely Mentally Ill: A Highly Vulnerable Population." In *The Homeless Mentally Ill: A Task Force Report of the American Psychiatric Association*, edited by H. Richard Lamb. Washington, D.C.: American Psychiatric Association, 1984.

Keskiner, Ali, Marilyn J. Zalcman, and Emily H. Ruppert. "Advantages of Being Female in Psychiatric Rehabilitation." *Archives of General Psychiatry* 28 (1973): 689–92.

Kirkland, Mrs. C. M. *The Helping Hand: Comprising an Account of The Home, for Discharged Female Convicts, and an Appeal in Behalf of That Institution*. New York: Scribner's, 1853.

Koenig, Peter. "The Problem That Can't Be Tranquilized." *New York Times Magazine*, May 21, 1978.

Koltuv, Barbara Black. *The Book of Lilith*. York Beach, Maine: Nicolas-Hays, 1986.

Komisar, Lucy. *Down and Out in the USA: A History of Public Welfare*. Rev. ed. New York and London: Watts, 1977.

Kozol, Jonathan. *Rachel and Her Children: Homeless Families in America*. New York: Fawcett Columbine, 1988.

Krauthammer, Charles. "When Liberty Really Means Neglect." *Time*, December 2, 1985, 103–4.

Ladies' Home Journal. Editorial. July 1933.

La Ferla, Ruth. "The Right Stuff." *New York Times Magazine*, September 30, 1990.

Landrine, Hope. "The Politics of Personality Disorder." *Psychology of Women Quarterly* 13 (1989): 325–39.

Laslett, Peter. *The World We Have Lost: Life in Preindustrial England*. New York: Scribner's, 1965.

Le Sueur, Meridel. "Women on the Breadlines" (1932) and "Women Are Hungry" (1934). In *Ripening: Selected Work, 1927–1980*, edited and with an introduction by Elaine Hedges. Old Westbury, N.Y.: Feminist Press, 1982.

Leather, Ella Mary. *The Folk-Lore of Herefordshire, Collected from Oral and Printed Sources*. Hereford: Jakeman & Carter; London: Sidgwick & Jackson, 1912.

Lemert, Edwin M. "Legal Commitment and Social Control." *Sociology and Social Research* 30 (May–June 1946): 370–78.

Levenson, Conrad. "Designing Homes for the Homeless." *The Livable City: A Publication of the Municipal Art Society* (New York) 14 (March 1990): 9.

Levitas, Mitchel. "Homeless in America." *New York Times Magazine*, June 10, 1990.

Lidz, Theodore. *The Origin and Treatment of Schizophrenic Disorders*. New York: Basic Books, 1973.

Lipton, Frank R., Albert Sabatini, and Steven E. Katz. "Down and Out in the City: The Homeless Mentally Ill." *Hospital and Community Psychiatry* 34 (September 1983): 817–21.

London, Jack. *The People of the Abyss*, edited and introduced by I. O. Evans. 1903. New York: Archer House, 1963.

Love, Edmund G. *Subways Are for Sleeping*. New York: Harcourt, Brace, 1957.

McCarthy, Mary. *Birds of America*. 1965. New York: New American Library, 1971.

Macdonald, Cynthia. *W(h)oles*. New York: Knopf, 1980.

Macfarlane, A. D. J. "Witchcraft and Conflict." In *Witchcraft and Sorcery: Selected Readings*, edited by Max Marwick. Harmondsworth: Penguin, 1970.

McGlashan, Thomas H. "Schizophrenia: Psychodynamic Theories." In *Comprehensive Textbook of Psychiatry*, edited by Harold I. Kaplan and Benjamin J. Sadock. 5th ed. Baltimore: Williams & Wilkins, 1989.

McIntyre, Marjorie. *The River Witch*. New York: Crown, 1955.

Marcuse, Peter. "Neutralizing Homelessness." *Socialist Review* 18 (1988): 69–96.

Marin, Peter. "Helping and Hating the Homeless." *Harper's Magazine*, January 1987, 39–49.

Marshall, Dorothy. *English People in the Eighteenth Century*. London: Longmans, Green, 1956.

Martin, Marsha A. "Strategies of Adaptation: Coping Patterns of the Urban Transient Female." Ph.D. diss., School of Social Work, Columbia University, 1982.

Martin, Marsha A., and Susan A. Nayowith. "Creating Community: Groupwork to Develop Social Support Networks with Homeless Mentally Ill." *Social Work with Groups* 11 (1988): 79–93.

May, Herbert G., and Bruce M. Metzger, eds. *The Oxford Annotated Bible with the Apocrypha*. New York: Oxford University Press, 1965.

Mayhew, Henry. *London Labour and the London Poor: A Cyclopaedia of the Condition and Earnings of Those That Will Work, Those That Cannot Work, and Those That Will Not Work*. 1861–62. 4 vols. New York: Dover, 1968.

Mead, Margaret. *Male and Female: A Study of the Sexes in a Changing World*. New York: Morrow, 1949.

"Meeting the Treatment Needs of Homeless Drug Users." *Safety Network: Newsletter of the National Coalition for the Homeless*, December 1989.

The Metamorphoses of Ovid. Translated and introduced by Mary M. Innes. Baltimore: Penguin, 1955.

Meyerowitz, Joanne J. *Women Adrift: Independent Wage Earners in Chicago, 1880–1930*. Chicago and London: University of Chicago Press, 1988.

Michelet, Jules. *Satanism and Witchcraft: A Study in Medieval Superstition*. Translated by A. R. Allinson. Secaucus, N.J.: Stuart, 1939.

Millett, Kate. *The Loony-Bin Trip*. New York: Simon and Schuster, 1990.

Mostoller, Michael. "A Single Room: Housing for the Low-Income Single Person." In *The Unsheltered Woman: Women and Housing in the 80's*, edited by Eugenie Ladner Birch. New Brunswick, N.J.: Center for Urban Policy Research, 1985.

Mowbray, Carol T. "Homelessness in America: Myths and Realities." *American Journal of Orthopsychiatry* 55 (1985): 48.

"Municipal Shelters under Attack Again." *Safety Network/NY: The Newsletter of the Coalition for the Homeless,* July 1990.

Murray, Gilbert, trans. *The Trojan Women* by Euripides. London: George Allen & Unwin, 1905.

Murray, Margaret A. *The Witch-Cult in Western Europe.* Oxford: Clarendon Press, 1921.

Murray-Aynsley, Mrs. "Scraps of English Folklore, XVI: Herefordshire." *Folk-Lore* (London) 39 (December 31, 1928).

The Nation. Editorial. August 9, 1933.

Neumann, Erich. *The Great Mother: An Analysis of the Archetype.* Translated by Ralph Manheim. Princeton, N.J.: Princeton University Press, Bollingen Paperback, 1972.

New Century Cyclopedia of Names. New York: Appleton-Century-Crofts, 1954.

Newall, Venetia. "The Jew as a Witch Figure." In *The Witch Figure: Folklore Essays by a Group of Scholars in England Honouring the 75th Birthday of Katharine M. Briggs,* edited by Venetia Newall. London and Boston: Routledge & Kegan Paul, 1973.

O'Brien, Patricia. *The Woman Alone.* New York: Quadrangle Books, 1973.

O'Connor, Philip. *Britain in the Sixties: Vagrancy, Ethos and Actuality.* Baltimore: Penguin, 1963.

Orenstein, Gloria Feman. *The Reflowering of the Goddess.* New York and Oxford: Pergamon, 1990.

Orlinsky, Harry M., ed. *Notes on the New Translation of the Torah.* Philadelphia: Jewish Publication Society of America, 1970.

Orwell, George. *A Clergyman's Daughter.* 1935. New York: Harcourt, Brace & World, Harbrace Paperbound Library, n.d.

———. *Down and Out in Paris and London.* 1933. New York: Harcourt Brace Jovanovich, Harbrace Paperbound Library, 1961.

Otwell, John H. *And Sarah Laughed: The Status of Women in the Old Testament.* Philadelphia: Westminster Press, 1977.

Packard, Mrs. E. P. W. *Marital Power Exemplified in Mrs. Packard's Trial, . . . or Three Years' Imprisonment for Religious Belief . . .* Hartford, 1866.

———. *Modern Persecution, or, Insane Asylums Unveiled, as Demonstrated by the Report of the Investigating Committee of the Legislature of Illinois.* Hartford, 1873.

Parsons, Ruth J. "Empowerment for Role Alternatives for Low-Income Minority Girls: A Group Work Approach." *Social Work with Groups* 11 (1988): 27–45.

Pearson, Karl. "Woman as Witch." In *The Chances of Death and Other Studies in Evolution,* vol. 2. London and New York: Edward Arnold, 1897.

Peiss, Kathy. *Cheap Amusements: Working Women and Leisure in Turn-of-the-Century New York.* Philadelphia: Temple University Press, 1986.

"Perspective: Missing the Point." *Safety Network/NY: Newsletter of the Coalition for the Homeless,* June 1990.

Pinkerton, Allan. *Strikers, Communists, Tramps and Detectives.* New York: G. W. Dillingham, 1878.

Piven, Frances Fox, and Richard Cloward. *Regulating the Poor: The Functions of Public Welfare.* New York: Pantheon, 1971.

Pomeroy, Sarah B. *Goddesses, Whores, Wives, and Slaves: Women in Classical Antiquity.* New York: Schocken, 1975.

"The Princess Who Loved Her Father Like Salt." In *Indian Fairy Tales,* compiled by Mulk Raj Anand. Bombay: Kutub, 1946.

Q., Annie. "The Homeless Movement: Can We All Work Together?" *Voices to and from the Street: A Newsletter Written by NYC Homeless, for NYC Homeless,* July 1990, 1–3.

Ram Dass and Paul Gorman. *How Can I Help? Stories and Reflections on Service.* New York: Knopf, 1988.

Reckless, Walter C. "Why Women Become Hoboes." *American Mercury* 31 (February 1934): 175–80.

Reitman, Ben L. *Sister of the Road: The Autobiography of Box-Car Bertha, as told to Dr. Ben L. Reitman.* 1937. New York: Harper & Row, Harper Colophon, 1975.

Ribton-Turner, C. J. *A History of Vagrants and Vagrancy and Beggars and Begging.* 1887. Publication 138, Patterson Smith Reprint Series in Criminology, Law Enforcement, and Social Problems. Montclair, N.J.: Patterson Smith, 1972.

Rich, Adrienne. *Of Woman Born: Motherhood as Experience and Institution.* New York: Bantam Books, 1977.

Riis, Jacob A. *The Battle with the Slum.* 1902. Montclair, N.J.: Patterson Smith, 1969.

———. *How the Other Half Lives: Studies among the Tenements of New York.* 1890. New York: Scribner's, 1939.

Ripperger, Henrietta. "Going Places and Doing Nothing." *New Outlook* 163 (January 1934): 51–54.

Ritzdork, Marsha, and Sumner M. Sharpe. "Portland, Oregon: A Comprehensive Approach." In *The Homeless in Contemporary Society,* edited by Richard D. Bingham, Roy E. Green, and Sammis B. White. Newbury Park, Calif.: Sage, 1987.

Roberts, Allen, and D. N. Pappas. "The Shopping-Bag Ladies." *Columbia,* February 1979, 13–21.

Roman, Paul M., and Harrison M. Trice. *Schizophrenia and the Poor.* Ithaca: New York State School of Industrial and Labor Relations, Cornell University, 1967.

Rooney, James F. "Societal Forces and the Unattached Male: An Historical Review." In *Disaffiliated Man: Essays and Bibliography on Skid Row, Vagrancy, and Outsiders,* edited by Howard M. Bahr. Toronto and Buffalo: University of Toronto Press, 1970.

Rorty, James. "Counting the Homeless." *Nation* 136 (June 21, 1933): 692–93.

Rosen, George. *Madness in Society: Chapters in the Historical Sociology of Mental Illness.* Chicago: University of Chicago Press, 1968.

Rosenhan, D. L. "On Being Sane in Insane Places." *Science* 179 (January 19, 1973): 250–58.

Rossi, Peter H. *Down and Out in America: The Origins of Homelessness*. Chicago and London: University of Chicago Press, 1989.

Roth, Dee, and Gerald J. Bean. "New Perspectives on Homelessness: Findings from a Statewide Epidemiological Study." *Hospital and Community Psychiatry* 37 (July 1986): 712–19.

Roth, Dee, Beverly G. Toomey, and Richard J. First. "Homeless Women: Characteristics and Needs." *Affilia* 2 (Winter 1987): 6–19.

Roth, Joan. "If I'm Not on My Milk Crate, You Can Find Me in My Phone Booth." *Ms.*, March 1977, 74–77.

Rousseau, Ann Marie. *Shopping Bag Ladies: Homeless Women Speak about Their Lives*. New York: Pilgrim Press, 1981.

Salerno, Dan, Kim Hopper, and Ellen Baxter. *Hardship in the Heartland: Homelessness in Eight U.S. Cities*. New York: Institute for Social Welfare Research, Community Service Society of New York, June 1984.

Sanger, William W. *The History of Prostitution: Its Extent, Causes and Effects Throughout the World*. New York: Medical Publishing Co., 1899.

Saxby, Mary. *Memoirs of Mary Saxby, a Female Vagrant*. Pamphlet 95. London: Religious Tract Society, n.d.

Scheff, Thomas J. *Being Mentally Ill: A Sociological Theory*. New York: Aldine, 1966.

Shapiro, Joan Hatch. *Communities of the Alone: Working with Single Room Occupants in the City*. New York: Association Press, 1971.

Shulman, Alix Kates. *On the Stroll*. New York: Knopf, 1981.

Sjoberg, Gideon. *The Preindustrial City: Past and Present*. Glencoe, Ill.: Free Press, 1960.

Snow, David A., Susan G. Baker, Leon Anderson, and Michael Martin. "The Myth of Pervasive Mental Illness among the Homeless." *Social Problems* 33 (June 1986): 407–23.

Soverow, Kathy S. "Creating a Safety Net: A Few Thoughts on Loss and Homelessness." *Moxie*, June 1990, 17.

Stamaty, Mark Alan. *MacDoodle St.* New York: Congdon & Lattès, 1980.

Stansell, Christine. *City of Women: Sex and Class in New York, 1789–1860*. 1986. Urbana and Chicago: University of Illinois Press, Illini Books, 1987.

Starhawk. *Truth or Dare: Encounters with Power, Authority, and Mystery*. San Francisco: Harper & Row, 1987.

Stark, Louisa R. "Stranger in a Strange Land: The Chronic Mentally Ill Homeless." *International Journal of Mental Health* 14 (Winter 1985–86): 95–111.

Stefl, Mary E. "The New Homeless: A National Perspective." In *The Homeless in Contemporary Society*, edited by Richard D. Bingham, Roy E. Green, and Sammis B. White. Newbury Park, Calif.: Sage, 1987.

Stern, Mark J. "The Emergence of the Homeless as a Public Problem." In *Housing the Homeless*, edited by Jon Erickson and Charles Wilhelm. New Brunswick, N.J.: Center for Urban Policy Research, 1986.

Stoner, Madeleine R. "The Plight of Homeless Women." In *Housing the Home-*

less, edited by Jon Erickson and Charles Wilhelm. New Brunswick, N.J.: Center for Urban Policy Research, 1986.

Strasser, Judith A. "Urban Transient Women." *American Journal of Nursing* 78 (December 1978): 2076–79.

"Street Level." *Safety Network/NY: Newsletter of the Coalition of the Homeless*, March 1984.

Struening, Elmer L. "A Study of Residents of the New York City Shelter System." New York State Psychiatric Institute, New York. 1987. Photocopy.

Stuart, Mary. "My Shadow: Why Couldn't I Get the Woman in the Park Out of My Mind?" *New York*, May 16, 1988, 70–84.

Szasz, Thomas S. *The Manufacture of Madness: A Comparative Study of the Inquisition and the Mental Health Movement*. New York: Harper & Row, Harper Colophon Books, 1977.

———. *Schizophrenia: The Sacred Symbol of Psychiatry*. New York: Basic Books, 1976.

Thomas, Keith. *Religion and the Decline of Magic*. New York: Scribner's, 1971.

"The Tiffany's Display." *Safety Network/NY: Newsletter of the Coalition for the Homeless*. August 1983.

"Tramps." *Railway Age Gazette* 12 (April 23, 1880).

Trevor-Roper, H. R. "The European Witch-Craze." In *Witchcraft and Sorcery: Selected Readings*, edited by Max Marwick. Harmondsworth: Penguin, 1970.

Tsuang, Ming T., Stephen V. Faraone, and Max Day. "Schizophrenic Disorders." In *The New Harvard Guide to Psychiatry*, edited by Armand M. Nicholi, Jr. Cambridge, Mass., and London: Belknap Press, 1988.

Tudor, William, Jeannette F. Tudor, and Walter R. Gove. "The Effect of Sex Role Differences on the Social Control of Mental Illness." *Journal of Health and Social Behavior* 18 (1977): 98–112.

"An Unsophisticated Hobo." *Railway Conductor* 18 (January 1901): 26–27.

U.S. Congress. House. Committee on Banking, Finance and Urban Affairs. Subcommittee on Housing and Community Development. *Homelessness in America*. Hearing, 97th Cong., 2d sess., December 15, 1982.

U.S. Department of Housing and Urban Development. *A Report to the Secretary on the Homeless and Emergency Shelters*. Washington, D.C., May 1984.

Vexliard, Alexandre. *Le Clochard: étude de psychologie sociale*. Brussels: Desclée De Brouwer, 1957.

———. *Introduction à la sociologie du vagabondage*. Paris: Marcel Rivière, 1956.

von Franz, Marie-Louise. *An Introduction to the Interpretation of Fairy Tales*. New York: Spring Publications, 1970.

———. *Problems of the Feminine in Fairy Tales*. Zurich and New York: Spring Publications, 1970.

———. *Shadow and Evil in Fairytales*. Zurich: Spring Publications, 1974.

Vonnegut, Kurt. *Jailbird*. New York: Delacorte Press/Seymour Lawrence, 1979.

Waisberg, Jodie, and Stewart Page. "Gender Role Nonconformity and Perception of Mental Illness." *Women & Health* 14 (January 1988): 3–16.

Walkowitz, Judith R. *Prostitution and Victorian Society: Women, Class, and the State*. Cambridge: Cambridge University Press, 1980.

Warner, Sylvia Townsend. *Lolly Willowes: or The Loving Huntsman*. London: Chatto & Windus; Toronto: Clarke, Irwin, 1926.

Watson, Sophie, with Helen Austerberry. *Housing and Homelessness: A Feminist Perspective*. London, Boston, and Henley: Routledge & Kegan Paul, 1986.

Welsford, Enid. *The Fool: His Social and Literary History*. 1935. Gloucester, Mass.: Peter Smith, 1966.

Westin, Jeane. *Making Do: How Women Survived the '30s*. Chicago: Follett, 1976.

Widdowson, John. "The Witch as a Frightening and Threatening Figure." In *The Witch Figure: Folklore Essays by a Group of Scholars in England Honouring the 75th Birthday of Katharine M. Briggs*, edited by Venetia Newall. London and Boston: Routledge & Kegan Paul, 1973.

Wilkerson, Margaret B., and Jewell Handy Gresham. "The Racialization of Poverty." *Nation*, July 24/31, 1989, 126–32.

Wilkins, Vaughan. *Fanfare for a Witch*. New York: Macmillan, 1954.

Willeford, William. *The Fool and His Scepter: A Study in Clowns and Jesters and Their Audience*. Evanston, Ill.: Northwestern University Press, 1969.

Wood, Margaret Mary. *Paths of Loneliness: The Individual Isolated in Modern Society*. New York: Columbia University Press, 1953.

Woolf, Virginia. *A Room of One's Own*. New York: Harcourt, Brace & World, 1929.

Wright, James D. "The Mentally Ill Homeless: What Is Myth and What Is Fact?" *Social Problems* 35 (April 1988): 182–91.

Wyatt, Richard Jed, Darrell G. Kirch, and Lynn E. DeLisi. "Schizophrenia: Biochemical, Endocrine, and Immunological Studies." In *Comprehensive Textbook of Psychiatry*, edited by Harold I. Kaplan and Benjamin J. Sadock. 5th ed. Baltimore: Williams & Wilkins, 1989.

Index

Compositor:	Wilsted & Taylor
Text:	10/13 Sabon
Display:	Sabon
Printer and Binder:	Edwards Bros.